Minority
Party

Minority Party

WHY DEMOCRATS
FACE DEFEAT
IN 1992 AND BEYOND

Peter Brown

REGNERY GATEWAY
Washington, D.C.

Library of Congress Cataloging-In-Publication Data
Brown, Peter, 1949–
    Minority party: why Democrats face defeat in 1992 and beyond /
Peter Brown.
      p.   cm.
    Includes bibliographical references and index.
    ISBN 0–89526–530–3
    1. Democratic Party (U.S.)—Public opinion.   2. Public opinion—
United States.   3. United States—Politics and government—1989–
I. Title.
JK2317   1991
324.2736—dc20   91–17420
                                                 CIP

Published in the United States by
Regnery Gateway
1130 17th Street, NW
Washington, DC 20036

Distributed to the trade by
National Book Network
4720-A Boston Way
Lanham, MD 20706

1991 printing
Printed on acid free paper
Manufactured in the United States of America

To my father, Philip Brown,
who taught me about politics,
and to Mary Beth, Stephen,
and Charlotte, who taught me
about life.

Contents

Introduction   ix

1. Middle America: Democratic Roots,
   Republican Hearts   3
2. Joe Lunchbucket Doesn't Live Here Anymore   29
3. The Elephant Is Smarter Than the Donkey   53
4. Losing Patience: White America, Black America   77
5. Different Thinking Is Reality, Not Racism   105
6. The Democrats and Liberal Guilt   127
7. Guilt Is a Political Loser   151
8. Minus-sum Politics   171
9. The Ostrich Syndrome   196
10. Suburbs and Democrats Don't Mix   214
11. Jesse Jackson Scares the Middle Class   237
12. The Minority Mirage   266
13. The Broader Democratic Problem   290
14. The Treatment: Painful But Necessary   311

   End Notes   337
   Index   341

Introduction

At the Democratic National Convention in 1988, which I attended as chief political writer for the Scripps Howard News Service, I witnessed Jesse Jackson end his prolonged teasing and endorse Michael Dukakis. The place went wild.

My colleagues thought Jackson's rapprochement would seal Dukakis' victory over George Bush in November. After all, Dukakis already led by seventeen points in the polls; Jackson's help would tip the balance even farther. This time, the Democrats had a sure win.

My interpretation was far different. I pictured how the 20-25 percent of Americans who make up the swing vote in any election would view things. These voters were white and middle class in their pocketbooks and values. They already resented the Democratic party they believed ran roughshod over their needs and desires in order to cater to racial minorities, the poor, and the elite liberal whites who ran the party. If the American public thought Dukakis had conceded too much in exchange for Jackson's help, the Democratic nominee was dead meat.

As I struggled to write my analysis, sorting out the reasons of my disagreement with my colleagues, my thousands of conversations with my father and the sight I had just witnessed converged and made me realize I had something to add to the public discussion.

This book is the result. It is about the forgotten middle class. Winning elections requires understanding middle-class people and, for the Democrats, regaining their allegiance.

★ ★ ★

Although my father is by no stretch of the imagination a swing voter, the political education I received from him over the years has gone far in helping me understand American politics. Without that advice and direction, this book would never have been written.

Countless others have given me help and encouragement; I have room to mention only a few:

Clay Richards, now of *Newsday*, and Arnie Sawislak, retired, were invaluable mentors during my years at United Press International.

Among my colleagues with whom I have covered national politics, one man stands out for his enormous—probably unconscious—help. The *Chicago Tribune*'s Jon Margolis, through his own reporting and analysis, taught me the most important lesson about political journalism: context is everything. Which is why, in looking at events that day in Atlanta in 1988, I was able to block out the fanfare and search out how they would play in November.

A debt of gratitude is also due to Scripps Howard, especially Senior Vice President for Newspaper/Publishing Bill Burleigh and Vice President/News Dan Thomasson, for allowing me to cover national politics and develop the expertise that led to this book.

Also, heartfelt thanks to the crew at Regnery Gateway, Inc.—Al Regnery who published the book, Trish Bozell who edited it, Megan Brockey who handled the publicity, Jennifer Reist who pulled it all together, and Carole Schabow who proofread.

But the real thanks that I owe goes to the hundreds of people who gave generously of their time. Without several of these, the book would never have existed. At the top of the list is John Pekkanen, an award-winning medical writer whose kindness and patience in helping me fashion the proposal and idea were invaluable. John's contribution cannot be overstated, nor my gratitude exaggerated.

More than a dozen friends and colleagues—some who disagree with my thesis and are uncomfortable with my analysis—spent scores of hours reading all or part of my manuscript.

Susan Feeney, Pam Maples, Ron Gallagher, and Stuart Rothenberg especially did yeoman duty and helped make great improvements in the final product. The suggestions of Juan Williams,

Reginald Stuart, Elaine Hooker, Marvin West, John Moore, Ruy Teixeira, Peter Copeland, Richard Cooper, Martin Schramm, S. W. Dunn, Betty Dunn, Al Tuchfarber, and Eloise Dunn Stuhr were also invaluable.

Other colleagues and friends who helped through writings or conversations that stimulated many of the thoughts in the book are Joe Klein, Tom Brazaitis, Thomas Hargrove, Andy Schneider, James W. Brosnan, Adam C. Condo, Bob Holland, and Mary Gray at the Stanley Foundation. Also Lou Peck, who edited the magazine piece that led me to write this book, and Steve Mills, whose computer expertise allowed me to finish it.

Unlike many books about American politics, this one is about real people. For that I owe a debt of gratitude to the many who allowed me into their lives:

—Geri and Tom Suma, Louise Renaud and Ken Kramer, Barry and Kathleen Marino in Macomb County; and Randy and Bonita Primas in Camden;

—Dennis Dyer, Curtis Jones, Howard Jeffers, Justin Darr, Richard Gordon, Nghia Tran, Jackie Barton, Frank Sullivan, and Robert Wilks, who allowed me to tell their stories;

—Pam Blips, who was surprised to discover she was the typical American, and her husband Mark, who graciously opened up their lives.

The cooperation of pollsters of all political stripes was essential as well. Special mention goes to Stan Greenberg, a Democratic pioneer who goes often without honor in his own party. He asked questions that needed to be asked before others dared. The Democratic party and its candidates would do well to listen to him. Other Democratic pollsters who were generous with their time and data are Paul Maslin, Harrison Hickman, Celinda Lake, Geoff Garin, Peter Hart, Rene Redwood, Michael Donilon, and Mark Mellman. A special thanks to Janet Howard, executive director of Democrats For The '90s, who went out of her way to help me. On the Republican side, Rick Reed at Market Opinion Research was a godsend, as were Kathy Frankovic at CBS, Andy Kohut and Diane Colosanto for Gallup and then Princeton Survey Research, Carol Bowman at *Times-Mirror*, and James Dyer at the Harte-Hanks/ Texas Poll.

A special thanks to Art Nolan of National Demographics & Lifestyle. He made available his firm's analysis of the lifestyles of various towns, counties, and zipcodes in America. In describing these, my information is based on NDL's figures.

Although I made no bones about the thrust of the book, Democratic officials and insiders for the most part allowed me to interview them. There was an understanding that none of the material from the interviews, which were almost all held prior to the 1990 election, would become public until after the voting.

Thank you to Senators Joseph Lieberman, John Breaux, and Charles Robb; Governors Bill Clinton, Evan Bayh, James Florio, and Doug Wilder; former Governors Jim Blanchard, Bruce Babbitt, Richard Lamm, and Richard Celeste; Congressmen Bill Richardson, Tim Penny, Mike Espy, Kweisi Mfume, John Lewis, and Bob Matsui; former Congressman Tony Coelho and former Congresswoman Geraldine Ferraro; former Mayors Henry Cisneros of San Antonio, Andrew Young of Atlanta, and Ed Koch of New York; Texas Attorney General Dan Morales, Iowa Attorney General Bonnie Campbell, and Los Angeles City Councilman Michael Woo.

The same goes for those at the Democratic National Committee, where Chairman Ron Brown was generous with his time, as was Vice Chairman James Ruvolo, Texas State Chairman Bob Slagle, and former Michigan Chairman Rick Weiner. DNC staffers Mike McCurry, Bill Morton, Mark Steitz, Ginny Terzano, and Jim Deshler also deserve heartfelt thanks.

Although this book argues that the Reverend Jesse Jackson has hurt Democratic chances of winning the White House, he granted me a lengthy interview for which I am most grateful. Frank Watkins, Steve Cobble, and Bob Borosage, who have been his long-time advisors, were helpful as well. A special note of thanks to Jerry Austin, who made available two chapters of his unpublished manuscript, in addition to long interviews.

Democratic activists, campaign staffers, and consultants who contributed to this project were Brian Lunde, George Burger, Terry Michael, Susan Estrich, Paul Conn, Bill Galston, Natalie Davis, Carol Darr, Tom Donilon, Al and Ginger From, Peter Kelly, Bill Carrick, Duane Garrett, Tom Herman, Mark Gearan, Bob

Beckel, Cleta Mitchell, Harriet Woods, Heather Booth, Ira Arlook, Frank Greer, Roz Wyman, Paul Soechting, Suellen Albrecht,
Joe Trippi, Will Marshall, Jim Quackenbush, Kay Patterson, Annette Polly Williams, Tom Schieffer, and Anne Eschoo.

Although this book is about Democrats, it would have been
impossible to write without the thoughts of Republicans. Sen. Phil
Gramm, Gov. Carroll Campbell, former Gov. Thomas Kean, and
House Republican Whip Newt Gingrich were most helpful. So too
was the late Republican Chairman Lee Atwater, and from his RNC
staff Mary Matalin, Norm Cummings, and Leslie Goodman.
Texas GOP Chairman Fred Meyer, Michigan Republican Chair-
man Spencer Abraham, and former Reagan White House political
directors Haley Barbour and Bill Lacy were also invaluable. Among
GOP insiders who helped me greatly were Doug Watts, Sara Long,
John Morgan, Karen Hughes, Tom Cole, Michelle Davis, Ed
Rollins, David Doyle, and Terry Gilsinen.

From the academic community, the insights of the brothers
Black, Merle and Earl—who probably understand the political
transformation going on in the South better than anyone—were
invaluable. So too was the help of Rafael Valdivieso, David Hayes
Bautista, Patrick Glynn and Don Nakanishi. Futurist Alvin Toffler
was also gracious with his time.

For the chapter on the 1990 elections, I depended greatly on the
reporting of Tyler Bridges of the New Orleans *Times-Picayune*, Jim
Morrill of the *Charlotte Observer*, and Cathy Decker and Bill Stall of
the *Los Angeles Times*.

Although I'm sure this book will provoke much criticism, let me
disarm it in three areas beforehand. Students of politics will notice a
contradiction between a quote from Lee Atwater in my book and
one in Kevin Phillips' *The Politics of Rich and Poor*.

Phillips picked up a quote from the *Boston Globe* in which Atwater is reported to have said, "The way to win a presidential race
against the Republicans is to develop the class warfare issue, as
Dukakis did at the end. To divide up the haves and the have-nots
and try to reinvigorate the New Deal coalition and to attack."

Although Phillips' book was not out at the time of my interview with Atwater, I asked Atwater about the *Boston Globe* quote because I had seen it elsewhere. In response, during a February 1990 interview in his office two weeks before it was discovered he had a malignant brain tumor, Atwater said, "You can't win a haves versus have-nots campaign in a relatively stable, healthy society. You can't tell them they aren't doing well if they are." In that discussion, attended by Mary Matalin, Atwater clearly felt class warfare was a foolhardy approach for the Democrats, and he hoped they would continue to use it.

Perhaps the remarks by Atwater—a keen student of Machiavelli—to the *Globe*, the hometown paper of Michael Dukakis, were meant to play with the Democrats' minds. We will never know.

On another matter, serious students of demographics will question my reference in some places to data for whites, blacks, and Hispanics. Hispanics can be either white or black, although roughly nine in ten are white. When I refer to figures for whites, it is meant to mean non-Hispanic whites, and when I refer to blacks, it is non-Hispanic blacks. The figures for Hispanics refer to those of both races.

This book should make it clear, but let me state the obvious. This is a book about practical politics: How Democrats can win presidential elections. Few of my suggestions are easy, and I understand some—perhaps many—will think me heartless. For those Democrats who will find the book infuriating, I can only say that I write what I perceive as reality. Think of me as a physician examining a patient and giving his professional opinion. I am offering a tough diagnosis and recommending tough medicine as the only road to recovery. That is how the book is intended—not to harm the party, but to help it.

And finally, this book would never have seen the light of day without the support and understanding of my family. My wife, Mary Beth—whose interest in politics was minimal before meeting me and has become only marginally greater since—was a constant source of love and encouragement. She not only tolerated my absence on the many nights and weekends when I secluded myself upstairs with the word processor, but read the entire manuscript and offered the invaluable perspective of a political outsider. She is also the computer whiz in the family, and without her expertise, I would not have been able to write the book. Stephen, who like any little boy wanted to know why I was spending so much time writing, became enamored with the project and rarely complained about my preoccupation with it. He showed the patience of the special child he is. It is truly my hope he will grow up in a world where ideas matter and a person's worth is determined by his own energy and ambition.

Minority
Party

1

Middle America: Democratic Roots, Republican Hearts

The yellow school bus might as well have said DEMOCRATS in big black letters. They were the ones Geri Suma blamed for trying to haul her son, Greg, past the neighborhood school to God knows where. Busing was what sparked Geri's rethinking. The Democratic party's ties to the 1960s' counterculture and her belief that the family's taxes were financing spendthrift Democratic programs cinched it. She rejected her once-cherished political heritage.

A similar process began in 1972 for Louise Renaud, a self-proclaimed liberal who earned a teaching degree after eleven years of night school. The catalyst for her estrangement from the Democratic party she too had once loved was her students. Many of their families were on welfare, yet they wore designer jeans while Louise made her own clothes to make ends meet.

Barry Marino's departure came in the early 1980s after years of frustration with what he saw as the Democrats' wimpy foreign policy. The trigger event was the 1979 takeover of the U.S. Embassy in Iran. Ronald Reagan's personality and toughness sealed the switch for the typical baby-boomer who had once supported George McGovern for president.

The Democratic party, the oldest and for a time one of the most successful political parties in world history, has a serious problem. As Walter Mondale, the Democrats' 1984 presidential candidate, put it in early 1991: "We're close to becoming a one-party presidential country."

Geri Suma, Louise Renaud, and Barry Marino explain why the Democrats have lost five of the last six presidential elections. For varying reasons and in different decades, they walked away from the Democratic party. In sum, they reflect the concerns that have led millions of Americans to do the same. Until the Democrats understand who these millions of people are and why they have left, the party will not win any presidential election. The Republicans may give away the White House through a scandal, as in 1976, or because of a bad economy. But the Democrats won't win it—or control their own fate—until they face up to their problem.

That, of course, is easier said than done. It involves the most sensitive issue in America—race. People in general, and Democratic leaders in particular, shy away from discussing the topic. But Democrats must if they are to remain competitive nationally, much less regain their stranglehold on American politics.

The key to the problem is to realize that most of the millions of Democratic defectors are white.

"The problem isn't that the Democratic party isn't getting enough black votes," asserted Sen. John Breaux, a Louisiana Democrat who ran the Democratic Senatorial Campaign Committee for two years following the 1988 election and saw the national scope of the issue. "It's that it's not getting enough white votes. White Americans are hemorrhaging away from this party."

Among Democratic presidential candidates since World War II, only Lyndon Johnson in 1964 carried white voters. In 1988, Michael Dukakis got 40 percent, and was competitive among whites only in states with few blacks. Although most Democrats cringe at any racial analysis, it is impossible to ignore the math. No party can win the presidency without a majority, or near majority, of whites, who are 80-plus percent of the electorate.

Democratic politicians are troubled because the attitudes behind the white flight are hard to reconcile with what they view as the inherited values of the Democratic party. Much less can they justify it to the millions of blacks who are the most loyal Democratic voters. They prefer to talk of a 43 percent strategy —the percentage of whites needed to win a national election assuming they get 90 percent of the black and two-thirds of the Hispanic vote.

These pages deal with the reasons why white Americans reject the Democratic party, its presidential candidates, and its policies. If Democrats choose to believe their problems merely stem from the popularity of President Bush's wildly successful 1991 Persian Gulf War, they will again be closing their eyes to the real reasons they risk political impotence. Some of the reasons involve overt racial conflicts with blacks. Others stem from class, value, and economic conflicts that largely parallel racial lines.

Geri, Louise, Barry, and others who opened up their lives for this project embody the values of middle-class America at the end of the twentieth century. They are solid citizens who work, pay taxes, and want to lead safe, decent lives. They are no longer on the outside of the economic system looking in. They either have a piece of the American pie or believe they can have one if they work hard enough. They no longer see the point of throwing in with the have-nots in the hope that everyone can have a little. They have made judgments based on their everyday life experiences.

Some will label their feelings, and perhaps this book, racist. I hope not, for those who do will again be failing to hear the voice of the American middle class. Whether these millions are justifiably fearful of crime and tired of what they see as abuses of welfare and affirmative action, or simply dislike people of a different color, is a judgment call.

For two decades now, Democratic leaders have tried to pretend that the feelings of the Geri Sumas, Louise Renauds, and Barry Marinos don't exist, or that if they do, they belong to bigoted people who don't deserve to have their views aired. The alternative is a conscious decision to lose the White House rather than appeal to these swing voters who decide the presidency. Whichever, the result is the slow but steady decline of the Democratic party that, beginning with Franklin Roosevelt's election in 1932, ruled America without serious challenge for almost forty years. The numbers are there. Pollsters have picked up the change from the days when whites were willing to give up something to help blacks in order to atone for past wrongs. That is in the past. They are not doing penance in the heartland anymore.

To understand the evolution of events that put Richard Nixon, Ronald Reagan, and George Bush in the White House is to appreciate the change in Macomb County, Michigan, a 700,000-person almost all-white suburb on Detroit's northern border. In 1960, it was the most Democratic suburban county in America. Today, Macomb—home to Geri Suma, Louise Renaud, and Barry Marino—is solidly Republican when it comes to voting for president.

In 1960, 63 percent of the county's largely Roman Catholic 167,670 voters backed John Kennedy. In 1964, 74 percent voted for Lyndon Johnson, and in 1968, George Wallace, a third-party candidate, got almost 15 percent, leaving Democrat Hubert Humphrey with just 55 percent of Macomb's vote.

And there the Democratic era ended. Since then, it's been solidly Republican at the presidential level. Reagan won two-thirds of Macomb's votes in 1984, Bush equaled it in 1988. By then, the county's voting population had almost doubled, as was the case nationally in suburbs from Long Island to Long Beach. In state and local races Republicans were also making inroads, although like the country as a whole, they still had a way to go.

The GOP presidential dominance was maintained in 1988 even though during the campaign Macomb's jobless rate was a little above the national norm; in the 1982 Reagan recession it had hit 17.6 percent. Macomb draws sustenance from the large and small manufacturing plants that dot the landscape, many of them tied to the auto industry. Michael Dukakis took his 1988 tank ride, ridiculed so effectively in Republican campaign commercials, at a Macomb defense plant.

But despite the slump in the domestic auto industry, entering the 1990s, a third of Macomb's workers toiled in factories and they produced half the residents' income. This put Macomb's median household income at $37,711, slightly above the national average.

But it was a meat-and-potatoes, rather than a wine-and-cheese type of affluence.

Macomb, with a land mass half the size of Rhode Island, has a greater population than five states. At the county's far end, along Lake St. Clair, the more affluent areas are sprinkled with apple orchards. But mostly, Macomb is dotted with the small, single-family houses, fast-food restaurants, and modest parks that stamp it as a typical American suburb.

For Geri, it all began to crystalize one spring day in 1968 when her 1960 Dodge Dart dripped transmission fluid onto the driveway. Greg, then four, was turning blue from asthma. She knew that if the Democrats put through their busing plan, suburban kids like hers would be sent into Detroit, right past Siersma Elementary School down the block. And she knew the family bank account couldn't afford to replace the ailing Dart. That meant that while her husband, Tom, took their other car to work at the Chrysler plant, she'd be unable to get to Greg many miles away at school if he should have another attack.

The Democrats, she felt, were playing with her life.

"At that time, I wasn't thinking so much about politics. I was thinking about busing. Greg was getting ready to start kindergarten. My main concern was what if he became ill wherever he was taken and how would I get there? I didn't know what I would do. I just didn't like the idea of my child being taken away from me, that's how I perceived it. I felt I would have no control over anything in my child's school.

"At that point I could see the way things were changing. Mostly some of the Democratic stands on some social issues, especially busing," Geri remembers. "Busing made me begin to think the Democratic party wasn't for us."

Once the process of disillusionment began, she decided that the Democrats had never met a tax they didn't hike, were weak in dealing with foreign powers overseas and criminals at home, had little regard for family values, and worried too much about the poor and minorities at the expense of middle-class people like herself. It destroyed her faith in government.

Geri's transformation did not come without emotional trauma. In the 1968 Democratic presidential primary she had backed

Eugene McCarthy, the darling of what would later become the quiche-and-brie set. But unlike most of Senator McCarthy's supporters, she supported him not because he opposed the Vietnam War, but because McCarthy's fellow Minnesotan and rival, Vice President Hubert Humphrey, Lyndon Johnson's designated successor, "just wasn't in my league." Humphrey favored busing.

When Humphrey won the Democratic nomination, Geri faced a dilemma. "I had voted Democratic top to bottom until then," she said. It was a lesson learned early in her family, imbued almost as strongly as their Roman Catholicism.

Her father, and most adult males she knew, was a staunch member of the United Auto Workers, then and now almost joined at the hip with the Democratic party. He had been a Democratic precinct delegate and was close to many of the party's local power brokers in Detroit's ethnic Hamtramck section. "My dad loved FDR. He thought the WPA saved him during the Depression."

But Geri, who proudly claims to have voted in every election, knew she couldn't vote for Humphrey. And of course she couldn't just sit it out.

She tried to pretend that her vote for Nixon "was an aberration and the Democratic party would come back. But from then on, it seemed to just go more and more to the left. The first time I voted Republican I did feel guilty, but it was the right thing to do. It was a message being sent. I thought things would go back, but they didn't, because the Democrats never got the message. By 1972, it began to dawn on me the Democratic party wasn't coming back. Instead they were falling apart."

Had Geri Suma been born twenty-five years later, she would have been a natural politician. She has a vivacious personality, a supple mind, and an even faster tongue. She is quick to say what she thinks and has the courage of her convictions.

But times were different when she grew up as one of four children in a traditional Polish-American family. A good student, she graduated from Detroit's Pershing High School in 1956, and although her father, Iggy Nadolski, had a good job doing trim work on Chryslers, there was no money for college.

Still, she liked her secretarial job with the Detroit Board of

Education and living at home. She began dating Tom, just out of the army, when they bowled in the same league. They shared the same interests and goals: sports, family, and the desire for an upwardly mobile life that would give them a chance to live the middle-class American dream.

Almost thirty years later, little of that had changed and it seemed they had achieved their dreams. Although never easily. Tom Suma is graying slightly atop his 160-pound frame. He remains the same proud and quiet man Geri married, the solid type mothers want for their daughters, the kind who wears a suit when he goes out to dinner, even at family-style restaurants.

Geri, a stocky 5'2" brunette, does most of the talking. They miss church only a handful of Sundays a year, and their kids, who worked part-time in high school, are college graduates. The Sumas are big sports fans, frequently attending Red Wings hockey games. They follow the Lions, Tigers, and Pistons on television, and sometimes watch two games on different sets. Outside of sports, their TV tastes run to public affairs shows, country & western music is their favorite on the radio, and *Gone with the Wind* and *Top Gun* lead their movie lists.

In 1964, two years after their wedding with Greg on the way, the Sumas, like so many other Americans, moved to the suburbs. They had lived in Detroit's Wayne County all their lives and were now part of the massive exodus of whites. Detroit's population peaked in the late 1950s at almost two million, but by 1990 the Census Bureau had trouble finding one million residents. Between 1960 and 1990 the Motor City's population went from 70 percent white to 75 percent black.

The Sumas settled in Warren, just over the city line from Detroit. Much of the Democratic erosion in Macomb from 1960 to the early 1990s stemmed from the county's changing demographic profile. The first wave of new residents was mostly made up of auto workers like Tom and those who lived off the car industry. They were not the white-collar types who lived in neighboring Oakland County, but blue-collar workers who in the fifties and early sixties took advantage of the security and prosperity that union contracts gave them to move to suburbia where houses were larger and more affordable. For Tom and Geri the move was simply a matter of finding the best housing value. Unlike many others, it had nothing to do with a change of image; they liked who they were.

The second wave was white flight after the Detroit riots in the late 1960s; those already in Macomb shared the new migrants' resentment and fear of blacks.

"The riots of the sixties probably turned off blue-collar America right before our eyes," sighed former Michigan Gov. Jim Blanchard, who ran the state from 1982-1990. "A lot of people believe Democrats created the riots by promising blacks too much."

That resentment made busing a flash point. And it was exacerbated by the suburban lifestyle. The latest wave of suburbanites either brought children with them or began having them once they had settled in.

Greg Suma was born in 1964 and Christine followed in 1965. Geri stopped working when Greg was born. They could have used Geri's salary, but she felt mothers with small children should stay home. Besides, she wanted to be with her kids.

The Sumas were like most of the others who bought three-bedroom, one-and-a-half-bath, brick ranch houses for $20,000 with every penny they could save, beg, or borrow. They assumed they would live there the rest of their lives, with a small vegetable and flower garden in the back, and that their kids would attend Siersma school, a half block from their front door.

For a while it appeared they would be only half right. Indeed, almost thirty years later they were still in the house, valued at $75,000. Roses, cucumbers, and tomatoes were pushing through the backyard soil. Even as they looked toward Tom's retirement, the Sumas had no thoughts of leaving. This was their home.

But schools had been another story.

The Sumas had moved to Warren before the federal courts began ordering students to attend schools miles from their homes in order to reverse racial segregation. But by the late 1960s, the school situation had changed, and with it the political mindset of Geri and countless others. Opponents called it "forced busing," a phrase that became synonymous with white opposition to the court-ordered plans.

What grated on Geri as much as busing itself was those who said busing was like castor oil: it didn't taste very good going down, but it would make everything better. But it seemed to her that few of the kids of Democratic liberals selling that line were being bused. Even now she says: "I thought the judges were dictating what should and shouldn't be done. It told me a little about the liberal philosophy. They thought they knew what was best for my son. I was crushed, angry. You can't make pawns out of little school kids and that was what they were doing.

"They think they know better than we do. Just because they tell me something is good for me doesn't mean it is. I have a sense they try to tell us how to run our lives."

The Sumas won their battle. The Supreme Court eventually overruled the busing plan that would have sent Greg and Christine into Detroit. But the intervening years had changed the Sumas' political outlook. During that time Republican Presidents Richard Nixon and Gerald Ford opposed busing, as did GOP Gov. William Milliken.

The Sumas and millions like them never forgave the Democrats for trying to bus their kids. In the end, some black kids were bused to Siersma, but that didn't bother the Sumas. Their position, they maintained, had nothing to do with race, but with wanting Greg at the local school. "The neighborhood school was half a block away," a still-bitter Geri pointed out. "That's what you live in a neighborhood for. You have neighborhood schools, neighborhood scouting, activities after school."

An admitted "straight-arrow," she thinks the liberal Democratic mindset that spawned busing set the country up for the problems it faces in the 1990s. "Back in the sixties, people with my views were told nothing was wrong with marijuana," Geri complained. "But after that, now we have heroin, cocaine, and crack. Kids were living together, communes, group living, then Woodstock and what took place there. The sixties was when this nation was corrupted, and it seems like we can't reverse any of this. Now we have an epidemic of drugs and AIDS. I just think liberals in general seemed to feel that stuff like that was all right. They knew best about what this country should be, and look what happened."

Tom, a Chrysler tool-and-die maker and strong UAW member,

left the union in 1964 to become a maintenance supervisor, a choice he has often questioned since. Some years, he felt, he could have made more money on the line because of the fat overtime checks. And the union benefits were better, too. But as a supervisor, he had security he didn't get from the union—he avoided the layoffs that came regularly for hourly workers. Still, he didn't feel like management. He considered himself working class and thought the UAW had done well for its members.

Politically, however, Tom and his colleagues on the line were going their own nonunion way. Ironically, many who worked in plants outside the county commuted via the Walter Reuther Freeway, a monument to the legendary labor leader who couldn't foresee a day when his workers and the Democratic party would not be as one.

Back in 1968, Tom's base salary, roughly $9,000, put him right at the average family income figure, although his sixty-plus-hour weeks during that boom period made him richer. Still, when he and Geri voted that year for Nixon, they thought it a treasonous step for working people like themselves. They were, in fact, middle class, but they didn't think of themselves that way. Not yet.

The inflation and stagnant economy in the late 1970s during Jimmy Carter's presidency dropped the Sumas' other shoe on the Democrats. The economic slide convinced them that the Democrats not only were out of touch with their values, but contrary to what they had always believed, with their pocketbooks as well.

Beginning to view themselves as middle class, the Sumas no longer responded to Democratic appeals to the little guy. They saw the Democrats becoming a party that focused on help for the needy at the expense of the middle class. Geri and Tom Suma felt their tax money was going to pay for other peoples' programs. And they resented it.

By the early 1990s, Tom was earning roughly $40,000, a solid middle-class income, and supervising a dozen workers at the Chrysler Mound Road engine plant, which makes V-8 car and truck engines.

His complaint with Democratic economics is best explained by his paycheck. Tom Suma estimated that in 1989 he paid $2,500 in property taxes, $8,000 in federal income taxes, $4,000 in Social Security levies, and another $4,000 in city, county, and state taxes. He had to work 125 days a year to pay the tax man before he and Geri got a dime. The Republican rhetoric—blaming the Democrats for raising taxes—struck home.

"It's outrageous. A lot of it is due to the Democrats. If the Republicans ran the country, taxes would be lower," says Tom Suma. "I think the Democratic party's idea of moving ahead is raising taxes to keep the economy going. Even though it's only trickle down, Reagan's economic ideas have worked. I don't like to be taxed to death. That seems to be the big thing with the Democrats. And I don't like the bureaucracy that develops out of that."

Never mind that Michigan's election law does not allow registration by party. The Sumas are now confirmed Republicans. Fittingly, the most enthusiastic party member is their son Greg, whose asthma attack began it all. He's now an accountant who worked days and got his college degree at night. The family proudly wears the GOP label and doesn't understand what happened to the Democratic party they once had loved.

"My values have never changed. I love this country, the flag. I've not changed that much. Democrats have," Geri insists.

As the years pass, they vote less and less often for Democrats in lower offices. Still, Geri keeps a bust of John Kennedy in her living room. And even now she gets a bit misty-eyed when she recalls how much she cried the day he died.

Louise Renaud can also pinpoint the beginning of her political metamorphosis. She walked into the voting booth in 1972 planning to vote for the Democratic presidential nominee as she had since her first election in 1956 when she voted for Adlai Stevenson against popular Republican President Dwight Eisenhower. But when she pulled the curtain behind her and stared at the machine, she just couldn't do it. Somehow, George McGovern seemed to embody everything she'd been taught to disdain.

It was the designer jeans worn by black kids from welfare families at Detroit's Kettering High School, where she taught, that finally made her decide to vote for Nixon.

For more than a decade Louise worked as a secretary while attending college at night to get her teaching degree. By 1972 she was thirty-six and a teacher earning $9,000, 30 percent more than she had pulled down as a secretary. Yet she couldn't afford such fancy clothes. "It was the straw that broke the camel's back," Louise decided. "I would see the kids, whose families were on AFDC [Aid to Families with Dependent Children], walking around in designer jeans, silk shirts, alligator shoes. And I'm breaking my buns." She asked herself, "What the hell is going on? I can't afford that."

McGovern's plan to give even more cash to welfare recipients stuck in her craw. She voted for Nixon but felt she'd betrayed her family and everything for which she had stood. She was so ashamed she didn't tell a soul.

"I guess that's when I realized I wasn't a Democrat anymore," she remembers. "I felt funny doing it. I just felt that I shouldn't be voting Republican. I guess I associated the Republican party with money and business, but not people like me.

"I considered myself working class, and working-class people didn't vote for Republicans. If you belonged to a union [as she did, the American Federation of Teachers] you didn't vote for a Republican. . . .

"I thought it was a one-time-only thing. I really wasn't voting for Nixon. 'I'm not really a Republican. This is just a protest. I'm voting for the man and not the party'—that kind of attitude. I thought McGovern was off the deep end. That was probably about the time I started losing my liberal views. I felt that I just can't stand the giveaways. McGovern symbolized that."

Then, at a 1973 New Years' Eve party, her brother Albert, a sheet metal worker four years her junior, alluded to Watergate and said, "Only an asshole would ever vote for Nixon."

"I said, 'That's not true because I voted for Nixon.' I can still see the way his mouth dropped open and he told me he would never talk to me again. To this day, when I burn bacon or something like that, he says, 'I never expected any more of you because you voted for Nixon.'"

Her brother's reaction wasn't all that surprising. Louise grew up in Roseville, another Macomb suburb, the ninth of twelve children. Theirs could have been a model for the traditional, blue-collar working-class family. Her father was a union electrician at U.S. Rubber and her mother worked briefly during World War II, but mostly she had her hands full with the kids. They were a typical family in Macomb, which was and remains 96 percent white, 1 percent black.

Louise, medium-height with a stocky build and light brown hair, is very much a middle-class person who takes pride in that identity. Comfortable in jeans, but with a soft spot for silk dresses in the right setting, she craves both the excitement of Las Vegas and the serenity of backwoods camping.

She and her husband have a two-bedroom, one-and-a-half-bath condo in Mt. Clemons, which they bought in 1977 for $37,000. Decorated in earth tones, it has a handful of antiques and more than a score of paintings, lithographs, and prints, some of them by Georgia O'Keefe, almost all of flowers.

While some couples use their savings to trade up homes, they spend theirs improving boats. Their pride is *Louisa,* a thirty-four-foot fiberglass boat for which they paid $40,000 in 1986. They spend most of their summer on it. She likes "Jeopardy" and "60 Minutes" on TV; she cried during *On Golden Pond* and laughed at *Ghostbusters.* One day she reads a Danielle Steele romance, the next a Robert Ludlum thriller.

The Depression was stamped indelibly on her parents' psyche and they passed it on to Louise, born in 1934 during the hard times. Actually, her father worked steadily and the family got by pretty well. What remained was a sense of self-reliance, a belief that if you worked hard enough, you would get by.

One week, Louise remembers, her parents borrowed $20 to make ends meet, and repaid it immediately. "They believed that was the ultimate degradation. They probably would have let their children go hungry before they went on welfare." When FDR died, her mother cried for days. "She didn't cry that hard when her father died. FDR was just an absolute hero in our house."

Louise began working early on, first baby-sitting, later at a variety of after-school jobs. She was both helping out and learning the family work ethic. She was a good student, but like Geri Suma, college was out of the question. There was no money. But that wasn't the only obstacle. "My mother," she admitted ruefully, "thought I would price myself out of the marriage market" if she went to college. In fact, Louise did not marry until 1981, after she and her husband, Ken Kramer, had lived together for a decade.

Louise's willingness to challenge social custom, such as cohabiting, showed up much earlier and at a critical time in her life.

After graduating from high school in 1952 she found what seemed like a dream job—at first. She worked for the phone company, sorting tickets for long-distance calls in precomputer days. Within months, she was the second-fastest sorter in Detroit. But her supervisor, a frumpy, fiftyish woman who behaved liked a school marm, was determined to make Louise fit the Ma Bell mold. In the fall of 1952, Louise was sitting in the phone company backroom out of the public eye, with her legs crossed, her skirt a full five inches below her knees. Her supervisor walked by and sharply told her that "Bell girls do not cross their legs." Rather than adhere to someone else's social norms, Louise gave her two-week notice on the spot. Her father was "so upset. He thought, here I had this wonderful job and was set for life, and how could I do that and toss it away."

Soon she was working as a secretary and bookkeeper, first for a stockbroker, then an insurance agency. But the incident at the phone company stuck in her head and she realized that she needed an education to protect herself.

Still working full days, she went to school at night, two years at Macomb County Community College followed by nine years at Wayne State University in Detroit. She moved from Roseville into an integrated neighborhood in Detroit near WSU. Her parents had since died and she was supporting herself on the $6,000-7,000 she earned annually, making most of her own clothes to save cash. She hung around the campus, marching in civil rights demonstrations and dating several black men. She was a liberal—wary of foreign military entanglement, pro civil rights, a firm believer in activist government. And proud of it.

"I recall the [Francis Gary] Powers incident" in 1961 in which an American spy plane was shot down over the Soviet Union. "I remember thinking, 'We ought to apologize for that,' and yet if someone had asked me that today I would say that's just something we have to do. I'm much more pragmatic. The world works a certain way and we have to adjust."

But, in one way, Louise is unlike many who have left the Democratic party. "I really don't mind paying taxes," Louise insists. "I don't want to see people abused, or go hungry. I want to have good roads, air safety. They can tax me for the drug war. That doesn't bother me. But I want something in return." She would support socialized medicine, an alien concept to conservatives, "because it would be for everyone."

Louise's defection is the direct result of her anger with a welfare system she believes has created and perpetuated a mostly black underclass. She blames the Democrats for setting up a system that rewards people for doing nothing. It is an insult to her parents' work ethic.

Welfare, Louise says, is "one of the things that absolutely just destroys me, and I feel the city [Detroit] has been destroyed and I think giveaway programs and blacks are responsible. I don't think we demand any responsibility. The attitude of the kids at school and in our neighborhood seems to be: 'It's mine. I have it coming. You owe it to me. I deserve this because I've been discriminated against.' That's a real problem for me.

"I find myself less liberal on race than I was," she adds. "Affirmative action just hasn't worked. It bothers me. I don't feel the blacks have taken advantage in a positive way of what they were given. It's a lot of money spent for it not to have worked. Maybe I wouldn't be so negative if I thought the policies were working.

"I would not mind welfare that said, 'We realize you can't support a family working at McDonald's, so take the job and we'll help support your family.' It's the giveaways I can't stand. It seems to encourage this idea that if they wait long enough they will get something for nothing. I think that attitude is there in the black community."

It really began to eat away at her in the late 1980s when she began to teach the children of children she had taught in the early 1970s. The original students dropped out of school, had babies, and went on welfare. Their children not only gave every evidence of continuing the cycle, "the students I have now are worse than their parents. They don't want to do anything."

Louise spent the last several years before she retired in the fall of 1989 trying to place her business students in jobs, a frustrating experience.

"They would say, 'I don't want to work at any janitorial or fast food job; I don't want to work where I get my hands dirty.' Then I tell them to fill out an application in case a vice president's job at General Motors comes open, and the kids say, 'You mean you can get me into General Motors?'

"These are kids with no skills. Only about half are literate. Our most successful placements were with school districts because their standards are lower than private industry. Educators are more tolerant.

"In 1987, one of the kids I placed was fired for stealing toilet paper from McDonald's. He said 'My mother said it was all right.' They were on AFDC . . . ."

Louise figured that about 60 percent of the students in her business courses—typing, accounting, and bookkeeping—dropped out of school, although the official Kettering High School rate for 1983-87 was 46 percent. In 1981, she did her own survey and found that roughly 70 percent of her female students were unwed mothers. One unmarried eighteen-year-old had four children under age five.

Kettering was built in 1965, five miles north of the Renaissance Center, the fancy, glass-towered riverfront area familiar to tourists. The students are almost all black, the staff half black and half white. The school has deteriorated, but looks new compared with the surrounding urban war zone. Almost a third of the houses in the immediate area are abandoned. Junkies and dope dealers—many of them students—line the streets. Louise often saw students with wads of cash easily totaling $5,000. She tried to interest her students in working, in getting off the welfare cycle, but she'd run up against a brick wall.

As she put it: "If they can wear Calvin Klein jeans and have babies by not working, then they say, 'Why should I go and flip hamburgers for $4 an hour?' . . . They think someone, the government, will take care of them. The more babies, the more AFDC. And the Democrats have perpetuated that system." The Democrats are "going in a whole different direction than I am." Surprisingly, Louise—whose sentiments are echoed by many who share her disgust with the Democrats—gets a lot more worked up about Teddy Kennedy than about Jesse Jackson who, she figures, is genuinely trying to help his people, albeit at her expense.

"I dislike Kennedy," Louise states flatly. "He's not like his brother [JFK]. I get the feeling he just wants to give away all the time to the poor and the blacks and underprivileged. I have a little bit of difficulty about crying 'round the poor when I had two jobs going through school." What really bothers her is the way Kennedy "and the other Democrats have a tendency to talk down to me when they try to tell me why I should think this or that."

She still keeps a picture of Harry Truman—"my hero"—in her sewing room. But Louise Renaud has become a Republican. Race is the reason.

"I don't like this attitude in myself. I don't like this streak of racism that's going through me. I don't think blacks are genetically inferior or anything; they just lack a work ethic and the welfare system has reinforced that. Ten years ago, I would have cut my tongue out before I said 'those people or those blacks.' Now, as I see the neighborhoods crumbling, I tend to generalize. I blame the Democrats, people like Teddy Kennedy."

Barry Marino didn't actually leave the Democratic party until the 1980s. But at that time, four years of foreign policy embarrassments and economic pain under Jimmy Carter finally impelled him to turn his back on the liberal ideals he'd held.

It began on a Sunday morning in 1979 when he heard about the embassy takeover as he got ready for church. Once it became clear the takeover was sanctioned by the Iranian government, Marino, like millions of other Americans, viewed it as a direct violation of the rule of diplomatic immunity that had been honored for centuries, even by Nazi Germany. When Carter didn't act aggressively, said Marino, "the light came over me. I realized I don't think like those Democrats. They just weren't believing the same types of things I believed in anymore. A Third World country was taking over our embassy—an act of war. And we stand by and let them do what they want."

He'd voted for McGovern and Carter during the 1970s because he believed in government activism. And he did it because that was what he'd been taught to believe.

When Barry was a youngster, his father, a crane operator and UAW member, made sure Barry understood that "the Republicans pick up the tablecloth from the four corners and don't let any crumbs fall. Democrats snatch the tablecloth off and let the crumbs fall to the little people." Today, he and his father, still a "dyed-in-the-wool Democrat," can't talk about politics without fighting.

In many ways, Barry is typical of the baby-boom generation. He doesn't like anything big—big labor, big business, big government. Like many of the Woodstock generation, he moved to the right once he married and had a family, and became a "born again" Christian in the early 1970s. "The maturing process generally makes you more conservative. When you start bringing up a family you generally want to keep what you have. You want to have the best for them."

Barry was born in Bluefield, West Virginia, and his family moved to Detroit when he was an infant. He graduated in 1968 from Hazel Park High School, on the border of Macomb and Oakland Counties. It was one of the most tumultuous years in American history. Vietnam, race riots, the assassinations of Martin Luther King, Jr., and Robert F. Kennedy shook the nation to its core.

Although his family was not appreciably better off than the Renauds and Sumas, times had changed. Everyone, it seemed, was going to college. Barry went off to Taylor University in Upland, Indiana. He stayed two years, but couldn't finance his junior year and went back to Detroit, where he got a job running a drill press at a TRW factory. He finished his degree studying at night at nearby Oakland University.

He remained on the line at TRW for eighteen years, earning a solid, middle-class living, until in the late 1980s he developed Carpal Tunnel Syndrome, swelling of a ligament, in his right hand. Unable do any type of repetitive factory work, he had to leave his job in the summer of 1988 and was forced to wear splints on his wrist. From an annual $30,000 plus benefits, his income dropped to $20,000—workers' compensation without benefits—on which he had to support his wife, Kathleen, and three teenage children. Kathleen went to work full-time while Barry, approaching forty, searched for a new career.

The second phase of Barry's political education began to take shape in the late 1970s, only a few years after Barry attended the Oakland County Democratic Convention to back McGovern. "The inflation was eating everyone up," he remembered. But Barry was lucky; he was not laid off. Overtime disappeared, however, and the advent of his two youngest children, born in 1978 and 1979, stretched the family purse strings further.

At around this time, Barry began to question his allegiance to the Democratic party because it always seemed to support the very causes that angered him, such as abortion and gay rights. But he remained a Democrat. Until the embassy staff in Iran—and the nation, in a sense—were held hostage. "That struck me. He's our leader, how can he sit on his hands? I just said this can't go on. We have to do something. But Carter didn't."

When the hostages were released unharmed 444 days later, Marino didn't soften his attitude toward Carter and the Democrats. In fact, he grew angrier.

"It would have been better to have done something even if the hostages were killed," Barry asserted. "Just think how many terrorist acts could have been forestalled. We have had so many in the last decade because the United States has been perceived as indecisive. Once they were taken I knew I couldn't vote for Carter again. After Reagan took office it took two years for me to decide I was a Republican.

"Basically, Carter's lack of leadership left a very bad taste in my mouth. I just couldn't believe anyone could flip-flop on so many issues. It was driven home by Reagan" and his unwillingness to compromise his principles. "I liked Reagan's domestic policy

—people went back to work, inflation became almost nonexistent.

"Liberalism is a very good ivory-tower philosophy, but it doesn't work in practice. Just like communism would be great if it worked, everybody would be taken care of, but it doesn't work. I haven't seen a strong liberal or Democratic leader in my lifetime," he added.

Actually, in September of 1991, five months before the blitzkrieg U.S.-led victory over Iraq restored America's credibility around the world and vanquished the Vietnam syndrome at home, Marino was already convinced that the Republican president would not allow America to be humiliated as a Democrat had a decade before in Iran. "I'm confident George Bush will get it done," he said shortly after Labor Day. "With Carter everyone was thumbing their nose at the United States. We had no political clout in the world. This time will be different."

Of course, Marino was right. And following the war, the stereotype of strong, competent GOP leadership in foreign affairs as contrasted with Democratic weakness and lack of resolve was further stamped in the minds of Marino and millions of other Americans. "I just knew Bush and the Republicans [were] different," he said after the fighting. "He's a much stronger man. I knew he was in charge and wouldn't back down. Republicans are just stronger when it comes to foreign policy."

Despite his philosophical and soft-spoken manner, Barry, a hefty man with a barrel chest, looks and lives like a man who works with his hands. He wears a mustache year round, grows a beard every winter and shaves it in the spring. His thirty-five-year-old, three-bedroom, grey brick ranch house in Warren has aluminum trim and a two-car garage, adorned with a basketball hoop. He's held on to the house, despite his drop in income, because it was bought in 1975 for $30,000 and the $327 mortgage remains affordable.

Barry's kids have Detroit Pistons posters around the house and he takes pride in the late nineteenth-century oblong table with heavy legs that he refinished—and in the numerous trophies won by his kids in Bible study contests.

It doesn't take a marketing study to establish that the Marino household is typical in Macomb. He likes to fish, but doesn't care for hunting; he enjoys watching sports on television, and his favorite show is "Rosanne," a situation comedy about a blue-collar family.

Barry's favorite pastime, though, is spending time with Kathleen and the kids. The couple met at the First Baptist Church of Hazel Park when he was eight and she was seven. They began dating when he came back from college and they were married two years later. "I still try to be a romantic," he mused, "but finances being what they are I can't go out and buy flowers on a whim."

After Barry became a Republican over foreign policy, he found himself reevaluating his support for the Democrats' domestic agenda. He echoes Louise Renaud on welfare, Tom Suma on taxes, and Geri Suma on moral values.

In 1984 he was a "Reagan Democrat." By 1988 he was a Republican precinct delegate. Unlike Louise and Geri, there are no Democratic icons from the past adorning his home, and there aren't likely to be in the future. "I don't think my true ideals have changed, but I approach problems from a much different aspect."

The problem for Democratic leaders is that Geri Suma, Louise Renaud, and Barry Marino are typical, and so is Macomb County. In fact, Denver-based National Demographics & Lifestyles, which examines the nation's 212 metropolitan areas, says Macomb's profile is close to being that of America's typical middle-class white family. Football is big there. Wine tasting is not. The "in" leisure sport is bowling, not tennis. They shop at K Mart, not Neiman Marcus. Breakfast is bacon and eggs, not croissants and champagne.

In all parts of Middle America the masses of Democratic defectors are unlike the traditional Republican stereotype. Neither wealthy nor WASPy, these people are middle class in their orientation even if not always in their pocketbooks. As the 1990s dawned, counties like Macomb represented the cutting edge of political change across America, and the Democratic party, once the confident and sure 500-pound gorilla of American politics, was looking remarkably like the poor little lamb that had lost its way.

What has happened is "true not only in Macomb, but all over the United States," affirmed former Governor Blanchard, a rare Democrat willing to acknowledge the change. "The behavior in Macomb is similar to suburban Cleveland or Chicago. I think the amazing thing is that the suburbs seem to be the same all over the United States."

The South is no different, agreed Sander Levin, a Democratic congressman from suburban Detroit. "We lost Michigan for about the same reasons we lost the states in the South. If you look at the patterns of suburban voting in Michigan, they are quite similar."

Macomb County became something of a laboratory for trying to understand the change in American politics. The county and its voters have been dissected, examined, and documented by Democratic researchers.

Shaken by the size of Reagan's victories in Macomb, Michigan, Democrats in 1985 commissioned Stanley Greenberg, a highly respected but partisan Democratic pollster, to assemble a series of focus groups to examine the situation. Greenberg, whose wife Rosa Delauro would be elected to Congress in 1990 representing the New Haven, Connecticut, area, had received much of his political training from the antiwar movement and the war on poverty. A former Yale professor and political economist who at one point took Marxism seriously, Greenberg, by the late 1980s, considered himself a Social Democrat on the European model. When he took on the Michigan project, he was not prepared for the intensity of the reaction of Macomb whites, but he was a pro and knew he was witnessing a new reality.

Focus groups have become the rage in American politics. They are generally made up of about a dozen voters, picked because of their demographic profile and the information they can provide about the larger group they represent. They give an insight into a participant's innermost thoughts, concerns, and emotions which traditional public opinion polling cannot do because of the multiple choice nature of survey questioning. Focus groups, for example, provided George Bush's 1988 campaign team with a powerful issue—Dukakis' program that gave convicted murderers weekend furloughs.

Greenberg brought three dozen Macomb County registered Democrats who had voted for Reagan to a Sterling Heights, Michigan, motel in March of 1985. The voters were broken into four groups. Each participant was paid $35 for two hours and fed cold cuts. The tone was set when Greenberg read a quote from Robert Kennedy, a man held in reverence by these heavily Roman Catholic voters. The quote was RFK's eloquent call for Americans to honor their special obligation to black citizens whose forefathers had lived through the slave experience and who themselves were the victims of racial discrimination.

It went over like a lead balloon.

"That's bullshit," shouted one participant.

"No wonder they killed him," said another.

"I'm fed up with it," chimed in a third.

Greenberg was astonished at their vehemence. The resulting report sent a shudder through state and national Democrats. It was the first of a continuing series of research projects during the latter half of the decade that explained the problem, quite literally, in black and white.

The votes for Reagan among these traditional Democrats, Greenberg reported, stemmed from a "profound disillusionment, a loss of faith in the Democratic party," a sense that "the Democratic party no longer responded with genuine feeling to the vulnerabilities and burdens of the average middle-class person. Instead the party and government were preoccupied with the needs of minorities. . . . They advanced spending programs that offered no appreciable or visible benefit" for middle-class people.

The perceived failure of the Democratic party to convince middle-class voters that it cared about them was a blow to those Democratic officials who believed their own rhetoric: They were the party of the people.

But the real kick to the groin was the racial analysis. Party leaders minimized it at the time, but it was real, even then. And it was destined to grow larger as the Democrats refused to deal with whites' deepest frustrations and the Republicans grew adept at responding to them.

"These white Democratic defectors express a profound distaste for blacks, a sentiment that pervades almost everything about government and politics," the report said. "Blacks constitute the explanation for their vulnerability and for most everything that has gone wrong in their lives; not being black is what constitutes being middle class; not living with blacks is what makes a neighborhood a decent place to live. . . . These sentiments have important implications for Democrats, as virtually all progressive symbols and themes have been redefined in racial and pejorative terms."

Greenberg's study continued: White voters "reject absolutely any notion that blacks suffer special circumstances that would require special treatment by employers or government. There is no historical memory of racism and no tolerance for present efforts to offset it. There is no sense of personal or collective responsibility that would support government anti-discrimination and civil rights policies."

Paul Conn, the political honcho for the Michigan House Democratic caucus which had paid for the study, said that those who saw the report were "shocked by the intensity" of the racial sentiment. Nonetheless, he and the Michigan party took heed.

Governor Blanchard, who as congressman had represented part of Macomb, was arguably the most politically astute Democrat of the 1980s because he understood suburbanites, who by that time had become the key to electoral success across America. Over the next few years, Blanchard devised a legislative program that went to the heart of voters' complaints: He pioneered government-guaranteed savings plans to ensure that people could buy homes and send their kids to college. And he did so despite complaints from black leaders that the plans didn't do much for their people who lacked the cash to get into them. Blanchard also went on a prison-building spree to reinforce his tough-on-crime image.

Less than two years after Greenberg's report, Blanchard was reelected with 68 percent of the vote, both statewide and in Macomb. But in 1990, Blanchard fell off the political tightrope. He lost narrowly because he was unable to keep both inner-city blacks and suburban whites in his corner. He only carried Macomb by 54–46 and got a much smaller than typical turnout of black voters in Detroit. Blanchard was also a casualty of that year's public frustration with incumbents.

The quirks of 1990 aside, Blanchard's astuteness was apparent even in the 1970s when he was beginning his political climb. Well before most in his party, he realized that voters thought the Democratic party and its social programs were out of control. In 1975, as a freshman congressman, he called Ed Muskie's office when he heard the Maine senator had backed "sunset" legislation that would require programs to be reauthorized periodically to stop them from growing out of control. "You don't know me, but you owe me one," Blanchard told a member of Muskie's staff. "I was your Michigan coordinator [when Muskie ran for president in 1972] and you never made it to the Michigan primary. I'd like to be the House sponsor of the sunset bill."

Blanchard got his wish and it was his top issue for several years until his crusade for the federal bailout of Chrysler gave him the prominence that catapulted him into the governor's mansion. But it was the sunset issue that helped him build the image that worked so well for years: a Democrat who understood middle-class concerns.

The Democratic party's national leaders, however, lacked Blanchard's political instincts; they treated Greenberg's Macomb study like a mistress at a family funeral. It was the first of many warnings they would ignore. Because they wanted to believe it wasn't valid. Some rationalized that the school busing furor in Macomb had made it atypically racist. Others hoped it would pass, laying it to the phenomenon of Reagan's personal popularity. Underlying the failure of party leaders to act on Greenberg's message was a simple fact. They had no powerful rebuttal.

"They just couldn't let go," Conn remarked wryly. "Whether it was liberal guilt, an inability to let go of their sixties' and seventies' mindset, or they had brainwashed themselves," he wasn't sure. "Maybe they had repeated the same things so many times to themselves, it had become an element of faith and assumed a religious atmosphere."

It was certainly true, as Democratic leaders inevitably charged, that some of the defections were due to old-fashioned racism. The problem was that these leaders refused to believe it was anything else. They didn't see that most middle-class people in Macomb, as in suburbs from Hartford to Houston, were very different from their parents. From 1920–1960, government intervention helped their parents to get jobs, forced management to deal with them fairly, enabled them to educate their children, and gave their families a better standard of living. But now, government intervention seemed to consist solely of special favors for blacks. A half-century before, wealthy WASPs were equally offended by what they perceived as unfair government handouts to the Poles, Italians, and Irish. Their grandchildren now ran Macomb and America.

But with one political difference: sheer numbers. A half-century ago, those who felt they needed government help far outnumbered those who didn't. By 1990, that had changed.

Democratic leaders, however, refused to focus on the problem, preferring to chalk the whole thing up to racism. And understandably so. Dealing meaningfully with these voters' deep-seeded resentment about welfare, crime, and racial preference programs would require Democrats to reexamine their traditional stance of giving priority to the neediest when the interests of the poor clashed with other groups.

So they ignored the problem. But corroboration of Greenberg's report soon surfaced in Democratic polls during 1986 in Macomb and elsewhere around the country.

In 1987, the *Detroit Free Press* asked a pollster to follow a representative sample of Macomb voters through the 1988 campaign year. The results showed that while voters gave Democrats every chance to regain their allegiance, when the election came they voted as before: Republican. Greenberg's own follow-up studies reached the same conclusion.

What the research reflected, above all, was values—specifically, that the Democratic party no longer shared the values of the middle-class. The voters in Macomb and around the country continued to view Republicans as better able to hold down taxes, contribute to their personal prosperity, and keep the United States out of war. Democrats always had complicated reasons not to endorse what these voters considered to be common sense issues—national defense, lower taxes, and a thrifty government.

What was showing up in Macomb County, and around the country, was decades of change in the United States, most of it demographic, part of it attitudinal. That tidal wave was crashing up against the Democratic party and washing it away.

2

Joe Lunchbucket Doesn't Live Here Anymore

Former New Jersey Cong. Millicent Fenwick, the model for Lacy Davenport in Gary Trudeau's "Doonesbury" comic strip, loved to tell those who learned at her political knee about a woman hitchhiker she picked up in 1940. The Great Depression still had the nation in its grip that fall day as she drove along Route 202.

The sixtyish, overweight woman was walking down the road carrying a live chicken, its wings flapping, inside a string bag. Mrs. Fenwick stopped to offer a lift to the woman, who looked as though life had been rough on her. Her black skirt and jacket over a gray sweater captured her mood. She was not a happy soul.

As they drove along, the aging woman seemed to agree as Republican Fenwick propagandized for Wendell Wilkie, the GOP nominee running that year against FDR. Fenwick talked about the free enterprise system and about how FDR's New Deal had damaged America. Slowing the car to drop the woman off, Fenwick turned to her and said, "I hope you'll vote for Willkie."

The woman, clearly among the half of all whites then living below the poverty line, demurred. She had believed for years FDR's charges that Republican "economic royalists" didn't care about people like her. "You know, I think everything you say about Willkie is right, but I just get a kind of a feeling that Roosevelt's on my side." With that she climbed out of the Chevrolet.

Despite all the blue smoke and mirrors that is American politics in this high-tech age, the winning candidate is still the one who makes average voters feel he or she is on their side.

In the last decade of the twentieth century it has become crystal clear that all across America, as in Macomb County, average voters no longer see Democratic presidential candidates as being on their side. But many Democratic leaders don't understand this, or if they do, are unwilling to face up to it. They persist in believing that their control of Congress and most state governments shows that Americans really prefer Democrats, the real kind that believe in standing up for the little guy. Winning the White House, they insist, requires a return to the old-time Democratic religion.

There is no better example than the last two weeks of the 1988 presidential campaign. It was as if someone had whispered Millicent Fenwick's story in Dukakis' ear. He launched a populist drive keyed to the "On Your Side" theme aimed at voters who thought Democrats who stood up for the little guy were standing up for them. As Dukakis' speeches became more fiery, the crowds swelled and grew more enthusiastic. And for a two-day period, the polls showed the race was tightening. This made Dukakis think that maybe, just maybe, the old Democratic formula could still work.

It didn't, of course. True, his class warfare theme stirred the emotions and brought out the votes of traditional Democrats who still believed they were being victimized by the rich and who had previously been put off by Dukakis' dry technocratic style. But his last-minute strategy did something else: it confirmed the feelings of a much larger group of middle-class voters that he wasn't their type of guy.

The results shouldn't have surprised Dukakis. Tom Kiley, who understood white voters better than anyone else in the Dukakis high command, had insisted for months that such a class-oriented approach was the out-of-date "45 percent strategy." It would have worked at one time, sure, but *before* those who considered themselves middle class reached critical mass in the electorate.

The Republicans, however, certainly understood. When Lee Atwater saw Dukakis' tactical turn, the 1988 Bush campaign knew the election was over. "You can't win a 'haves versus have nots' campaign in a relatively stable, healthy society. You can't tell them they aren't doing well if they are," said Atwater during a February 1990 interview, two weeks before doctors discovered he had a malignant brain tumor that killed him a year later.

Dukakis had zeroed in on a target, but it was too small. He drew the core Democratic vote, exit polls showed, perhaps as no one had since Harry Truman. Those voters still bought into the class warfare mentality: Republicans only cared about the rich; Democrats looked after the little guy. But in this new age, that core vote just wasn't large enough to elect a president. By 1990, only one in ten white voters lived in poverty. The message the Democrats had geared to working-class people just didn't resonate with the middle class, which most workers now considered themselves to be.

Dukakis simply did not speak their language.

"If we lead with class warfare, we lose," explained Arkansas' Bill Clinton, who though only forty-five was the nation's senior governor in 1991, and a likely future presidential candidate.

"The traditional formula for the Democrats has been 'It's us versus them,'" said former Arizona governor and 1988 Democratic presidential candidate Bruce Babbitt. "Now we are victims of our own success. The argument, I think, is resolved by numbers. There are more of them than there are of us. It is a class-oriented pitch which has wonderful intensity for less than 50 percent of the people. That's the reason candidates like Jesse Jackson, Ted Kennedy, and Mario Cuomo simultaneously generate so much intensity among Democrats and have such a difficult time coming close to winning a [national] majority."

ABC News' 1988 exit poll explained why. Half of those who voted in the 1988 presidential election were middle class, with family incomes between $20,000 and $50,000 annually. Among those voters, Bush won roughly 55 percent of the vote.

Dukakis won six in ten votes from those with family incomes of $10,000 or less—but they were only 13 percent of the voting population. Bush won six in ten from the 22 percent of the voters who had family incomes of $50,000 or more. The two men basically split the 16 percent of voters with incomes from $10,000–$20,000, the remaining working-class vote.

Babbitt, a state attorney general who became governor by a fluke (one governor resigned and the next one died), dropped out of the 1988 Democratic presidential race after a dismal showing in the New Hampshire primary. He was nevertheless one of the few Democrats to emerge from the 1988 campaign with greater stature than before he began. In his two-plus terms as chief executive of the heavily Republican state, Babbitt made a tacit deal with the GOP-dominated legislature: "You give me the money to fund programs for the needy and I'll run a fiscally tight ship." It worked. Babbitt, who became an enormously popular figure in Arizona, balanced budgets and pioneered child care and environmental programs later adopted by other states.

But when he turned to national politics where communication skills were critical, Babbitt was out of his league. His body language was lousy and his delivery only marginally better. Even when he switched to contact lenses and took hours of media coaching, he still looked, by his own admission, like "Mr. Ed" on TV. But those who knew him loved him. He was genuine. He believed that politicians must tell the whole truth, even if voters didn't want to hear it. The media made him a cult figure, and even though he was the first to drop from the race, he became a celebrity among politicians, journalists, and academicians.

And it wasn't just Democrats who admired his sharp mind and straight-shooting character.

Bill Lacy, Reagan's top White House political aide for a time, when asked how the Democrats could ever win back the presidency, said, "They've got to find a Bruce Babbitt who is from a larger state and who is more articulate."

Babbitt understood what few Democrats did: that the demographic and attitudinal change in America over the past quarter century had reshaped the electorate. The majority of voters no longer saw themselves as a have-not constituency, nor believed that the Democratic party was willing to meet their needs.

"In 1950, we were a nation of economic classes," Babbitt explained. "The extraordinary success of the American economy has made us a classless society, so that the kids of labor leaders go to college listening to the same music, taking in the same popular culture" as the children of managers. "In 1950 you could spot the cultural differences between a steel worker and an aerospace engineer. That's very hard to do now. There are differences in the workplace, but there aren't anyplace else. They both tow their boats to the lake on the weekend. They all expect their kids to go to college. Economic stratification has been all but obliterated, not for everybody, but for 80 percent."

Most people, and perhaps most importantly, most voters thought they had a piece of the pie. In fact, more than two out of three 1988 voters, according to CBS-*New York Times* exit polls, had incomes of $25,000 or more, and almost as many owned their own homes. On the eve of World War II only a few more than four in ten Americans owned their own homes and almost half of all whites and nine out of ten blacks lived in poverty. Home ownership was especially critical to understanding the change. Not only was it symbolic of the American dream, but it also intrinsically changed behavior in the direction of middle-class values.

The increase in living standards was a two-step process. In the two decades after World War II, average family income doubled, taking inflation into account, and those living in poverty dropped from a third to about 15 percent of the population.

Peggy Noonan, who penned moving speeches for Reagan and Bush and was a celebrity after her book *What I Saw at the Revolution* became a best-seller, grew up during that era. "I was born in the Democratic precincts of Brooklyn, New York, in 1950," she told a Republican National Committee meeting in the summer of 1990, "and I grew up with people, the children and grandchildren of the immigrants of Europe, who thought—as I was taught to think—that the Republican party (forgive me) was the party of rich dullards. In our neighborhood, Democrats were cops and firemen. Republicans had profoundly uninteresting jobs like . . . insurance company vice president. They always seemed like the great cliché—country club guys, fat, a little self-satisfied, kind of snoozy."

By 1989, the Census Bureau said, the median family income, adjusted for inflation, grew to $34,210. For married couples, the norm was $38,547. Given the correlation between income and voting, the median family income of voters was much higher. Even more important to the partisan equation, the Congressional Budget Office said there had been roughly a 10 percent growth in median family income in Reagan's eight-year presidency, precisely the years during which millions of Democrats like Macomb County's Barry Marino cemented their GOP allegiance.

Other studies showed much slower income growth for the middle class, but they shared one fundamental flaw. They generally compared the median incomes of the late 1970s to those of the late 1980s, which for political purposes was unfair. The years 1978-1980 not only included a recession, but Carter's presidency as well. To understand how voters felt about Reagan and the GOP you had to realize they understood the distinction between the Carter and the Reagan years, and voted accordingly.

The numbers, although slightly stacked, also showed that there was some truth in Democratic complaints that Republican economics didn't help those on the bottom very much. That, however, gave the Democrats little political comfort for two reasons: Those on the bottom—the poverty rate remained 13 percent at the beginning of the 1990s—were too few of the total population; and they comprised an even smaller slice of the voters. A Census Bureau analysis of the 1988 voting patterns showed that voters with family incomes over $50,000 were almost twice as likely to vote as those with family incomes of less than $15,000. Besides, even among the poor, there was significant evidence of middle-class values— especially among the one in three below the poverty line who owned their own homes.

Political reality notwithstanding, many Democrats believed it was their role to continue to stick up for the downtrodden. And besides, it was popular at chic cocktail parties in the Boston-Washington corridor during the late eighties and early nineties to talk gleefully about how Reagan, Bush, and the Republicans had blown their chance. Any talk of a realignment in which the Republicans would become the true majority party had died, they boasted.

During the first two years of Bush's term, they waited for the economic catastrophe that would return the nation to its New Deal senses. And in 1990 the economy did indeed enter a recession. But times had changed. Even though voters didn't like the economic downturn, they were no longer beguiled by the Democratic class warfare message.

To a large degree that could have been because the Democrats had another class problem—the growth of a "new class," those involved in politics, law, journalism, and government. Although this group was small and disproportionately affluent and elitist, it was also disproportionately Democratic and influential within party councils.

And it was heavily composed of baby-boomers. But not the typical ones who had trouble making ends meet and worried about how their kids would be cared for and schooled. The members of this "new class" declared they understood the needs of the middle class, and intellectually they did. But in their guts, they couldn't relate because this "new class" was composed of those who were by definition out of the mainstream. They were more likely to be single or, if married, childless; more likely to live in cities than suburbs, and if in the suburbs, invariably in the atypical close-in liberal kind; more likely to watch PBS than "The Simpsons."

Their lifestyle showed what they valued—an easy commute and classical music over safe streets and country-western. That alone stamped them as out-of-touch with average folks. They always seemed to be the ones who didn't understand why the Republicans picked up votes on values questions—like the Pledge of Allegiance.

That was because this "new class" had different values. On the margin they were more prone than average folks to worry about civil liberties—because invariably they were steeped in constitutional law—or not to care about taxes—because they could afford the increased levies. If some few Republicans were members of the "new class," they would hardly make a dent in the GOP. Within the GOP political apparatus they never achieved the same power as their counterparts did within Democratic councils.

The "new class" and the traditional Democratic class warriors shared at least one thing in common: a Marxist view of the world. They were consumed by the thought that money was the primary driving force in political life. That was why the Democratic establishment, top-heavy with members of the "new class," bought into the 1990s version of class warfare—tax fairness.

The issue had been boiling within liberal think tanks for some time. Ironically, the spark that set it off was a book by Kevin Phillips, a Nixon strategist in the 1968 election. Phillips' 1970 book, *The Emerging Republican Majority*, predicted the GOP presidential era.

But this time around he was wrong. His 1990 book, *The Politics of Rich and Poor*, argued that the increasing gap between the rich and poor in America stemmed from the Reagan tax cuts which reduced the tax code's progressivity and gave the rich a break at the expense of the middle class and the poor. It was questionable whether the middle class suffered in the 1980s. Studies, many from those with political axes to grind, tried to make that point. But in early 1991, a Census Bureau study, assumed to have less political bias, found otherwise.

Its comparison of household wealth between 1984 and 1988 found that the portion of the nation's wealth held by the richest 20 percent of Americans actually *fell*—from 47.5 percent to 44.4 percent. During that same period, the Census said, the percentage of wealth held by the poorest 20 percent of Americans fell negligibly, from 7.2. percent to 7 percent. Meanwhile, the share of wealth held by the three middle quintiles—the American middle class—increased.

What's more, in the spring of 1991, the Bureau of Labor Statistics (BLS) did a little-noticed study that went a long way towards undercutting Phillips' basic premise—that real incomes hadn't gone up much for average families.

In 1983, the BLS had refigured the Consumer Price Index used to measure inflation. It modified the existing formula aimed at calculating the cost of housing for average people by beginning to figure in only price increases for residences, not investment real estate.

But it wasn't until 1991 that the BLS went back and refigured inflation for the years before 1983 using the new, and it was agreed, more accurate measure. When that was done it revealed startling results: Since the new formula showed inflation had been a good deal lower than previously thought, much more of the gain in median family income was actual, rather than the result of inflation. In fact, between 1970 and 1989—roughly the period Phillips argued had seen stagnant middle-class incomes—the increase in the median standard of living in real terms had been 39 percent higher than previously thought.

But even if Phillips had been correct—that the rich were getting richer—his thesis that the Reagan tax cuts were responsible was badly off base. A Congressional Budget Office (CBO) study found that among the richest 10 percent of American families, incomes rose $16,000 between 1980 and 1988, but only $1,200 of that total came from the tax changes. Phillips nevertheless maintained that income disparity would almost certainly lead to a populist revolt that would puncture the GOP's success.

Democratic leaders loved the book because it reinforced their basic beliefs. The same Kevin Phillips who a decade before had been excoriated by Democrats became their new patron saint. They figured that he couldn't be wrong. After all, he was a prominent Republican. But, in fact, by 1990 Phillips hadn't been near a Republican strategy meeting in more than a decade. The GOP had changed, his Northeastern wing of the party was a bit player, and he was no longer an insider.

Facts notwithstanding, the media sought Phillips out for comment because, identified as a Republican insider, he gave their stories the look of authority. The media could as easily have gone to Democrats, who would have said the same things, but Phillips' past gave his words weight and his book became a best-seller.

Because Democratic leaders wanted so badly to believe Phillips was right they didn't look carefully at the evidence—he, too, used data that included the Carter years in calculating his claim that the middle class fared poorly in the 1980s. So in 1990, they made his arguments the center of the Democratic program to reduce the federal budget deficit. Democrats, complained Republican Senate Leader Robert Dole, tried to "cast this as Republicans for the rich and they're for everybody else. . . . That's the same old Democratic lie that's been out there for twenty, thirty, forty years."

The Democrats got a break when Bush bungled the budget

negotiations, and for a while it looked as if the charge might stick. Bush took a nose dive in the polls and the Democrats dreamed of a big year at the ballot box. They quickly ran TV ads that portrayed the GOP as the party of the rich and waited for the GOP scalps to fly. But they were wrong. They had misunderstood.

Just because the polls showed that Americans believed the wealthy did not pay their fair share of taxes did not translate into their believing that the rich ought to be punished. And that's because polls showed that Americans generally believed the wealthy had earned their money through intelligence and hard work. Besides, who was rich and who was comfortable was in the eye of the beholder. Everyone wanted at least to be comfortable. In fact, a *Washington Post*-ABC News poll in October 1990 found that one in four Americans (also 45 percent of those aged 18-30) thought it likely they would someday be rich.

It wasn't hard for the average guy to figure it out. Democratic calls for soaking the rich would make it potentially more difficult for him to become comfortable—and stay that way.

In 1990, the GOP enjoyed the best showing in a generation by the party holding the White House. In elections since 1954, the party in the White House had averaged a loss of twenty-six House seats, three Senate seats, and five governorships. In 1990, the party of the president lost one Senate seat, nine House seats, and one net governorship, but only because two former Republicans running as independents took the state houses in Connecticut and Alaska. Without Bush's screw-up on the budget the GOP would have probably picked up some seats—almost unheard-of by the party in the White House.

But like tabloid reporters, Democratic leaders decided they wouldn't let the facts get in the way of a good story. They declared it a huge victory, and to some degree the media bought it.

"The American public has awoken to what really happened in the 1980s," Democratic National Chairman Ron Brown said the day after the 1990 balloting. "The 1980s were not a glory period for America as Ronald Reagan and George Bush tried to tell us. They were a disaster. The rich got richer, the poor got poorer, and the middle class got squeezed. This is going to be a telling message as we move toward 1992 . . . . That's what the debate is going to be about over the next two years leading up to the 1992 presidential race."

And Brown wasn't alone. The three congressional Democrats who, along with Brown, spoke for the party—House Majority Leader Richard Gephardt, House Speaker Tom Foley, and Senate Majority Leader George Mitchell—all boarded the fairness train.

It was as though they had forgotten that in 1980 Jimmy Carter had lost with a party platform that declared "in all of our economic programs, the one overriding principle must be fairness," or that in 1984 Walter Mondale was buried alive when voters rejected the view of America expressed in that year's platform that "a corrosive unfairness eats at the underpinnings of our society."

Some Democrats did realize what was going on. But they were outshouted, outranked, and pretty much ignored by the media. "Kevin Phillips' view of an extreme populism is a siren song," said David McCurdy, elected at age thirty to Congress representing the Oklahoma City area. By 1990 McCurdy had ten years seniority and a gut understanding of why his state and district went heavily for Republican presidential candidates. That's why he survived. "I don't believe that is a platform for Democrats to win on. It has a certain sex appeal, a certain flash. But when you really start to examine it, I think it falls short."

But good sense lost out and the party's congressional leadership sided with Brown—and against the majority of American voters. It reinforced the prevalent view that Democrats wanted to create a society where everyone could dream of being comfortable/rich, but, once there, no one should stay that way. Democrats seemingly believed that having money was intrinsically bad, that those who had it must have done something wrong on the way.

In short, Americans agreed with Democrats that keeping the poor from getting poorer was good. But they didn't agree that keeping the rich from getting richer was equally good.

Americans, that is, rejected the Democratic view that income equality was a desired goal. In October 1990, when the Democratic tax fairness campaign was at its height and supposedly moving millions of one-time Democrats back to the fold, a *Washington*

Post-ABC poll showed that more than eight in ten people interviewed agreed "it's important to allow people to make as much money as they legally can because that's what makes the economy grow."

Americans understood that capitalism by definition meant that some people did better than others. The system rewarded effort and they believed that was right. In 1985 a survey by the National Opinion Research Center at the University of Chicago asked people if they agreed: "It is the responsibility of government to reduce the difference in income between people with high incomes and those with low incomes." Only 22 percent did so.

The middle class no longer considered the rich the enemy. Instead, they saw the black underclass as the enemy—the chief obstacle to the security of their daily existence—because of the tax money it consumed. Any tax increase was bad: first, because even if it began with the rich, the middle class knew such levies couldn't raise very much money so, inevitably, the Democrats would raise their taxes too; and second, because the middle class had lost patience with government programs for the poor, which only wasted their tax money. This racial tension, fueled by differences in economic status, lifestyle, and values, made class warfare a political loser for the Democrats.

"What had existed in the sixties and seventies was a fad whose time has gone," explained Mike Espy, Mississippi's first black congressman since Reconstruction. "Middle-class people are really concerned about their own lifestyle and their family's lifestyle. In their mind the nation's resources are diminishing, the pie is growing smaller, and the people are becoming more conservative to safeguard what they have."

Despite all their rhetoric, Democrats, as Sen. Sam Nunn, D-Ga., put it, had begun to accept that "in presidential elections, Republicans are now the de facto majority party. Democrats are the minority party in presidential elections." They knew, as Nunn said in 1989, that "with reapportionment coming up, the picture is likely to get worse as electoral votes migrate to the South and West where we are the most vulnerable."

Sen. Bob Graham of Florida understood earlier than most that the status quo—in which the GOP held the White House and the Democrats most everything else—was bound to change. "If we do not move quickly to deal with the issue at the presidential level," he told a meeting of the Democratic Leadership Council in March 1989, "we are no longer going to have the ability to be the successful party at the state and local level. We are not just talking about the important goal of electing national leadership. My friends, we are talking about survival."

The view from those without a real stake in the party is even harsher. Ira Arlook was the executive director of Citizen Action, the national umbrella organization whose economically populist citizen groups have two million members in twenty-five states. And it not only bought into the class warfare message, but actively tried to sell it. Although the organization's leadership, like Arlook, generally supported Democrats, its members were more likely to be independents. They, like everyone else, were moving toward the Republicans.

"The Democratic party is a shell. It's not what parties used to be. It's not machinery. Look at the DNC [Democratic National Committee]. What do they have? You can run an excellent operation and still have it mean less than it once did because there are fewer Democrats.

"The battleground statewide is more and more with independent voters," he added. "It's the candidate who can appeal to the independent voters, not the party apparatus. A good Democratic party operation can bring out the Democratic vote, but that frequently isn't enough to win anymore. Michael Dukakis did not have trouble winning Democratic votes, even among those who had voted for Reagan. The Reagan Democrats came home. The problem is there aren't enough Democrats anymore, even with conservative Democrats. And the rest could not be appealed to by Mike Dukakis' message."

The Democrats' own polls showed that even those who called themselves Democrats trusted the Republicans more than their own to run the country.

Dave Barry, the Pulitzer Prize-winning humorist, caught the public attitude about the Democrats nicely, describing them as "the kind of people who'd stop to help change a flat [tire], but would somehow manage to set your car on fire. I would be reluctant to trust them with a Cuisinart, let alone the economy."[1]

A survey in the spring of 1989 by a consortium of the Democratic party's best polling minds found that the Democratic argument that their electoral ineptness was due to the candidate, not their message, was flat-out wrong.[2] The study found that voters didn't agree with Democrats on the issues voters considered important, and, probably significantly, didn't trust them. Of the 37 percent of the electorate that still considered themselves Democrats, only 57 percent had a positive opinion of the national Democratic party.

In 1988, according to National Election Studies polls, 78 percent of those who voted for Bush called themselves Republicans, and he won a comfortable victory. By comparison, that same academic consortium's data in 1964 showed that GOP nominee Barry Goldwater got 76 percent of his votes from self-identified Republicans and was beaten badly. The conclusion is inescapable: Today, Republicans can win by relying mostly on their voters, rather than winning over Democrats as had been the case for decades. The tables have turned!

And all of this is the result of changing lifestyles among the mass of white voters that have rejected class warfare. The Democratic party's leaders not only don't share this view, they do not even comprehend it.

It was the first week of the 1984 fall campaign. Beginning with a Labor Day parade through empty streets in New York, Democratic presidential nominee Walter Mondale suffered through the type of incredibly bad week that could provide a case model for campaign managers.

Trailing badly in the polls and fearing that his support among the Democratic members of the House of Representatives might begin to crumble, he met privately with the House Democratic caucus.

As was fitting, House Speaker Thomas "Tip" O'Neill presided at the session, held on the ornate floor of the House of Representatives, with the press and public galleries closed off, allowing candidate and members of Congress to vent their feelings freely. Mondale's words, low, sad, and reflective, echoed what had countless times come out of O'Neill's mouth: "I go out and campaign among these guys whose parents went to school on the GI bill, got their first house on FHA housing, whose life has been made by these Democratic programs. Then they go out and make $20,000 a year and start voting Republican." It didn't take a rocket scientist to realize neither man understood what was happening to the electorate, nor how to reach it.

Neither one understood that upward mobility didn't stop at $20,000 a year. It was almost as if Democrats believed that as their constituents became more affluent, they should vote out of past loyalty rather than self-interest. Mondale's campaign manager, Bob Beckel, remembered that "for him the notion that blue-collar workers could go any place but the Democratic party was a shock."

But Mondale wasn't alone. It was symptomatic of an entire generation of Democratic leaders. "When you looked at the audience," Beckel continued, "a lot of the older guys who had been in the Democratic party a long time were with him nostalgically on it. But the younger guys, you could see them looking at him and realizing times had changed and Mondale didn't realize that. Fritz happened to step into American politics during the single largest transition period the Democrats have gone through since the 1920s."

Although he wasn't elected to Congress until 1986, John Lewis, a black congressman whose Atlanta district is split between blacks and whites, understood. "The people who are not middle class are trying to become middle class. And those who are in the middle class are trying to do better. The Democratic message doesn't appeal to their aspirations."

In November of 1984—as in the last several presidential elections—the traditional Democratic voters who were now middle class gave Mondale, O'Neill, & Co. the back of their hand.

ABC News' exit polls showed Mondale got less than 38 percent of voters in the middle class—those with incomes of

$20,000-40,000. When only whites with those incomes were counted, his share dropped a couple of points.

One component of that loss was that Mondale, who probably personally knew every union official this side of Gdansk, got just 54 percent of the votes of union members and their families. Among white union members, and among all blue-collar workers regardless of union status, Mondale only drew 49 percent.

Mondale lost in the biggest political landslide in American history. Class warfare didn't work anymore.

Unions were dying and with them the largest constituency for class warfare. The reason was apparent. During the quarter century beginning with World War II, the phenomenal growth in the American economy was in the big corporations and their unionized blue-collar work force. But in the midsixties that began to change. Economic growth over the next twenty-five years was fueled by the small entrepreneurs in technology and nonunion service industries.

To understand the impact of this economic evolution all you have to do is look at Pittsburgh. The one-time home of the steel industry had been a labor stronghold. But people and jobs have been leaving the metropolitan area for decades. By 1989, only 1 percent of Pittsburgh's residents worked in steel mills, and no operating mills existed within the city limits.

The situation is the same in almost all the heavy industries throughout the "Rust Belt" states that stretch from New York to Missouri. As a result, the proportion of Democratic voters who come from families containing a union member fell from 22 percent to 14 percent between the 1950s and 1988.[3]

In 1988, ABC's exit polls showed Michael Dukakis received 64 percent of the union vote—enough for victory in the heyday of unionism, but not anymore. By 1990, just 12.5 percent of the work force in private industry was unionized. Only the growth of unions among public employees—37 percent of government workers were unionized—allowed unions to claim just under 16 percent of the total workforce. That was little more than half the 30.5 percent of the workforce it had represented in 1968, before the Democratic coalition began unraveling.

Even among the rank-and-file there was a sense that the union leaders' political priorities often differed from the average Joe's once the labor bosses left the bargaining table. This was especially true as the labor movement, aware of its diminishing base, began associating with such liberal causes as abortion rights, feminism, and gay rights.

As the union share of the electorate shrank, the number of voters for whom the union label carried a negative taint increased. Partly, it came from a diminished understanding among young people—who are suspicious of big institutions like labor anyway—of the unions' part in building up the middle class. What showed up in opinion polls was a sense among the electorate that the unions were greedy and often pursued their goals to the detriment of the national good.

The slow erosion of union strength reinforced the loss of class consciousness for union members and further undercut the Democrats' class warfare theme. With only one in eight workers in the private sector belonging to a union, wage gaps developed among people of similar age, qualifications, and skills doing the same job.

Since there were no unions to keep salaries uniform, companies paid higher wages to the most productive employees. The new American economy saw the growth of jobs in which a worker's initiative and creativity mattered. In the old days, from the employer's point of view, there wasn't much difference between an excellent assembly line worker and a mediocre one, as long as the product didn't fall apart. But with the U.S. economy entering a new, computer-driven era, that changed. Education and productivity were rewarded. The casualty was the sense of worker solidarity.

When voters begin to look at the rich/comfortable guy with the big house as someone like them who had just worked a little harder or better, it became political suicide to focus on him as the enemy. In 1990, a Gallup Poll showed that only half of those surveyed felt an income of $95,000 made you rich.

Democratic class warfare didn't work anymore because there were many more Americans who thought they were closer to being rich than to being poor. Beckel believed "the most significant political event of the last two decades" was the GOP's ability "to convince middle Americans that their interests were best served by attaching themselves to wealthy people and divorcing themselves from poor people. Reagan made it by convincing them that as a poor person goes up the ladder one rung, the middle class comes down one, whereas when wealthy people go up they pull the middle class with them."

And, conceded Democratic National Chairman Ron Brown, "we missed that tilt." Democratic leaders didn't realize what was happening until too late. They still talked about more government programs. "For years they [Democratic leaders] looked upon the vast, sprawling landscape of government spending and stood for a one-word platform: more."

The perceived fiscal irresponsibility, especially concerning programs for the poor, clashed with middle-class values of frugality and reinforced its resentment. What's more, by the 1990s polls showed that even those not in the middle class shared the same values, aspirations, and resentments. American society, it seems, was not made up of static economic classes. In a 1990 study, the Census Bureau found that three out of four Americans saw their incomes rise or fall at least 5 percent annually, often a good deal more. This income mobility fostered middle-class dreams—the hope that the upside growth would in their case prevail.

Because average voters no longer saw the greedy rich (Republicans) trying to take advantage of them, they didn't think they needed government protection. Politically, this was the crucial attitudinal change.

The new middle class thus no longer considered it necessary to bear the tax burden and the government bureaucracy that provided such protection. This antitax sentiment, which spawned a host of tax rebellions across America in the late 1970s, was the spark that fired the GOP electoral rebirth.

The middle class' frustration with taxes and its belief that the bureaucracy was stupid—and possibly evil—fueled its growing cynicism about politics.

Tom Brazaitis, Washington bureau chief for the *Cleveland Plain*

Dealer, Ohio's largest and most powerful newspaper, had for some time grasped the disillusionment intellectually. But in 1990, it hit him right between the eyes. That spring, in his weekly column, Brazaitis castigated taxpayers for not checking off the box on their returns allowing $1 of their taxes to be used to finance presidential campaigns. The response from his readers—the crowd that defines the American middle class—was overwhelming. Virtually all of them told Brazaitis he was hopelessly naive.

"They all said, 'But you don't understand! This is the only way we can say no to the government,' " remembers Brazaitis, who is confident that almost all the response came from whites. The federal fund that finances presidential elections was facing bankruptcy in the early nineties precisely because whites were turning off the political process in large numbers.

There has been massive publicity about how minorities feel politically powerless, and no doubt they do. But simple logic suggests that change in the last quarter-century, when political cynicism took center stage, has been among whites.

Roughly 61 percent of the eligible electorate voted in the 1968 presidential election. By 1988 the figure was down to 50 percent. But during that same period voting by minorities increased dramatically. The inescapable conclusion is that there has been a steep drop-off among whites.

Another conclusion can be drawn: Since the standard of living among whites has risen steadily, the voter drop-off has come from the middle class, not the poor. By not voting, the middle class was giving government the finger figuratively. The reason stemmed from a mental and emotional transformation. The parents of voters like Tom Suma had never paid much in income taxes and seemed to benefit from government programs because they had low incomes. But now the Tom Sumas, the middle-class wage-earners, were paying up to half their income in taxes and felt they weren't getting much at all in return. This feeling was especially powerful in the South, and in the bulging Northern suburbs.

Equally devastating to the class warfare issue, particularly in the South, was the intense state competition that developed during the 1980s for economic development projects. Public officials couldn't woo companies to set up shop in their states if they were running class warfare campaigns, because firms wouldn't do business in states where politicians used the private sector as their whipping boy and banker of their social programs. Most Democrats who dropped the populist financial theme prospered.

One was Bill Clinton, the boy wonder of the Democratic party when elected governor at age thirty in 1978. He became the preeminent Democratic voice on education reform, emphasizing private sector involvement rather than massive new federal panaceas. For that reason, Clinton was invited to Bush's 1990 State of the Union speech. Bush put his stamp on the education reform Clinton had helped develop in concert with both Republican and Democratic governors, who acknowledged that massive amounts of new federal money were not the answer.

This put Clinton at odds with an angry Ted Kennedy. He recalls that Kennedy took him aside and lectured him about the evils of dealing with the Republicans because they were The Enemy: "He said, 'Bush is trying to be the education president and is trying to minimize his own responsibility. Those of us who are trying to fund these programs feel like we are being boxed in because you guys are giving your credibility over to him.' He was pretty critical of that. I understand where he was coming from, but I told him Bush was the only president we've got. How can a Democratic governor refuse an invitation from a Republican president who is at least entering into a serious dialogue?"

The lack of understanding between two Democratic generations—Kennedy and Clinton—was not an isolated incident. Nowhere has this difference been clearer than between father and son Indiana politicians Birch and Evan Bayh.

The elder Bayh was a typical New Deal liberal. As a U.S. senator (1962-1980), he always voted with labor and minorities. That was what Democrats did. When he sought the presidency in 1976 Bayh was the darling of the liberals. But he did not comprehend what was happening. Carter won the presidential nomination that year by deviating from the Democratic Holy Crusade, class warfare. Insult piled on injury. In 1980, Bayh lost his Senate seat to a young Republican, Dan Quayle, who rode Reagan's themes of smaller government and lower taxes. Yet Birch Bayh, private citizen, remained—and remains—a liberal.

Evan Bayh won the governorship of Indiana at age thirty-three in 1988, the same year Bush easily carried the state. But Bayh's politics were a world apart from his father's. He enjoyed labor support and was on good terms with minorities. But, because he didn't automatically equate their interests with those of average voters, he also opposed them at times.

"The answers of the nineties can't be the same as the answers of the sixties," Evan Bayh asserted. "People who two decades ago had considered themselves have-nots now have a material stake in our society. They are more interested in being protected from government than being assisted by government. In my father's day his impulse might have been, 'Here's a problem, it needs to be solved. Let's create a department.' That's not my first reaction. Mine would be to get the private sector to work on it, or through incentives give individuals some encouragement to help with this. Only then would I think about creating a governmental entity. That is a significant difference in perspective."

Unlike most party leaders, Bayh recognized something fundamental had changed in how average voters reacted to political questions. Aspiration had become the dominant emotion, and even those who weren't quite middle class thought they could be. More important politically, they behaved as though they already were.

In the spring of 1989, pollster Greenberg, whose warnings based on Macomb County four years before had been ignored, put it bluntly to whoever would listen: "There is no longer an enduring electoral majority in America centered on a coalition of production workers, low-income families, minority and aging communities," Greenberg said. There were not enough voters who viewed themselves as "have-nots" to win the November election, he insisted.

In 1985, the size of the economic transformation was brought home to Al From, head of the Democratic Leadership Council, a group set up by moderate party officeholders such as Graham and Nunn to move the party back to the ideological middle. Al From had understood intellectually what was happening, but attending his wife's twentieth high school reunion drove home the message.

Ginger From graduated from Banks High School in Birmingham, Alabama, in 1965, before desegregation. When she was
in high school, it seemed to Ginger that most fathers worked in the
city's booming steel mills or in other blue-collar jobs. She lived in
the East Lake neighborhood that even twenty-five years later remains one of the city's white bastions.

The night of the reunion was not what From had expected based
on his wife's memory of the neighborhood: "They had a roster of
what everyone was doing now. Of the two hundred people on the
roster, I only found a half-dozen blue-collar jobs. The rest were in
the service sector and new collar jobs" which meld traditional blue-
collar tasks with the modern economy, such as a Federal Express
route driver. "The point is, there isn't a working class," From
explained. "Everyone now thinks they are middle class."

Ginger also attended a reunion of her high school sorority, Sigma
Chi Delta. "Most of the girls had come from blue-collar families,
but although we didn't take a vote or even discuss politics I would
bet you every single one of them was now a Republican," she
reported.

The decreasing effectiveness of class warfare delivered an especially
heavy blow to Democrats in the South, where it formerly had great
appeal. The South had by far the largest share of the nation's poor
whites and had been the country's most staunchly Democratic
region since the Civil War.

But the South changed: From a stagnating, agriculturally dependent region that lost people to the Northern cities, it became a
vibrant industrial and demographic magnet. Air conditioning,
cheaper land, natural beauty, and a less complicated lifestyle attracted millions to the South—and the West. The two areas became
known as the "Sun Belt." During the 1970s and 1980s growth rates
reached fifteen times higher there than in the Northeast and Midwest, the largest population shift in U.S. history.

There was no better proof than the emergence of Wal-Mart
stores, an Arkansas-based chain that built its business in the South
and West during that period as the nation's leading retailer. Wal-

Mart took the title from Sears Roebuck, the Chicago-based firm with stores located heavily in the declining cities and close-in suburbs of the Northeast and Midwest where there were no longer as many potential customers.

If business didn't lead the wave, it certainly went along. Labor was lower and material costs were cheaper than up north. In 1900, two-thirds of the South's labor force had been in farming and mining and almost all its manufactured goods had come from the labor-intensive North. But by 1985, only 5 percent of the region's workforce farmed or mined. Between 1960 and 1985 the South gained 17 million new jobs and the West added another 11 million. The Northeast and Midwest combined added just 13 million during that same period.

This migration also meant that voters were literally moving in the Republican direction. The North and East had been home to Democratic traditions of government doing for people. The Sun Belt disdained governmental activism. Haley Barbour, a former Reagan White House political director, believes that "realignment in the South is not a product of just conservatives in the South leaving the Democratic party, but it's migration into the South and industrialization of the South. The in-migration frankly affected more voters than the philosophical movement from Democratic to Republican party, but that is what has probably given the thing critical mass."

In 1952, almost eight in ten white Southerners called themselves Democrats.[4] In 1988, George Bush won the Southern white vote by more than 2-1, and by a 53-41 margin white Southerners identified themselves as Republicans. In short, by 1988 white Southerners made up only 23 percent of the Democratic party nationally, compared with 31 percent in 1960.[5] As a result, the generally conservative Southerners had a shrinking role in party affairs, including the selection of presidential candidates. And that in turn drove more of them into the Republican ranks. It was a destructive cycle for the Democratic party.

The Institute for Southern Studies, a Durham, North Carolina-based nonpartisan think tank, found that Southern counties that had voted for Bush in 1988 by more than a 2-1 margin were growing two and three times faster than those that had backed Dukakis. It was not surprising since Bush carried the white, suburban middle-class areas, while Dukakis did best in the inner cities. "You see a real problem across the board," conceded Susan Estrich, Dukakis' 1988 campaign manager. "Whatever the issues were this time and that time, we've got a continuous problem in the last three or four [presidential] elections, running in the 30 percent range among white Southern voters."

Progress was slower at the state than at the national level, but anyone who didn't think the Republicans would control the Sun Belt by the turn of the century had probably also bought an Edsel. The population shifts combined with Sun Belt political attitudes resulted in a 1990 census that required redistricting, which would benefit Republicans. In the fifty congressional districts that grew the most in the 1980s, Bush got 60 percent of the vote in the 1988 election. Of the fifty that lost the most, Dukakis got 55 percent of the vote in 1988.

A total of nineteen Electoral College votes—and congressional seats—will move to the Sun Belt from the North and East by 1992. That means that Republicans have almost a lock-tight grip on more than 220 of the 270 electoral votes needed to win the White House.

While Democrats see the population, economic, and electoral vote numbers, they seem unable to understand how the three worked together to defeat Democrats. "The leadership in the national party," laments Lewis, the black congressman from Atlanta, "and people in Washington have failed to keep up with the white South and how it has changed." Lewis, a thoughtful man and civil rights pioneer, knows that, unfortunately for the Democrats, it was not just a Southern problem.

The party has been unable to understand that politicians who can't deal with change are destined to be overwhelmed by it. And this lack of insight will turn out to be just as responsible for the Democratic deterioration as the death of class warfare.

3

The Elephant Is Smarter Than the Donkey

America's economy and way of life were changing rapidly as the new century neared. But the Democratic party was hanging on to the past for dear life. The Speaker of the U.S. House of Representatives summed it up well: "The Democratic party is like a man riding backward in a railroad car. It never sees anything until it has got past it."

Maine's Thomas Reed was talking about the turn of the twentieth century, but he could just as easily have been describing his party today.

In the last decades of the 1800s, America moved from an agrarian to an industrial economy. The assembly line replaced the plow as the symbol of the American economy. Democrats either didn't, or refused to, comprehend the immense changes in the offing. They threw in with the Western and Southern agrarians against the industrialists—a decision that with historical hindsight was incredibly shortsighted. It was as if the Democrats thought they could hold back the hands of time.

The preeminent conflict of the day was over the relaxed money policies that farmers and ranchers wanted to keep interest rates down and reduce their ever-present debt burden. But these policies guaranteed inflation, and that ran counter to the interests of the Northeast and Midwest, home to the new industries and the vast majority of voters.

The Democrats opted for relaxed money and paid a heavy price for their miscalculation: From 1860 to 1932—when the Depression created fertile ground for the class warfare mentality—the only Democrats to win the White House were Grover Cleveland and Woodrow Wilson, both capitalizing on GOP fratricide.

Yes, there were other reasons for Republican dominance. It certainly helped that the GOP was the party that "won the Civil War," in a sense the GOP's nineteenth-century version of being tough on defense. But at its core, the virtual GOP monopoly on the White House during that period was because it better understood the change America was undergoing and moved with it.

A century later, as the twenty-first century neared, yet another new order was taking hold. And the Democrats had not learned from their mistakes. This time, the industrial age was being lowered into the ground. Computers and microchips were the engines of this economic change. The information age was dawning.

In fact, by the early nineties, almost three out of five workers were classified as either professional, technical, or white collar—which meant they were toiling in the jobs of the future.

Fewer than one in three were blue-collar workers. And the clout in American economics and politics was moving South and West.

Once again the Democrats opted for the past. Whenever they were forced to choose between policies that helped the changing society or those tied to the past, they opted for the latter—mainly because the two remaining parts of FDR's coalition were having difficulty dealing with the changing economy. Union jobs were disppearing in older Northern and Midwestern industries and being created at a much slower rate in the new entrepreneurial Sun Belt economy which was fueled by small business growth. And blacks were at a competitive disadvantage in this new age, on the whole they lacked the education needed to compete effectively. So, in order to protect their core constituents, Democrats gave away the high ground on the question of change.

But GOP strategists, aware that American society was moving from an industrial to an information-based economy, were better equipped to deal with the political ramifications of the demographic shift. In 1985, Bill Lacy, head of the Republican National Committee's political operations and later Reagan's top White House political aide, circulated a memo to GOP officials airing John Naisbitt's and Alvin Toffler's futuristic views of an evolving society to alert them to the change. Whether the GOP consciously geared itself to the societal shifts or was in the right place when the tide turned, the result was the same.

Naisbitt's best-selling *Megatrends* that hit at the beginning of the 1980s spotlighted ten societal trends that he correctly predicted would dominate the decade. None of them advanced the Democrats, but several helped the GOP, some enormously. The decentralization in all walks of life was custom-tailored to the Republican philosophy, as was the increasing emphasis on self-help and the movement of the economy from a heavily unionized industrialized society to a nonunion informational age.

At the same time over at the Democratic National Committee (examined in detail in Chapter Nine), officials spent $250,000 for a massive report on the motivations of the electorate, then threw it into the trash when the findings disturbed them.

The Democrats were so far off target that *American Demographics* magazine in December 1989 listed them among the decade's ten worst misreaders of their own market. The magazine, the bible of the marketing business, compared the Democrats' bullheadedness to Coca-Cola's foolish attempt to kill Classic Coke just as a generation of baby-boomers wanted to be reminded of their youth, and to the fashion industry's decision to bring back the mini-skirt when the bulk of women were dressing for business careers.

In the marketing area Republicans have a definite advantage. Their political people generally have some business background. Early on they invested in computers, using the new technology in their campaigns more effectively than Democrats. In 1988 the Bush campaign used an IBM mainframe to pick through a decade of ratings and demographics from the nation's 212 TV markets to figure out the most effective way to reach voters. Unlike the

Democrats, GOP meetings traditionally feature a discussion of the changing electorate. GOP campaigns view the electorate as if it were a commercial marketplace. Voters, Republicans figure, evaluate a candidate as a variation of a consumer deciding which detergent to buy.

"They come from the Madison Avenue school of campaigning," (DNC) Chairman Brown reproved. But he had to acknowledge that "they have used those techniques very effectively."

Even when the political marketplace rejected a bedrock position of the GOP coalition, such as abortion, the Republicans understood how to go with the flow of public opinion. Shortly after the 1989 Supreme Court decision threw the touchy issue back to the states, the GOP began a drift to the middle. There was no way, given the GOP 1988 platform that called for a constitutional amendment to outlaw abortion, the Republicans could become the abortion rights party. Too large a part of their coalition, especially evangelical Christians and other social conservatives, viewed abortion as murder. Slowly but surely, however, the Republicans moved toward the public opinion center from their perch on the far right. Some GOP (and Democratic) candidates who had opposed abortion suddenly changed their minds—three in five voters believed abortion was murder, but the same percentage also thought it should be legally available. More in evidence were the Republicans who, having favored a constitutional amendment to ban abortion, now couched their opposition and supported more popular restrictions, such as requiring parental consent for teenage girls wishing to abort.

President Bush proclaimed the GOP tent big enough for all regardless of their position on abortion and conspicuously campaigned for prochoice GOP candidates in 1990. He and party leaders made sure that the GOP candidates in some of the highest profile races were for abortion rights. It showed just how quickly and adroitly the Republicans could shift with the political currents, in stark contrast to the more dogmatic approach of the Democratic hierarchy on most issues. Critics may have questioned the GOP's commitment to its stated principles, but they kept winning the White House; they preferred to sacrifice their principles rather than sacrifice their necks.

Not only do Republicans better understand the marketplace, but they are light years ahead of the Democrats when it comes to the technology of reaching it: television.

"You have to understand the impact on politics that television has had," said Tony Coelho, until 1989 third-ranking in the House Democratic leadership. Coelho earned House Republican Whip Newt Gingrich's genuine compliment of being the "smartest Democrat in America," and Republicans generally credit him with stopping them from taking over Congress in the 1980s. Coelho took personal command of the Democrats' House electoral apparatus when Reagan's popularity had them on the defensive. He twisted the arms of business lobbyists, making them cough up big money for Democrats in exchange for access to those who controlled Capitol Hill. Criticism of his ethics did nothing to stop him; Coelho used the money to modernize the campaign machinery and fund the counterattack which, combined with the 1982 recession, stopped the GOP offensive in its tracks.

"People in the past read their local newspaper. Often they had a tendency to be a couple of days late, and they could analyze it, but there were no pictures. Today, 60 percent of the American public gets 100 percent of their news from TV. That is staggeringly important. Democrats still don't understand that yet," sighed Coelho in 1990, after a cushy junk bond deal arranged through his business connections became public and forced him to resign his House seat.

"The Republicans have understood it for some time. People don't listen to the news, they watch it," Coelho continued. "That's very important because people make gut decisions on their politics based on images, based on feelings as opposed to reading it through and trying to understand it. We have not accepted that in our approach to national politics."

The key to television's impact on politics is the power of pictures, which people remember far more than the words spoken by reporters. This shouldn't have been news to Democrats. After all, TV pictures of Southern cops beating civil rights demonstrators and freckle-faced American boys coming home from Vietnam in body bags was what so dramatically shaped public opinion a generation ago.

In this new age, pictures are even more important because watching television is how Americans distract themselves while they do something else—eat dinner, wash the dishes, play with the kids. Thus they don't always pay close attention.

The White House under Reagan understood this perfectly. Marty Schramm, in *The Great American Video Game*, his book about the impact of television in the 1984 election, tells of CBS White House reporter Lesley Stahl doing what she considered one of the toughest stories ever on Reagan. Her story told how Reagan delegated everything to others, of his faulty grasp of detail, his having to read everything from cue cards. As she watched the piece, she was proud: she had brought the real Reagan to the American people. She braced for the protest from the White House high command and, sure enough, the phone rang inside her tiny cubicle in the White House press room moments later.

It was one of the president's senior aides, but to her utter surprise he was jubilant. "Great piece. We loved it."

"What do you mean, you love it," Stahl gasped, thinking she was being conned.

No, really, the Reagan man assured her, he was more than satisfied. Watch the story over, but turn down the volume, he advised. "We're in the middle of a campaign and you gave us four and a half minutes of great pictures of Ronald Reagan. And that's all the American people see. They don't listen to you if you are contradicting great pictures. They don't hear what you are saying, if the pictures are saying something different."

After watching the piece again, she understood. The visuals showed a smiling Reagan going in and out of rooms shaking hands, performing his official functions, basking in the adulation of flag-waving supporters. The words she had scripted about his shortcomings didn't match the message of the pictures: and the pictures won hands down.

On the campaign trail, the differences between the two parties are like night and day. Republicans worry about pictures above all else. Democrats say they do, but they always seem to come in second out of two.

There was no better example of this dynamic than on September

6, 1988, the second day of the fall campaign between Bush and Dukakis.

After trailing by up to 17 points over the summer, Bush had come up even by Labor Day, in large part by projecting an image of strength and instilling doubts about Dukakis' manliness. The pictures on the evening news shows of the candidates that day were just what the Republicans wanted America to see.

Bush, visiting the Northwest Marine Iron Works in Portland, Oregon, was jeered by union shipyard workers. Dukakis, speaking in a Polish community center in suburban Chicago, was confronted by antiabortion protesters.

Bush, his sleeves rolled up, challenged the overalls-clad crowd of hard hats, chanting "George go home" and "union buster," to let him speak. Combatively, he pulled out of his pocket a United Steelworkers of America union card from 1950 when he sold oil-drilling equipment in California. He wanted not only to show that he understood union concerns, but also to signal the millions who would watch the incident on the TV news clips that he wasn't going to take any crap.

By contrast, diminutive Dukakis, faced by demonstrators, many of them women shouting "abortion is murder" and "what about the unborn," was clearly rattled and stepped back from the podium. As he watched linebacker-sized bouncers carry out the protesters, one of whom was beaten up when he tried to explain his views to reporters, Dukakis stood with his arms folded, looking like the Harvard intellectual Republicans claimed he was.

That night viewers heard their TV reporters talk about how both men had been heckled, but the pictures showed two very different men: Bush the strong fighter, Dukakis the wimp.

To Tom Donilon, once the boy wonder of Democratic politics, and, in the early nineties, a "thirtysomething" veteran of three losing Democratic presidential campaigns, it was just more proof of the differences between the two parties. As he put it, "The Republicans understand the most important dimension in the presidential campaign is strength versus weakness. Everything they did was calculated to show Bush as a strong man."

Donilon had been around the track many times in the previous decade, and his candidates had been stepped on at every turn. He worked in the Carter White House as a college student, and in the 1980 Carter campaign against Ted Kennedy, he served as Carter's chief delegate counter. Later on, he was the main briefer for Mondale and Dukakis for their debates against Reagan and Bush in 1984 and 1988 respectively. Now a Washington lawyer, Donilon believes the Republicans have mastered presidential politics and it saddens him.

"The Republicans understand that themes and simple messages move people," he says. What Donilon doesn't say, but clearly believes, is that, at least in 1988, the Democratic candidate didn't understand that strength was the main issue. And if he had, he wouldn't have had the faintest idea how to use it.

"We are learning slowly," admits Democratic Chairman Brown. "We are a grass-roots party. Grass-roots politics is still important, but is not as absolutely dominant as it used to be. Media-dominated politics is of much greater importance, and [the Republicans] had a jump start on us in that area. The use of the media in politics is more of a business-oriented, upper-income-oriented technique. We relied on our strength, which was people at the grass-roots level. They relied on their strength—a Fortune 500, Madison Avenue, top-down approach—and it did give them a significant head start."

Republicans borrowed the techniques of product marketers. They foresaw that focus groups reveal how voters make decisions. They soon applied the "clustering" technique used by marketers to politics, dividing the nation's neighborhoods into one of forty types based on lifestyle. This allowed political messages to be carefully targeted. They were years ahead of Democrats in developing highly sophisticated polling techniques.

Democrats, on the other hand, came from labor or political backgrounds and generally lacked commercial training. Even though they had the same data on the changes taking place, they were ill-equipped to use it.

"The typical Democrat doesn't look at the technical side of politics," said Peter Kelly, a top party fund-raiser and formerly the party's national treasurer. "He's not poll-oriented. There are real differences in techniques. Democrats tend to be real seat-of-the-pants flyers. Republicans tend to be more jet fighters. Democrats think the people they know are typical, while Republicans look at demographics."

Kelly, a mountain of a man at 6'7" and 330 pounds, and a moderate, was probably *the* Democrat in America who understood the huge difference. He had an extra edge. At one time he had wanted to be Democratic national chairman, but when he saw the way the party was headed, he knew that wasn't in the cards.

Kelly became a partner in a wildly successful Washington, D.C., consulting firm set up by many of the top young politicos from the 1980 Reagan campaign—Roger Stone, Charlie Black, and Paul Manafort. Later they brought in Atwater. The firm made its money representing business and made its reputation staging campaigns. Kelly was useful as an entree to the Democrats in Congress. He in turn saw the GOP techniques up close and learned from them. He came to understand fully just how far behind the Democrats had slipped. It wasn't that the Republicans were all rocket scientists and the Democrats all morons. But there was a chasm between the two parties' ability and desire to understand a changing society.

The shifting political landscape threw up a series of obstacles for a Democratic party that had come to power under FDR on the votes of the young, Northern big-city ethnics, Southern rural whites, unions, minorities, and those who felt left out. It was always an odd coalition because, other than empty bellies, Southerners and rural whites had little in common with unions and blacks. The addition of cultural minorities, unknown as voting blocs in FDR's days, eventually brought another element to the Democratic base—hardcore feminists, homosexuals, and civil liberties activists.

Yet, for decades the Democrats were like a multisided crystal, and presidential candidates successfully reflected the side each of the constituent groups wanted to see. Southerners saw them as economic populists, minorities as their civil rights champions, Northern ethnics as their shield against the ruling WASPs. Until it all began to unravel in the late 1960s, diversity was an asset. The various ethnic groups may have feuded, but they had the same political agenda—upward mobility.

But in the seventies and eighties—although Democratic support among black voters remained rock solid, and the number of minority voters had grown greatly since the New Deal—the coalition was shredding. Millions of former laborers were now middle class and content with their lot in life, and this shattered the Democratic coalition that had been held together by bailing wire. The communications technology, moreover, provided a constant flow of information that convinced Middle America that its own interests clashed with the Democratic party agenda.

Macomb County symbolized the national mood: white Democrats were reacting negatively to the impact of cultural and racial minorities on the Democratic party. "Mass communications hurt the Democrats because before [television] they could be all things to all people," Sen. Phil Gramm (R-Tex.) remarked. "They could be talking about values in a traditional family setting. They could be talking about tolerance to alternative lifestyle people. They could be everything to everybody. When television came, you only could have one message. You couldn't go to Cleveland and deliver one message and go to Atlanta and deliver an opposite message. What you did in Cleveland showed in Atlanta."

Those who lived in the suburbs of Atlanta or Cleveland had more in common with suburbanites elsewhere than with people who lived in the city adjacent to them. Besides, there just weren't many big city ethnics anymore. Like former Reagan speechwriter Peggy Noonan's family, they had all moved to the suburbs. They were now suburban ethnics, or if they remained in the city, they shared the suburban mindset—which was a Republican view of the world.

At the beginning of the 1990s, a CBS-*New York Times* poll showed the American people were almost evenly split between the GOP and the Democratic party—a post–World War II Republican high. Ten years earlier, the month that Ronald Reagan was elected president, the same poll gave Democrats a 46-24 advantage. Even more distressing for Democrats was the clear pattern: whites were abandoning the party. In early 1990, whites identified as Republicans by a roughly 5-to-4 margin: the strongest white support of Democrats came from the oldest voters. During that same period, in countless traditionally Democratic states from Minnesota to Alabama, statewide polls showed GOP pluralities. Although Democrats edged ahead in the states and nationally in the fall of 1990, when Bush's handling of the budget created waves, the GOP surged ahead in the spring of 1991 following Bush's success in the Persian Gulf War. Whatever the events of the day, two things were clear: the Democrats 20-25 point lead was long gone, and the long-term trend favored the GOP.

Ohio, the symbolic home of Middle America—and other than California, the most important state in presidential elections because of its almost eerie ability to back the winner—showed how dramatic the change had been. In 1990, Al Tuchfarber, a University of Cincinnati pollster who surveys the Ohio electorate regularly, looked back and found that white Ohioans who had called themselves Democrats by a 49-38 margin in 1981 ended the decade identifying as Republicans by a 45-39 margin. In California, where in 1976 Democrats held a twenty-seven-point lead in identification, the two parties were almost equal.

Voters told pollsters that the GOP could better handle the economy and keep the peace—the two key issues in presidential voting.

The GOP made large inroads among the young, especially during the Reagan years. The change in voting behavior from past generations of young people stemmed from the simple fact that in the adult lifetime of these young people, Republicans had brought economic security and foreign policy stability. If they remembered a Democratic president it was Carter, whom they considered a failure. By 1992, three-fifths of the electorate will have been born since FDR died.

For decades, young voters were the most liberal age group in the electorate. Although they didn't vote much, when they did, they went heavily Democratic. In 1980, voters aged eighteen to twenty-nine called themselves Democrats by a 54-33 percent margin, said CBS-*NYT* data. A decade later the same poll found that Republicans held a 51-40 lead in that same age group. Tuchfarber found in 1990 that white Ohioans twenty-four years and younger were Republican by a 64-25 margin.

More telling was a Gallup poll taken simultaneously. It showed that 63 percent of the under-twenty-nine age group described the GOP as the party likely to do "a better job of keeping the country prosperous," while only 23 percent said that of the Democrats.

Ronald Reagan, moreover, made it fashionable to be a Republican. On college campuses, where a generation before "GOP" had been a four-letter word, young people liked his toughness on crime, foreign policy, and welfare. It was even more true of the young who were in the workforce. There was less enthusiasm among the young for Bush until his Gulf War success gave him at least a temporary 90 percent approval rating. Given the historical pattern—that voters become more Republican as they age—the GOP was in fine shape. As the 1990s began there had been signs that the youngest voters—those of college age—were veering to the Democratic party. But this "baby bust" generation—much less numerous than their older siblings—found the GOP record of success seductive.

"I'll tell you what chills the blood of liberals," said Sen. Daniel Patrick Moynihan (D-N.Y.). "It was always thought that the old bastards were the conservatives. Now the young people are becoming the conservatives and we're the old bastards."[1]

Although Democrats might have deluded themselves that the young don't vote in large numbers, time would inevitably change that. And although voters change as they move through life—baby-boomers were liberals during the sixties and conservatives during the eighties—the evidence shows that the pressures of families, jobs, and mortgages convert more voters to the Republican party as they age than go the other way.

As Bob Teeter, Bush's pollster, would often tell audiences: For the GOP, "the bad news is that there are still more Democrats in the electorate; the good news is they're dying off."

Republicans did more than joke about this change. They assembled aggressive college-level recruitment campaigns and marketed themselves as the party of the future, with Reagan, and then Persian Gulf victor Bush as their hero. Democrats tried to recruit young voters by invoking past Democrats who were only names from history class, a stale come-on.

Young voters, moreover, did not share the guilt for past injustices felt by many Democrats. This generation went to desegregated schools, they felt the world was mostly color-blind, and they were therefore unmoved by the continuing Democratic call to give minorities special treatment.

The same trend among young people was even more evident in the South. Even before the Persian Gulf War, Natalie Davis, a member of the DNC and professor and pollster at Birmingham Southern University, found that 52 percent of young Alabamians said they were Republicans, while 33 percent called themselves Democrats. Among white men 18-24, the core future electorate, the GOP lead was 68-14. Davis told state party officials if they did not make 1989 "the year of the white male," they could forget about the future.

They didn't, of course, but they may have to.

As jobs moved from the industrial sector to the service and information industries, they moved from the North and Midwest to the South and West. Those changes sealed the fate of unions, because the new industries and new workers were at best skeptical, and at times outright hostile, toward organized labor.

Moreover, the number of people who chose to work part-time grew phenomenally. Technological advances, especially computers, allowed many to work from their homes. This new breed of worker found itself at odds with unions, which showed a dinosaur-like inability to adapt to the changing environment. The union's whole mission was to retain the status quo, to keep the rigid work rules. But flexibility had become the watchword in society. "[The unions] saw no distinction between the poor and oppressed textile or sweatshop worker and people who today are using technology to work at their own speed on their own schedule in their own home," said futurist Toffler, himself a former union activist and former Democratic leader. "It's sad for me because there is nobody visible in the Democratic party who understands or has come to terms with where the society is going."

When the man who symbolized the future turned away from the Democratic party, there was no better indication of what was happening.

Republicans, unfettered by historical ties to unions, have embraced the new technology and the lifestyle it has brought.

The migrants to the South, as well as those who moved from the Northern cities to the suburbs, were the modern version of pioneers who joined a wagon train going west more than a century earlier. They were by nature optimists willing to risk whatever security they had for opportunity and a better life. Republicans seemed instinctively to understand that, but Democrats were another story.

"I don't think there is any question that we are guided by the notion of security, protecting what we have, and not by the whole issue of expanding our base, expanding our economic opportunity," worried Bob Matsui, an astute six-term Democratic congressman from Sacramento, California Matsui realized the Democrats had missed the boat on this key point and felt it was the primary reason the Republicans were eating the Democrats' lunch. Republicans marketed themselves as the party that provided opportunity for success rather than security. The tug-of-war hadn't existed earlier. Democrats had formerly offered both security—unemployment compensation, Social Security, and welfare—and opportunity— college loans and federally subsidized mortgages.

By the early 1990s, the average middle-class voter wasn't nearly as concerned about security as had been his parents, who lived through the Depression. And he felt that the Democrats were too security-oriented in their appeals to the unions and blacks.

"What has happened is Democrats became trapped by their traditional constituency [unions and blacks], which has the least ability to move flexibly," said Henry Cisneros, the former mayor of San Antonio and America's best known Hispanic Democratic politician. The party was caught "protecting that constituency which is less capable of change."

Cisneros could see that change was everywhere, especially in the Sun Belt. "Democrats are going at the pace of change of the slowest rather than the fastest . . . . Democrats are trapped into defending groups that are at the rear both in income and ability to adapt to change."

The trade issue in the late 1980s and early 1990s is a perfect example. Democrats worried about protecting the jobs in industries that were being hurt by foreign competition, about their constituents' shrinking piece of the pie, and talked about limiting imports of foreign goods. Republicans, whose constituents focused their sights on making the pie grow, viewed trade as a way of developing additional markets for American products. They knew that U.S. restrictions would produce retaliatory levies on American products overseas.

In addition, Republicans looked to technology as a sign of economic opportunity, a feeling shared by the vast majority of Americans. But those very technological changes were the ones that directly threatened the remnants of the Democratic coalition—unions and blacks.

"Democrats conceded to a kind of fuzziness and laziness of thinking about how to extend beyond the neediest," said Cisneros. "A certain righteousness sets in about the protection of the neediest, and a certain disdain sets in for the middle class. What has happened in some sense is that the refuge becomes a certain demagoguery about protecting the poor. . . . That is not winning politics, and it isn't even what's best for the poor."

Finally, the increasing strength of public employee unions—the only growing sector of organized labor—further pressured Democrats to emphasize government's role at a time most American voters saw it as featherbedding and harmful to the national interest. The Democrats' very success in making government the instrument of their political party became a political liability, because they were viewed as an instrument of government.

"That is a huge constituency, but is not now and never will be a majority," says Arkansas Gov. Bill Clinton, one of the few Democrats willing to take on the public employee unions. Clinton faced down the teachers' unions in his state by insisting on teacher competency testing, and the voters stood by him. "How [government workers] think, how they talk, how they view things is much different [from] the way most taxpayers do."

Republicans didn't worry about those content with their present rung on the ladder, but concentrated on the new middle-class majority who looked to climb higher. They caught the wave of change and rode it. As they did, a kind of intellectual rigor mortis set in among the Democrats.

What happened in Bruce Babbitt's Phoenix neighborhood was typical of what was happening across America. Babbitt, his wife Hattie, and their two young boys moved into their ranch-style, brick-and-cinder-block house in 1977.

Babbitt was Arizona's attorney general, in his late thirties, and with a lifestyle much like the other residents of this Phoenix suburban neighborhood. The neighborhood was similar to those that had emerged across the country in the great post–World War II building expansion. The neighborhood was built around schools.

Aside from the cactus, warm temperatures, and Squaw Peak Mountain visible in the distance, it looked like many other major metropolitan areas in America. The quarter-mile cul-de-sac, adorned with basketball hoops and skate boards, was the kind of place young professionals with new families moved to, raised their kids, and left when their children did.

It was an upper-middle-class neighborhood, but not blatantly so. Babbitt was a bit better off than some of his neighbors because he had inherited money. When Babbitt moved there, homes cost $60,000-70,000. A decade later they had doubled in price. Despite the high average income, most homeowners weren't Republicans. At least not then in the late 1970s.

"My neighbors used to be Democrats for cultural and economic reasons," Babbitt remembered. "They identified with what they perceived to be economic issues advocated by Democrats. They were perceived to be opportunity issues. Their kids were more likely to get a college education, to find jobs in a prosperous economy. The Republican party was perceived as the country club party, and we somehow identified with family values. That perception has changed."

Today, Babbitt says, "My friends in Phoenix ask me why any middle-class American would vote for the Democratic party. Now they say they are Republicans, again because of economic and cultural values. They believe our economic policy is to spend more money irrespective of the results. They see the [Democratic] expenditure of money creating dependency rather than growth" and the GOP as the party providing opportunity. "Now my neighbors say the Republicans are tougher on drugs, are more oriented to family values."

But, as Macomb County showed, the Democrats' suburban problems weren't restricted to the Sun Belt. While the population and job growth rates in the North were smaller and the cities and rural areas were shrinking, the suburbs were growing. And those new suburbanites shared many of the values of those who had migrated to the Sun Belt. Suburbanites were suburbanites.

Between 1950 and 1990, the number of suburbanites more than doubled. By 1992 the suburbs had more than half the nation's voters.

The suburban migration began forty years ago. A generation of newly married veterans profited from the Democratic-inspired government mortgage programs and moved to the new subdivisions on what had been woods or farmland. Business soon followed.

The movement picked up in the seventies as baby-boomers began having families. They left the cities to raise their children in safer places, where their dollars could buy the roomy single-family homes that were not available in the cities.

And baby-boomers—who make up the largest age group in the electorate, almost one in two eligible voters—were different from their economically insecure parents.

The baby-boomers realized they lived in a competitive world where they would have to fight to retain the prosperity they had enjoyed as children. The deep recessions of the seventies, as many of them were entering the job market and buying homes, drove that message home. Moreover, their generation was so large that there was often a shortage of schools, jobs, or good housing. In many cases, an older competitor with more seniority, or union protection, won the promotion these boomers felt should have been theirs. Sometimes it was affirmative action. Republicans spoke the language of this opportunity-centered group.

And as the 1980s ended, a second belt of suburbs even farther out, known as "exurbs," spread from coast to coast. Businesses had found it cheaper and safer for their employees to locate in the suburbs, and as more jobs were created in the near suburbs, commuters could and did move even farther from the center cities.

But it wasn't just changing demographics that hurt Democrats. It was changing attitudes and the Democrats' inability to adapt. "A lot of Democrats were stuck in the sixties. They didn't realize America had changed," said Sen. Phil Gramm. The Republicans not only understood the change, they also knew how to exploit it politically.

The Vietnam War as well as the civil rights and women's movements of the sixties, followed by the economic ravages of inflation and the newly discovered dependence on foreign oil of the seventies, produced a cynical country that wasn't quite so cocky as before. This was exacerbated in the eighties by the twin shocks of the budget and trade deficit which left many Americans uncertain about the country's future.

American students scored in the bottom third on a wide range of international exams and measurements; males ranked a low 15th and women 8th in life expectancy, 20th in infant mortality, 27th in cardiovascular health, and 13th in cancer illnesses.[2]

Out of this came a retrenchment. American public opinion went "back to the future."

The boomers reached child-bearing age, a major factor: Nothing ensures a yearning for the sure and the steady like becoming a parent. The share of the population in the 35-54 age group—the years when people worry about protecting their family, property, and community standards—rose from 21 percent in 1980 to 25 percent in 1990; and it is projected to hit 30 percent by the turn of the century.

Drugs, considered relatively benign in the 1960s, became Public Enemy No. 1 in the 1990s. Millions of Americans seemed to be saying that maybe the straight and narrow lifestyle, the same that had inspired a cultural rebellion in the 1960s, wasn't so bad after all.

People like Geri and Tom Suma, who considered the student protests, sexual liberation, and alternative lifestyle as deviant behaviors, never changed their tune. But as the 1970s became the 1980s, they were joined by converts like the Sumas' Macomb neighbor Barry Marino, baby-boomers who had grown conservative with time and children.

In conventional political terms the Republicans were the original opponents of the sixties movement. The addition of the new converts allowed them to achieve critical mass. In time, this GOP coalition of the eighties would run against the sixties, castigating the decade as a time when the Democratic notion that government should not uphold any moral values had run amok. And once again, Republicans were on the right side of public opinion.

"This has not been, and may well not be for some time, one of those periods in which the wind is blowing strongly in our direction," conceded Ira Arlook of Citizen Action, and a veteran of the sixties culture, in a gigantic understatement.

On social issues, Republicans took advantage of the change in the electorate by sitting on the sidelines and letting the Democrats dig their own graves.

"In a large sense we got carried away with the politics of change and protest," said Babbitt, himself a 1960s civil rights marcher in Selma, Alabama. "The civil rights movement, the war, the cultural changes—the pendulum simply swung too far in the eyes of the average American. We became the party of permissiveness rather than tolerance. There is a very thin line, and the judgment of the American people is we went beyond tolerance to permissiveness."

It seemed, moreover, even in the 1980s, that every time a prominent politician marched to call attention to the complaints of blacks, gays, or feminists, he was a Democrat. That became the Democratic image. The party was increasingly dominated by minorities, symbolized by Jesse Jackson, and white limousine liberals, like Teddy Kennedy.

Sen. Joseph Lieberman of Connecticut, one of the few social conservatives to rise to national prominence as a Democrat in the late 1980s, put it best.

"The presidential Democratic party," Lieberman said, "has been seen too often as a party that has tolerated or encouraged those different values and lifestyles that are inconsistent with the traditional role of the family." And, added Jim Slattery, a Kansas Democratic congressman, the Republicans "are moving millions of Americans on this issue."

Again, this dynamic became most apparent in the South, a genteel place where being flashy is almost a sin in itself, and in the Frost Belt suburban neighborhoods, where ethnic Roman Catholics have migrated from the central cities.

"Going hand in hand with the cultural conservatism of the times was crime," remarked Bill Galston, a University of Maryland professor who was Mondale's 1984 chief domestic advisor, "and a perception on the part of many conservative-to-moderate voters that the judicial system and many of the leaders in the Democratic party had tilted against what they regarded as an appropriately tough attitude towards criminals and crime."

Republicans realized that crime was on the public's mind and made tough enforcement and the death penalty their credo. Too many Democratic candidates confused being tough on criminals— of whom a disproportionate number were black—with racism, and soft-pedaled the issue by, for example, opposing capital punishment. But Macomb County's attitudes were prevalent, and Democratic candidates suffered.

But none of those issues would have spelled disaster. The lethal blow came when Democrats presided over the worst economic slide since the Depression and the biggest foreign policy embarrassments in recent American history.

The late 1970s, when Carter was president, turned out to be the trauma for many Americans that the Depression had been for their parents. The economic dislocation wasn't nearly so bad as the 1930s, but it was nevertheless a great shock to the new generation. After all, the seventy-six million boomers had grown up with a rising standard of living. An economic downturn made it seem as if their world were crumbling around them. They stopped trusting the Democratic approach—that government was the answer.

"The world that America helped rebuild at the end of World War II," Democratic Chairman Brown remembered, "suddenly seemed to be spinning out of control. Here at home you could feel the growing anxiety and frustration."

"Our party seemed to lose its gyroscope," Brown continued. "We were at our best in the decades after World War II when we understood and felt the fears, anxieties, dreams, and hopes of average Americans. Government was the tool we used to shape America's future. By the late 1970s, however, we seemed incapable of using that tool wisely . . . Some Democrats, obviously carried away with programmatic government, even began to sound a little silly. . . . Things had really begun to go too far."

Living through the Carter years in which inflation peaked at more than 13 percent, with interest rates of 21.5 percent, had a profound influence on personal and national behavior. People bought goods fearing that tomorrow they would be more expensive. So too, the country lived on credit cards. And that mentality brought the record budget deficits of the 1980s.

That ended the traditional Democratic argument that Republicans preside over bad economies and Democrats take care of the average guy. Under Republican Reagan's program of lower taxes and less government spending, the economy reached a post-World War II record of more than seven years of economic growth. Interest rates and inflation were cut in half or more, and unemployment rates plummeted.

Carter also presided over the Iranian embarrassment—which drove millions of Barry Marinos out of the party—and he was forced to admit he had been naive in trusting the Soviets. Here, too, Reagan offered a new tough line that fit the mood of voters. In fact, his toughness brought about a new foreign policy

By the 1990s everything had come up roses for the Republicans. For the first time ever the Soviets offered to destroy a whole class of nuclear weapons. The former archenemy seemed to have been tamed, and democracy was breaking out from Central America to Krakow. The one-hundred-hour U.S. victory in the Persian Gulf was the crowning achievement.

"Ronald Reagan changed America. The things Ronald Reagan fought hardest with the Democrats about are over," crowed Newt Gingrich. And he was basically right. Few politicians wanted to be identified with ballooning government spending or taxes, and even Democrats were trying to be tough on drugs and crime.

But the Republicans understood something else: that the changes did not mean people had rejected many traditional Democratic middle-class ideas.

Unlike their former instinctive, some say knee-jerk, rejection of any sort of governmental activism, the Republicans no longer opposed Social Security, environmental clean-up, or spending on education. They had learned their lesson. They decided to win presidential elections. They spoke of solutions that allowed the private sector to play a larger role in government. "I have always said I favor active government, but that doesn't mean I favor state bureaucracy," said Gingrich. And that became the GOP cry. It allowed the Republicans to slide toward an activist approach to government without forsaking the cornerstone of the conservative philosophy.

As the 1992 election dawned, American voters faced two competing alternatives:

- A Democratic party that has been out of the White House for more than a decade, that blew it the last time at bat, and that doesn't seem to understand why.

It is, opines Democratic Senator Robert Graham of Florida, as though the Democrats were losing a fast-food war. Their top menu item—the presidential candidate—just doesn't stack up to the competition.

"The United States is going through the process of the McDonaldization of American politics," Graham explained. "People are increasingly forming their partisan identification by what they see on television . . . a national party dominated by its presidential candidates or that individual fortunate enough to be elected president. And when they look at our fast-food franchise and look at the Republicans' fast-food franchise on television they are electing to buy their hamburgers at the other stand."

As if the Democrats hadn't enough of a problem, they are also badly split internally. Some think their old ways are just fine. Others feel, in the words of Jim Jones, former head of the House's budget committee who became chairman of the American Stock

Exchange, that "the Democratic party could go the way of the British Labour party unless we make some very fundamental changes in our message and image."

Democratic pollster Paul Maslin thinks the Democrats have not even hit bottom: "I'm not optimistic about 1992. It could be 8, 12, or 16 years down the road. The party's still got to find what its soul, what its roots are. The next four years are going to be extraordinarily difficult for the Democratic party."

The comparison with the British Labour party is apt. The Labour party became electorally inept by going hard left, concentrating on economic redistribution and foreign policy isolationism.

"We're kidding ourselves if we think the national Democratic party is a nonideological party," Maslin says. "It is perceived to be a party that is liberal, and of the poor and wealthy"—but not the middle class—"and that is not one that wins presidential elections."

- A Republican party on a winning streak because it has adapted to changes great and small.

No one argues with New Jersey GOP Gov. Tom Kean's assessment. "There are things you can always find that we Republicans don't unite around, but we unite around so much more these days than Democrats do. You can find 80 percent of the issues that unite almost all Republicans. It's hard to find 50 percent of the issues that are Democratic issues that you can unite Democrats on."

Living proof is the way the Republican establishment co-opted the supporters of evangelical Christian Pat Robertson's 1988 campaign for the GOP presidential nomination. Robertson was very critical of Bush during the primaries, but by 1989 Marc Nuttle, Robertson's former campaign manager, had become the executive director of the National Republican Campaign Committee and Robertson's followers had been integrated into the GOP establishment. Not so on the other side of the aisle, where the other preacher, Jesse Jackson, seemed to be constantly thrashing about, trying to find a place for himself in the Democratic party.

Still, the major reason Democrats are split on many issues has to do with the other major demographic change in the electorate.

The civil rights laws of the 1960s produced huge numbers of new black voters, both in the North, which had received 4 million black migrants from the South, and in Dixie itself.

In 1952 about 20 percent of the South's population, but only 6 percent of its voters, were black. By 1980, blacks were still 20 percent of the population but almost the same percentage of voters.[3] In 1988, census data showed that nationally blacks were one-eighth of the population and network exit polls found they made up one-tenth of the voters. And almost 90 percent of blacks voted Democratic.

By 1988, 22 percent of Democratic voters in the November election were black—compared with 9 percent in 1960—and their influence in Democratic primaries grew proportionately greater as more whites left the party.[4]

As the 1992 election approached, it became increasingly clear that the Democratic hold on black voters worked both ways: it could be counterproductive. The party's historic role as the protector of minorities was a political minus as white America began to change its racial attitude.

4

Losing Patience:
White America,
Black America

Randy Primas spent July 4, 1988, like millions of other Americans, watching the local fireworks. For him, that was in Camden, New Jersey, a once-prosperous city that is perhaps America's best example of urban decay. A chance encounter that night erased any doubts he had about the gap between white and black America, between city residents and suburbanites.

Primas, then Camden's mayor, had put together a joint fireworks display with Philadelphia, which lies directly across the Delaware River. In Camden, the site was Wiggins Waterfront Park, a product of urban renewal and an oasis amidst the squalor.

Roughly 20,000-25,000 people were there that night, many of them suburban whites. Primas, shedding his official role, walked to the top of the grassy hill that overlooks the river. He wore shorts, sandals, and a T-shirt and looked just like everyone else.

He found himself standing behind a middle-aged white couple. The man wore shorts and a yellow Izod shirt, the woman a sundress. He couldn't help but overhear their conversation, and as the discussion progressed, Primas began to listen intently. "She told him, 'Aren't you glad we came in?' referring to coming into Camden. The man admitted, 'I would not have believed we could have this kind of [pleasant] experience,' " Primas recalled.

"It was the kind of thing that made me realize the severity of the problem," he went on. "He couldn't believe that he could come into the city of Camden, have a good time, and not get mugged."

All this occurred about the time Primas' wife Bonita, who teaches social work at Camden County Community College in the heart of suburbia, about twelve miles from downtown, asked her almost all-white classes if they had ever been to Camden. "Easily three-quarters of them said no, except perhaps to drive through on their way to Pennsylvania," Mrs. Primas related. She now asks that question of her classes each semester, and "that kind of response is pretty much the rule."

Randy Primas continued his tale. "I realized that other than coming to the criminal justice system, the hospitals, or the Rutgers-Camden campus, there is no reason to come into the city. And most of those are not pleasant reasons to come in."

Primas, a bushy-haired veteran of two decades of political infighting between his city and its burgeoning, prosperous, and mostly white suburbs, can be blunt about the problem because he is black. What these and countless other similar experiences during his 1981-1990 tenure as mayor drove home was that among too many whites "there's a perception the cities are just a black hole."

And, as depressing as it is, Primas articulates the opinion of most white Americans in the 1990s.

Whether it is tourists being stabbed on the New York subway; Detroit residents setting their city ablaze every Halloween; D.C. Mayor Marion Barry using crack; D.C.'s congressional delegate Eleanor Holmes Norton not paying her taxes for most of a decade; Philadelphia facing bankruptcy; or Los Angeles's gang wars, urban/black America evokes the hostility and fear of most middle-class whites.

It isn't that most whites are racist. It is, rather, that they do not realize that the poverty and illegality they have come to associate with blacks only constitutes a small slice of black America. It isn't any ridiculous notion of white superiority or black inferiority, but rather, as black broadcaster Tony Brown put it so cogently, that "most white people want nothing to with us because they are convinced it will reduce the quality of their lives."

It hadn't always been that way.

In the 1960s, white America decided to make reparations for the historic wrongs done black America. In the early part of the decade, night after night, TV showed dogs attacking black children at civil rights demonstrations, blacks beaten for drinking from a water fountain, blacks murdered and dumped into shallow graves.

"There were such horrendous acts that anyone with any human kindness was repulsed," the 1984 Democratic vice presidential candidate Geraldine Ferraro remembered. "[White] people felt it was necessary to reach out. They looked at it and said, 'Oh my God. How can you do that to another human being?' "

It was this sense of outrage then shared by the vast majority of Americans that provided the moral authority for the changes that government rightly proceeded to engineer. No one could reasonably argue that something needed to be done—and few did.

Laws guaranteeing voting rights and access to public accommodations, facilities, and housing were among the high-profile results of that public will. There was a second thrust also—to provide economic parity for blacks. Most white Americans rejoiced, hoping that the injustice could be ameliorated by legal means. After all, times were good. And one of the most admirable qualities of Americans is their generosity. They cringe at the thought that while they are doing well, others are not. Few considered the long-term ramifications of programs aimed at giving minorities a step up in competing for their share of the American Dream. They thought the programs were both needed and justified.

Before the 1960s those whites who had cared about what was happening to blacks had seen themselves as the great white father. They would look after those blacks who followed a prescribed path; those who did so would, moreover, reap the fruits of American life.

So perhaps coincidentally, perhaps because of the change in racial attitudes by the white majority, the American idea of fairness underwent a change of definition, and for the first time America sought to include blacks into the equation.

America had seen waves of immigrants carving out their place in society. Before the 1960s, fairness had meant that a person received what his sweat earned him. The family that emerged from Ellis Island to work six-day, twelve-hour shifts in sweat shops deserved to move up. It had played by the rules. Just so, the less industrious did not deserve to do so well. While this applied to whites who were lazy, in the minds of most whites it stereotypically described blacks and explained their lack of progress—not, that is, the legal barriers of segregation.

The 1960s witnessed a fundamental change in American thinking.

Perhaps it was the widespread prosperity. Millions of white Irish, Italians, Poles, Jews, and others whose grandparents had climbed out of poverty had earned a solid place in the economic mainstream. Fairness took on two new meanings: A person was entitled to an equal opportunity to succeed or fail regardless of race, and a person was entitled to some things based on need, not necessarily on achievement or effort.

It meant that education, jobs, health care, and more should not be handed out according to who could pay for them, but based on who needed them. It was as close to socialism as the fiercely individualistic American spirit had ever come.

In one effort, government and business created minority set-aside programs to guarantee a certain percentage of government contracts to minority-owned firms. Government and industry also instituted affirmative action programs to force schools and employers to increase their recruitment of minorities.

The two-pronged drive—for basic rights and for economic parity—occurred under Democratic auspices. Although many Republicans played key roles in the bipartisan legislative efforts, and in fact some civil rights measures were actually beefed up under GOP President Richard Nixon, the programs would forever be considered a Democratic legacy. Liberals would point to them with pride two decades later during their years in the political wilderness.

Some Democrats understood the political impact of these programs, even then. President Johnson remarked privately moments after signing the 1965 Civil Rights Act: "I think we just delivered the South to the Republican party for a long time to come." He underestimated the geographic impact. A quarter-century later, from California to New York, much of white America felt the statute of limitations had expired for its past crimes against blacks. Whites believed they had helped blacks achieve equal rights and were unwilling to provide the extra financial help that blacks said they required to achieve economic equity.

"Once it shifted to the cost factor, America was not willing to pay for equality," Jesse Jackson stated. "It considered freedom horizontal movement. But it would make no concession on the cost of vertical equality."

Poll after poll showed that big chunks of white voters were saying "enough." An Associated Press–Media General poll in August of 1988 found that four out of five voters overall, and even a higher percentage of whites, opposed giving preference to minorities in hiring. Three out of four were against preferences in college admissions. In a Gallup poll done for Times Mirror Co. in May 1987, 46 percent of whites agreed that "we have gone too far in pushing equal rights."

Furthermore, those who agreed the civil rights efforts had gone too far were disproportionately the traditional Democratic working- and middle-class folks like those of Macomb County. They felt victimized by such policies and were easy targets for GOP charges that the Democrats had forgotten the white middle class.

In the eyes of most white Americans, a level playing field now existed. They believed that the original and worthy goals of the civil rights movement had been met. But now, they felt, special efforts to help blacks had permeated most aspects of American life and were not justified by the wrongs committed by a previous generation of whites against a previous generation of blacks, especially if that meant they had to pay the price for their forefathers' crimes.

But, the Democratic bigwigs agreed with black leaders who argued the existing programs for blacks had only produced tokenism. These same Democratic leaders refused to appreciate how widespread was the belief among whites that they were being assessed for the crimes of others. Democrats kept describing the glass as half empty, while most white voters thought the glass was half full, with the level rising. This vital change in white attitudes eluded the Democratic leaders.

The political implications of this sea change in white attitudes—justified or not—cannot be overestimated. It changed the terrain on which virtually all political battles were fought in the final quarter of the twentieth century.

Bill Clinton's fifteen-year record in politics established him with civil rights groups as a strong supporter. A born-and-bred Arkansan, his youthful good looks, Yale Law School degree, and Rhodes Scholarship gave him a star quality that early on pushed him into the national limelight. Friends joked he was America's only political rising star for three decades—the 1970s, 1980s, and 1990s. But Clinton kept in touch with the average person, and that won him five terms in the governor's mansion despite his continual raising of taxes.

Thus Clinton was troubled, but not surprised, by a conversation he had one night in 1990 with an old friend, the type of conservative Democrat who had once been the bulwark of the Arkansas party. The federal courts were at the time looking into school desegregation in Little Rock with an eye towards increasing the racial mix. They were also reviewing the state's legislative plan to create more districts with black majorities in order to elect more black lawmakers.

"Bill, I just don't understand the world I'm living in," his friend said. "We need the federal courts to integrate our schools by race, but we need the federal courts to segregate our legislative districts by race."

Clinton realized his friend was voicing the frustration and puzzlement felt by millions of white Americans. "His feeling," said Clinton, "was that the federal courts want to take over the political process" with "no underlying principle other than a liberal bias in creating these political solutions to racial problems, which he thinks are going to undermine the ability of blacks to really take responsibility and really change their own future. I think his attitude is fairly typical of what is going on."

Some have worried that even to discuss such notions will label them "racist." But ignoring the issue has only exacerbated the political problem for Democrats—and increased racial polarization in America, because the remedial programs of which Democratic liberals are so proud haven't helped black America enough. Whether that is because the programs are inadequately funded as liberals charge, or because they have perpetuated black underachievement as conservatives argue, the dismal fact is that by the early 1990s, a third of all blacks lived in poverty, three times the per capita rate of whites and a larger percentage of blacks than did so in 1969.

The median black family income, adjusted for inflation, has remained flat over the past two decades, in large part due to the changes in the U.S. economy. The blue-collar jobs that require strong backs went first. The low educational levels among blacks meant they were the hardest hit by the economic evolution.

Whites were doing better economically, but they weren't feeling secure. The economic pie was not growing as it had during LBJ's Great Society. Middle-income whites felt they were working harder and had less to show for it. They were partially right.

Median white family income was $35,980 in 1989, roughly a 10 percent boost over the past twenty years. But whites had expected the 50 percent real increase in their standard of living they had experienced during the 1950s and 1960s to continue. In fact, many families needed two wage-earners to keep up with their middle-class lifestyle—the two cars, VCRs, microwave ovens, and serious vacations—much more than their parents had enjoyed.

Meanwhile, prominority programs begun in the 1960s had become a fact of American life. By the 1990s, whites believed preferential hiring of minorities was making equally and better qualified white candidates suffer for wrongs long past. Moreover, the poor seemed to be falling further behind, while blacks who profited by the programs did so well that many whites felt they were the victims of reverse discrimination.

"I don't think there is any doubt the Democratic party has been typecast since the sixties as the party that favors big government and benefits poor people, a disproportionate amount of whom are black," remarked Bob Beckel, Mondale's former campaign manager.

Actually, white resentment over tax money subsidizing blacks was somewhat misguided. In 1990, programs primarily aimed at the poor—welfare, Medicaid, food stamps, public housing—took 12 percent of the federal budget, or roughly 15 percent of total program spending when interest on the national debt was taken out of the equation. Such programs took a larger share of state and local government revenues. In fact, the poverty rate was higher in white, rural America than in heavily black and Hispanic urban America. Little public discussion of those numbers emerged because both media and politicians preferred to ignore the subject. But the resentment was simmering away in Middle America. And to blame this attitude solely, or even mostly, on white racism was unfair.

"The average white voter is not racist," stated Sen. Joseph Lieberman (D-Conn.), who has a rare understanding of the middle class. "The average white voter is protective of what he has . . . . They associate black people with poor people and they don't want to be pulled back down the ladder that they have worked so hard to come up."

Lieberman, the first orthodox Jew elected to the U.S. Senate, identifies with the immigrant experience and the pre-1960s definition of fairness. When told about Macomb County's Louise Renaud, he called her a "great example" of what was going on across America.

"She knows something is wrong. There's a sense of injustice here that is beautiful. I don't think it's racism. It's more, 'You are making a fool of me. What am I, a chump? I'm breaking my back, my wife is too. And you're going to give my money to these people who don't even work and are pulling the wool over your eyes. What are you, fools?' "

Ronald Reagan fed the fire.

"Reagan convinced whites the civil rights movement had taken advantage of them," said Jesse Jackson. Reagan's 1987 quip that "we waged a war on poverty, and poverty won," resonated throughout white America.

Further, whites didn't understand why. By the beginning of the 1990s, federal, state, and local governments were spending $150 billion annually to eradicate poverty.

Whether fairly or not, many whites wondered why blacks as a

group continued to fare so poorly; perhaps, they wondered, the reason was blacks themselves. In short, they turned their backs on the 1960s' belief that society was to blame for black problems.

In 1991 the University of Chicago's National Opinion Research center reported that among whites nationally 78 percent thought blacks were more likely to prefer living on welfare, 62 percent thought blacks were less likely to be hard working, 56 percent thought blacks were more likely to be violence prone, and 53 percent thought blacks less intelligent.

A good example was the public reaction in the late 1980s to CBS's decision to suspend Andy Rooney and fire "Jimmy the Greek" Snyder for their separate comments about why blacks had problems in society and excelled athletically. The two men were pummeled by the media, but public opinion took their sides.

By the 1990s it was clear only a shrinking group of liberals and blacks blamed society solely for black problems. "People just don't jerk their knees anymore when you sing 'We Shall Overcome,'" stated former Colorado Democratic Gov. Dick Lamm.

Lamm won a well-deserved reputation for bluntness in 1984. At that time, discussing the skyrocketing costs of health care, he suggested the elderly have a "duty to die" to make way for succeeding generations. Although senior citizens groups bristled, he remained popular in Colorado because of his direct way of dealing with this as well as other problems.

A former civil rights lawyer, Lamm is just as direct when it comes to race. White voters, in his opinion, "look at the welfare and crime rates among blacks and they feel there is not reason to discriminate, but reason to be cautious. And then you have the Democratic party whose only explanation of this is a need for stronger and more civil rights laws. It just didn't ring true with what they saw in reality."

Meanwhile, a two-tiered black America was emerging. To a much larger extent than among whites, millions of blacks had climbed the economic ladder in the past generation. These upwardly mobile blacks moved to the suburbs, further destabilizing inner-city neighborhoods where millions more blacks were left behind.

By the early 1990s, one in eight blacks had incomes above

$50,000 in real terms—two-and-a-half times the 1968 rate. Another third earned between $25,000 and $50,000. And again, that growth in income had been much higher among blacks than whites. Roughly four in ten blacks were middle class by the early 1990s compared with seven in ten whites.

The aggregate income in black families where both parents worked, and when government benefits were included, was roughly 85 percent of a comparable white family's. The average black married couple had a solid middle-class annual income of $30,650.

The problem with black America, however, was that too few families included both a mother and a father, let alone two paychecks. In 1940, at the end of the Great Depression, which hit blacks worse than whites, only 18 percent of black families were headed by women, and that was mostly because of the death of the husband. By 1990, the Census Bureau said, the figure was 44 percent and rising. Moreover, 61 percent of those black families with children under age eighteen were single-parent households.

Among the poor, black fathers living with their children were a rarity, in part because for decades the welfare bureaucracy barred benefits if a man lived in the house. Typical of America's black inner-city matriarchy were the Chicago Housing Authority projects where among the 27,178 families with children, only 8 percent were headed by a husband and wife. An astounding 92 percent were headed by just one parent, almost always the mother.[1]

It was, said CHA Chairman Vince Lane, a black man who began trying to clean up the mess in the early 1990s, a situation "exacerbated by well-intentioned but misguided social policy which has driven working families from public housing [and] created islands of desperate poverty."

And the situation has grown much worse, much faster. The Centers for Disease Control said in 1988, 64 percent of black babies were born to unwed mothers, with four in five of the births to women ages 15-24. In most cases both mother and child wound up on welfare. Compare that with the 17 percent of white children born out of wedlock. In addition, the black divorce rate was almost twice that of whites, adding to the growth of single-parent black families. More than anything else, this phenomenal escalation of single-parent families fueled the growth of the underclass. The situation became a powerful symbol of the problem.

Ed Koch, the three-term New York mayor, neatly captured white America's frustration: "Government cannot take the place of a mother and father. We tried, but we cannot take their place, we cannot be the surrogate family."

And it wasn't just white conservatives, whose credentials liberals questioned, who voiced those concerns. Health and Human Services (HHS) Secretary Louis W. Sullivan, the black member of Bush's cabinet, in the spring of 1991 began a campaign to drive home the message: "Many of the root causes of the disintegration of child health and welfare are directly traceable to the unprecedented and precipitate rise in single parenting due to the lack of family formation and rise of divorce . . . beyond the question of resources, there's the matter of values that families and communities teach, that government cannot teach, that are critical for human survival."

A line of thinking that had been previously limited to avowed racists began to seep into polite middle-class white society: The welfare culture spawned by LBJ's Great Society was responsible for the increase in single-parent households by enabling young ghetto girls to have children and support them without either a man or a job. In 1960, 22 percent of black children were born out of wedlock; that figure grew to 35 percent in 1970 and 55 percent in 1980. The comparable rates of out-of-wedlock births for whites were 2 percent, 6 percent, and 11 percent, respectively.

Although blacks were only about 12 percent of the population, they made up a third or more of the welfare caseload. A University of Michigan study found that of black children born in 1967, at least 72 percent spent a minimum of one year on welfare before their eighteenth birthday. The comparable figure for whites born that year was 25 percent.[2] Liberals, however, argued that a majority of welfare recipients were white, and that the middle class was racist to focus only on the blacks on welfare. But the argument didn't impress many middle-class whites who still saw the black share as disproportionate.

And it was not just whites who felt this way. A Gallup poll

commissioned by the Joint Center for Political and Economic Studies, the nation's leading black think tank, found in 1988 that 57 percent of blacks and 54 percent of whites felt women were having babies in order to collect more welfare. The study also found that 65 percent of whites and 49 percent of blacks believed "welfare benefits make poor people dependent and encourages them to stay poor." Meanwhile, only 19 percent of whites and 28 percent of blacks believed "welfare benefits give poor people a chance to stand on their own two feet and get started again."

Moreover, as the 1990s dawned, polls showed that white voters increasingly accepted Reagan's explanation for black poverty. (Actually, he could have been quoting Louise Renaud of Macomb County.) Government social programs, Reagan said, had created "a kind of bondage in which people are made subservient to the government that is handing out the largesse, and the only people who prosper from them is that large bureaucracy that administers" the programs. "Too many [poor people] become dependent on government payments and lose the moral strength that has always given the poor the determination to climb America's ladder of opportunity," he added.

The Republican aversion to large federal programs was percolating in the middle-class consciousness, and for good reason. "In the last twenty-five years, we have spent over a trillion dollars in federal, state, and local programs to aid the poor. Twenty-five years ago, 70 cents of every dollar went to the poor, cash transfers from government directly to individuals," Robert Woodson stated. Woodson is black and the president of the National Center for Neighborhood Enterprises, which promotes black community development. In 1990 he was awarded a $320,000 MacArthur Foundation "Genius Grant" for his work. "However," Woodson continued, "in the past and recent times if you look at where the money goes, 70 percent of every dollar goes to those who serve the poor. I call them the Poverty Pentagon."

Woodson's figures were somewhat exaggerated because the 70 percent represented money for such things as payments to doctors, hospitals, and nurses involved in Medicaid services. But he nevertheless communicated the frustration with the welfare bureaucracy that exists among blacks and whites.

What Reagan implied, and many whites believed, is that blacks were unwilling to make the sacrifices to pull themselves up. A study of white voters during the 1988 election found that by more than a 2-1 margin, whites thought that "if blacks would only try harder they could be just as well-off as whites."[3] Most whites no longer believed that past discrimination was a valid reason for the current lack of black progress. Blacks, however, insisted that it was.

But surveys of this sort weren't widely reported, largely because, in the main, only academic pollsters asked these question directly. Media pollsters knew if they did, the resulting news stories might be more incendiary than they cared to handle. Thus, while these attitudes were becoming prevalent in much of white, middle-class America, they were not discussed publicly.

Ironically, the white frustration with black progress was voiced more openly by black Democrats. Kweisi Mfume, a Baltimore congressman, understood what was going on in white America even though he didn't agree: "There was always an expectation that the underclass needed an opportunity. And if the opportunity was presented, the underclass would work itself out of that situation. Now things have become a little bit different. I think most [white] people . . . feel, 'They have the tools to do it, we've given all these opportunities. Why isn't it being done? We're not prepared to give any more.' "

Most white politicians were afraid to examine why blacks were unable to climb the economic ladder as had countless immigrant groups before them. They worried they might be called racist if they said drugs, welfare, and crime were disproportionately a black problem. Most black leaders were no more helpful. They worried that acknowledging the problems would encourage whites to lose patience with blacks.

But talk radio, the vox populi of today, made clear that in Middle America voters were way ahead of the politicians. From Detroit to Denver, callers voiced their beefs for all to hear. Many whites seemed to be saying they couldn't understand why, after what they considered a quarter-century of special treatment, so many blacks seemed to be choosing such a destructive lifestyle.

But the underclass was only a small slice of the black community. Two-thirds of blacks were not poor, and the majority of the others were working to lift themselves out of poverty. Many blacks believed that white America was not making any distinction. Jesse Jackson expressed their feelings when he remarked that whites "watch television. They see us projected as less hard-working than we are. That's why they call us lazy. They see us as less patriotic than we are. As less universal than we are, less hard-working than we work. They see us as more violent than we are, and less worthy and less American than we are."

Less than half of the 33 percent of black Americans who are poor—perhaps 10 percent of the roughly 30 million blacks—made up the underclass. Yet many whites believed that most blacks lived in a dirty, ugly, and dangerous world inundated by drugs where people eschewed regular work for the allure of crime and big money.

Behind the TV pictures, moreover, were some troubling statistics that stoked whites' qualms. Of black men aged 20-24 who were not in school, 17 percent did not work at all in 1987, the government said. During that period of almost full employment nationally, the black unemployment rate topped 11 percent and the figure for black teenagers reached about 30 percent.

Middle Americans knew those youths weren't living off trust funds. They understood how difficult it was for them to get jobs without even a high school diploma—in New York City, three out of five blacks were dropouts. But facts were facts. Despite government efforts, the situation had worsened. In 1976, 34 percent of blacks with high school diplomas went to college; by 1985 the figure had dropped to 26 percent. A 1988 study by the W.T. Grant Foundation concluded that a college graduate could expect to earn double the salary of a high school graduate and more than triple that of a high school dropout. Thus, as a group, the next generation of blacks would be no better off than their parents.

The downward spiral seemed certain to continue.

Nowhere was all this more evident than in Camden, New Jersey. On the eve of World War II, the city had three hundred factories, plus a shipyard that employed 35,000 workers. There were 118,700 people living in row upon row of well-kept, flat-roofed brick homes. The city hummed: RCA-Victor turned out radios and phonographic equipment, Esterbrook produced millions of pens, and forty-two plants cooked and canned Campbell's Soup for the world's kitchens.

A half-century later those same city blocks resembled post-World War II Berlin—crumbled and collapsed houses, ruptured sidewalks, and ten thousand abandoned residential buildings. Children played amidst shattered glass, junkies openly used and sold drugs—even the Mafia had moved to the suburbs. At the beginning of the 1990s, Camden's population was more than 85 percent black and Hispanic, and very poor. Two-thirds of its residents received some form of welfare. Only one factory remained, and unemployment was 12 percent—three times the statewide rate. And that didn't account for the thousands who had stopped looking for work.

As real estate prices boomed throughout the rest of New Jersey, Camden's plummeted. The average house went for $35,000, some for as little as $1,000. No one wanted to live there. Those who did had no place else to go.

Camden's fate was sealed by the same forces that emptied scores of other major cities. World War II veterans used federally subsidized mortgages to buy larger homes on farmland outside of town. Business soon followed. In the late 1950s, James Rouse, the developer who would later redevelop Boston's Faneuil Hall and Baltimore's Inner Harbour, began work in suburban Cherry Hill on one of the nation's first giant shopping malls. Before long, other suburban retail meccas were siphoning customers away from Camden's downtown stores.

"At first those who moved to suburbia weren't rushing away from minorities. It was the desire to be part of the American Dream and own a single-family house," recalled Primas, who was the state's commissioner of community affairs in 1990. Born in 1949, when Camden was 20 percent black, Primas grew up in a lower-middle-class black enclave. "I didn't know what unemployment was. During my childhood Camden was a city that worked. I can't think of anyone I knew who didn't come from an intact [two-parent] family."

A riot in 1969 began the real change, both in the city's racial composition and in its economy.

"After the riots the white flight was exacerbated," Primas continued. ". . . I thought when I graduated from Woodrow Wilson High School in 1967 the population was probably 40-50 percent minority, but when I went back and looked at my yearbook there were only about fifty blacks and Hispanics out of five hundred." His wife Bonita graduated from Camden High School (the city's only other public high school) that year and she estimates her class was three-quarters white. Randy Primas went on the city council in 1973 and "at that point, I started regularly attending graduations and could see how few whites there were. When the white flight came, it happened very, very quickly."

In short, the suburban boom turned the city's nine square miles into an economic ghost town and racial ghetto without even a supermarket or movie theater.

Camden led the nation in some troublesome statistics. Three in five children lived in poverty, one in three was born to a teenager, and 90 percent of these teenage mothers were unmarried. Drugs and violence were epidemic.

"Many of our residents believe government's job is to take care of them from birth to death. But who is going to pay for it?" Primas wonders.

To white America and especially the suburbs around it, Camden's residents contributed to their own misery and now they expected someone else to bail them out. Most of the almost 500,000 residents in the middle-class suburbs surrounding the city—which had shrunk to about 75,000 people—felt they were footing the bill.

They were right. In 1989, of the city of Camden's $70 million budget for city government services—but not welfare or school costs—only about $12 million came from city residents. The rest was paid by state and national subsidies. In short, suburban taxpayers paid most of the costs.

The suburbs were different. Life was stable, jobs were available, and real estate values climbed. The average suburbanite's income was three times that of a Camden city resident. The only reminder suburbanites had of Camden came with their tax bills. In 1989, the average suburban homeowner paid 35 percent of his $3,600 annual property tax bill for jails, courts, and hospitals that he felt were used mostly by Camden residents.

His state and national income taxes paid the city's welfare costs.

Although Camden was a stark example of the economic gulf between city and suburbs, it nevertheless accurately portrayed the national picture. Census Bureau demographer Larry Long found a similiar situation in cities ranging from New York to Detroit, from Chicago to Atlanta. On average, 1960s' census data showed that median family income in those cities was equal to 85-93 percent of the median family income of their surrounding suburbs. By the late 1980s, Long found, those cities had median incomes of 50-60 percent of their surrounding suburbs.

The political impact of cities like Camden was best explained by former New Jersey Governor Thomas Kean, a moderate Republican admired by both Democrats and Republicans, who left office in 1990. In the suburban-dominated state that, not coincidentally, had voted for a GOP president ever since 1964, Kean accomplished the extraordinary feat of winning a majority of the black vote in his 1985 reelection bid. He even carried Camden. He was the image of the forward-looking Republican the party tried to cultivate.

Looking back at his eight years in office, Kean saw a major change in white political attitudes: "It's become increasingly more difficult to sell programs to help urban areas, more so than when I first came to office. People say basically they've had enough. They say, 'Our people are sick and tired of voting money for those people' or whatever expression they use. They say, 'We've given too much to the cities.' "

That, Kean added, represented a major change in public thinking. "That wasn't the case when I first came into office eight years ago . . . . They think the programs set up to help black America haven't worked. They use expressions like 'pouring money down the rat hole.' People are much more likely to view the worst as far as stealing and corruption. There's just a lack of credibility. There's a racial side to it."

The increasing chasm between white and black America was especially frustrating for middle-class blacks who felt whites based their judgments on race, not class. These blacks believed that their lives could be on the line if they were stopped for speeding by a white cop in a bad mood. They told of being unable to get taxis late at night. Successful black executives sensed that women held their purses tighter as they walked by on the street and spoke of subtle, but genuinely unfair, racial stereotyping. Most whites were so bombarded with negative images of the black underclass that they stopped making distinctions among blacks, feeling it was not worth the perceived risks. This exacerbated the sense of victimization in black America, especially among middle-class blacks who otherwise might have been more prone to believe, like their middle-class white counterparts, that a level playing field really did exist.

James Graham's experience was typical. A husky six-foot black man with a neatly trimmed mustache, Graham was the president of the Birmingham, Alabama, Urban League. He was a "Buppie"—a black Yuppie—and a community fixture who mixed with whites and blacks. Yet, although nattily and conservatively dressed, he too faced hostility.

He had countless experiences like the time he was driving home from work through Birmingham's downtown business district in his shiny, four-month-old maroon Cadillac during the spring, with hours of daylight left. As he pulled up to a red light, he noticed in the next lane an old Chevy with a dented fender driven by a white woman in a work shirt. She looked over at Graham in his suit and tie.

"I glanced over, didn't stare or anything," Graham recounted. "I could see her visibly move in her seat as though she was trying to move away from me. She reached back and first locked the door on her side, then locked the passenger side door, and then rolled up her window and made sure the others were up. I remember thinking, 'I can't believe this, here I am minding my own business.' It left a bad taste in my mouth. The thing was that given, my car and how I was dressed and her car and how she was dressed, I ought to be the one locking my door. But it's something you get used to seeing if you are a black male."

Because whites saw Asian immigrants make phenomenal strides, they didn't see the discrimination that blacks said still existed against nonwhites. Polls reported that roughly two out of three whites concluded that blacks didn't work as hard as the new immigrants. Gallup and the Joint Center found that a similar percentage of blacks agreed.

Even though they had been the last guys off the boat, so to speak, Asians became the new Jews. By the early 1990s, their incomes were 20 percent higher than whites and twice that of blacks. Their children dominated American education, winning academic prizes and seats in the best colleges in numbers five times the 3 percent share of the U.S. population that Asians constituted. Asians seemed to be opening a new business on every block and were more likely than whites, and several times more likely than blacks, to become entrepreneurs.

Meanwhile, blacks were floundering. And most whites blamed blacks for their situation. By almost a 5-1 ratio, white America believed blacks needed to pull themselves up one rung at a time, as had millions of Jews, Irish, Italians, and earlier immigrants.[4]

And it wasn't just the attitudes of whites about race that were becoming more polarized. Blacks were moving just as quickly in the other direction. At its core, the difference was a dispute over one simple question: Who was responsible for the problems of black America? Whites increasingly were seeing blacks as responsible for their own situation, and were therefore unsympathetic to calls for further special help. Blacks believed that the racial discrimination in white society was the reason, and continued to push for government to do even more.

During the early 1990s across black America, it became fashionable to repeat—and in many quarters to believe—Nation of Islam leader Louis Farrakhan's charge that "the epidemic of drugs and violence in the black community stems from a calculated attempt by whites to foster black self-destruction."

Some blacks even charged that the white establishment was working with organized crime to supply blacks with enough drugs to kill off the race. But that of course ignored the reality that in the major cities many of the drug lords and most of the dealers were black. So too were the mayors and/or chiefs of police in many of the cities with the worst drug problems: New York, Los Angeles, Washington, Detroit, Philadelphia, and Baltimore.

At first, most whites thought Farrakhan's charge bizarre. But then the media and the polls showed that it was being accepted in much of black America.

A more improbable accusation was in the offing.

A *New York Times*-WCBS poll of New York City blacks in the summer of 1990 found one in ten believed AIDS was "deliberately created in a laboratory in order to infect black people." Another two in ten said they thought that might possibly be the case. The same poll showed six in ten blacks either believed or thought it possible that "the government makes sure that drugs are easily available in poor black neighborhoods in order to harm black people." And almost eight in ten blacks in the survey believed or thought it possible that "the government singles out and investigates black elected officials in order to discredit them in a way it doesn't do with white officials."

To whites those ideas seemed like the height of folly. But they stopped laughing in 1990 when a heavily black jury refused to convict D.C. Mayor Barry on most charges for smoking crack, even though he was videotaped in the act. The jurors believed Barry's argument that the federal government had entrapped him.

Because most whites by now resented the black insistence on victimization, black cries of racism, which had worked years before, fell on deaf ears. Whites felt that blacks seemed to think blacks could not fail on their own, but only because they never had a chance to begin with. "The 'racist' epithet, like the little boy's cry of 'wolf,' is a charge so often invoked these days that it has lost its historical moral force," said Glenn Loury, a conservative black Harvard professor who has been labeled an "Uncle Tom" by the black establishment. But Loury's thinking, although still unpopular, slowly began to spread to others in the black community.

Washington Post columnist William Raspberry, a spokesman for the black middle class, put it this way: "Racism has become our all-purpose explanation for every disadvantage. . . . I think our reliance on race as the universal explainer does more harm than good. It inhibits our achievement by limiting our ability to try. It oversimplifies complex interpersonal relations and reduces our own role in their improvement. . . . I can't say too clearly that the racist explanation may often be the correct one. But it is, in my view, frequently a damaging one."

In this new age, whites agreed that many of those on welfare were indeed victims—not of racism, however, but of their inability to take responsibility for themselves. Most whites, for instance, didn't see the unwed teenage welfare mother, whether black or white, as a victim. They figured that she, at least in part, was responsible for her plight. But they saw themselves as the victim, since they were footing the bill. Enlightened whites realized that the real victims were the children: the welfare babies who seemed doomed to a life like their parents, and the middle-class kids destined to live in an increasingly two-tiered society. But because blacks constituted such a disproportionate share of unwed welfare mothers, class and racial antagonisms were jumbled together.

The frustration in white America was captured by a black man, Joshua Smith, who had built one of the nation's largest black-owned businesses, the Maxima Corporation, a computer services firm.

"As long as society feels we're a drain," Smith stated, "then we're not going to be liked. But when we turn that around and contribute, we're going to be desired. I think the Vietnamese have proven that. Nobody talks about those boat people. Now everyone sees the valedictorians in the classes. They see the business people, the role models."

The growing racial polarization of America became a defining problem for the Democratic party. John Lewis, the black congressman whose Atlanta district has chunks of middle-class white suburbs along with homeless shelters and public housing projects in the city, could feel the tensions: "Race played a significant role. The party got the image of being the party . . . carrying the civil rights banner. You cannot escape that. I think it's a problem with bringing back those white voters that left." It has been made worse, he added, by Jesse Jackson's role in the Democratic party.

Inside the Washington beltway, where, as Huey Long once remarked, "the heart of America is felt less than any place I have ever been," most Democrats either weren't as perceptive or as candid as Lewis. They tried to believe the fallen-away whites were just a fringe element that shared Reagan's view that welfare programs perpetuated black poverty, a racist—or at least insensitive—position. They remembered the outcry that greeted Daniel Patrick Moynihan in 1965 when he warned that black problems stemmed from the disintegration of the black family. He was called a racist then, and for some years afterward.

But by 1990 Moynihan was seen as prophetic.

"I talked with him at the time," Ed Koch remembered. "Moynihan was hurt, politically and personally, by the attacks made on him for simply saying the major problem in the black community was the lack of family structure. For twenty years he was in the doghouse. You can't get Moynihan to talk about black families now. Public officials, seeing how Moynihan had been treated, shied away from any discussion of reality in that area."

Despite Moynihan's experience, or perhaps because of it, during the first half of the 1980s no Democrat of any consequence was willing to concede that Reagan might have had a point about the welfare system. But as the decade closed, even Democrats were beginning to come around. A Democratic Congress passed welfare reform in 1988 aimed at cleaning up the mess that by then everyone agreed the system had wrought.

The reforms contained provisions that liberals only a few years before had considered Draconian. One was a work requirement for welfare recipients, albeit a watered-down version. Another allowed women to collect welfare benefits even if a man was in the house—an effort to rebuild black families.

Still, the black civil rights establishment was little changed in its outlook. Its leaders—the NAACP, Jackson, the Congressional

Black Caucus—looked at government as financier and protector of black progress and regarded any deviation from that view as treasonous.

Many of these same black leaders had changed the aim of the civil rights movement of the 1960s from integration to black empowerment. The black power movement was a boon for black politicians. If true integration ever became a reality, the power of black leaders would be diluted in the larger group of whites.

Thus, these black leaders took up the cry of affirmative action, which has kept the black power structure almost intact. Lewis, a pioneer of that period, laments the transition although he, like virtually all black leaders, supports affirmative action programs as a means of securing equal rights and opportunities for blacks.

"We made a serious mistake when the movement turned against its first principle: integration," said Lewis, a short and stocky sharecropper's son. "The seeds that were planted twenty years ago have borne very bitter fruit. We started going our separate ways. So many black elected officials, so many black would-be politicians got caught up in this whole idea of 'give me a piece of the pie' . . . . rather than talking about the common good. I think we missed the boat. There was a perception blacks wanted to take something from someone else in order to have something."

Some black politicians were able to appeal across racial lines to the middle class. Virginia's Doug Wilder, for example, was elected the nation's first black governor in 1989 in a state with only a 15 percent black population. He ran on a platform that differed little from that of his two white predecessors, Charles Robb and Gerald Baliles. And they, by almost all standards, were conservative Democrats. Wilder believed the civil rights establishment had badly served black America by not recognizing change.

"It's to a lot of people's advantage to say things aren't any better," Wilder said. "What worked in the sixties won't work in the nineties. Because what was, was. Things change. People change. Walking around proclaiming our ethnic identity doesn't solve problems."

The silver-haired governor underwent a huge philosophical transformation between his election as a liberal state senator from a black Richmond district in 1969 to the man who made history two decades later. Wilder had cut his Afro, trimmed his mustache, and become a political insider.

Wilder, with his eye on the national spotlight, was the unusual black politician who was popular with whites because he made them feel comfortable. And he practiced a fiscal conservatism unique to black Democratic officeholders. "People have said we [blacks] have not made any progress in the last twenty years and I dispute that," Wilder contended. "There are more opportunities in this country than ever before. There has been great progress. The question of why more people are not taking advantage of these opportunities has opened the great debate."

But few black politicians succeeded as he did in majority white areas because they were unwilling to adopt his agenda—supporting government spending cuts over tax increases and emphasizing an individual's responsibility to help himself. And on one issue Wilder came on strong—he switched his previous opposition to the death penalty. It may have been the most important step of all.

A fundamental emotion influenced the attitude about blacks in middle-class America: fear. Crime was rampant. Or so it seemed to almost everyone, rich or poor.

Arkansas' Clinton, whose state was hardly a crime capital, spoke for almost all Americans when he said: "I hardly know anyone who has not been victimized by crime or has someone in their immediate family [who has] not been victimized by crime in the past ten years."

In the spring of 1989 a young woman jogger and a model citizen became the national symbol of that middle-class fear. Graduated from Yale, she had done volunteer work with the poor and was climbing the investment banking corporate ladder when she was savagely beaten and raped while on her nightly run in New York's Central Park. The assailants were a group of black and Puerto Rican teenagers who newspapers reported told police they had been on a "wilding" spree out looking for a white girl.[5]

The incident created a storm even among hardened New Yorkers. Some black leaders said the white community was prejudging the black youths, although a few had admitted their guilt. But what really got under many white voters' skins was the attitude of Democratic leaders who tried to skirt the racial angle, who refused to acknowledge the reality of black crime.

New York Gov. Mario Cuomo was one of the few politicians willing to discuss the racial aspect of the attack. But he quickly retreated to the mushy liberalism of many Democrats when he was asked by the *Washington Post* about data that showed 91 percent of prison inmates were black or Hispanic in a roughly 40 percent black and Hispanic city.

"Behind closed doors, there are undoubtedly a lot of white people who see [crime] as a problem caused by black people," Cuomo stated. "It's all wrong talk, counterproductive talk. You are not more apt to be in organized crime because you're Italian, and you are not more apt to be a mugger because you're black. . . . This is a dangerous game to play with those statistics. You can say most of the people executed for murder are black, therefore most murderers are black. But maybe the white people could afford better lawyers . . . that kind of generalization has been used as a pseudo-relevant factor to punish people for generations."[6]

Whether or not crime was increasingly becoming a black problem, the point was that most whites thought it was. Democratic leaders, whom white voters viewed as being politically beholden to blacks, refused to deal with that perception. They also refused to deal with the stark figures and images that caused whites to feel the way they did.

Nationally, one in four black men in their twenties was either in jail, on probation, or on parole—four times the rate for whites and more than twice the rate for Hispanics. Murder has become the largest single cause of death among young blacks. Blacks made up roughly half the inmates in U.S. prisons—about four times their share of the general population. In 1990, half of the nation's twenty largest cities set records for the number of murders.

Largely because of the violence and drugs, men in Bangladesh, one of the poorest countries in the world, had a better chance of living past age forty than men in Harlem. "There are some locations [in America] where it's now more likely for a black male between his fifteenth and twenty-fourth birthday to die from homicide than it was for a soldier to die during his tour of duty in Vietnam," said Robert G. Froehlke, of the U.S. Centers for Disease Control.[7]

White America laid the country's murder spree at the door of a whole generation of young black men, adrift and lawless, and had little sympathy for them. It was no accident that the only Democrats willing to articulate what white, middle-class America thought of explanations like Cuomo's were those like former Colorado Governor Lamm. Because he was outside the political arena, he could say what he believed. And he believed Cuomo's rationale was hogwash.

"When you are faced with the incredible rise in crime rates and growing welfare loads, people look at the Democratic party and reject the Democratic party's blind defense that criminals are victims of a racist society," Lamm declared.

Cuomo's response did nothing but reinforce white America's belief that Democrats would always find a way to blame white society for what it figured was a black problem. It didn't help that liberal Democrats invariably shifted the argument to show, accurately, that blacks were more likely to be the crime victims.

In the 1960s, that explanation might have worked, but the thinking of white voters had changed. Most just tuned out anything that smacked of black victimization. The preponderance of black crime stuck in white America's craw. Being scolded for such thoughts only made them more angry.

Democratic pollster Greenberg, who became the party's expert on such matters, explained that middle-class voters "link the fact that they think Democrats are soft on crime and welfare with their black base. The fact that they are indulgent of criminals, are indulgent of people on welfare which they see largely as a minority question, means to them that Democrats don't understand that the people who are supposed to be rewarded are the ones who work. And they [the white middle class] have made a racial connection."

What became fixed in white minds was that violence seemed to be a way of life in the black community. The drug scourge that terrorized America accentuated that impression, and television coverage fanned the flames. The statistics said drugs were as prevalent in white neighborhoods as in black, and that when economic factors were taken into account, blacks were no more violent than whites.

"I would venture to say there's as much drugs in [heavily white and affluent] Georgetown as there is in [heavily black and poor] Anacostia," said black District of Columbia Police Chief Isaac Fulwood, Jr., in August 1989. "But it's not on the street corner. And the people don't tend to resort to violence. The difference in black neighborhoods is the violence that has come with it."[8]

Yet, as the streets of America's cities became more violent, most whites became more race sensitive and, in turn, many blacks grew more angry. And still, few politicians were willing to talk about the problem. Republicans saw no need to. They benefited from the status quo. The task fell to the Democrats, who were behind the political eight-ball. Yet most white Democrats were just plain scared. Given their tenuous position with whites, they worried that discussing the issue might be confused with racism and they would lose most blacks as well.

And, in fact, those who did paid a price, like Moynihan had twenty years before.

Sen. Charles Robb, a Virginia Democrat, suggested in 1986 that "while racial discrimination has by no means vanished from our society, it's time to shift the primary focus from racism—the traditional enemy without—to self-defeating patterns of behavior." He said that "by doing nothing in the face of these realities, the federal government had created a de facto social policy of welfare dependency for women and prison for men."

For his candor, Robb was assailed by liberals for being insensitive to blacks. But a lesson lurked for the party in his experience. Robb was deemed the most popular politician in a state that had voted Democratic for president exactly once since 1952. Despite openly speaking of the white middle-class frustration, he had retained his black support.

And that is the key for Democrats who want to win presidential elections. Although white resentment is periodically shown in tax-payer revolts, the largest manifestations come every four years when Democratic presidential candidates can't get the white middle class to take them seriously.

"There is some sense in this country that the Democratic party, or at least some of the activists, may be more interested in helping them [blacks] than helping me [white middle-class voters]," acknowledged Susan Estrich, Dukakis' 1988 campaign manager. "It's not that 'I'm against them,' I've heard in focus groups. 'It's just that . . . I want to get a decent job, send my kid to a good school.' It's not the kind of race issue that no one wants to say blacks should get jobs, it is 'in tough times whose side are you going to be on?' Worse still, 'Are you the party that is going to bend over backwards for blacks when the rest of us just want to walk straight?' "

5

Different Thinking Is Reality, Not Racism

Howard Jeffers and Justin Darr were an unusual team. Only a year apart in age, both grew up in the South and pretty much made their own way in the world. They used their hard-muscled bodies to earn solid middle-class livings from the hard hat construction industry in North Carolina's Raleigh-Durham-Chapel Hill area.

Jeffers, a large, quiet black man with hands as strong as the steel he welded, grew up in the rural South, near where he works. Darr, a pipe fitter, was a white suburban kid from Memphis.

During the years that the two men built new power plants and shut down those with problems, they often worked together as a unit. It was extremely dangerous work and their mutual dependence established a bond that spanned real differences in their personalities and views.

They are friends. They think the world of each other, although they don't socialize outside of work. During those long, hot, sweaty days, when they take their breaks, the two men talk sports, complain about this or that, and sometimes discuss politics. They don't agree much on politics, but that never seems to matter.

They earn about the same salary—roughly $28,000 annually plus overtime. Their wives' more modest incomes supplement the family bank accounts. Darr has a daughter and they both have stepchildren. Both like the simple things in life, and neither minds driving a distance to work. For them, living outside of town has its rewards.

Darr lives in Sanford, North Carolina, about thirty-five miles from the Research Triangle. His well-kept, grey, ranch-style house with a small pond and woods behind is snuggled into a neighborhood of similar suburban homes.

Jeffers lives in Roxboro, another Research Triangle suburb thirty miles north of Durham, in a similarly sized brown, wood-frame, three-bedroom, two-bath home that he built on land his father gave him. Jeffers grew up on a nearby family tobacco farm, one of eleven children. He barely discussed politics with his parents, but he knew they were staunch Democrats. Jeffers' childhood was much poorer than his stepson's. He graduated from high school, worked in nearby textile mills for five years, then learned to weld. He is in demand, and can work as much as he wants. Despite the unflattering image of black America often presented on television, it is hardworking, law-abiding people like Jeffers who make up most of black America, and an even larger share of black voters.

Darr's story is less linear. He grew up in a Catholic family with a Republican father and a Democratic mother. He spent two years in a Benedictine monastery as a teenager before leaving for an on-and-off mixture of college and jobs that took him across much of the country for the better part of a decade. When his odyssey began he was a "cool" but scrawny 1970s teenage hipster with beads and hair halfway down his back. In 1972, he stuffed envelopes for George McGovern's presidential campaign.

By the time he got his undergraduate degree from the University of North Carolina in economics and philosophy he was a solid 6'1", two hundred-pound hard hat with a trim beard and a new way of looking at life. His joy is being a dad after his prolonged bachelorhood. Once married he became assistant head of his stepson's Boy Scout troop in order to take a crash course in children.

Jeffers, a strapping 6'2", 215-pound man with a small mustache, didn't get to play football when he was in high school because he had to harvest tobacco. He makes up for it now, in a sense, parked in front of the TV watching pro games. He's naturally quiet, and often needs a little prodding before he'll speak his mind. But he knows what he thinks, and he doesn't mince words when the guys sit around in their slack moments.

"I agree with the Democrats 100 percent in that they want government to do things for people," says Jeffers. "Government should help the homeless. The government should provide jobs, that's the main thing. Fair wages. Government should get businesses to pay better. They probably don't get enough involved in telling business what to do. Government should look out for people's welfare. Business often takes advantage of people."

Darr, by contrast, is a strong believer in the free market. He thinks government too often sticks its nose in where it doesn't belong, and when it does often screws up. He believes federal plans to institute child care programs are an intrusion into family responsibilities and will further weaken the American family, a trend that stems from the Great Society's effort to shape society in the Democratic image.

"I think during the Carter administration is when I began seeing the proper role of the government as more of a policeman for society rather than a great equalizer," Darr states. "I think the Democrats have tried to socially orchestrate the country too much through government programs."

Dennis Dyer and Curtis Jones also have a great deal in common, although they don't know each other and live several hundred miles apart.

Both come from Northeastern working-class families. Both worked their way through college, have white-collar jobs, and earn over $50,000, which puts them on the highish side of the middle class.

Dyer manages a software development office in Reading, Pennsylvania, about fifty miles northwest of Philadelphia, and lives in a wood-frame, stucco house with white and brown siding. Although fairly typical of his city of 75,000, the house is another world from the 10'-by-54' trailer he grew up in near the United States Military Academy at West Point, New York. His dad was a civilian welder, his mother worked nights as a nurse.

Dyer was the family's first college graduate—with a degree from the Ivy League's Brown University—but not the last. Two other brothers, part of a tight-knit family that would make Norman Rockwell proud, have degrees from Cornell University and the Massachusetts Institute of Technology. Like Justin Darr, Dyer had shoulder-length hair as a teenager. But he too grew more conservative, not only in appearance, but in his general outlook.

He and his wife Jeanne are testimonies to perseverance. Dennis was an offensive lineman on his high school football team. At 5'8", 140 pounds, he blocked defenders who sometimes topped his weight by one hundred pounds. Jeanne's story is a screenplay waiting for a producer. In the mid 1960s, as a teenager, she was stricken with Hodgkin's Disease. Despite several recurrences, she is one of the first persons ever cured of the once-fatal form of cancer.

They live in the ninety-year-old house in which she grew up. Shortly after Dennis got his MBA from Syracuse University, he met Jeanne at a firm in Reading where they both worked. She now takes care of blond, blue-eyed Stephen, who is adopted and yet a dead ringer for Dennis.

Jeanne was always the more conservative, but since their marriage in 1978 Dennis has moved steadily right. "I consider myself a conservative," he says, "because I tried the liberal point of view for a long time and I don't think it works. It's time for people to do things for themselves instead of waiting for the rest of the world to do things."

Curtis Jones, chief of security for the 100,000 residents in Boston's public housing projects, agrees with Dyer's call for individual responsibility. He's also a walking advertisement for the benefits of hard work. He worked his way through Northeastern University, and, like Dyer, took advantage of government aid to get through.

Jones is a solidly built black man of average height who grew up in Boston, one of five children of a metal worker and a social worker. His upbringing was similar to Dennis Dyer's. "My parents were hard-working, very independent people. We grew up with the fact that you do things for yourself because you are the only ones who can make a difference."

Jones, who lives in a three-story, nine-bedroom Victorian-style home in Boston's integrated Dorchester section, is an example of the good things that government programs can provide.

As a youth, beginning in the early sixties his parents availed themselves of a voluntary plan that sent black kids out of Boston's all-black Roxbury section to suburban schools. That plan was less controversial than the forced busing of both whites and blacks a decade later.

Every day for six years Jones got up earlier, and home later, than his neighborhood friends. He rode a bus more than an hour each way to Marblehead, on Boston's north shore. He was one of forty-two blacks out of nine hundred students there, and he was elected sophomore class president.

Jones now sends his children to a school in the western, lily-white and affluent Boston suburb of Weston, an even longer ride than he had as a child. "The welfare state has lulled a lot of people to sleep to believe the government will give them what they need," he asserts. "It sometimes destroys individuals to believe government will always be there for them."

Yet when it gets to specifics about the legitimate use of government, Dennis Dyer and Curtis Jones disagree almost as much as Justin Darr and Howard Jeffers. Jones sees a need for government programs which Dyer doesn't. Jones is much more willing to spend his tax dollars for programs to help the poor, or those on drugs or in prison. He considers it an investment. Not Dyer.

Jones thinks his approach is pragmatic. "Look at welfare mothers. They have been receiving welfare since they were born. One family could cost the nation several hundreds of thousands of dollars, or millions over time. If we could educate them, give them opportunity," they could become productive members of society and save tax money. Dyer, and much of white America, has heard that rationalization for the last quarter century and no longer buys it.

The attitudes of Dennis Dyer and Curtis Jones differ, as do those of Justin Darr and Howard Jeffers, even though they share common economic situations. The reason is race. It is no coincidence that of these four members of the "thirtysomething" generation, Jeffers and Jones are black and solidly Democratic, and Dyer and Darr are white and conservative Republicans.

In short: Most black people and most white people in the country think very differently about political issues. This notion has been established beyond doubt by polling data, and it violates the concept of equality and color blindness that permeates American, and especially Democratic, thought.

It's also something of a taboo subject in polite conversation. Witness the way Fortney "Pete" Stark, a liberal California Democratic congressman, was treated when he lost his temper in the summer of 1990 with Bush's Health and Human Services Secretary Louis Sullivan, a black. Stark called Sullivan "a disgrace to his race" for not favoring big government solutions to urban problems. He quickly apologized, but everyone knew exactly what he meant. Stark had assumed—as do the American people—that blacks believe in governmental solutions. And he was right. Sullivan is the rare exception.

Those unwilling to confront the reality—that blacks generally want government to do more, and whites want it to do less—have repeatedly argued that it logically stemmed from differing economic perspectives. But the reality is not nearly so true, nor so comforting. Clearly, as a group white voters are better off than most blacks. But the ideological difference exists just as strongly between blacks and whites of similar economic status. It is vital to remember that the majority of black voters *are* middle class, they *are* people like Howard Jeffers and Curtis Jones. The average black voter is *not* a welfare mother.

ABC's exit polls from the November 1988 elections showed that among black voters, 56 percent had incomes of $20,000 or more, one third had college degrees, while another 28 percent had had some college instruction. The comparable figures for whites were higher: 74 percent, 37 percent, and 29 percent, respectively. But the difference is not as large as might be expected.

Republican leaders, better attuned to demographics than Democrats, understand perfectly the differences between white and black political attitudes, but they keep mum about it. They see no reason to risk their edge with white voters. Sure, they would like to increase their black vote, but they know they don't need it to keep the White House. What they must do is hang onto the whites who make up 80-plus percent of the electorate, which means to remember how much most whites oppose new taxes and distrust the government.

And because Democrats have been afraid to deal with the different political attitudes of blacks and whites, they have failed to understand why their message is not selling sufficiently to win. The different attitudes between blacks and whites are stark.

Blacks attribute to government the ending of slavery and segregation, and therefore overwhelmingly favor expansion of the federal role. They think it is a legitimate government function to improve, and in some cases provide, a suitable standard of living for those who can't make it in the marketplace. "There's a history there," explains Atlanta congressman John Lewis. "We saw the national government during the height of integration as a sympathetic referee for civil rights. We saw the government as a shepherd, a bridge over troubled waters. We won't let that go. Sometime that may change, (but) the great majority of blacks, because of our recent past, tend to see the federal government as the leader, as the shepherd. Not as big brother, but to create the climate and environment for greater social change."

Whites lack the sense of debt to government felt by blacks, and worry more about the cost of government than its benefits. Even affluent blacks are more likely than whites to support almost any kind of tax proposal, even sales taxes that hit the poor hardest. The same is true on the spending side: Blacks habitually favor federal programs, even in areas like farm subsidies from which few blacks benefit.

Phil Gramm was born poor in rural, red-neck, "yellow dog" Texas, so named because the residents at one time would have voted for a canine if it were the Democratic nominee. Gramm was the first in his family to graduate from college. He earned a doctorate and taught economics at Texas A&M. When he decided to go into politics, naturally it was as a Democrat.

Gramm, whose intellect is equaled only by his ego, media savvy, and instinct for the political jugular, was among the most conservative Democrats in Congress when elected in 1978. That was fine at home, because in Texas conservative Democrats were the rule, not the exception. But on Capitol Hill, Gramm's politics stood out in the House's liberal Democratic caucus even more than his Texas twang.

So, in early 1984, Gramm switched parties. But unlike most others, he resigned his seat in order to force a special election in which he ran as a Republican. He argued that voters should get another pass at him now that he had switched parties. Three months after winning easily as a Democrat, he was reelected as a Republican with 55 percent of the vote. Later that same year, he was overwhelmingly elected to the Senate as a Republican.

But Gramm, who had a 2-1 favorable rating among blacks in his district when he was a Democrat, lost one all-black precinct 202-0 as a Republican. Gramm was curious. He had been no more conservative as a Republican than as a Democrat. He hadn't voted any differently on black issues. Why, then, had black support disappeared once he shed his Democratic label?

"I couldn't understand it," Gramm recalled. "Then I realized what it was. What has happened in the black community is that 44 cents of every dollar of income comes from government [in salaries from government employment and benefits from government programs]. If you figure that money turns over once in the black community, which would be a fairly conservative estimate, then another 44 cents is the first turnover. You are talking about 88 cents of every dollar in the black community coming from government."

"I couldn't figure out why the black merchants weren't supporting me. They were middle class. But what I realized is they are indirectly on welfare. The guy who comes and puts the quarter in the slot for their washing machine, the small merchants, they are dependent on the government check. While they are not on welfare they are beneficiaries. People who are getting almost 90 percent of their income either directly or indirectly from government are going to vote for the party of government. Period."

Actually, the Census Bureau puts the amount of money in the black community that comes from government at 36 cents per dollar, but that doesn't account for the value of noncash government programs like food stamps and medical care. If Gramm's numbers are slightly off, his analysis isn't. The corresponding figure for whites is 21 cents.

No better evidence exists of the attitudinal differences between the races than the yearly public opinion surveys conducted during the last half of the 1980s by the Gallup organization and the Joint Center for Political and Economic Studies. Because blacks are roughly 12 percent of the nation's population, it is difficult to get a well-defined picture of black public opinion because most national polls generally only sample 1,000-1,500 people. That yields black subsamples of 120-180 people, too small to be meaningful. But to compare attitudes, Gallup and the Joint Center began surveying samples of roughly 650 black and 650 white voters, which provides a margin of error of less than 4 percentage points.

Their 1988 survey, which was consistent with similar polls, showed that 66 percent of blacks, compared to only 23 percent of whites, thought government should guarantee a job and a good standard of living for all. It is impossible to overestimate the significance of that difference. Those who back government involvement will inevitably support higher taxes and larger bureaucracies. In short, every major domestic political question revolves around that difference. Gallup also did a much larger 1987 research project for the Times Mirror Co. That survey found blacks much less likely than whites to believe people can work themselves up the economic ladder if they try hard enough. Blacks are also much more suspicious of the private sector.

These differences translate directly into partisan politics: Democrats are viewed as wanting a big government and Republicans as wanting a small one.

ABC's 1988 exit polls showed that black and white voters of the same average family income saw things differently. Essentially, poor whites are less likely than poor blacks to view big government as their friend; similarly, middle-class whites are less likely to hold that view than middle-class blacks. ABC's poll also found that among the 15 percent of all white voters who earned $10,000-$20,000 annually, Bush won 55-44, but among the 19 percent of the blacks in that income category, Dukakis won 90-9.

Among the 51 percent of white voters who earned $20,000-50,000, Bush won 59-40, but among the 42 percent of black voters who earned the same, Dukakis won 87-11.

Among blacks there are exceptions, of course, like Secretary Sullivan, or Gary Franks, elected in 1990, from Waterbury, Conn., the first black member of the U.S. House in a half-century to represent a 4 percent black district. Conversely, there are many whites who share the predominant black view of what government should do, but not nearly enough to constitute a voting majority.

These liberal Democrats, however, have views far different from the mass of white voters. They tend to support candidates like Ted Kennedy. They also have great control over the Democratic presidential nomination—and that explains the Democratic losing streak. It was said of the New Democratic Coalition, a group of liberal Democratic activists of the 1970s known as the NDC, that their initials stood for "November Doesn't Count." In their search for ideological purity, they lost sight of the November election.

There are relatively few blacks who don't fit the liberal philosophical profile, which explains why Republicans have so much trouble recruiting black voters, even those whose educational and economic profiles would likely have made them conservative had they been white.

Dennis Dyer and Curtis Jones, two proud, hard-working men, illustrate many of the differences between black and white voters. Both are economically comfortable and middle class—a far cry from the selfish Yuppie lifestyle.

Dyer is able to help finance his in-laws' trips to family reunions. His wife's brother, who has Down's Syndrome, lives with them. He gets to the office by 7 A.M. during the spring and summer so he can get on the golf course in the afternoon. He and Jeanne are religious people.

Although Jones realizes his $54,000 salary puts him solidly in the middle class, "I would actually say I am upper class in mental state, although not in dollars," he asserts. "Look what I am capable of doing. Can I play golf when I want? Yes. I can go on vacations. . . . I have never wanted things I couldn't achieve. I don't worry about money. I never had to. I don't have a lot of it, but I have enough. The issue is how do you use your money."

Dyer is sympathetic toward the poor and Jones doesn't like the idea of new taxes. But at the margin, Dyer's instinct makes him skeptical of government programs, while Jones' tends to support them. Dyer thinks they have created a dependency among welfare recipients that prevents them from functioning on their own. And he has lost patience with the programs themselves. Jones agrees government programs have produced a minority population that expects government help. But he thinks better management of the programs is the answer.

"I don't feel as though one part of America owes something to another part of America because I'm better off than they are," says Dyer. "I don't think Rockefeller owes me a check every month because he's rich and his grandfather abused people when he built his fortune."

Again, at the margin, there is a disparity between the two, as there is between blacks and whites, on criminal justice matters. Dyer's general attitude is that society should take criminals off the streets and throw away the key. Jones leans to using the penal system to rehabilitate wrongdoers.

Perhaps Jones views prisoners more leniently because he knows some of them personally. Various of his teammates from youthful games played amid shattered glass have wound up in trouble. "Prisons don't work. What happens is a prisoner gets older, he gets out and can't get a job," Jones explains. "He has no opportunity and commits a crime again. And we're paying for his life all over again, at $30,000 a person, per year. The 'throwing away the key' syndrome never works. It's costing us dearly as a nation."

For much the same reason—and because the death penalty has been used disproportionately against blacks—blacks are much more likely than whites to oppose capital punishment. Whites worry much less that an innocent person will be executed and much more that a criminal might be paroled too early. Whites are less likely to know people who have been accused of murder; blacks worry about the system's fairness. Whites see statistics; blacks see the faces of defendants.

Foreign policy and economics are other areas where blacks and whites have diverse opinions.

The Gallup-*Times Mirror* survey found that on a host of theoretical questions, blacks, compared to whites, are more wary of U.S. military involvement overseas and less likely to believe that a strong military ensures peace and to consider themselves "very patriotic."

When President Bush ordered the U.S. attack on Iraq in January 1991, that difference in public opinion quickly surfaced. In the months following the August 2, 1990, Iraq invasion of Kuwait, almost weekly Gallup polls showed blacks generally 25-35 points less willing than whites to back Bush's tough policy. And when the president ordered the U.S. to launch an attack on January 16, 1991, a slew of polls showed that, generally, three-quarters or more of whites, but fewer than half of blacks, supported the decision. In some polls, the gap was as large as forty points.

The reasons were clear. Blacks thought the money for the military effort could be better spent on America's distressed cities and, moreover, were concerned that the U.S. soldiers at risk in the Persian Gulf were disproportionately black.

When it comes to money matters, the attitudinal differences are not just because of the relative size of black and white salaries. In truth, the salary differential is in many ways a smaller problem for black America.

The experience of Jones' parents is an all-too-true example of the financial fallout black families face as a result of bigotry. His parents scraped together enough money to buy a home in the heavily white West Roxbury section of Boston. In 1970, they paid $19,000 for a five-bedroom, two-bath home on a wooded half-acre tract. They were among the first blacks in the neighborhood. But instead of the Welcome Wagon, they were met with hostility. In 1974, during the furor over school busing that rubbed the city's nerves raw, someone hurled a firebomb at their home. No one was injured, but it was the straw that broke the camel's back. The next year, after five years of tension, his parents sold the house for $29,000 and moved into a rented apartment in a more liberal integrated suburb. But that house was easily worth $250,000 by the end of the 1980s, money that should have been in his parents' bank account.

Clearly, the legacy of racial discrimination created the economic disparity that gives the average black household one-tenth the assets of the average white household, and holds black family income to two-thirds that of white households. This means even middle-class blacks feel—and are—more apt to lose it all because of a layoff or a major expense. It explains why blacks are so concerned with economic security, even when they appear to be doing well. And why they support government programs—their safety net.

The other part of that legacy is that the entrepreneurial spirit is not strong in black America. The focus is on security that government can provide, not only in benefits, but in employment.

Fully half of all black managers and professionals are government workers.[1] Even when the income of blacks and whites is similar, their economic and psychological profiles are not. Many blacks with middle-class incomes have benefited directly from government programs set up to help minorities. In fact, it is the black middle class, not so much the poor, that has benefited from affirmative action. Black middle-income families are much more likely to live in cities than their white suburbanite counterparts.

Whites in the $24,000-$48,000 income range are only 15 percent more likely than blacks of similar incomes to own their own home. But those whites are between two and three times more likely to own investment real estate and part of a business or to play the stock market.[2]

The reasons are obvious. Blacks historically have had less money to invest than whites, and members of the black middle class have been less likely to have discussed investments with their parents. Moreover, blacks are wary of the private sector which had to be prodded by government to open its doors to them. Naturally, then, blacks are much less likely than whites to back economic policies based on the concept of shifting money from government to private investment. Jones opposes lowering the capital gains tax rate because he doesn't make such investments; Dyer is for cutting capital gains taxes because he does.

Actually, on this and most other matters, blacks like Curtis Jones and Howard Jeffers have a lot more in common philosophically with Robert Gordon than they do with Dennis Dyer and Justin Darr. Gordon is white and lives in the suburbs, but he is the prototypical white liberal.

For race is not the only thing gnawing away at FDR's New Deal coalition. As the polling data show and the 1988 campaign illustrates, a host of values questions separates most white voters from the white activists who run the Democratic party.

It is the attitudinal differences between most middle-class whites on the one hand, and blacks and the minority of white liberals like Gordon on the other, that explain much about the Democrats' political impotence.

Gordon, forty-six, is a foreign language teacher at a Columbus, Ohio, prep school who lives in Worthington on the city's northern side and has voted Democratic all his life. Slim and short with brown hair and beard, Gordon realizes that the liberal philosophy of his Unitarian Church is out of step today, not just with the country but with his own family. Much like the 1980s' TV sitcom "Family Ties," he finds himself at odds with his two grown sons over politics, yet he revels in the liberal label. "The ideas that were predominant in the sixties are still with me," Gordon claims. "I haven't seen any reasons to change those principles. I believe we can do things collectively and that means in many cases with government help and with public funding."

Gordon is not an atypical Democratic activist, just an atypical white, and he embodies the major differences between those whites who vote in Democratic primaries and caucuses and the mass of white voters who vote in November. On most matters, these liberal whites align closer to blacks than to other whites.

Evidence of this is available, although it took a massive project of 11,000 interviews done by Gallup for Times Mirror to provide large enough samples of blacks and likely Democratic primary voters to be meaningful. Of the total white sample, about 11 percent fit this criteria—being strong Democrats and likely primary voters. Blacks were about 12 percent of the sample.

The poll showed that white Democratic activists, white primary voters, and blacks, were significantly more likely than the mass of whites to believe that:

- Labor unions have not become too powerful
- Blacks haven't seen much real improvement in their status
- The government should guarantee every citizen enough to eat and a place to sleep

- The government should help the needy even if it means adding to the deficit
- Hard work offers little guarantee of success, which is determined pretty much by forces outside of the average person's control
- Government regulation of business is worthwhile

Even Bob Borosage, Jesse Jackson's top issues advisor, concedes that "the Democratic primary voter and activists are much to the left of the general party members and even further to the left of the general electorate."

Moreover, using the *Times Mirror* data, a demographic analysis of these white liberals shows they are more likely to be female, Jewish or Catholic, age fifty or older, part of a union family, unemployed, retired or working part-time, widowed or divorced, and have no children.

What the data shows is a Democratic primary electorate disproportionately made up of those either not competing in the economic marketplace, or protected from it by unions or government service. Being older, the group remembers the Democrats fondly from their era of prominence. What stands out is the relative absence of middle-class white people.

There is no appreciable difference between white Democratic activists and other white voters when it comes to income. But when it comes to lifestyle, Democratic primary voters are roughly twice as likely as other Democrats, in the preceding six months, to have read more than six books for pleasure or enjoyed classical music, and four times as likely to have attended the theater or ballet. In general, Democratic activists and average voters just have different priorities.

That was driven home forcefully to Evan Bayh shortly after he was elected Indiana's governor in 1988. Bayh is tall, with striking looks that Yuppie women like to call "drop-dead gorgeous." Within months of taking office, he was thinking about an eventual run for the White House. He knew he was young enough to wait for a more favorable political climate, and thus began trying to create a Democratic party more in tune with middle-class attitudes.

To that end he spoke to a meeting of the Democratic Business

Council, those who had given the DNC at least $5,000, in many cases much more. Presumably such a business-oriented group should have appreciated Bayh's mainstream message delivered in April 1989 at the Boca Raton Hotel and Club, a lush but aging Caribbean-style resort with pink stucco walls and outdoor fountains on Florida's inland waterway. "I asked for questions and the first hand that went up, the individual said, 'Governor, I think the most important issue of the nineties and the years beyond will be animal rights and I want to know what your position is on that,' " Bayh said, with part chuckle and part dismay.

Were that an isolated instance of Democratic insiders being out of touch, the chuckle could win out. But in truth, those people who are the core of the Democratic party—blacks, unions, government workers, issue activists—think differently than most Americans. They think of the Democratic party in terms of Franklin Roosevelt whipping the Depression, or people like themselves fighting in the 1960s for civil rights and against the Vietnam War. They view the solutions of that period—basically, a larger federal domestic role and a shrinking foreign one—as equally valid for the 1990s. But their view of the world is set in time. What's more, they are dying off much faster than they are being replaced by the young.

As a group, the Democratic liberals are more than twice as likely to think well of Jesse Jackson, Jimmy Carter, and Ted Kennedy, are four times less likely to have softened toward Richard Nixon, and are more avid fans of CBS' Dan Rather than are whites in general.

These are the people who nominate Democratic presidential candidates.

A *Washington Post* analysis of Democratic convention delegates shows just how out of touch they are.[3] Among the delegates to the 1988 Democratic convention that nominated Dukakis, 41 percent called themselves liberal, twice the figure for all Americans. And a total of 21 percent of the delegates were black, compared with their 10 percent share of the 1988 voting electorate. They were, moreover, much wealthier than the Democrats they represented, confirming the limousine liberal charge: more than half, 55 percent, had family incomes over $50,000—$20,000 above the national average—while only about 15 percent of Democratic voters earned $50,000.

The *New York Times* (July 17, 1988) said a whopping 55 percent of Democratic delegates were lawyers, teachers, union members, or government employees. And seven in ten had college degrees. In a period of Soviet Union belligerence, 63 percent wanted to chop defense spending as opposed to only 28 percent of voters in general.

The good news for the Democrats was that their 1988 delegates were more in touch with Middle America than they had been four years earlier, when more than half the delegates called themselves liberals and three-quarters wanted to cut defense spending. In 1984, the primary voters and their delegates were so far left that virtually all the Democratic presidential contenders were required by political reality to support a proposal to make homosexuals eligible for protection under affirmative action laws.

As time passed, not only did the spectrum of those who voted in Democratic primaries narrow, but their number decreased. Although most pronounced in the South, it was happening everywhere.

Florida was so Democratic that fully 20.2 percent of the states' voting age population participated in the 1976 Democratic presidential primary. But by 1988 so many Democrats had either left the party or stopped voting in primaries that the figure fell to only 13.2 percent. Since Jackson's candidacy ensured a high turnout of blacks and white liberals, the vanishing Democrats were clearly white moderates.

In Illinois between 1984 and 1988, turnout in the Democratic primary dropped by 158,497 persons, and the turnout among those with family incomes above $50,000—limousine liberals—grew from 5 percent to 15 percent of the vote. In North Carolina, turnout dropped by 281,000, but $50,000 income voters increased from 9 to 13 percent of the total. In Pennsylvania the drop was 141,000 voters and the rise in the wealthy share rose from 3 to 10 percent of the electorate.[4]

Democratic candidates and the people who run their campaigns are captives of the same out-of-touch mindset that handicaps Democratic primary voters. In 1984 it was Mondale's Minnesota-

Washington, D.C., mafia—a collection of politicos from two liberal, atypical places.

In 1988, it was Dukakis and his Boston mafia. Dukakis' crew, despite all the polling data, never understood how out of step they were with what their candidate called the "real America." Boston, despite a history of continuing tension between blacks and whites, is one of the most liberal cities in America on civil liberties and cultural matters. A marketing survey, moreover, showed it was the least religiously attuned city in America. Its upper-middle-class suburbs to the west, including Dukakis' Brookline neighborhood, have an openly homosexual congressman, Barney Frank. On foreign policy, the memory of Vietnam still hangs heavy and an almost instinctive opposition to use of U.S. troops overseas is the norm.

Dukakis and most of his campaign team came from Boston, went to Harvard, and did not understand how out of touch they were. That was made crystal clear a few weeks after the election by Dukakis' campaign chairman, Paul Brountas, speaking at a Harvard seminar: "I disagree with the characterization of the campaign being run by Boston pols. I don't think Susan Estrich is a Boston pol. I don't think I am either."

But Brountas had been a Harvard Law School classmate of Dukakis, had chaired Dukakis' previous gubernatorial campaigns, and had lived most of his adult life in Boston, where he was a prominent attorney. Campaign manager Estrich went to college at Wellesley, the exclusive women's college in the Boston suburbs, and graduated from Harvard Law School, where she later taught.

Brountas mistakenly thought that the country envisioned a Boston pol as a cigar-smoking Irish ward heeler. Those in the Dukakis inner circle, in fact, would have done better if they had had a touch of those they regarded as traditional Boston pols. It would have given them a much better feel of America. At least they would have understood why they were beaten about the head by their handling of the Pledge of Allegiance and the American Civil Liberties Union during the 1988 general election campaign.

In May 1977, Governor Dukakis vetoed a bill that would have required school teachers to lead students in the Pledge of Allegiance. He felt it was unconstitutional, and a state Supreme Court advisory opinion agreed with him. The matter lay dormant until Bush raised it eleven years later, saying he would have signed the law no matter what the court said.

Incredibly, when Bush took up the issue, Dukakis didn't understood that average voters couldn't relate to his logic. Who cared about the legal technicalities! The Pledge of Allegiance *is* America. In fact, four of ten Bush voters told *Times Mirror's* postelection poll that the Pledge was a very important factor in their decision. Among those who thought it was an important factor, nine in ten told ABC's exit pollsters they voted for Bush. Dukakis' retort, that Bush's position raised "very serious questions" about his understanding of the law, won him the votes of lawyers, but no one else. And not even all of them.

"I—and, I think, the rest of the campaign—never really understood that what the Pledge was about was the nerve it was hitting with blue-collar America in not being sufficiently respectful and sensitive to the flag," said Carol Darr, Dukakis' chief campaign counsel and one of the few members of the campaign hierarchy from outside Boston. "A Republican," she said, "explained to me that it recalled the image of the 1960s' Democrats—long-haired rebellious kids with the flag on the seat of their jeans." And she was right. The problem was that Dukakis—especially Dukakis, but also many of those who ran his campaign—didn't see anything wrong with using the flag in that or any other way.

The reality that the issue was killing them just never sank in. In mid-September 1988, Arkansas Governor Clinton, who had a personal bond with and respect for Dukakis that grew from their years together at governors' conferences, was invited to sit in on Dukakis' preparation for his first debate with Bush. By this time, the Pledge of Allegiance issue was hurting Dukakis badly in the polls. Clinton felt his most valuable contribution would be to offer a non-Harvard perspective.

"How are you going to answer this Pledge of Allegiance thing?" Clinton asked Dukakis during the prep session in a plush suite in the Lexington Hotel across the street from Dukakis' Boston campaign headquarters.

"The general consensus around the table," Clinton recalled,

"was, 'Do we need to spend a lot of time on this in this debate?' And Mike, bless his heart, and this wasn't being liberal, this was his government mindset, said, 'What does that have to do with being president?' Dukakis said, 'It's hard for me to believe it's going to be a big deal.' I told him it is a big deal," Clinton replied. "Where I come from, people will not vote for a president who doesn't like to pledge allegiance to the flag. He felt his program for college scholarships, or his program for star schools, that was what being president was all about—the initiatives you could take by the spending of tax money that would change people's lives through specific programs. But words matter, values, symbolism matters. We had this long talk, and finally I sat down and wrote out a proposed 56-second statement about this Pledge issue and how you could argue it in terms of values." But Dukakis never used it. "To him, his values as a citizen were not relevant to his campaign for president, because the president was the person who did government. That is a huge problem for the Democrats," Clinton lamented.

The ACLU controversy was much the same. Dukakis had bragged during the primaries that he was a card-carrying member of the American Civil Liberties Union. And most of the people who vote in those contests think the ACLU's hard line on individual rights is not only acceptable, but praiseworthy. During the summer of 1988, when the ACLU, the flag, and Willie Horton were hurting the Democrats badly everywhere, one perplexed member of Dukakis' gubernatorial cabinet asked naively, "I don't understand what the controversy is about. Isn't everyone a member of the ACLU?"

The answer was a Big Fat No. In the rest of America, the ACLU was seen as favoring criminals over victims, and backing scraggly protesters over the U.S. government.

But what set these hard-core Democrats apart was not only their belief that government should solve problems. It was their belief that those who differed—who raised issues that required moral value judgments—were sadly lacking in their moral and civic responsibilities.

Nothing better illustrated that preachy, condescending trait than the Democrats' inability to understand middle-American values when it came to Bush's plan to meet human needs through grass-roots volunteer efforts around the country. Bush called it "a thousand points of light" and said it would help solve America's social problems. It involved little federal money and created no new bureaucracy. Whether it would do much once Bush was president was open to question; but it certainly sounded good.

Yet at their final debate during the 1988 campaign, Dukakis openly mocked Bush for his statement. More devastatingly, Dukakis mocked the independent "let's all pull together and get something done" values that prevail on Main Street, USA. He and everyone around him thought it was a dodge, Bush's way of saying, 'I gave at the office.' Dukakis also made fun of Bush's comments about being "haunted" by the pictures of poor children and the homeless.

In fact, across America, Democratic liberals thought the "thousand points of light" idea was one big joke. "Being haunted—a thousand points of light—I don't know what that means," Dukakis complained. "I know what's happened over the course of the past eight years. These programs have been cut and slashed and butchered, and they've hurt kids all over the country." And it hit home—with the shrinking few who, like himself, think government is the only answer.

It was, sadly noted Clinton, one of those things that spoke volumes. Democrats like Dukakis felt "the only legitimate action that a politician takes is not what he says, or what he feels, but what he does in terms of a program or a bureaucracy." The rest of the country simply disagreed. In the words of Sen. Phil Gramm of Texas, middle-class voters believed "compassion is not what you do with someone else's money, it's what you do with your money."

It was Bush's message that resonated with the vast majority of voters, even some who thought the Reagan years hadn't done enough for the poor. After all, a 1990 Gallup study showed three in four adults had donated time or money to help the needy that year, and more than half of all households did volunteer work that averaged sixteen hours a month.

"What troubles me," Bush said of Dukakis, "is that when I talk of the voluntary sector and a thousand points of light and a thousand different ways to help on these problems, the man has just said he doesn't understand what I'm talking about. And this is the problem I have with these big-spending liberals. They think the only way to do it is for the federal government to do it all."

Score one for Bush. A big one.

6

The Democrats and Liberal Guilt

As the 1990s dawned it was easy to see how differently Democrats and Republicans viewed America. Their national chairmen, in their politics and personas, told the tale.

Republican Lee Atwater, a prototypical baby-boomer whose taste ran to barbecues and blues music, could have easily sold insurance in any Sun Belt suburb. Atwater was a bantam rooster with a South Carolina twang whose hawkishness, both in personality and appearance, was honed when Southern Republicans needed every edge they could find. Atwater's aggressiveness made enemies who often charged he not only played rough, but also played dirty. Patricia Schroeder, a Democrat and liberal Colorado congresswoman, spoke for many inside her party when she labeled him "probably the most evil man in America" for his campaign tactics. Yet even his opponents acknowledged that Atwater probably had the sharpest political mind of his generation.

What Atwater understood was that reaching white middle-class voters required identifying with their everyday lives. To that end, he would watch MTV, the rock music video channel, in order to grasp what moved young people, or would literally disappear into suburban and rural America to visit with "Joe Six-pack."

The insights he garnered led him to harp constantly on Reagan's

1980 question that defeated Jimmy Carter, "Are *you* better off today than you were four years ago?"

Democratic Chairman Ron Brown, a black New Yorker by birth, was, in contrast, as smooth as Atwater was jagged. It wasn't his color that made Brown less in tune with average voters. Ironically, given his Harlem—albeit middle-class—upbringing, it was his lifestyle. He skied in Aspen, vacationed in Europe, and ran among Washington's Democratic power brokers. Always impeccably groomed and coiffed, Brown had a smooth-as-silk appearance—monogrammed shirts, opal cuff links, and stylish suspenders—that reflected his years as a high-priced Washington lobbyist-lawyer.

Brown's climb up the ladder of the liberal establishment was aided by mentors ranging from Mario Cuomo to Ted Kennedy. They, more than his identification as Jesse Jackson's 1988 convention manager, won him the chairmanship of the Democratic National Committee.

The differences between Atwater and Brown were paradoxically symbolized by their common admiration of Lyndon Johnson. Atwater, a disciple of Machiavelli, respected LBJ's use of raw political power to get what he wanted. Brown, on the other hand, fixed on LBJ's burning desire to be remembered as the president who stamped out poverty.

"Republicans ask, 'Are *you* better off today?' Very selfish, very self-serving, a very nasty kind of question, although it gives an indication of their perspective," Brown states. "The questions Democrats ask, and the questions that ought to be asked are, 'Are *we* better off? Is our country better off?' And I think that series of questions, juxtaposed against theirs, really does give a clear distinction between the two parties."

Brown is right. There is no better explanation. Although Brown is more mainstream than Kennedy, Jackson, or Cuomo, he shares with them the political disease that has crippled the Democratic party for a quarter century: Liberal guilt.

This guilt is the belief that those who have prospered in American society have somehow done so at the expense of those who have not, regardless of whether or not the successful person acted wrongly. In racial terms, it is known as white guilt—the belief by some whites that the mere fact of being white gives them an unfair edge over blacks, an edge that can only be made right by atonement.

Black officials are much more open than whites in admitting that liberal guilt or white guilt has disappeared from most of America. In Atlanta, which has one of the nation's largest black middle-class populations and better race relations than most black cities encircled by white suburbs, it is an article of faith that both guilts are a thing of the past.

"Within the leadership of the Democratic party and within white liberals there's a feeling we have not done enough," says John Lewis, the black congressman from Atlanta. "You may want to call that white guilt, that people have been sensitized to the point that if we fail to make certain moves then the problem is going to get worse rather than better. But that is not shared by most white voters."

Andy Young, Atlanta's mayor for eight years, is even blunter: "It doesn't exist in most peoples' minds and it shouldn't. The liberal guilt syndrome is probably a Cambridge-Minneapolis-San Francisco syndrome. But most Democrats who run the national party have grown up with this liberal guilt. It's not even personal guilt, but a collective guilt of previous generations, a feeling you have to feel a conscience through guilt. It's one of the reasons the Democrats whom we have nominated for president do poorly. But it is totally irrelevant everywhere else. Most people don't feel guilt themselves and there is no reason why they should."

But Democratic leaders cannot discard that crucial piece of ideological baggage. It is there whenever they fail to focus on creating more wealth for society rather than redistributing what exists, mock the middle-class' obsession with its own woes, or blame their own failures on racial problems.

The Democrats are out of sync with voters because they are lost in time, thinking that the idealism that moved America in the 1960s is still flourishing today.

"What we are a victim of is not having the wrong attitude, but keeping that attitude too long. In the 1950s and 1960s that was the appropriate attitude. There is a liberal orthodoxy that has not changed," says former Colorado Governor Lamm. "The Democratic party is peopled by people out of the sixties who have not realized the dreams of the sixties can't be financed by the economy of the nineties. The social dreams of the sixties with their pat solutions have become unworkable. No one believes them anymore. We have a great variance between the orthodoxy of the people who run the Democratic party and the average voter, especially over race issues."

The Democrats put themselves in the same box as blacks in their social outlook—always viewing those who were unable to be part of the economic mainstream as victims. After all, this guilt-driven belief argued, if America truly is an egalitarian society, then everyone should be able to succeed. If, however, a pattern of nonsuccess exists, then look for a sinister force. Simple failure is not acceptable.

"The Democratic party has been locked into the victims theology: Even criminals are victims; minorities are total victims," Lamm believes. "The only explanation for minority failure is they are being discriminated against. The public realizes that is an inadequate explanation, while there is truth in it. We still tragically live in a society with racism. But you see throughout America people coming from Vietnam and Korea, people from Cuba, Pakistan, and succeeding beyond all measure. The idea that the Democratic party is out there still pushing busing and affirmative action and, to a degree, quotas" falls on deaf ears in middle-class America.

"The Democratic party always fights the last war, and it's very difficult for it not to," Lamm adds. "Most of our generals were trained in that war—the labor movement, the idealism of the sixties, the antiwar movement. That became the biggest thing in their lives. The biggest challenge of public policy is to understand when the world has changed and why."

This in many ways is reminiscent of the militarism that dominated the Soviet Union for forty-five years after World War II. The Soviet leadership was so mindful of Hitler's near victory that it emphasized defense concerns over the domestic population's economic needs. Domestic dissatisfaction, not an invading army, led to the ruptures within the Soviet Empire.

So too with the Democrats. Economics is a perfect example of the liberal guilt syndrome at work in American politics. Democrats are so tied to their habit of blaming the greedy rich for society's problems, they fail to see that the middle class no longer agrees.

Senator Gramm of Texas is largely correct in saying that Democrats "try to create this guilt feeling with the fairness issue" by arguing that because some groups do better than others the system is unfair.

But even Democrats finally began to realize they could no longer sell a national guilt trip and be nothing but the party of redistribution. Having spent millions of dollars on polls and focus groups telling them just that, the message by the early nineties finally began to sink in. Economic growth was the key issue. But for some, that meant advocating something they had always despised.

"It's embarrassing for a lot of Democrats to talk about creating wealth. It's an example of liberal guilt," states Lamm. "The liberal orthodoxy coming out of the 1930s-1960s was that the major role of public policy is to create a just society. Reagan and the Republicans realized that, whatever the validity of that, the new equation is you can't distribute what you don't earn. That a just society has to be rooted in an economically successful society. The idea that the Democratic party would be talking about wealth creation just goes against the last forty years of history. They will talk about jobs, but not the larger question of creating a competitive economy. Wealth isn't a dirty word, but they are schizophrenic. They have spent so much time talking about dividing wealth and the extremes of excessive wealth, that the idea of how you create wealth is very difficult for them."

It was never clearer that Democrats were out of step than during the 1988 presidential campaign when George Bush used the case of Willie Horton to charge Michael Dukakis with being soft on crime.

Horton, convicted of first-degree murder in 1974 for brutally killing a young gas station attendant, was sentenced to life in prison. Under the Massachusetts furlough program—set up by a Republican governor but supported by Dukakis—Horton was given ten furloughs. On his last one in June 1986, Horton fled to Maryland, where he raped a white woman and knifed her fiancé. Dukakis refused to apologize or to meet with Horton's Maryland victims, and brushed aside objections by averring that such incidents were part of the acceptable risk that came with furlough programs.

Bush used the issue on the stump and in TV commercials. He did not use Horton's picture in his ads, but a Republican group, operating independently of his campaign, did. Willie Horton was black.

The issue was a major factor in moving Bush from a seventeen-point deficit in the summer of 1988 to an eight-point victory in November.

Bill Lacy, former Reagan White House political director, was sent by Atwater to run the California campaign in June of 1988 when Bush was eighteen points behind in the state. "I have seen hundreds of polls during my career, and I have never seen an issue cut against a candidate like that," Lacy said after testing the Horton issue.

But it wasn't only in California, where crime is big, that it worked so well. It melted Dukakis' support nationally because for years Democrats seemed to be the ones who worried more about due process for criminal defendants than the victim's well-being. They were the ones who cried police brutality and thought prisons should reform criminals rather than keep them off the streets.

But most of all, it worked because many Democratic officials — including Dukakis—opposed the death penalty, a punishment favored by four out of five voters in certain cases.

Liberals worried that the jury might make an irreversible mistake, agreeing with the Founding Fathers that better a thousand murderers go free than an innocent man be punished. But Main Street America in the 1990s thought otherwise. Not that most Americans wanted to punish the innocent. It was, rather, that they believed the criminal justice system had become slanted in favor of defendants.

"A claim that was based on thin air would not have been persuasive," sighed Virginia's Senator Robb. "You can't convince the American people that the Democratic party or a Democratic candidate is soft on any of those issues without some tangible evidence to support your accusation. But if you have a party and a candidate who has clearly taken some visible stands, then you can ridicule the party and the candidate . . . then it's very easy to create doubt, and that's what the Republican campaign did very effectively."

At first Dukakis ignored the Horton issue, accurately claiming that a president has little to do with state furlough programs. But soon even his own people saw the political weakness of their case.

Two weeks after the 1988 Democratic convention most of the party's top political minds were summoned to the Lafayette Hotel on the edge of Boston's Chinatown to allow the Dukakis high command to pick their brains concerning the fall campaign. It was early August, and although Bush had been using the Horton case on the campaign trail, the TV commercials had not yet begun to inundate the air. During the give-and-take, someone asked campaign manager Estrich how Dukakis planned to defend a program that gave a weekend pass to a cold-blooded killer who had no incentive to return to prison.

"Estrich admitted they had no real answer," recalled pollster Stan Greenberg, a participant. "What they looked for was a political answer. But what they didn't understand was how serious the charge was and their need to calm people's anxieties."

With no substantive answer to an issue that was increasingly damaging the campaign, Dukakis' Harvard Law School graduates followed the legal profession's time-honored adage: "When the law is on your side, argue the law. When the facts are on your side, argue the facts. When neither is on your side, argue emotional issues that change the subject."

And so the Dukakis brain trust unleashed their secret weapon. They brought Jesse Jackson before television cameras to denounce the Horton issue as "clearly a racist ploy." Vice presidential candidate Sen. Lloyd Bentsen and Dukakis pushed the same line—that the Horton issue was racist since it played on white Americans' stereotype of black crime.

Their rationale, as articulated by Geraldine Ferraro after the election, was: "I think most people seeing that ad would feel that they were in more danger because Willie Horton was black. I don't think people will articulate that or admit it. I don't think there would have been the same reaction if Willie Horton were white. And the reason is Willie Horton stared down at you and Willie Horton became the guy at the corner you are afraid of. Willie Horton became every single black anybody was afraid of when you walk down a street at night."

Because, to Democrats, leaders being called a racist was the moral equivalent of being charged with child abuse, they figured it would shame average voters into feeling Bush had played dirty. For a brief period the Republicans held their breath while in millions of living rooms across the country the white middle class considered the Democratic charge of racism.

It didn't take. The average voters just didn't go for the Democratic, liberal-guilt mindset. They just plain didn't feel guilty for being scared of black criminals and of perceiving them as a serious problem.

"Most white Americans did not think they were racist," said former New Jersey Governor Kean. But voters saw the Democratic charge of racism "as a product of liberal guilt and the average guy in the suburbs looked at the Willie Horton ad and said, 'It's true. There isn't anything here that's not true. And if it's true, what's wrong with it? I don't react that way to it.' I think the Democratic criticism of the ads did as much to publicize the ads and get people thinking about them as the ads themselves.

"I think the natural reaction [of] the liberal leadership of the Democratic party . . . was very different from the reaction of the American people," Kean felt. "They said the problem with the ad was the picture of Willie Horton. Why was it wrong? 'Well [they said], he was black and therefore that made the ad racist.' I don't think the average American reacted that way."

The Democratic counterattack failed. In fact, it just reinforced the white middle-class perception that Dukakis wasn't their type of guy, because they didn't understand why it was racist to talk about reality, and they saw black crime as a chilling reality.

"It's not that Democratic liberals dismiss it [the black crime rate] but they feel they are able to justify it as an outgrowth of conditions, poverty, and deprivation," explained Mike Espy, the black Mississippi congressman. "They see that as a valid excuse," but most "white Americans don't . . . ."

During the 1988 campaign, it was almost impossible to find prominent Democrats who would buck the party line that called the ad racist. But as the story faded, some of the more courageous Democrats began to air their opinions.

Invariably, they were moderates like Sen. Joe Lieberman of Connecticut, Gov. Jim Blanchard of Michigan, or former San Antonio Mayor Henry Cisneros. Quietly, some of these Democrats disagreed with the party line calling it racist for voters to act on stereotypes if those stereotypes, such as black criminals or welfare recipients, were validated by statistics.

Back in 1986 Blanchard, aware of the Democrats' ongoing problem with the crime issue, had wanted to distance himself from them. During his first term, he ended an early release program for prisoners, and in his reelection campaign he used a TV commercial that showed him slamming the prison door shut.

"To this day I think [Bush pollster Bob] Teeter [who lives in Michigan] saw it and borrowed it," says Blanchard.

When Blanchard first saw the Bush campaign's use of Horton he knew Dukakis was in deep trouble; the key issue was not race, but softness on crime.

"Being tough on crime is not a racist message," Blanchard stated in an interview months before he was defeated for reelection. Was the Horton ad racist? "I don't think the viewers looked at it that way. I don't think the people in Macomb County viewed it that way. People saw it, saw Dukakis let this guy out. They said, 'I don't like this kind of a guy. He's soft on crime. He's a soft-headed liberal. He doesn't think like me. It's the same soft-headed Democratic baloney.' I don't think anyone came up to me and said it was a racist commercial."

Cisneros was even blunter. "What they were saying was that Dukakis was not sufficiently strong on crime. It would have worked almost as well, and maybe better, if Horton had been white, and therefore it had nothing to do with race. I think the ad was fair politics at the margins. It was a legitimate public policy question. It basically described a true situation."

Lieberman, whose suburban-dominated state is much more moderate than the liberal bastions of neighboring New York and Massachusetts, feels that middle-class voters "resent the charge" that they are racist. "They have a right to resent it," Lieberman claims. "Most of these people consider themselves decent law-abiding people who are not racist. They don't like to be demeaned by a bunch of fancy-pants, self-righteous politicians who think they understand what motivates people.

"I don't think it is racist" for voters to respond to images that conform to their experiences and reality as they understand it, Lieberman continues. Liberals argue that "more people on welfare are white, but there are more white people. The same is true when it comes to crime. All you have to do is go to a jail. Clearly something has happened. You can give reasons—poverty and all— but the average man and woman . . . don't want those excuses. They just see the facts. They don't want a social sciences dissertation. I don't think there is racism in that sense."

But party leaders clung to their belief like members of the Flat Earth Society. Even after the election, most Democrats continued the argument. It spurred Republicans like South Carolina Gov. Carroll Campbell to mutter about "the new McCarthyism. What was so bad about McCarthy? He said that 'anyone who disagrees with me is a communist.' Now what happens? If anyone takes on anything the Democrats disagree with, they are a racist. Now who wants to be called a racist? It is the new defense. It is the same way McCarthy went up the ladder."

At a seminar held at Harvard's John F. Kennedy School of Government a few weeks after the 1988 election, the Bush and Dukakis brain trusts literally got into a shouting match over Horton. In the modern conference room Atwater and Roger Ailes, Bush's ad man, kept asking the Democrats: Would the Horton ads have been acceptable if Horton had been white? Were they unacceptable because he was black?

Estrich, fittingly seated almost directly across from Atwater, ducked that question, claiming the entire issue had not been fair play, as if a referee in a striped shirt should have thrown a penalty flag against the GOP.

But that really *was* the question. And there really *was* a referee. The voters. And they didn't see a violation. If they had, Bush wouldn't have won.

"Most white voters said, 'This is true, this is fact. It's not a matter of race,' " agrees a much calmer John Lewis, the black Georgia congressman. "None of us, no Democrat, no decent human being, would support what Willie Horton did. But to defend him, or identify with Horton by arguing that it was racist, was a loser politically."

When it comes to political losers, liberal guilt on the Willie Horton issue pales in comparison to liberal guilt on another matter. That is, do past wrongs against blacks and other minorities still demand remedial action? Should minorities receive preferences in jobs and education?

The idea grew out of LBJ's Civil Rights Act, which was passed with the understanding that the equal opportunity it guaranteed would not mean racial preferences. But, in fact, the act set up a federal Equal Employment Opportunity Commission (EEOC) to investigate complaints of discrimination in the workplace. Federal courts were authorized to order employers to take steps to overcome the effects of past discrimination, and told businesses and schools to take affirmative steps to seek out qualified minority applicants. It became known by its proponents, mostly Democrats, as affirmative action. Thus, despite the guarantees given by the authors of the civil rights laws, the EEOC broadened its mission. From enforcing antidiscrimination laws, it began to promote social engineering.

There were many statistical successes.

"The great equalizer in America is entrepreneurship," Peter Kelly, the former DNC treasurer, opined. "In the construction field, which is my special area, it's been very difficult to get minorities involved because it requires capital, bonding, technical know-how. If we didn't have an affirmative action program in the cities, there would be no black subcontractors. We have been working hard at it for twenty years. When we first started, we could find no subcontractors qualified to do the jobs, zero. Now, twenty years later, in Hartford, Conn. [Kelly's hometown], we've got about fifty that do quite a good job. That would never have happened were it not for affirmative action. That's largely because minorities entered late into the economic scene and that's the only way we can get them in. Now, does that disadvantage majority [white] contractors? To some degree it does. But they have more than their share of opportunities."

Until the economy began to sour in the mid-1970s, polling showed public support for the programs. But, inevitably, the time came when there weren't enough good jobs or places in prestigious colleges to go around and the resentment that had been bubbling below the surface broke through into the open.

The issue of minority preference soon came to the fore and white cries of "reverse discrimination" changed the political landscape. Those who opposed the programs called them "quotas." They especially seethed at systems that created different standards—one for blacks and other minorities, the other for whites—in order to guarantee jobs and college admission for minorities. Most whites, rightly or wrongly, believed times had changed and blacks could compete equally. Racial preferences were now unfair. After all, they argued, they hadn't personally discriminated against blacks nor profited from past discrimination. Why should they be made to suffer?

The final straw, as far as the white middle class was concerned, came during the Carter years when the Democrats controlled the government. A Democratic administration, with the approval of the courts, created guidelines that effectively changed the rules: Employers and educators no longer had to provide equal opportunity as originally intended by the social planners of the Great Society, but equal results. In practical terms, if blacks constituted 20 percent of the employees in an organization, and if they did not get 20 percent of the promotions, the courts would start looking for discrimination.

Fittingly, the resentment in white America was highlighted in a situation at the University of California at Berkeley, the crown jewel of America's public education system. Located on Telegraph Hill across the bay from San Francisco, Berkeley led the student uprisings against American society during the 1960s and symbolized, in the eyes of middle-class America, student excesses of that time. A quarter-century later, burnt-out hippies still hung out on the periphery of the campus, and more natural food stores dotted the landscape than anywhere else in America.

While the current crop of students was more conservative than the sixties generation and business courses were the rage, the university faculty and administrators still lived in the past. Their mindset illustrated what twenty years of Democratic programs had wrought and why white America was seething.

In June 1989, although 61 percent of the state's high school graduates was white, only 33 percent of the entering freshmen at Berkeley was white. The reason: in an effort to give minorities a fair shake, the school had undertaken a two-tiered admissions system. All blacks and Hispanics in the top eighth of the state's public high school graduates were admitted, while much tougher standards were applied to whites and Asian-Americans.

The result? In 1989, more than 2,500 white and Asian-American applicants who were straight-A students in high school—records far superior to the minority requirement—were denied admission. In 1991, Berkeley officials began to change the admissions process, but by then serious alienation had already taken place among California students and parents. And the federal government was investigating whether the university was discriminating against whites and Asian-Americans.

Other colleges mirrored the Berkeley situation.

At the University of Virginia's stately Charlottesville campus that same fall of 1989, more than one out of two blacks with an average SAT score of 1023 was admitted, while only one in three whites with an average SAT of 1253 got in.

Admissions wasn't the only area with two sets of standards.

Many whites were especially enraged by the well-intentioned efforts of administrators to improve black graduation rates. At Penn State, a black student—regardless of need—who maintained a grade average in the C to C plus range received $550 in financial aid. If he or she did better the prize was $1,100. White kids might have better grades and greater financial need, but their race automatically disqualified them for these awards. Poor white students with good grades could often find financial aid elsewhere, but that didn't erase the anger. At Florida Atlantic University, which is state-funded, black students who qualified for admission were given free tuition, regardless of their economic situation. Whites, Hispanics, or Asian-Americans from poorer families weren't so lucky. When, despite preferential admissions, black graduation rates nationally remained far below whites, white resentment deepened.

An internal report that Berkeley won't release to the public showed that roughly only one in five admitted in 1982 under that program—those who would not otherwise have qualified for admission—had graduated five years later. And the Berkeley figures were no aberration. U.S. Department of Education figures showed that blacks and Hispanics were twice as likely as whites and Asian-Americans to drop out of college for academic reasons.[1]

And it wasn't just in education that a system of different standards for different races flourished. Perhaps the most glaring example of racial preferences was a program run by the federal government. Since the early 1970s the U.S. Department of Labor's Public Employment Service had used the General Aptitude Test Battery to rate candidates for jobs in private industry and in some state governments. The test is multiple choice and measures reading, math, vocabulary, spatial, perceptual, and dexterity skills.

But the social engineers in the Carter administration were dissatisfied with the results, because blacks did not score well. They decided the way to overcome the reluctance of employers to hire blacks was, in effect, to lie to them about how blacks did on the exam. And so, under the bureaucratic rubric of "within group score conversation," they changed the way scores were reported. Each test-taker was graded on how many questions he or she answered correctly, and then the score was compared to the nationwide pool of applicants—*of his or her race.*

In short, if a black person, an Hispanic, and a white person took the same test and got the same number of correct answers, they got widely different scores. For instance, if they were applying for what the government called "family four" jobs—those for auto mechanics or bookkeepers—and scored 300 points on the exam, black candidates would be listed as in the 83rd percentile, Hispanics, the 67th, and whites, the 44th. When the applicants' scores were sent to a potential employer, there was no indication of the person's race, only the percentile rank.

Because of bureaucratic sluggishness, this process, called "race-norming," didn't actually take effect until 1981, when the Reagan administration was in power. In 1986, the Justice Department threatened to bring suit against the program on the grounds that it discriminated against whites.

Roughly 16 million people had their GATB scores "race-normed" during the 1980s. In addition, an even larger number met a similar fate in private industry which "race-normed" the results of tests that companies designed themselves to evaluate job-seekers. If Democrats thought no one knew what was going on, they were right in part. It was so complicated that few understood its intricacies, but the public down deep knew that something was askew. And it brought out a sentiment Democrats should have been familiar with—aversion to special privileges.

Larry Holman, forty-seven, typified that resentment. In the fall of 1989, the lanky, gray-haired six-footer was in his fifth year as a shipping supervisor at Preis Enterprises in Waterloo, Iowa. He could see the state's economy was deteriorating and figured his job was likely to be the next casualty. So he moved in with his sister in Richmond, Virginia, and began looking for work. He soon found an opening at the James River Co., where he was told they could use his years of experience. But, they said, there was this technicality. He had to take an exam (the GATB) required of all applicants.

Holman, a high school graduate with some college credits, wasn't worried. In short order he received his score and a letter from the company saying they were putting his letter in the "inactive file" because of his low score. He threw it in the trash, so it's not known exactly how he did since those scores are confidential. But his sister, Maxine Ford, was there when he opened the letter.

"I'm nothing but a dummy," she remembers him saying when he opened the letter. "It was one of the hardest things I can ever remember in my life," is all Holman, a Vietnam veteran, will say of the experience. It never occurred to him that the score was anything but an accurate rate of how he did versus all test-takers.

Of course, since the results were "race-normed," that isn't what the score represented. Whether he would have gotten the job or not without the racial curve will never be known, nor is it known who got the job and whether that person was black, white, or Hispanic. What is clear, however, is that Holman—who subsequently found out about the scoring system—is bitter: "It's as if I only get two points for every touchdown I score and someone else gets twenty-four."

The political effect on Holman, a self-described independent, is predictable. "I blame the Democrats for these kinds of programs," he says.

This sort of resentment should not have surprised the Democrats. After all, Democrats have championed the fight against special privilege for decades. Historically, they have fought against special treatment for the rich, such as tax breaks for capital gains income, which they perceived as disproportionately helping the wealthy. But now, in the eyes of white, middle-class America, these same Democrats have become the advocates of special rules, first for blacks, later for women, or Hispanics, or whatever group might claim it needed help to compete equally in the marketplace.

White middle-class voters insisted they weren't being racist in opposing preferential treatment and, in fact, the majority weren't. The best evidence was the overwhelming opposition among them to Reagan's ill-conceived effort to give tax-exempt status to private segregated schools. White Americans did not want to go back to government-sanctioned discrimination against blacks; they just didn't like government-sanctioned policies they perceived as discriminatory against them. They felt that although those policies might once have been justified, times had changed.

Nita Lowry, a rare Democrat elected to represent the middle-class suburbs of New York's Westchester County, explained that people simply wanted to take care of themselves and their families first: "In middle-class America, where people feel they are struggling to make it on $30,000 a year, $40,000 a year, you don't want to be generous with the next job up the ladder and say, 'Give it to a black, I can wait.'"

Perhaps nowhere in the United States were the tensions created by such policies felt more strongly than in a two-story, Spanish-style building on the south side of Birmingham, Alabama. The changes in Fire Station #10 illustrate the split that decades of affirmative action/quotas have created in America.

The once prosperous all-white Avondale section of town has been declining for some time. Like Birmingham itself, the area has become increasingly black. And its fire station is not aging gracefully. The sleeping quarters are upstairs, as is the living area, where cactus plants grow in the large window planter in the fire-fighters' day room. On cold nights a fire blazes in the brick fire-place, and on rainy nights, the roof in the sixty-five-year-old building leaks.

The fire captain is Jackie E. Barton, the son of a railroad worker and clerical worker who grew up in an all-black neighborhood in Birmingham and graduated in 1967 from a segregated high school. The civil rights confrontations in Birmingham—some of the most tense of that decade—left an indelible mark on Barton, whose memories of childhood are filled with physical and economic injustices heaped on blacks, himself included. In 1969 he moved to Los Angeles because "I wanted to get away from Birmingham. There wasn't any opportunity here."

Soon afterwards, Barton, tall and solidly built with salt-and-pepper hair, a mustache, and silver wire-rim glasses, joined the air force. He spent six years as a military firefighter in Vietnam, Thailand, Korea, and the Philippines, and returned to Birmingham as a civilian in 1975. He began working as a firefighter for a military contractor and pursued that career in the Air National Guard.

He never thought much about working for the city when he got out of high school—blacks just didn't get those jobs then. The first black fireman was hired in 1968, the next in 1974. There were no black supervisors until 1982.

But by the early eighties things had begun to change. A consent decree was signed in 1981 settling a discrimination suit brought by blacks, and a system of racial hiring and promotion preferences was set up aimed at giving the fire department a work force and leadership that mirrored the local population—in other words, 28 percent black.

Barton, of course, took and passed the Birmingham Fire Department exam in 1976 well before the consent decree and was hired as a fireman in August of 1977. In 1985, when the directives of the consent decree were in effect, he was promoted to lieutenant, and in 1988 he made captain.

Assigned to the same firehouse are Robert Wilks, eleven other whites, and three other blacks. A year older than Barton, Wilks—who is white—has been a Birmingham fireman since 1967. With a decade more experience and much higher test scores than Barton, Wilks was passed over several times for lieutenant. One year he ranked third in the department on the exam while Barton ranked eighty-sixth. Wilks finally made lieutenant and worked under Barton, but he also scored higher than Barton in the captain's exam. (Charles Brush, also white, is the other lieutenant at Station #10 and has held that rank since 1977. Brush is president of the local firefighters union which has challenged the preferential hiring system.)

Wilks would like to be a captain and earn the $4,000 or so increase in salary, but he knows the city's policy obstructs his promotion. For a while city officials were promoting two blacks for every white, regularly passing over many top-scoring white candidates in favor of blacks with lower scores.

Barton and Wilks don't talk much. They work different shifts and often replace each other as the officer in charge, but Barton is the boss. There is no overt hostility. But there is lots of tension.

"If they want to be equal that's fine," Wilks states. "But the one who takes the test and comes out on top should win. I don't have any problems having a black lieutenant or captain providing he does as well as I did. Then he deserves it. We just carry on our regular business. I don't mention it to him and he doesn't either. There's always some tension," Wilks admits. "I am being penalized for what happened in the past. If you are going to be compensated, be compensated one time. He got the job because of affirmative action, then he got promoted because of it twice. That's three times he's been compensated. I didn't have anything to do with it. The middle-class white male is taking the brunt of affirmative action. It doesn't affect the lower class and the rich. It's the middle-class working man who has carried the brunt and that's not right. When they passed those civil rights laws, it's like saying everyone else has civil rights but the white male."

Barton, who was one of ten blacks in the six-hundred-member Fire Department in the predominantly black city when he was hired, figures it's only fair: "When I was growing up in Birmingham, I was discriminated against because I was black.

"It's hard for me to put myself in their shoes," Barton says of people like Wilks. "I'm trying to advance and never had a fair shake. It's hard to put yourself in their case. If it's not his fault, it was the fault of other whites who put the system in like that." Barton thinks there "was more resentment in 1985 [when he became a lieutenant] than when I made captain in 1988 or now. They have had time to see my performance. I'm sure there is still some resentment, but I can't let that stop me."

Besides, Barton believes that if the city hadn't formerly discriminated against blacks, he would have joined right out of high school like Wilks did. He has been a firefighter for just as long as Wilks, but the city's previous hiring policies prevented him from working there. As for the exam score, Barton doesn't say much. Some argue the exam is racially discriminatory, which brings howls from Wilks and white firefighters.

Bill Gray, a white who looks like the stereotype of the "good ol' boy" and is the size of an NFL linebacker, was once head of the local firefighters union. Gray is now a Republican state lawmaker representing an aging, heavily white section of Birmingham. He left the department—and, not coincidentally, the Democratic party also—because he felt he was "beating my head against the wall" looking for a promotion. He was fifteen years older than Wilks and he knew the dual system meant he'd probably never make captain.

"I know my daddy didn't, and I don't think my granddaddy owned any slaves [and] I don't think I [have] discriminated against blacks in my life," said Gray. "And if my granddaddy did, I'll tell 'em where he's buried and they can go out and stomp on his grave all they want. But don't take it out on my son. The black may be a superior athlete, not always, but he may be, and that's good. And my son may beat him on the fire department exam. But whatever exam, if he beats him on ability, my son ought to have it."

Most white Americans agreed with Gray.

"It's almost a nonissue in that it comes out regularly in focus groups we do with middle-class voters" throughout the country, Democratic pollster Greenberg stated. "There is no debate on affirmative action. Everybody's against it. There is a very small share of the [white] electorate—zero—that believes they have personal responsibility for this. That they ought to be paying for the injustice. They will acknowledge there was injustice. But people do not feel they are personally responsible and that they ought to be paying for it. They can't even begin to understand the logic on it. It does not even reach the level of common sense for the majority of Americans. They think they are being asked to pay a bill that is not theirs. There is no convincing them, particularly if they have not lived through the civil rights movement, why they should have to pay this bill. There are not two sides" to white public opinion. "It's odd that the Democratic party takes it as an accepted principle, whereas the base which we need to reach in order to win elections takes it as a conventional wisdom that it's an injustice to the middle class. It's a political problem of historic proportions."

The middle class went so far as to adopt the Republican description of the Democratic programs—"racial quotas." By the early 1990s, the huge majority of white voters agreed with Republicans like former New Jersey Governor Kean, who argued: "The Democratic party often starts with results and thinks they can guarantee them by changes in the law. You cannot do that; you cannot guarantee success. You cannot guarantee results, nor should you. Everyone ought to be brought up to the starting level, and then after that it's a race. Some people are going to fall behind, some move ahead. That's what capitalism is all about. I think Democrats reject that. If people are losing they try to find ways that fix the race. They want to take the guy who is winning and bring him back."

Seemingly aware of this, the centrist Democratic Leadership Council (DLC), headed by Senators Nunn and Robb and Governors Clinton and Blanchard, sought to give the party a facelift on the issue. It took on squarely the question of equal opportunity versus equal results and came out for the former. Yet at the very 1990 meeting in New Orleans where the position was announced, the DLC invited Jesse Jackson to speak, and he had a different message.

"Lyndon Johnson said we must fight for equal results. To me there must be a commitment not just to try, but to make it happen," Jackson told reporters. "If there is not a commitment to equal results, you will have the opportunity to enter school, but no real commitment to graduate children. It's not enough to demand equal opportunity for those who have been disadvantaged at the point the game is restarted. For those who have been the victims of negative action, there must be affirmative action. For those who are deprived at birth, there must be a head start to bring some equality to the situation. I tend to subscribe to Lyndon Johnson's position of a commitment to equal results, not just equal opportunities. To say you stand for equal opportunity, but not for equal results, is either a non sequitur, or a statement based on racist or sexist assumptions."

Any attempt to change the party's image on the issue became hopelessly muddled—a casualty of Jackson's ability to dominate the media.

In city after city, state after state, the Birmingham pattern existed—blacks were getting jobs over whites who scored better on the qualifying exam. Those who backed such programs felt that the instances in which better qualified whites were passed over were limited, but as time passed, it became a more pervasive practice. Blacks felt that they needed such programs because they didn't trust whites who made most of the hiring and promotion decisions to be fair unless forced to meet numerical targets.

As a party, Democrats were slow to understand. They believed they held the moral high ground, and thought that continued racism explained black misfortune and justified special treatment. They just saw a different 1990s America, one whose continued racism explained black misfortune and justified special treatment. "I think that if people conclude that they don't want to pay any longer for the misdeeds of their parents and grandparents, and therefore affirmative action and set-asides and those programs aren't appropriate, I can understand their thinking," DNC Chairman Brown remarked. "But I think their thinking is wrong. But I argue you still need those programs because there is at present racism and sexism that is not related to their parents and grandparents, but is related to an existing, recurring problem."

But Democrats like Brown focused too heavily on the big picture and not enough on the individual voter. New Jersey Gov. Jim Florio, when asked about Birmingham's Fire Station #10, refused even to discuss the issue from the perspective of those like Wilks. "I'm inclined to not want to deal with it on a micro-level because it's a trap," he said.

Actually, Jesse Jackson, when asked about Barton, Brush, and Wilks, said what white Democrats who supported such preferential programs believed, but were afraid to vocalize: "Those two white guys inherited the prerogative of a racial default."

Simply put, the Democrats viewed the Wilkses and the Brushes, who had benefited from being white most of their lives, as casualties of war, an unfortunate but necessary sacrifice to the altar of black progress.

It might be good philosophy, but it's lousy politics.

And that's why Florio was correct in saying the issue was a trap, and Democrats were the ones being caught. Because they blindly stuck to their position that the almost lock-step white opposition resulted from a misperception: "If affirmative action was interpreted properly," Brown explained, "there would be much greater support from people. The assumption now is that affirmative action means that unqualified people are now getting jobs or admitted to colleges."

In many ways it was like busing. Democrats believed the overall goal of having all children grow up in an integrated society justified forcing kids to pay the price—in terms of busing—for wrongs done by previous generations.

Supporters of the concept clung to Jackson's explanation that "affirmative action doesn't negate whites. It is designed to expand and make room for those who have been locked out historically."

But he was wrong, at least in the eyes of white America. Whites didn't necessarily think that unqualified blacks were getting jobs ahead of qualified whites. White America thought *less* qualified blacks were being preferred over *more* qualified whites as, for example, those who sought jobs through the Labor Department's Public Employment Service. Brown, Jackson, and the Democratic establishment never recognized that distinction, though it was critical.

The problem was that in an economy that wasn't growing dramatically, such as in the late 1980s, there just weren't enough good jobs to go around. The early battles had been over entry-level positions. But as the baby-boom hit middle age, the competition was for promotions, and it boiled down to blacks like Barton and whites like Wilks.

Yet even those like Peter Kelly, as politically in tune with Middle America as any recent Democratic national official, felt that the issue, whether called affirmative action or quotas, was worth the price the party was paying politically: "It may or may not be death for the party, but it's got to be done. In some regards it's being abused to death, in some it's working well. It's just one of those things you are going to have your fingers broken on."

What it boiled down to was the almost unanimous sense in the upper echelons of the Democratic party that government could dictate what initiative, hard work, and talent could produce. In their view, it was perfectly just for whites to suffer to help blacks because blacks at one time had been victims of legal discrimination. It truly was liberal guilt.

Nowhere was this double standard more apparent than on the 1988 campaign trail in which Jesse Jackson was the symbol for the aspirations of 30 million black Americans. Jackson's politics were well to the left of the political mainstream—his willingness to cut defense and embrace some of America's most contentious foes, as well as his wish to raise taxes and spend for social programs as if the Great Society were still in bloom.

Yet virtually none of the other six Democratic candidates for the presidential nomination dared criticize him, although they regularly chopped up one another.

"The handling of Jesse Jackson during the campaign debates was the most striking example. Liberal guilt played a big role," Bruce Babbitt, one of the six white candidates, recalled. "If you go back and look at those debates, Jackson was never challenged by any of us. It was a microcosm of the whole problem. I was really struck by the reality of being in a presidential debate in which a black American was a major candidate.

"It seemed nearly impossible that it could occur in my lifetime and that I could be on stage where there was such an extraordinary symbol of the progress that we had made. I was with him in the streets of Selma [Alabama] as a young man [marching for civil rights], and it never crossed my mind that the day would come in my lifetime, twenty-five years later, in which he would be a candidate for president of the United States with a large amount of white support.

"He's entitled to the benefit of a double standard. Although [at the time] my thought wasn't that explicit. There has been so much racism in this society and so much willingness to belittle blacks, that I am saying I am not willing to take that risk . . .

"All of the other candidates shared my sense of pride that this was a piece of history and he was entitled to have the fullness of the moment without being subjected to the sort of nit-picking standard we were all applying to each other."

7

Guilt Is a Political Loser

No one in America has more liberal guilt than Ted Kennedy. It oozes out of him. In word, deed, and lifestyle, the Massachusetts Democrat symbolizes the worst aspects of limousine liberalism, liberal guilt and all.

The senator was born into a family that, by the 1960s, was being mistaken for the American monarchy—one brother became president and a second might have been but for an assassin's bullet. As for the third, well, much was expected of Teddy.

But he was different from his brothers. He was neither so smart, so driven, nor nearly so responsible. Unlike brothers John or Robert, moreover, Teddy Kennedy had no feel for the middle-class man or women. Robert Strauss, former Democratic National chairman and party elder statesman, is reputed to have said: "Rose [Kennedy] didn't have no triplets."

In 1961, at the young age of thirty, Teddy was tapped to take over his brother's Senate seat. But once on Capitol Hill, the first clue appeared that he was politically different from his brothers, who enjoyed making fun of mushy-headed liberal Democrats. Whereas his brothers had always considered the Senate just a handy steppingstone to the White House, Teddy actually liked the clubby atmosphere and became an insider. And once his much-ballyhooed 1980 run for president failed, Teddy settled comfortably back into the Senate to make his mark.

He soon became one of—if not *the* most—polarizing figure in American politics. Detractors had a field day with his personal life. But for liberals Kennedy has become a hero who for three decades has carried their water on every imaginable cause.

So it was fitting that he would become the point man for the congressional effort to legitimize racial preference policies even further at the very time white America was beginning to express its distaste for those already on the books. But then no one ever accused Kennedy, or the Democrats of that era, of having the political instincts of his brothers.

By 1989, the Supreme Court was speaking with a more conservative voice because of Ronald Reagan's appointments. The nation's highest bench reshaped its decisions in ways that infuriated liberals, especially on civil rights matters. Liberals had assumed that the courts would continue to approve hiring programs like that of the Birmingham, Alabama, fire department, which promoted black firefighters over whites who had more experience and higher test scores. But instead, the Reagan-influenced court allowed Birmingham's white firefighters to challenge the consent decree that had originally set up the program.

Thus, in 1990, Democratic leaders decided to speed up their death wish by rubbing some more salt into the middle-class wound.

With Kennedy in the lead, they put together the Civil Rights Bill of 1990 aimed at overturning a number of Supreme Court rulings which had made it more difficult for minorities to win discrimination suits. Once again, the Democrats were perceived as pushing the needs of minorities at the expense of the middle class.

For their part, Democratic leaders figured no politician could oppose a civil rights bill in an election year and get away with it. But they were wrong.

This legislation was vastly different from the landmark 1964 and 1965 Civil Rights Bills which provided equal rights to all people— basic human rights like voting, access to public accommodations, and housing. The 1990 bill, on the other hand, was aimed at providing economic equity to specific groups at the expense of the middle class—the *white* middle class. Any way you looked at it, the white middle class would pay the price.

Intentional discrimination was already illegal under the law. At issue in the 1990 legislation was the much more complex matter of how an employee could prove discrimination with no evidence of employer intent. Also crucial was how an employer could justify having a work force with a racial composition that did not mesh with that of the labor pool.

The basic thrust of the bill was to instill in law the guiding principle that the goal was the proportionality of results, not the equality of opportunity. It would create a presumption in the law that racial, sexual, or ethnic imbalance in a work force or school population was the result of illegal discrimination. In practical effect, the bill would treat bottom-line statistical imbalances as proof of illegal conduct. If a business was operating in an area where the labor pool was 20 percent black, the presumption under the law was that 20 percent of the employees at all levels should be black, regardless of differences in skills, quality of education, or training.

The legislation would allow as an employer's defense only the argument that the challenged business practice bore "a significant relationship to successful performance on the job." In other words, a university might have difficulty in defending its decision to hire a white professor with a PhD over a black without one because the lack of a doctorate does not necessarily prevent teaching success in the classroom, although such a degree is considered a crucial mark of academic competence. Or a businesses might be held liable if it promoted a white with outstanding ratings over a black with good ratings since good ratings might be sufficient for the performance of that particular job. In other words, objectively measured standards would be less important than race.

President Bush desperately wanted to sign the bill as part of his effort to woo black voters. He therefore offered a compromise that would have allowed practices that produced a work force different from the labor pool if that force bore "a significant relationship to a significant business objective." Congressional Democrats said no.

The differences in wording were crucial. Employers said the legislation as it stood would force them to hire by the numbers—in other words, to institute racial quotas—if they wished to avoid being endlessly tied up in court any time a minority member did not get a job that he or she felt was deserved.

Kennedy denied that the 1990 bill would require quotas, charging that the quota argument was a smokescreen for racial bigotry. He claimed that "there is not one iota of credible evidence that the anti-job discrimination laws were forcing any employer in America to resort to quotas," and to fortify his assumption, he included language to that effect. But that language, the White House presumed, would have as much weight with the courts as had the guarantees of Hubert Humphrey a generation before—that is, no weight at all.

Humphrey was the floor manager of the 1964 Civil Rights Bill. During the Senate debate on that measure he pledged that "contrary to the allegations of some opponents of this title, there is nothing in it that will give any power to the commission or to any court to require hiring, firing or promotion of employees in order to meet racial quotas or to achieve a certain racial balance. That bugaboo has been brought up a dozen times; but it is nonexistent."[1]

Almost thirty years later, it was clear to the vast majority of white Americans that the government had twisted the 1964 bill at will to impose policies that not only allowed, but encouraged racial preferences. Although in 1964 no one argued with Humphrey because of the widespread belief that blacks had been badly treated, by the early 1990s it was a different story. From Boston to San Francisco whites were using civil rights laws on their own behalf—to right what they believed was reverse discrimination. And they had plenty of encouragement from the Reagan and Bush Justice Departments.

Public opinion notwithstanding, Democrats used their large majorities in the House and Senate to ram the new civil rights bill through Congress in the summer of 1990. Even moderate Democrats from the Democratic Leadership Council—like Sens. Sam Nunn, Chuck Robb, and John Breaux—got behind the bill, somewhat surprising given that the DLC only months before had tackled the affirmative action/quotas issue with a declaration that it stood for equal opportunity but against guaranteed results. Still, when it came to the crunch, the DLC members fell into line.

Privately, some DLC insiders said it had been a close call. But members didn't feel strongly enough about the issue to risk fracturing their party—and an opportunity to send a meaningful message to the white middle class was lost.

This lack of courage was not confined to Democrats. Some moderate Republicans in both the House and Senate used the bill to curry favor with minorities.

When Bush's compromise efforts with the Democrats failed, the president vetoed the "quota bill" because of the pressure it would put on employers. The Senate sustained his veto by one vote.

But what even Bush didn't realize at the time was the language hidden in the bill's legislative history that would do much more than pressure employers to hire by the numbers in order to avoid lawsuits. In the fine print—much like that which allowed the previous racial preferences despite Humphrey's guarantees—lurked the requirement that employers demand racial balance in job candidates' test results.[2] In other words, it required the similiar type of arbitrary raising of black and Hispanic candidates' test scores as had the "within group score conversion" policy that the Labor Department's Public Employment Service had employed. If the bill had passed, the practice of giving minority candidates jobs and promotions over whites with higher test scores would have been the law of the land.

That issue never came out during the debate.

And, privately, many Democratic leaders were happy with the veto. They figured Bush had given them a prime campaign issue for the 1990 elections, then only a month away.

The average white middle-class voter, of course, had neither the time nor the inclination to wade through the legal language in the proposed legislation. Since the debate was not about basic rights, it became a question of which side to believe. No contest. History was on the GOP's side. Bush and the Republicans won hands down over Kennedy and the Democrats.

"The issue was lost for the 1990 election cycle when George Bush proclaimed it a quota bill," said Michael Donilon, a Democratic pollster who in 1990 handled surveys for Harvey Gantt, a black former mayor of Charlotte, North Carolina, who lost a Senate run to arch conservative Republican Jesse Helms precisely on this issue.

Because, that is, it reinforced the middle-class belief that Democrats cared more about minorities than about themselves.

But it was more than that. It refocused the issue for a new generation of Americans and cemented their frustrations. Those of baby-boom age and younger had grown up thinking that a level playing field existed for everyone. They had gone to school and worked with blacks. They were much less likely to hold the ugly racial stereotypes about blacks that were held by their parents who had grown up in a segregated society.

Donilon believed that there was a clear perception among older voters that Democrats cared too much about minorities and not enough about whites: "With younger voters I do not believe that has been a disabling perception. But this issue [affirmative action/quotas] is moving" in that direction.

There were two major reasons why these younger, middle-class voters were the most annoyed at this latest ploy: (1) the younger middle class didn't feel guilty at having contributed to a society where blacks were overtly abused, as had their parents; and (2) more importantly, the entire middle class realized that if the law encouraged hiring and promotion by quota, it was they who would be shortchanged.

"Younger voters," Michael Donilon explained, "do not have a personal experience with many of the discriminatory practices which have led to the development of these [affirmative action/quota] policies . . . . why it may or may not be necessary. They, in fact, believe that nondiscrimination is the proper policy to pursue and they do not perceive affirmative action or racial quotas as a nondiscriminatory policy."

That the average white folks believed these affirmative action/quota programs were a new brand of racism seemed lost on the Democrats pushing the legislation. They preferred to blame the opposition on the GOP's alliance with business against the mass of Americans. Or that it stemmed from a right-wing conspiracy of a small number of people.

But the opposition to the concept embodied in the bill was real in mainstream America. In the spring of 1990, a *Times-Mirror* poll of more than three thousand people nationally showed that only 16 percent of whites agreed "we should make every possible effort to improve the position of blacks and minorities, even if it means giving them preferential treatment." And most middle-class whites also believed that blacks had been getting special treatment from federal laws.

After their 1990 defeat, in 1991 Democratic leaders tried to refocus the debate on another provision of the bill that was still in dispute between Bush and Congress: Whether the option of punitive monetary damages for racial harassment on the job should be extended to victims of sexual harassment.

"It was not something that just helped racial minorities, but helped a majority—women in particular," argued Louisiana's Senator Breaux. Breaux's statement was a good example of Democrats who, understanding the resentment in white America towards them, tried to find a more politically popular defense of the program. Their best shot, they decided, was to argue that the aggrieved parties who would benefit from the bill included persons other than blacks.

It was a good try, but it didn't work. For it to work politically, the mass of white middle-class women had to believe they would be better off with than without the bill. Their sense of being victims wasn't strong enough to make the political difference. When they thought of the idea of quotas they were just as angry as white men.

And that was because the programs didn't put white women in the same category with blacks, but with other whites. It was their daughters with strong credentials who were passed over for minorities at schools like the University of Virginia and Cal-Berkeley. And white women were classified as "white" on exams like the Public Employment Service's GATB, in which blacks with lower scores on objective tests were boosted above whites with higher scores.

The other alternative for Democrats was to argue that legislation giving special help to blacks was no different from other government programs that singled out special constituencies, such as subsidies for farmers or small businessmen. But that argument was even a tougher sell. Farmers and small businessmen of any color were eligible for special help, if they met the programs' criteria.

More importantly, there wasn't the mass of opposition to those programs from consumers or big companies who felt they were disadvantaged by government's intervention.

Once again Democratic leaders were wrong. Dead wrong. The issue blew up in their faces because they did not understand the middle class. When Sen. Brock Adams (D-Wash.) said Bush's 1990 veto was "a cold political decision," he meant it as a jibe. But in truth, the decision was a political masterstroke. Once it was an open campaign issue, it became clear just how big an edge the GOP had.

Democrats had hoped the civil rights bill would be an issue they could control. They planned to use Bush's 1990 veto as a vehicle to inspire a large turnout of black voters against GOP candidates that November. As Democratic pollster Stan Greenberg put it the day Bush vetoed the bill, "it only becomes an issue if Republicans are articulating the Democratic weakness on quotas."

Democratic leaders, who possessed large amounts of liberal guilt, truly believed that it was unfair for Republicans to use the civil rights bill as an electoral weapon. And they tried to kid themselves the public agreed with them. Republicans had no such qualms and were under no such illusions. By and large, Republicans understood the middle-class frustration. And they used the issue for all it was worth. And it was worth a lot.

In a close election for governor of California—the most important race of the 1990 political cycle—this issue may have made the difference. Sen. Pete Wilson, R-Calif., had been pressured by everyone from President Bush on down to return home and seek the governorship. If the Republicans didn't hold the governor's mansion, they would get rolled in the 1992 reapportionment in which California would pick up seven more congressional seats.

Once Wilson agreed to run, the GOP felt confident. They expected that California Attorney General John Van de Kamp would win the Democratic nomination. Van de Kamp was a standard liberal, and the Republicans figured he would be relatively easy pickings in November. But former San Francisco Mayor Dianne

Feinstein came out of nowhere in the primary. And she won as a moderate—tough on crime, for the death penalty, and promising to hold down spending. She had charisma and the national media were making her a star. The GOP strategists had a problem. They had to find a way to stamp her as just another Democrat. And, as she cruised through the last week before the primary, she gave Wilson the opening he needed.

"Fairness is part of the dream," she told a black audience in Los Angeles during the Memorial Day weekend. "That is one of the reasons we have pledged an open and accessible administration. That is one of the reasons we have pledged to appoint women in proportion to their parity of the population—50 percent. To appoint people of color in proportion to their parity of the population."

She had made the remarks during the primary to please liberals, who make up a disproportionate share of the primary electorate. Problem was, such a message was exactly the wrong signal to send out during the general election. She had, that is, initially attracted the swing voters because they thought she was a different kind of Democrat. But with her comments about appointments, she sounded just like all the rest.

The moment they caught those comments, the Wilson brain trust knew it had an issue. Wilson let the Feinstein boomlet run through June. The national publicity about California potentially electing its first women governor convinced the media that Wilson was the underdog—and in fact he was in the polls—which was helpful.

Then, in mid-July, Wilson began his campaign. In California, campaigning means TV ads. Wilson began airing a commercial that showed a *Los Angeles Times* headline on Feinstein's pledge: "Feinstein Vows Hiring Quotas by Race, Sex," while an announcer commented, "Dianne Feinstein has promised as governor to fill state jobs on the basis of strict numerical quotas. Not experience, not qualifications, not ability . . . but quotas."

Feinstein claimed Wilson was distorting her words, that she really was talking about goals, and she responded with her own ad that claimed Wilson, as mayor of San Diego, had himself ordered a quota plan. But Feinstein failed to make the case.

"That ad sent us into a tailspin," said Bill Carrick, Feinstein's campaign manager. "It not only blunted our momentum, but it put us in a hole. We were well into the fall digging out of that hole."

The Wilson ad ran heavily during the summer and he quickly closed the gap with Feinstein. By October, Wilson had begun to pull away—polls showed he held a small but discernible lead. It was also the time when Congress would vote on whether to override Bush's veto of the Civil Rights Bill. Wilson had voted against the bill originally. As for Feinstein, when the Senate sustained Bush's veto by one vote, she decided to try to use the issue to energize her constituency.

"We had a turnout problem," Carrick explained, because the party had poured all its resources into the battle of TV commercials. Feinstein knew the risks of raising the issue again, but she felt strongly about it. Besides, without a massive minority turnout, she figured she had no chance.

So, she brought in Kennedy to feed red meat to the Democratic faithful. "It was one vote. . . . Pete Wilson's vote . . . If he didn't even show up, under our rules of the United States Senate, we would have overridden the veto. But he made sure he was there to vote no," Kennedy proclaimed. "Quota–schmota. All we were doing was returning to what the law was for seventeen years. But Pete Wilson voted no . . . I say we ought to veto Pete Wilson."

Kennedy assuredly energized blacks and feminists for Feinstein, but many of them would have voted for her anyway. What he also did was to cement the impression of mainstream whites that she wasn't as moderate a Democrat as she claimed. Given the results, Wilson probably would have paid Kennedy to come to California. The TV news that night showed Feinstein with Kennedy talking about an issue that President Bush had just told the country boiled down to quotas. In fact, the president took the issue head on in California, telling a Los Angeles rally for Wilson in the final two weeks of the campaign that "we wanted to eliminate prejudice in the workplace, but we do not want quotas." Bush and Wilson were hammering it in, and the Democrats knew it.

In the final week, Feinstein picked up the message and focused on it: "Because of Pete Wilson's vote, the 1990 Civil Rights Act is dead and the same civil rights protections that applied today to people of color were not, by his vote, extended to women. I say a state that is 51 percent female can't afford Pete Wilson as governor. I also say that a state that's 42 percent people of color can't afford Pete Wilson as governor."

The Census Bureau may agree that California's population in 1990 was 42 percent nonwhite, but on election day exit polls showed the voters were 81 percent white. Wilson knew this, and in the final days of the campaign he used the issue to make himself out as a strong leader willing to stand up for principle.

"I despise discrimination," he told reporters who asked about Feinstein's charges. "It would have been easy and expedient" to have voted for the bill. "But I voted against this one, whatever it is called, because it was a quota bill."

Feinstein campaign manager Carrick believed, "In retrospect, it clearly did more good for Wilson than it did for us." The *Los Angeles Times* poll taken a week before the election proved the point. It found white voters disagreed by a 57-35 margin with the following statement: "California's governor ought to see to it that the number of women and minorities appointed to state government jobs is in proportion to their share of the population." Even white women disagreed by more than a 5-4 margin.

But the power of the affirmative action/quota question was even more clearly demonstrated half a country, and an entire culture, away from California.

If it is possible—although wrong—to look at the Feinstein-Wilson race and explain his victory as having little to do with the issue, David Duke's showing is quite another matter. It gives testimony to the power of his message, which focused upon black crime, welfare handouts, and job programs perceived as preferential to blacks.

"I spoke out loud what a lot of people say around the dinner table," Duke claimed. "People were so impressed by the ideas that they voted for me despite the controversy of my background." Even granted that the 1980s had witnessed almost a ten-year recession in Louisiana, producing the despair that gives rise to demagogues such as Huey Long, the inescapable conclusion is that Duke said the things average people believe. They accepted his message despite his background.

Duke is a former grand wizard of the Knights of the Ku Klux Klan. He flirted with neo-Nazi groups at one point, didn't file his tax returns for 1984-87, and authored a sex manual for women on how to please men in bed. But the six-foot, sandy-haired Duke is also quite good-looking, having undergone plastic surgery and chemical peels to improve his blow-dried TV image. And on television, he has few peers in the political world. He was elected to the Louisiana House of Representatives in 1989 as a Republican and immediately began his campaign for the 1990 U.S. Senate election. The Republican party did everything in its power to repudiate him nationally, but by then he had a head of steam.

The night before Louisiana's 1990 Senate primary in which he would get an astounding 60 percent of the white vote—44 percent overall—Duke wound up his campaign at the Lions Club hall in the New Orleans suburb of Harahan. The crowd was a mix of older folks, who typically attend political rallies, and a healthy number in their twenties and early thirties, who generally find better things to do on Friday nights. There were young families with small kids and singles. In one way it was homogeneous. It was all white.

Many that night were in jeans and Duke T-shirts. A few wore coats and ties or dresses. Conversations with a random handful found a laborer, a truck driver, a housewife, a real estate broker, and a public employee.

All said they agreed with his message, but several said they weren't completely keen on the messenger. One even said she had voted for Michael Dukakis for president in 1988. All were angry at the political establishment, especially the Democratic party. And when Duke began to talk they responded enthusiastically— interrupting him with chants of "Duke, Duke, Duke."

"We live in double-speak times," Duke stated. "To me those liberal welfare programs with their quotas and goals discriminate against whites. But it's not called discrimination as it was when they used to do it to blacks. It's called affirmative action. And when jobs are given out on the basis of race, it's called equal opportunity. There is a double standard, ladies and gentlemen. You know it, I know it, everybody knows it. Are we polarizing the races? Blacks have voted in a bloc since they could vote. But if whites do it, it's polarizing. When they gave preference to whites, it was bigotry and hatred. When it's blacks, it's love and brotherhood. I'm for equal rights for everyone, even white people."

Duke raised roughly $2 million, mostly through a sophisticated direct-mail operation, and used the money to blanket the Louisiana airwaves with *thirty minute* commercials aimed at convincing voters he didn't have horns.

Duke stressed four themes:

1. Require welfare beneficiaries and public-housing residents to pass drug tests
2. Require workfare in exchange for a welfare check
3. Do not increase benefits to a welfare mother who has additional illegitimate children
4. End racial preference programs, whether they are called affirmative action or quotas

Duke was subtle as a sledge-hammer when it came to the 1990 Civil Rights Bill.

Sen. J. Bennett Johnston, seeking his fourth term, at first considered Duke nothing more than a nuisance, but he quickly changed his mind. Johnston, who ironically had been something of a segregationist in the 1960s, voted for the 1990 Civil Rights Bill. And Duke made a big issue of it.

"Many of us are angry now," Duke said on his TV shows. "We feel betrayed by the civil rights movement. Its leaders said they were dedicated to the goal of equal opportunity for all. They said racial classifications should have no place in public policy. They said they dreamed of a color-blind society in which people would achieve according to their merits as individuals, and not because of their race. How can they reconcile what they said with what has happened? Equality of opportunity has been replaced by preferential treatment and racial quotas. Free association has been replaced by forced association. Racial classifications are now the very heart of public policy. The principles of the civil rights movement lie broken and battered, the victims of liberals who now profess with straight faces that the perfect remedy for past discrimination is more discrimination. They should be indicted for intellectual mal-practice."

Since there were no exit polls of Louisiana voters, it is impossible to determine precisely where Duke's support came from. But there are more than enough indications from analysis of the precinct-by-precinct returns to make solid generalizations. Doug Rose, a Tulane University professor, used a computer analysis to estimate that Duke got 66 percent of the white Democratic vote, but only 51 percent of the Republican vote, which is almost all white. Duke ran best in the rural areas, worst in the cities where blacks predominate.

Almost a month to the day after Duke's showing, North Carolina reelected Jesse Helms to a fourth Senate term. There too, race was a big issue. If possible, it was even less subtle than in Louisiana. That's because Harvey Gantt, a black, was the Democratic nomi-nee.

Gantt desegregated Clemson University, where he became an architect, more than a quarter century before. He won the nomina-tion against a pack of white candidates and was pretty much an unabashed liberal. Unlike Virginia's Doug Wilder, Gantt didn't waffle or try to move to the middle. Gantt was against the death penalty, believed government had a large role in fostering the pub-lic's well-being, and embraced the support of gay and lesbian groups. Gantt also, of course, strongly supported the 1990 Civil Rights Bill.

Helms went into the election as one of the most disliked politi-cians in America. Democrats especially hated him, but many Re-publicans also not-so-secretly wished he would just go away. Helms took pride in being known as "Senator No." He voted against anything he believed conflicted with his "North Carolina values," whether abortion, public funding of art he considered obscene, or the, to him, too liberal foreign policy of Presidents Reagan and Bush. And he, of course, firmly opposed the 1990 Civil Rights Bill.

Even Helms' strongest supporters believed 1990 might be his undoing—his negatives with the voting public were so high that 45 percent of the North Carolina electorate might easily have voted for anyone but Saddam Hussein against him. And they worried that Helms' right-wing antics might have turned off enough soft supporters to make the difference. Two weeks before the election the *Charlotte Observer*'s poll had him eight points down.

That was when Helms unveiled a TV ad that would saturate the state in the final days of the campaign. It was aimed directly at the affirmative action/quota issue.

The ad showed a white man's hands crumpling a job rejection letter. "You needed that job," the voice commented, "and you were the best qualified. But they had to give it to a minority because of a racial quota. Is that really fair? Harvey Gantt says it is. Gantt supports Ted Kennedy's racial quota law that makes the color of your skin more important than your qualifications." Gantt dropped five points in his own polls within the first twenty-four hours of the airing.

Helms also ran ads that highlighted Gantt's quick sale of a television station at a huge profit through alleged use of federal laws that gave preference to minority applicants. Helms charged it was an example of Gantt taking unfair advantage of a minority set-aside program.

But it was the quota ad that really struck home with white North Carolinians. Helms was easily reelected with 53 percent of the vote, roughly a thirteen-point swing in two weeks, if polls are to be believed. Exit polls found that 61 percent of those who decided late said they voted for Helms. That is highly unusual. The undecideds almost always break strongly against the incumbent because he is the known commodity and that type voter is presumably not keen on the current office-holder. Clearly, the quota ad made the difference.

"It swung the election," said Donilon, Gantt's pollster. "Before Helms raised the racial quota issue we had him beat. Once he raised it, the issue produced a dramatic change in the election."

The question for Democrats is how to fight this issue if, as it appears, they are unwilling to switch. Johnston ignored the issue in his race and was almost run over by it, despite Duke's glaring faults. In the final weeks of that campaign, while Duke ran his ads on quotas and welfare, Johnston spoke of the many public works projects he had brought home and ran a home video of Duke burning a cross. He never got into the merits of the issues that Duke had articulated because he understood that if he did, it would just worsen his situation.

That was because Johnston's pollster, Geoff Garin, had asked Louisiana voters the pertinent question about affirmative action. Did they think it hurt them? Whites answered with a resounding yes. Garin asked voters to choose between one of the two following statements:

1. Affirmative action programs are still needed to counteract discrimination against minorities who continue to have less income, less education, and fewer job opportunities
2. Affirmative action programs have gone too far in favoring minorities, have unfairly discriminated against whites, and should be phased out

By a 53-30 margin whites agreed with the second statement— echoing Michael Donilon's reading of sentiment in North Carolina. And, given the 60 percent showing Duke got among whites in the election, although polls showed him doing much less well, it's safe to assume the support for the statement was probably understated.

Gantt tried a slightly different tactic. He called the Helms attacks "divisive" and told crowds to keep from being "diverted to the extraneous side issues that, at the end of the day, don't make much difference in your pocketbook, the education of your child, the care of your environment." He accused Helms of trying to "divide people along the lines of race," as if the Republican's appeals were somehow less legitimate than Gantt's to black voters to vote because of racial pride. But he never debated over whether the programs he favored constituted quotas, or over the legitimacy of racial preference programs.

Democrats in North Carolina, Louisiana, and Washington, D.C., made much of the fact that Duke and Helms voters were disproportionately poorly educated. As if the votes of people with a high school education count less than those with a masters degree. In fact, despite the increase in the educational level in America, there remain an awful lot more high school graduates than those with postgraduate degrees. It was another sign of the "new class" mentality.

There were other troubling signs for Democrats about the returns: voter turnout in North Carolina and Louisiana was over 60 percent, near records for off-year elections, rivaling the turnout rates for presidential contests. The issue brought out both whites and blacks, but there were many more whites to begin with, and the evidence showed the issue spurred whites more than blacks. Outside those two states, moreover, Democratic attempts to make the 1990 Civil Rights Bill a rallying cry for black voters failed miserably. Exit polls done by the pool created by ABC, CBS, CNN, and NBC found that GOP candidates did better among black voters in 1990 than they had in more than a decade. Furthermore, postelection analysis showed black turnout had been the lowest in a decade.

The deft use of the issue by Wilson, a moderate Republican who at times had been at odds with party conservatives, proves how effective it could be when used by a mainstream candidate whose background didn't brand him a racist. "Wilson played it subtly and effectively. He is much more the case history for the future than Helms or Duke," predicted Carrick, who ran House Majority leader Dick Gephardt's 1988 presidential campaign. Carrick believes the troublesome issue will not go away.

Yet even after the convincing 1990 evidence, some still clung to the belief Helms and Duke had won votes because of rather than despite their racial insensitivity. And that the issue could not be raised by anyone other than an outright racist.

Nothing could be farther from the truth, as those Democrats who had been on the front lines understood.

"The perception that arose out of the campaign between Helms and Gantt is that Helms used a 1950s–style racist campaign to defeat Harvey," said Michael Donilon. "That's not the case. He took the cutting racial issue of the 1990s and put it squarely in the political debate in ways that haven't been done anywhere else. There is an argument in the Democratic party that Republicans" will not "use this issue in the future because it has been associated with David Duke and Jesse Helms. I don't believe that's true. I believe moderate Republicans will use the issue and it will be a problem for us."

No logical reading of the returns can yield any other conclusion, especially in the case of Duke. "By a great degree he won the votes despite being a Klansman," opined Louisiana's Senator Breaux. "There was a [desire to] send them a message in Washington, that 'they' are not listening to 'my concerns' on a variety of things—the economy, welfare, affirmative action." But, Breaux insisted, the appeal of Duke's message was not limited to Louisiana. "It would be picked up in a large number of states. There's a strong feeling out there, it's not just in Louisiana, it's throughout the country."

Despite all the data, Democratic Chairman Brown labeled the Helms ad—and implicitly any GOP effort to present their side of the affirmative action/quota debate in a politically useful context—as beyond the bounds of fair play. "It is one thing to argue issues, one thing to talk about your positions on the bill," Brown asserted. "What [Helms] did was despicable. He clearly injected race deliberately into that contest. It was a scare tactic."

In Brown's view there was no legitimate way for a candidate who opposed the civil rights bill to raise the quota issue. "I haven't seen one yet," he said. Just as Brown had maintained after the 1988 election that the Republicans had a "special obligation" not to use a black man to illustrate the flaws in Dukakis' furlough program, so he and most other Democratic leaders felt it wasn't fair to raise the issue of the 1990 Civil Rights Bill because "there are some things that are just out of bounds."

But they did not hesitate to maintain there was nothing wrong with a Democrat, black or white, stigmatizing opponents of that bill as racist.

Here, again, was a belief that seemed to be as much a part of Democratic doctrine as it was alien to the middle class: that there were two sets of rules when it came to racially divisive issues. It was, that is, acceptable to appeal to blacks along racial lines because, after all, they had been the victims. But for whites to respond along racial lines was reprehensible.

When pressed, Democratic leaders insisted they weren't for quotas; they were for affirmative action; and the middle class shared their sentiments. But it was another ostrich-like rationale that just didn't hold water.

Mark Mellman, the pollster who has worked mostly for liberal Democrats, understood that the middle class does not make any distinction between quotas and affirmative action. It might have at one time, but too much had transpired in the last quarter century for that still to be the case. "Quotas are perceived as attempts by government to restrict the opportunities of white working people," Mellman said early in 1991. "The middle class views affirmative action the same way. People assume affirmative action equals quotas and preferential treatment."

Democratic leaders realized the issue was here to stay, but ignored experts like Donilon who told them "we need to develop a defense" on the issue. Otherwise, it would continue to defeat Democrats at every turn.

In early 1991, the Leadership Conference on Civil Rights, the umbrella group pushing a new version of the vetoed 1990 bill, asked Stan Greenberg's firm—who else?—to gauge the problem. When the report found what Greenberg had been reporting for years—that many whites believed civil rights advocates wanted special preferences for minorities rather than equal opportunities for all-in the finest American tradition of Democratic liberals, the group buried the document and ignored the public attitudes it documented.

And on Capital Hill the Democrats proceeded to push the same civil rights bill Bush had previously vetoed despite the increasing awareness of the change in middle-class political attitudes across the country evidenced in the 1990 voting. They had no better success in 1991 than in 1990 voting. Slowly, a new consensus emerged: Not only *could* politicians survive voting against a civil rights bill, but there was political profit with the middle class for those who did.

Yet Chairman Brown, for some reason, seemed to believe raising the issue would be healthy for Democrats. "The 1980s were a disaster, a period when the clock was turned back on civil rights and human rights. And Democrats are going to fight to reverse that trend."

What sweet music to Republican ears!

"The American people do not want a quota bill . . . and when the president says it's a quota bill, it's a quota bill, notwithstanding what Teddy Kennedy may say about it," asserts Vice President Dan Quayle. And he is correct. "The American people will believe the president, and they will not believe Ted Kennedy on this issue."[3]

The affirmative action/quotas issue is fast becoming the divisive and politically profitable issue for Republicans that busing was twenty years ago.

8

Minus-sum Politics

Mike McCurry woke up feeling like a million dollars that hot, muggy morning in Abbeville, S.C. McCurry, the Democratic party's communications chief, was enjoying a much deserved holiday after helping to run the party's 1988 nominating convention which had adjourned just sixty hours earlier in Atlanta.

As he got up on July 24, 1988, at his grandmother's house in the middle of the Piedmont, ninety minutes south of the bustling Greenville-Spartanburg area, his spirits were sunnier than the clear blue skies. After months of doubt, Jesse Jackson had given his blessings to Michael Dukakis and shown the nation a unified party. Before live network television cameras, Jackson had delivered the endorsement. In exchange, Jackson had received some substantive but unimportant concessions—or so it seemed at the time. Jackson could also show his followers he was being treated like a major player.

McCurry and every other top Democrat thought they had pulled it off just fine. Happy days were here again. Right after the convention, polls showed Dukakis with an eighteen-point lead over Bush. Even McCurry, who knew the feel of a losing campaign, having served as the media chief for John Glenn and Bruce Babbitt in their unsuccessful 1984 and 1988 Democratic primary races, viewed the convention as an unqualified success.

Until McCurry went to Sunday services at the Sharon Methodist

Church, a traditional, steepled, red brick church with fifty or so regular worshipers. The men were in shirt sleeves because of the heat, but they wore ties. The women sported cotton print dresses. Like many such congregations in rural America, it shared a preacher with other churches.

After the service, the men gathered outside the church and swapped stories about politics, fishing, and the weather. Even though he was a Yankee by their standards (actually, McCurry was a Californian who had come East to attend Princeton and by 1988 had become a veteran Washingtonian), the church crowd pretty much considered him one of its own. He had been coming there since he was a child and knew the townspeople, most of whom toiled in a variety of textile and other light manufacturing plants.

Abbeville, where South Carolina adopted the original Articles of Secession following the 1861 attack on Fort Sumter, was like thousands of American small towns. Its residents were by and large married and owned their own homes. TV sports programs, home video games, hunting, and fishing were their hobbies.

"When they heard I had just come from Atlanta, they rolled their eyes and said they were glad they had been as far away from it as they had," McCurry remembered. "Finally, it dawned on me that the dominant impression they had of the convention was of Jackson. 'All the sweating and hollering on TV' that they talked about were code words for Jackson. What was clear about these voters, the persuadable voters who had voted Democratic most of their life, was that their dominant impression of the convention had been of a Jackson celebration.

"I came there thinking we had a great convention and helped our guy, and found out otherwise. That was the first time I had dealt with the possibility that by giving Jackson so much of a forum he probably had made more of an impression than Dukakis in some people's minds," said McCurry, who left the DNC in 1990.

But Republicans had known this all along. "I think a lot of people are going to be surprised when they look at the convention this summer and see that one-third of the delegates are black," commented Bob Michel, the GOP leader in the U.S. House, in a rare moment of candor three weeks before the convention opened.[1] The

Bush campaign got a great deal of mileage that fall by portraying the Democratic ticket as a three-headed monster—Dukakis, Bentsen, and Jackson.

The Democrats were taken aback.

"We thought it was successful because of unity and harmony," McCurry recalled, "and because we thought the party looked like it had its act together. All that didn't register at all in the minds of voters. And these were not redneck racists. They are average income white folks."

Abbeville's whites, who later gave three-quarters of their votes to Bush, reflect the "minus-sum" nature of American politics. Simply put, Democratic appeals to their liberal base, black and white, often turned off a larger number of white middle-class voters. Minus-sum shows itself in two interrelated ways:

1. Whatever Democrats do to solidify and energize their base in respect to the issues stressed and the treatment of Jackson alienates the white middle class
2. The tactics and issues Democrats employ to win their party's nomination turn off a vast number of voters in the November election

"A lot of white voters view Jesse Jackson as someone who has too much power within the Democratic party," says Merle Black, an Emory University political scientist and an expert on Southern politics. "To the extent that Jesse Jackson emerges as a major figure, it is a reason for them to look away from the Democratic party. The more visible Jackson and Jackson's agenda become, the more whites may be driven from the Democratic party, and that makes it more difficult for the average white voter to take the Democrats seriously."

"In some ways, voters even seem to judge the strength and skill and character of a Democratic candidate on how effectively he gets along with—or copes with—Jackson," agrees John Sasso, Dukakis' campaign manager and alter ego in 1988. "It becomes an unending litmus test."

Democrats begin every presidential campaign by digging out of the hole they have created for themselves over the years. "One of the things Dukakis failed to realize was that even though his favorable-unfavorable ratings looked good, once he was the nominee, he acquired baggage of about twenty years that was an incredible burden," former Michigan Governor Blanchard avers. "Unless you can somehow shrug off some of that baggage in the process of getting nominated—the baggage that the Democratic party doesn't represent average people, that it's just preoccupied with the clients of government and doesn't hold any opportunities for average people—" a Democrat can't win.

The monumental attitudinal differences between blacks and most whites, and between white liberals and most whites, are at the root of the seemingly insoluble problem.

"There's just no good answer to this," former Colorado Governor Lamm believes. "To be compassionate is to be supportive of the black agenda and to lose the critical middle class. In most states it becomes worse than zero sum. When you look at places like Illinois and Michigan, there has been a corresponding loss in the middle-class vote that's eaten up and more than erased" any increase in black votes. "It's minus- not zero-sum."

Democratic pollster Geoff Garin explains that "in places where race is a political fact of life, there are a whole range of value-laden sensitivities that come into play, that in fact probably make life more difficult for Democrats among white voters. If you're sitting in a Democratic strategy meeting the crucial question may become, 'Does the Democratic party have to become less associated with blacks in order to win elections?' My answer is no. But that is the crucial question."

Garin's livelihood depends on business from Democratic politicians, and they would shun anyone who publicly answered yes. But the very fact he raises the matter underscores its existence.

We live in an increasingly complex world lacking many of the traditional signposts—a union endorsement, an ethnic affiliation—that average voters once used to make their decisions. And with the virtual disappearance of the class warfare mentality, economic status no longer substitutes for that service.

But other issues have emerged to fill the role: race and a number of value-laden symbols—capital punishment, homosexual rights, abortion, gun control, the flag, taxes. In large part, each of these gives voters a chance to rate candidates. And because of the huge emotional content of these symbols, voters can easily and quickly categorize politicians. Additionally, given the current combative political climate, candidates can use these symbols to send negative messages about their opponents.

In short, voters use those emotional issues as a litmus test to discover which politician seems to be in the pocket of someone who doesn't share that voter's priorities. For that reason, "there is probably an inconsistency with having 90 or 95 percent of the black vote and getting significant numbers of new [white] middle-class votes," Democratic pollster Greenberg asserts. "The reason why Democrats get 90-95 percent of the black vote is that they are seen as a party of black voters" primarily serving black interests.

The evidence on the racial aspect of the "minus-sum" equation is overwhelming and heavily linked to the increasing tension over public funding of programs for minorities.

"There's competition between blacks and whites in states with big black populations, and there are white people who feel black people are going to take away what they have," former Jackson campaign manager Austin maintains. "In states where that is not an issue, they vote for candidates up or down based on what comes out of the candidate's mouth and whether they believe in that. There's no fear in those states."

And that, quite simply, explains the 1988 voting pattern. The only states where Dukakis won a majority of white votes, with the exception of New York where the large Jewish population is instinctively Democratic, were those states where blacks were 5 percent or less of the population: Iowa, Minnesota, Wisconsin, Washington, Oregon, West Virginia, Rhode Island, and Massachusetts.

"In counties, states, regions of the South, the more black a particular county, state, or region is, the fewer white votes the Democratic candidate receives, and vice versa," says Democratic pollster Paul Maslin. "Therefore, the states where we can win white votes—Arkansas, Tennessee, Kentucky—those states don't have enough blacks to supply a base to win. Where we do have enough blacks—Alabama, South Carolina, and Georgia—we can't get the whites." In the North the same dynamic "works, but in a slightly different scale" among suburbanites who fled the cities.

It's no coincidence that Jackson did best among whites in the Democratic primaries and caucuses in Oregon, Vermont, Wisconsin, and Minnesota, states which are mostly white.

In 1988, minus-sum politics centered around Jackson.

Inside the Dukakis campaign headquarters, which filled most of a ten-story renovated building in a marginal neighborhood, campaign manager Susan Estrich sat in a well-lit corner office about as large as an average living room. The view of a seedy parking lot from her bay windows was about as attractive as her alternatives.

She was, by any measure, an extraordinary woman. A nice Jewish girl from suburban Boston with chin-length, dirty-blond hair, she typified the "superwoman" who emerged from the seventies women's movement. She seemed slated to become the first woman ever to run a major presidential campaign.

Having, as expected, made the dean's list at Wellesley and Harvard Law School, she became a Harvard Law School professor at age twenty-eight, one of the youngest in the school's history. She also climbed the political ladder with key jobs in the 1980 Kennedy and 1984 Mondale presidential campaigns. When Dukakis needed a campaign manager in the fall of 1987 after Sasso was forced to quit for spreading dirt about fellow candidate Joe Biden, Estrich took over.

During the 1984 election, she met and later married Marty Kaplan, Mondale's witty chief speechwriter. Since his job was in Los Angeles as a vice president of Walt Disney, Estrich seemed to spend most of her life on airplanes hopping from coast to coast.

In the spring and summer of 1988, as she tried to focus on the upcoming battle with Bush, Estrich felt as if increasingly the subject everyone wanted to discuss with her was Jackson's role at the convention and in the fall campaign.

Blacks felt that Dukakis had snubbed Jackson by not offering him the vice presidential nomination, and worse yet, by not notifying him in advance that he had picked Bentsen. After the convention, by a 42-38 margin, blacks told the 1988 poll done by Gallup for the Joint Center that they felt Jackson had been mistreated—he had not been accorded sufficient respect and deserved to be handled differently from the other losing primary candidates. This raised the specter of blacks sitting on their hands come election day unless Dukakis visibly courted Jackson and blacks.

"We got calls from blacks saying we can't go into our communities if there is a perception you have treated Jesse unfairly. The view in the black community was that we were not being forthcoming with Jesse. We tried to walk the line on Jesse. Anyone who tells you it's not a line to walk hasn't gotten enraged calls from black leaders," Estrich remembers.

On the other side, white Democratic moderates were telling her that offending Jackson was the best thing Dukakis could do to impress white voters. By a 67-10 margin, whites told that same Gallup-Joint Center poll they felt Jackson had been treated fairly. They thought the Democrats were too close to blacks, and therefore not sympathetic to the plight of the white middle class. An ABC News-*Washington Post* poll that spring showed that if Dukakis had picked Jackson as his running mate, it would have driven away twice the number of voters as it would have attracted.

"I would go to meetings with white leaders who would tell me, 'we've got to get tough and tell him to get off the train.' There were those in the white community who say my folks don't like Jesse and want to see you stick it to him," Estrich recalled. "Who could be against dealing firmly? But it became 'how far are you willing to go?' It was a public game of chicken."

The problem was that, when the Dukakis high command sorted out the conflicting demands, their analysis lacked the cool-headed logic of a numbers cruncher.

"The dominant thinking, as with Mondale in 1984, was that we need to buy his peace," said Duane Garrett, a San Francisco attorney and top Democratic fund-raiser. "That obviously was a misperception of the political situation; it was a carry-over of the liberal guilt of all of the key people from the candidate [Dukakis in 1988, Mondale in 1984] on down."

Garrett, a chubby and savvy baby-boomer with a passion for politics, the San Francisco Giants, and high-priced art, spoke from experience. He was Mondale's national campaign cochairman in 1984, and that drubbing made him realize sooner than most in Democratic politics how bleak the future appeared.

Garrett believed that "the key thing that would have helped Dukakis enormously would have been to go to war with Jesse at the convention. Not to be mean-spirited or petty, but to make it clear that Dukakis was the guy in charge. What they did was to so delude themselves, that millions of voters peeled away during that process because Dukakis was bowing to the beck and call of Jesse Jackson. Whether it's true or not, that's how voters perceived it. The implication was that there were private deals, that Jackson would become part of the government. The proper way to have played it politically would have been to stand up to Jackson and hope Jackson or a small group of his supporters would have walked out. Then that would have said to the American people about Dukakis, 'He's different. He has the toughness.' The problem Dukakis had is they didn't even understand the politics of it. Because of the liberal guilt mindset they could not have even come to grips with that alternative."

"The tragedy," remembered Blanchard, who chaired the Democratic Convention's Platform Committee and was a party to the backstage Jackson-Dukakis negotiations, "is that, behind the scenes, the Dukakis people decided to draw the line on four or five things and they were very tough but they didn't want people to know it. If the American people had seen how tough they were on some of the issues it would have helped Dukakis. But there was still this notion that if everyone wasn't happy in Atlanta we could not win. What happened there was that because everyone was accommodated, we wound up in much worse shape than we realized."

"The trick," sighed Dukakis' chief campaign counsel Carol Darr, a rare Southerner in that heavily Harvard environment, "is how do you get the lower-middle and middle-income whites, the so-called 'Bubba vote,' without selling out the blacks."

And that, at least in 1988, was an impossible task, because blacks and whites disagreed about almost everything, both substantively and stylistically. Unfortunately for the Democrats, there were roughly eight times as many white as black voters. Moreover, Democrats failed to understand that the white swing voter they lost to the GOP was worth two votes—one the Democrats didn't get and one the Republicans did. Blacks who didn't vote Democratic because they felt Dukakis mistreated Jackson were only a single loss—they just didn't vote. There was little chance they would vote Republican.

Even after the smoke cleared from the 1988 Democratic debacle, nothing seemed to change.

"There has been a flight of white voters *because* Democrats have reached out to blacks," conceded Roland Burris, then Illinois' comptroller and, in 1990, attorney general, the highest ranking elected black official in his state's history. Yet even Burris, who has won in heavily white electorates and knows how to count, didn't seem to understand.

Given the history of race relations, blacks saw negative motives where whites meant none. Blacks, in their constant demands for special assurances that none exist, have rubbed nerves raw, even among friends.

A group discussion run by *Harper's* magazine in the fall of 1989 and published in its January 1990 issue proved the point. The magazine, hoping to focus on the party's underlying problems, invited seven prominent Democrats to the Tabard Inn, a favorite of Washington's Yuppie set. Among them were Burris, California congresswoman Barbara Boxer, a street-smart liberal, and Barney Frank, known to America as Boston's gay congressman, but viewed throughout Washington as perhaps the sharpest liberal of them all.

There, with Burris on one side and Frank and Boxer on the other, the issue that symbolizes the Democrats' racial problems was played once again.

FRANK: Jesse was not mistreated. He didn't win.
BURRIS: People [blacks] make a lot out of Dukakis not calling Jackson about the vice presidency.

FRANK: Then I'd say to black voters, "If you are going to refuse to vote for someone for president who'll act demonstrably more in your interest because somebody didn't phone somebody, I wash my hands of the situation." I am serious. We have encouraged people to be self-indulgent in our various groups. I say, "You have it in your power to keep us from winning if you react this way. If you do, there is nothing I can do about it; we will never win."

BURRIS: Right now, the party says, "We don't want to highlight or flaunt a Doug Wilder or an Andy Young or a Bill Gray."

FRANK: Roland, look at the party. Ron Brown is the chairman, Bill Gray the House whip.

BURRIS: We do not market that to the black community.

BOXER: Our convention [the one after which McCurry visited Abbeville] markets our diversity. How many million Americans watch that on television?

BURRIS: We may see Jesse and all of this togetherness on stage, but if Jesse says, "I was mistreated . . . "

BOXER: That's his problem.

BURRIS: It's our problem. Treat it that way and I say we will never win the presidency.

FRANK: There *has* been a recognition of black Democrats in many positions. That's as much as can be done by any institution. When you say that they don't market it, there is no *they*. The individuals themselves have to do it.

BURRIS: There's now a move to undercut Ron Brown. He has run into power plays, and he's not been given proper status as the chairman of the party.

FRANK [describing the typical DNC maneuvering that had plagued Brown's white predecessors]: You're setting an impossible standard and, by that standard, we all fail.

If three liberal Democrats who basically agree about most things have so much trouble with this issue, finding common ground between liberals and the rest of America on such matters becomes, if not an impossible task, certainly a daunting one. Although Democrats for decades have bridged that gap at the state level while losing regularly for president, things have changed.

Increasingly, those Democrats who are winning governors' mansions and Senate seats in states that vote for a Republican president are doing so as moderates. In many cases, they don't have to compete for the Democratic nomination, or are entrenched incumbents. That is, they can concentrate on the November election.

Perhaps the best example is Virginia's Doug Wilder, the nation's first black governor. He was unopposed for the nomination and ran a campaign in which he played down race to such a degree that state political insiders joked that, if you closed your eyes during Wilder's campaign speeches, you'd think you were listening to past governors Gerald Baliles and Charles Robb, both conservative white Democrats.

But even Wilder's election was extremely close. He won by a fraction of a percent. Had he been forced to run in a primary with liberal issues dominating the agenda, he would have found it vastly more difficult to avoid the type of statements that could have been turned into Republican campaign commercials used against him in the fall.

On the presidential level, Democrats do not have the same luxury. Their presidential primaries have featured long bitter fights that inevitably provide ammunition for the GOP.

And despite paying lip service to the notion that Democrats who vote in primaries are different from average voters, activists don't really appreciate the distinction. Simply put, Democrats focus too much on party primaries, thus handicapping their candidate for the fall campaign.

This dynamic does not hamper Republicans to nearly the same degree.

The most obvious reason is that Republican primary voters, although more conservative than the overall electorate, are much closer to the middle-class center than the left-leaning ideology of Democratic primary voters. And where Republican activists do split from the general electorate it is usually not over the big economic and foreign policy issues that dominate presidential campaigns, issues that are part of the Democratic Holy Grail, but not acceptable in middle America.

Haley Barbour, formerly President Reagan's top White House political aide, explains how "minus-sum" works on campaign issues in the Democratic primaries to the GOP's advantage: "[Democratic] campaigns tend to create cleavage on these very issues. . . . [For instance], white Southerners have always tended to be very promilitary and see that as very important. Black voters view that as soaking up resources that could be put into social programs. The Democrats tend, because of who dominates the Democratic party, to make the fault lines these issues, and it does drive the mainstream Southern voter further away. I think that's true of white suburbanites in the North also."

Less obvious, but probably just as important, the GOP keenly understands the crucial difference between the primary and November electorates. The Republicans realize that even though their activists are closer to the middle-class mindset than the Democrats', they need as much time as possible to court the November voter.

And the way they do that is to select the party's presidential nominee, unite the party, and begin the fall campaign as quickly as possible. The 1988 campaign was the perfect example. Bush had wrapped up the GOP nomination by mid-March; Dukakis had to wait until late July.

While Bush ran unopposed in the GOP contests, Dukakis dueled Jackson in meaningless weekly primaries even after having effectively wrapped up the nomination by mid-April. In short, between mid-April and the mid-July convention Dukakis had to campaign to win the Democratic activists, the very ones who would vote for him in November no matter what. But he never had the breathing room to talk to the "swing voters," those who don't vote in Democratic primaries but who can make the difference in November.

Bush, on the other hand, campaigned through those same primary states starting in mid-March. Using the money budgeted for the primary, he spent much less time on Republican activists and concentrated instead on wooing middle-of-the-road voters. Perhaps more importantly, by early April his brain trust was putting together the strategy for the fall, something the Dukakis camp couldn't do for months.

An early end to the primary battle has become almost a GOP trademark. In fact, the one year the GOP took its nomination battle to the convention, 1976, was the only time since 1964 the Republicans lost the White House.

The reason for the difference is that the Democrats take their name seriously. They think the paramount goal is to have a truly democratic process, keeping as close as possible to the concept of one man, one vote. Sometimes it seems they agree with Henry Clay that they would rather be right than president. They fail to understand that the main goal of the nomination is not to embody democratic principles, but to win in November.

A memo to Democratic Chairman Brown in 1989 from Steve Cobble, who was running Jackson's political action committee, illustrates the point. Cobble supported a rule requiring each candidate to receive the same percentage of delegates in a state as he or she received of the popular vote in the primary or caucus. In other words, if on primary day in Ohio 150 delegates were at stake, a candidate who won a third of the popular vote would get fifty delegates.

Most, but not all, state Democratic parties allotted their delegates that way in 1988. On the Republican side, in most places plans provided substantial bonuses to the winner, which meant that losing candidates did much worse in delegate allocation than in the popular vote.

"Proportional representation is the symbolic demonstration of the difference between Democrats and Republicans," Cobble wrote. "We consistently argue that we care about fairness, and they don't. Clearly, it is fairer to count everyone's vote the same, and not to deny a candidate a fair share of his or her delegates."

Before the 1988 convention, the Jackson forces demanded a deal from Dukakis requiring that all 1992 delegates be allocated on a strictly proportional basis. To most party leaders it was a deal made in hell, but they had no say. Dukakis and Jackson controlled the convention, and the presidential nominating convention can set the rules for the forthcoming primary process, they knew they could do whatever they wanted.

And at that point, Dukakis was willing to do almost anything to buy Jackson off. Besides, if he won the presidency he could change the rules later. If he didn't, he'd be long gone and it would be someone else's problem. Jackson wanted the change for strategic reasons. He was already eyeing the 1992 race. But party leaders unconnected to the two camps fumed, and in the aftermath the DNC changed its charter to prohibit the presidential candidates from striking such last-minute deals in the future. The Democrats are nevertheless stuck with proportionality for 1992.

Strict proportionality sounds great on paper. But if, as in recent Democratic primaries, a sizable number of candidates enter the race, there is no incentive for the losers to drop out. They stay in to increase their bargaining power should a deal be cut for the vice presidency, or other political goodies. "At some point you have to discourage candidacies that are no longer viable," Senator Robb stated. "That's what happened to Jesse in 1988. He didn't fold his tent, and that certainly hurt Dukakis."

The primary race therefore continued on to the convention, as had also essentially happened in 1984, 1980, 1972, and 1968.

With the Democratic rules remaining as is, in 1992 you will, in effect, "end up with a situation where a guy who has no conceivable chance of winning the nomination would be equally as stupid to drop out," said Republican Chairman Atwater, who grinned every time he talked about the Democratic process. "What that does is guarantee their process goes down to the wire. If you think that's good, then it's a plus. In my experience, the sooner you can consolidate your party the better off you are. If you want to really get out to that 15-20 percent in the middle, the sooner you consolidate your own party, the sooner you get out after that vote. I think the Democratic party process pretty well guarantees a knockdown, drag-out battle to the finish line."

It is fashionable within the Democratic party to argue that rules don't matter. If Democrats believe that, they deserve their losing streak. McCurry's story about Abbeville underscores this problem. "Our convention had merely ended a primary campaign, whereas a month later, the Republicans used theirs to begin the general election campaign," he remarked. "This was the reminder to me of how dangerous a game Democrats play with our national convention. We use conventions to end primaries rather than begin the general election."

In addition to showcasing Jackson, the Democrats in 1988 used their convention to bash Bush. "Where was George?" was red meat for Democratic partisans unhappy with eight years of Reagan. But to most of the 70 percent of American households who watched the convention on TV and thought the 1980s had been pretty good, the Democrats did little to tarnish Bush's image, less to project a positive picture of themselves.

That's the key. The vast majority of Americans, and especially the swing voters, begin paying attention during the summer conventions. Republicans used the 1988 GOP convention to showcase their fall campaign themes. Remember George Bush's "kinder, gentler" speech aimed at those middle-class voters who liked the previous eight years of prosperity, but thought Reagan might have been too insensitive to the needy?

In a nutshell, the GOP system is far superior to the Democrats'. The GOP's primary rules provide substantial bonuses for candidates who win primaries. That gets the losers out of the race and gives the eventual nominee room to maneuver. Under this system, the candidate in some cases can get all or virtually all the delegates in a state by winning only a plurality of popular votes in a multicandidate field. This system, which pertained throughout much of the South in 1988, allowed Bush essentially to wrap up the nomination on Super Tuesday, March 13, five months before the Republican convention. The Republicans have a much more pragmatic view of the nominating process. They will do almost anything to each other in a primary fight, but once it's over, it's over.

In 1980, Atwater was running Reagan's southern primary campaign. Much attention in South Carolina was focused on making sure that former Treasury Secretary John Connolly, who had the support of Sen. Strom Thurmond, the patriarch of the South Carolina GOP, did not score a breakthrough.

Atwater, however, was worried early about a longshot named

George Bush, and he turned out to be right. Bush won Iowa and finished second to Reagan in New Hampshire. As the campaign headed to South Carolina, Bush was Reagan's only credible foe. Atwater knew Bush had once cast a vote that could be construed as being pro gun control while he was a member of Congress in the late 1960s. Atwater figured that vote could be the kiss of death for Bush among South Carolina Republicans. But that was before presidential candidates ran negative ads against their primary opponents. And besides, money was tight. But he also knew that Harry Dent, who was running the Bush campaign in South Carolina, listened to only one radio station. So Atwater got F. Reid Buckley, who lived in South Carolina and sounded just like his brother, conservative godfather William F. Buckley, to record a radio ad.

In the ad, an announcer asked: "Mr. Buckley, what do you think about George Bush's vote not wanting people to have guns?" Reid Buckley responded, "Mr. Bush shouldn't have voted against people having guns," but he was never identified by a first name, giving the clear impression it was his better-known brother talking.

Atwater had the ad played regularly for a few days, but only on the one station Dent listened to, where a thirty-second spot only cost $25. Soon after, Bush came to South Carolina. As he got off the plane, Dent rushed over to tell him the Reagan campaign was in the middle of a major media buy stressing Bush's gun control vote. Moments later, as Bush stepped in front of the TV cameras, he tried to explain a gun control vote that no one in the press corp had heard about. Bush, that is, made a factor out of a nonissue. Atwater had hurt the Bush campaign, badly.

Bush, however, understood that was just the way the game was played. When he became vice president in 1981 and began looking eight years down the road to the time when he would seek the presidency, one of the first things he did was to look up Atwater. Bush wanted him on his side.

And that was not an isolated instance. After Bush won the 1988 nomination in a campaign that featured tough tactics against him by leading challengers Sen. Bob Dole of Kansas and Rep. Jack Kemp of New York, all was forgotten. Within weeks, Bill Lacy from the Dole camp had been recruited to run the single most important state, California, while Kemp strategists Ed Rollins and Charlie Black were given senior positions in the national Bush campaign.

Meanwhile, the Dukakis campaign suffered from the Democrats' quadrennial affliction. Losing campaign operatives complained that the nominee was unwilling to bring in people from the other camps. And it was more than semantics or sore losers. Unlike the Republicans, there were serious differences among Democrats on major issues, making it more difficult to close ranks behind the winning candidate.

In 1992 the contrast between the Democratic and Republican delegate selection rules will be the greatest ever, much to the GOP's delight. If the Democrats have a host of candidates, their rules guarantee a lengthy intraparty fight.

"To the extent both parties have adjustments that need to be made for the general election, the Republicans have a tremendous advantage," Estrich believes. "They get to start in March and do so in an atmosphere which by June is without opposition. We have created a situation in which we are handicapped for those three months and risk that our most important forum—our convention—will be one in which we will be pulled the way opposite from the general electorate."

Those who understand are mostly officeholders, many of them from the South, like Democratic Senator Breaux of Louisiana: "The political realities of the 1990s dictate that we are going to have to change our ways in how we select our presidential candidates."

But Brown, Jackson's 1988 convention manager who negotiated the proportionality deal with Dukakis, refused to budge. That was his stance throughout the late 1988 and early 1989 campaign that won him the chairmanship. He blocked efforts to allow state parties to pick their own delegate allocation methods by claiming the party couldn't renege on a deal once struck.

But the irony of Brown's "a deal is a deal" stance is that he was part of a secret agreement between the Dukakis and Jackson camps before the 1988 convention. The two sides agreed to reopen the whole rules questions after the 1988 election—the agreement by Brown and Estrich that finally brought peace to the convention.

The agreement was demanded by Jackson, who apparently wanted to change the 1992 rules even more to his liking once the election was over. But Jackson decided to keep mum about the agreement after the election because, with Brown heading the DNC, Jackson figured his interests were protected.

Thus the impetus to change the rules after 1988 came from party moderates opposed to Jackson, and they were destined to fail. Privately, they admitted they were just setting the stage. They were betting Bush would be overwhelmingly reelected anyway, and were looking to modify the rules for 1996.

Clearly, winner-take-all systems, or systems just short of it, hurt candidates like Jackson because of the concentrated nature of his vote. In those states where it was used, Jackson did not get nearly the same percentage of delegates as of the popular vote. In Pennsylvania, where Jackson got 28 percent of the popular vote, he won only 8 percent of the delegates. For while he got a huge turnout in black areas of Philadelphia and Pittsburgh, those areas constituted just two congressional districts. Although his popular vote in these areas dwarfed Dukakis' popular vote totals, Dukakis won every delegate in the state's other twenty-one heavily white districts where turnout was lower.

The Jackson forces, in their attack on winner-take-all systems, argued that they were racially discriminatory. They claimed that housing patterns, which produce a small number of heavily black voting districts and a larger number of white districts, required proportionality in order that delegate allocation represent the voting pattern fairly.

While the argument has merit, it raised a problem: its effect creates another handicap the Democrats don't need. Once again, the party is putting its principles above victory. The matter is complicated by the fact that most proportionality opponents are also Jackson opponents who desperately want to stop him from winning the nomination.

The bottom line is that, in the general election the Electoral College also allocates each state's electoral votes on a winner-take-all basis. This gives residents of less populous states like Alaska and Wyoming much greater per capita clout than those in New York or

California. And whites are heavily concentrated in small states, minorities in the larger ones. Thus, unless the Electoral College is also changed—a highly unlikely prospect—proportional representation doesn't put the Democrats any closer to the White House; in fact, it handicaps their candidates.

Frank Fahrenkopf, Republican national chairman for six years under Reagan, understands this: "Our campaign operatives . . . go into primary states and caucus states realizing it's a winner-take-all ball game. They go into each state with an attitude and approach to reach out and touch every corner that they can, realizing that if they win the nomination, they will already have in place an experienced team in dealing with the winner-take-all approach—which is the Electoral College approach. I think when you go into a proportional fight to win delegates you have a different approach. . . . What may be an effective campaign organization for a Democratic candidate in the primaries may not be an effective campaign organization, or may even be a defective campaign organization, to meet the contest in the general election. You've really got to change, change dramatically."

The ultimate impact of the "minus-sum" game hits in the general fall campaign. Perhaps Fahrenkopf is right, maybe the rules stop Democrats from reaching their target constituency. Whatever the reason, the way Democrats frame their issues shows they don't understand the tension between the party's black and liberal base and the largely white and moderate general electorate.

Either that, or they can't count.

In 1988, Dukakis spoke out for national health insurance, arguing no one should be without basic medical coverage. A central part of his campaign, it helped him in the Democratic primaries. But it would only directly benefit the 11 percent of American workers— and smaller percentage of voters—who didn't have health insurance already.

It was one more example of Democrats giving priority to the perceived needs of the poor and minorities under the assumption that the middle class would either support the notion or could fend for itself. It was not that the middle class thought providing health insurance to the working poor—the ones without it, because the poor have Medicaid—was an unworthy idea. It was just that they were ruffled at the thought that not since Medicare was passed in 1964 have the Democrats engineered a major program that would benefit all Americans, not just the needy.

Meanwhile, Republicans were identified with programs of broad appeal—tax cuts, military buildups, and a return to traditional values—concepts often in conflict with those of particular Democratic interest groups, but in sync with middle America.

In 1988 the Democratic challenge was clearly to convince skeptical middle-class voters that Democrats could use government in a fiscally responsible manner to solve problems. But deep in the heart of suburbia, skepticism about Democrats was compounded by worries about college costs. It was a ready-made opportunity, but once again, the party failed the test. Dukakis had a variety of policy options, and he picked the one least attractive to the middle class and most attractive to the poor. The one he picked would have created a government program under which students could borrow as much as they wanted for educational purposes and repay it over their working lives, the amount of repayment based on their earnings.

Dukakis was intrigued by the notion that those who struck it rich would in effect subsidize the education of those who had no work or who chose low-paying public service careers like teaching.

"We felt it would appeal to a broader constituency," explained Tom Herman, Dukakis' deputy issues director. It was attractive because "lack of financial means will not preclude one from going to college."

The Dukakis camp was oblivious to a major public relations problem. Those who chose not to work—such as housewives— would not have to repay the costs of their education. No income, no repayment, and never mind the fiscal problems of the middle class.

Nor did they see any political problem with the concept of student borrowing based on financial needs, and repayment based on the ability to pay—a plan bordering on socialism.

Finally, Democrats actually thought it a plus to have the loan repayments collected by the IRS. They were totally ignorant of the deep loathing the middle class has for the IRS and, therefore, for anything that might expand its power.

One idea rejected by Dukakis was a national version of a plan pioneered by Blanchard in Michigan. Under it, parents could pay the state a set amount of money on the birth of their child—$6,756, in 1988 to guarantee four years of tuition when the youngster was ready for college. The idea was so popular in Michigan that other states scrambled to follow his lead. They understood the political appeal of relieving middle-class anxiety about their kids' future, while at the same time not spending more government money or redistributing middle-class money to the poor.

But not Dukakis. He and his camp, deep with liberal guilt, were put off by the thought that poor families would not have the money to make the prepayment. If it didn't help the poor, what good was the program?

A third option was to require all college students to do two years of national service, civilian or military, before they could receive for federal student aid.

This plan was the brainchild of Democratic moderates like Sen. Sam Nunn who saw it as getting the Democrats away from a welfare-like program where only the poor and portions of the middle class could qualify for federal college aid. Backers of this alternative argued that its political benefits were enormous; it would move Democrats from supporting "entitlement" programs to advocating "earned benefits." Nunn's plan would have given those who performed national service vouchers worth from $10,000-12,000 per year for college costs or for a first home.

But the cost would put an end to all other federal college aid programs. In effect, students without family college funds would have to participate if they wanted a higher education.

In the Dukakis high command, that argument stopped the Nunn idea flat.

"The impact would fall much more heavily on minorities, who have much less of a choice," Herman commented. "If they want student loans or grants, they would be forced to go into public service. You can hear the echoes of black people serving in Vietnam."

The Democrats' inability to understand the "minus-sum" equation is not limited to losing presidential campaigns. Even in the halls of Congress, where Democrats still rule, it routinely rears its head.

Coelho in 1989 was an acknowledged comer in the party hierarchy. His ties to the campaign committee made him as aware as anyone on Capitol Hill of the severity of the problem. He came from the central valley in California, the agriculturally rich region that stocked the nation's salad bars. His district, stretching from Modesto to Fresno, was populated by political moderates who voted Republican for president.

The first-generation son of Portuguese immigrants who became dairy farmers, Coelho had planned a career in the Roman Catholic priesthood, but at age twenty-two he learned he had epilepsy. Canon law, which has since been modified, barred him from becoming a priest. Devastated, he thought of suicide. But a Jesuit friend introduced him to Bob Hope, the comedian and staunch Republican, who took Coelho under his wing and helped him apply for a job with his local congressman, B.F. Sisk. Coelho worked for Sisk for thirteen years and won his seat when Sisk retired in 1978.

Coelho soon began channeling his energies, once directed toward the religious life, into efforts to rebuild the Democratic party. A natural politician and schmoozer, he won his leadership post after transforming a dormant and backward Democratic Congressional Campaign Committee into a modern, computer-driven operation.

Coelho saw the political opportunity for a raft of Democratic ideas on family-centered problems, such as child care and parental leave for workers. Yet he realized that such legislative items were doomed unless the Democrats could change their image of being so sensitive to black demands that they would scuttle the interests of the middle class should the two interests conflict.

Thus in late 1988 and 1989, Coelho convened a task force of powerful House Democrats who control the fate of social legislation. They were to draft a statement of principles that would act as a foundation for the Democratic social agenda. House Education and Labor Chairman Augustus Hawkins, Barbara Kennelly of Connecticut, Steny Hoyer of Maryland, Dale Kildee of Michigan, and George Miller and Barbara Boxer of California were among those present.

They met more than twenty-five times behind closed doors in one of the Capitol's oldest rooms. Chief on the agenda was a declaration that the work ethic was, in the Democratic view, the core value of society. It stressed that people who work ought to be rewarded and get ahead. It was aimed at the millions of white middle-class voters who felt their government cared a lot more about the guy on welfare than those who were paying the freight with their tax dollars.

But: "What should [have been] a consensus value was rejected. I was surprised to discover that was not a consensus position," remembers one Democratic participant.

The reason: Hawkins, a diminutive black lawmaker who represented the Watts section of Los Angeles, dissented, and refused to budge. Hawkins—born in 1907 and elected to Congress in 1962—was the most senior black member of Congress. He had been saved from poverty by FDR's WPA jobs program and continued to believe in such solutions a half-century later. He may have been only 5'5", but his seniority gave him a giant's clout. And he used every bit of it.

Hawkins thought the high-profile statement envisioned by Coelho would be seen as a slap in the face to welfare recipients. He was running true to form. During the 1970s Hawkins had teamed with Hubert Humphrey on legislation that would guarantee a job for whoever wanted one. Even in the late 1980s, Hawkins brushed off arguments that welfare operated as a disincentive to work. He almost killed the 1988 Welfare Reform Act that had pleased both Democrats and Republicans because he wanted more generous welfare benefits.

Kildee, a Flint, Mich., liberal who represented perhaps the nation's most heavily union constituency, also balked. But Kildee, who is white, had neither Hawkins' leadership clout nor his ability to use guilt as effectively on the other white lawmakers.

Then too, Coelho and Hawkins had been compatriots for years, and Hawkins had been the only black to support Coelho's bid for the leadership post.

Finally, Coelho's resignation from Congress over unrelated ethical matters sealed the document's fate. Once again, Democrats who had the power in party councils were so worried about the people they were offending that they forgot about the people they needed to court.

But Hawkins wasn't a happy victor. He could see the tide was turning, and he gave up his seat at the end of the term.

"He felt very strongly that the party and I were trying to walk away from the urban poor," said Coelho. "He felt I was being antipoor. It got very hot. He got very irritated. He was very, very frustrated. He didn't realize the New Deal was over. I tried to tell him you had to look at things today. Politics have changed dramatically. A Democrat has to recognize that a lot of people don't care about the poor. You need to accept the fact that the poor need to be helped, but not at the expense of the working middle class. There has been a tendency to say we only help the poor."

Indeed. The Democratic agenda in recent years is replete with examples of efforts to help its base at the expense of the middle class. As recently as 1989 an effort to place a straight-forward statement putting the party squarely behind the work ethic was edited out at the DNC for the same reason Hawkins blocked Coelho's statement of principles.

"It's not surprising . . . , every week there is another example," commented Tim Penny (D-Minn.). "I just don't think we're talking the same language [as most of the American people]. We have a majority of Democrats who tend to be liberal and who feel they have an absolute right to dictate the agenda. They are a minority in Congress and in terms of the general electorate. Yet they insist on controlling the issues and refuse to make compromises that would bring all Democrats aboard. We end up with more liberal positions than the public supports. This makes it easier for the Republicans to pick off Democrats in order to defeat Democratic bills. We get the worst of both worlds."

The Democratic congressional effort to pass the 1990 Civil Rights bill fell in that category. As did its emphasis on raising the minimum wage, which does nothing for the middle class except, according to some economists, increase inflation. The Democrats once-ambitious child care plan finally became law, but the final version was a hybrid of the Republican alternative and the Great Society-style program Hawkins and Co. first envisioned.

All of which proves that the Democrats really haven't learned their lesson. They still did not grasp the very real conflict of interests over economics and values between their base and the middle class.

Democratic pollster Maslin predicts: "When you look ahead it's very clear the results of 1988 put the racial question so front and center in the Democratic party that it may delay a majority in a presidential campaign for at least another cycle and maybe more."

9

The Ostrich Syndrome

Fittingly, the meeting was held at Disney World.

Democratic party leaders gathered in that fantasyland on November 21, 1985, for a state chairmen's meeting that would become one of the most pivotal in party history.

The agenda gave little hint of the gravity of what would occur. The meeting minutes have mysteriously vanished from the party files, so no official record of the two-day session exists.

Only a handful who weren't there, and a few who were, have ever understood the importance of that meeting. For on that day, the Democrats charted a suicidal course that would produce at least one, and probably several more, presidential defeats.

On that day the party had the chance to deal with the underlying causes that had forced Democrats off Main Street America. But its leaders muffed the opportunity and continued down a dead-end alley. Ignoring the mass of voters, they pitched their message to the nation's racial and cultural minorities, and to the dwindling number of white liberals who refused to believe the 1960s were over.

What actually happened was that National Chairman Paul Kirk, a politically timid man, decided to suppress the party's most exhaustive research project ever. In blunt language, this report described why Democrats were losing the White House. Simply put, the issue was race.

White voters—more than 80 percent of the electorate—felt left out, the research showed. They felt the Democratic party had become captive to black America and the politics of Jesse Jackson. They felt the Democrats neither understood their hopes and dreams, nor cared.

To a lesser extent these voters also resented Hispanics, homosexuals, radical feminists, labor, and the poor. They felt that those groups had also helped to take over the Democratic party and made it a place that no longer had room for them.

Dukakis' 1988 defeat can be traced to the deaf ears the party turned to the message delivered that hot November day at Disney World. Ironically, the Democratic elite felt a sense of serenity. They were an eclectic collection of men and women who bore little resemblance to the portly, cigar-smoking male pols who had run the party twenty-five years earlier. The "new breed" were aging New Dealers, occasional good ol' boys from the South, and some Democratic Yuppies—successful baby-boomers who, unlike their more numerous Republican counterparts, felt some guilt about their affluence.

As their taxis pulled up to the sleek Contemporary Hotel on the grounds of Disney World, they exuded optimism. After all, they had survived Ronald Reagan's forty-nine-state landslide just a year before and retained their control of Congress. The Democratic party was still standing. "There is nothing quite so exhilarating as being shot at—and missed," quipped North Carolina Democratic Chairman Wade Smith.

They were, in effect, in no mood to deal with the racial aspect of the upcoming report. The whole notion terrified most Democratic leaders because they understood its explosive character. Their largest remaining bloc of loyal voters was black. The party leaders wouldn't consider risking the alienation of their base, particularly since they still didn't understand they had a real problem with white America.

But it was more than that. The mostly white party leaders were filled with liberal guilt. They couldn't understand why the white middle class felt the way it did. Democratic officialdom was troubled by anything that challenged its doctrine that all people were the same regardless of race. It smacked of racism, they argued, even to acknowledge the statistics about black crime and welfare. And—even more ominous for their political future—they refused to understand the crucial attitudinal differences between blacks and whites.

But worst of all for the party, the state chairmen never heard the specifics of the report that day since it wasn't yet finished. They were given a general briefing, and that was more than enough to scare them silly. Maybe, had they known exactly how bad things were, they would have demanded that the party address the problem. But Kirk, guilt-ridden and scared of confrontation, never let it get that far.

Brian Lunde, the party's executive director, had pushed the research project to the forefront of the Democratic National Committee's priorities in 1985. His North Dakota roots and Southern political experience made him realize as 1984 rolled by that Walter Mondale hadn't a clue of what most voters thought. The report was Lunde's baby and, soon after Kirk tossed it in the trash, he resigned. Lunde had run Kirk's campaign for chairman and been rewarded with the top staff job. But he and Kirk came from different places and would go their separate ways because they viewed politics differently.

Lunde was an unusual Democrat. He believed in marketing: Politicians must understand what motivates the voters just as business people must know what makes consumers buy. In early 1985, when the DNC was in the red, he persuaded a skeptical Kirk to spend $250,000 on a five thousand-person national survey combined with thirty-three focus groups, an unusually large number. Furthermore, to ensure the party got a fresh perspective unhindered by Democratic sacred cows, Lunde went outside the traditional political community and chose a well-regarded Washington, D.C., commercial marketing firm, CRG Research, for a no-holds-barred picture of how voters viewed the Democratic party. The study remains CRG's sole foray in the political arena.

Now, in Mickey Mouse-land, Lunde stood on an elevated podium in the huge hotel ballroom and briefed the state chairmen in general terms. His watered-down summary largely avoided the specifics which no doubt would have offended virtually every Democratic special-interest group.

Lunde was flanked by DNC direct-mail chief Frank O'Brien and political director George Burger. The three staffers were more than a decade younger, on average, than the chairmen, who sat facing them in rows of rectangular tables, with each state's party chair, vice chair, and executive director grouped together. Kirk significantly sat among the state leaders, thus signaling his distance from the findings. At that point he knew few of its specifics, but enough to make him uncomfortable.

Lunde argued that the anti-Reagan rhetoric, then the rage among Democrats, was counterproductive: "The public has moved beyond Ronald Reagan. They have already put him in the history books." Voters wanted politicians to address *their* economic problems, he went on. For the vast majority of whites that meant helping them to buy houses, educate their kids, and take care of aging parents.

At that point Burger, a pudgy but savvy twenty-nine-year-old pol who was sweating profusely from the television lights, put it succinctly: "People are telling us, 'Please don't ask us to care for people down the street before we take care of our own family's economic security.' "

"Middle-class voters all over the country read Democratic calls for 'fairness' as 'not me, but some other guy,' " O'Brien, thirty four, one of the inventors of the Democratic party's direct-mail operation, said in his strong Boston accent. "When party leaders talk about fairness, middle-class voters see it as a code word for giveaway." And, he pointed out, 90 percent of voters consider themselves middle class.

What the three DNC staffers didn't tell the chairmen was that the report found that middle-class voters felt the "Democrats are the giveaway party. Giveaway means too much middle-class money going to blacks and the poor." They didn't have to. Kirk certainly understood the implications. He had read the results of Stan Greenberg's research in Macomb County a few months earlier. And even his partial knowledge of Lunde's project was enough for him to view it as a ticking political time bomb that could blow apart the coalition that had made the Democratic party great—a Democratic party he mistakenly thought still existed.

As if his actions could change public opinion, Kirk ordered the original report destroyed, leaving only a handful of copies, one of which, with enormous effort, was obtained for this book.

The CRG report said, in effect, of the two main white voting blocs the Democrats had lost—Southern moderates and Northern, mostly Catholic, urban and newly suburban ethnic voters: They see "a dual identity of the party; liberals on the one hand and special interests (blacks, gays, Hispanics, feminists, and labor) on the other hand. These two sets of 'owners' trade the party between themselves, leaving the common man out of the picture."

The Southern moderates and Northern white ethnics "are no longer part of the party identity. They feel betrayed by this constituent pressure to eject [them]," it added. "They view gays and feminists as outside the orbit of acceptable social life. These groups represent, in their view, a social underclass . . . that threatens to violate or corrupt their children. They feel threatened by an economic underclass that absorbs their taxes and even locks them out of the job, in the case of affirmative action. It is these underclasses that signify their present image of the Democratic party."

Kirk argued in 1989 that the study was not "well enough done to make it the Bible or road map for the future. I thought a better way to go was on the positive track on what we do stand for and do believe, rather than what the guy in the bowling alley is saying about us."

But the guy in the bowling alley had always been the party's best barometer. Because the Democrats did not tackle the racial, economic, and values concerns of Kirk's mythical bowler, that guy in the bowling alley had his say in 1988—and he voted Republican.

Whether Dukakis would have behaved any differently had there been a thorough discussion of the report's finding will never be known. But it's clear that without such a debate, Dukakis committed the same mistakes Democrats had made for two decades: pitching to "have-not" voters, who were already heavily Democratic, while ignoring middle-class concerns.

Lunde's experience in the South and rural Midwest had showed him that Democrats were too closely identified with interests that alienated white middle-class voters. Kirk's was in liberal Massachusetts, where the Democratic sacred cow priorities were never questioned.

It wasn't that Kirk, forty-eight, was as far left as Teddy Kennedy, for whom he had long toiled and from whose shadow he would never escape. But he did come from the same *noblesse oblige* background. Kirk's father was a Massachusetts Supreme Court justice. He himself had gone to Harvard, and he had his own Cape Cod summer home. Government, he believed, was to help the needy.

In short, Kirk personified the Democratic dilemma.

Intellectually, he understood what was needed. But he had a heavy heart. He was already smarting from the flak he'd taken from blacks, labor, and feminists for trying to dispel the image that Democrats were just a collection of special-interest groups. Those groups didn't know that he had been bowing to pressure from Lunde and like-minded staff when he'd taken those actions. He had, for example, lectured organized labor not to endorse a candidate in the primaries because to do so would be counter-productive, and he had withdrawn official recognition of the various special-interest caucuses (blacks, gays, Hispanics, etc.) within the DNC. He hadn't made his old friends happy, either, by canceling the 1986 midterm mini-convention that activists traditionally used to demand ideological purity from presidential candidates.

So, during that weekend in Orlando, Kirk told reporters—who even from Lunde's briefing saw the potential uproar it could create within the party—"I don't want to be chairman of a party that would leave these people behind." Shortly after Lunde walked off the stage, Kirk strode over and whispered to him, "Let's put a moratorium on this until I can get up to speed on it." At that point, all Kirk knew about the report was what he had just heard, but he could smell trouble.

Kirk had never been keen on Lunde's project. His one contribution had been to change a poll question. He made sure Jackson and Kennedy were deleted from the question asking voters to rate major figures. He didn't want a party document to show that voters disliked the party's two best-known figures.

After returning to Washington, Kirk finally read the entire CRG report. And, despite his later public denials, he recognized that it was on target, though he felt it was a simple answer to a very complicated question. More importantly, he believed the party could not, without going through unparalleled turmoil, appear to endorse a report that voiced what the core elements of the Democratic party considered racist doctrine. It would ruin what appeared to be a strong chance to reclaim the White House in 1988. Kirk showed the CRG report to Democratic congressional leaders and they concurred. They had their own fiefdoms and they were doing fine. Why rock the boat?

Moreover, Kirk felt that to follow Lunde's plan to circulate the research to party leaders around the country would give the media a field day.

There was also, of course, the other, overarching problem, the painful one that nobody wanted to deal with: How could a Democratic party, focused on have-nots, retool its image and appeal to enough voters to win the White House if the middle class didn't think Democrats were sticking up for them?

Kirk took the easy way out by altogether avoiding the racial issue. A month after the Disney World meeting he deep-sixed the report and assured the media that Lunde's comments about middle-class resentment had been taken out of context.

Kirk wasn't alone. Most of the state chairmen had also misjudged the electorate and were equally unwilling to deal with the sticky question of race. The state chairmen were the adult equivalents of a high school student government: well meaning and full of self-importance, but with little real power. Moreover, they had no appetite for internal combat.

The erosion of the state chairmen's power came about in direct proportion to the growth in clout of the various party constituencies: blacks, Hispanics, feminists, gays, labor, and peace groups. These groups had come to dominate the primaries which in turn nominated the Democratic presidential candidate and thus shaped the party's general election message. The state leaders now either came from the interest groups or, at the least, depended on them for their political survival. In short, they were likely to be part of the problem and thus lacked the courage to admit it and take a broom to it.

But that day in Disney World, the state chairmen, seeing the tip of the iceberg, panicked. Most of them, however, worried more about the immediate publicity than the ominous message. They knew that the handful of reporters at the back of the room, expecting the usual drivel of such meetings, had smelled a story, a real story. For Democrats to take an implicit shot at their black base was the political equivalent of man-bites-dog. Where journalists saw a good story, the chairmen envisioned internecine warfare on a grander scale than the battles of the 1970s, when reformers fought regulars.

Iowa Democratic Chairman Arthur Davis led the counterattack. Davis, fifty-seven, a successful, silver-haired Des Moines lawyer, served on the U.S. Holocaust Commission with Mario Cuomo when Cuomo was New York lieutenant governor and a noncelebrity. The two were friends and shared a deep passion for helping the needy. Davis was genuinely offended by the report's recommendations. "It may help us elect more people," Davis told his fellow chairmen, "but it is not my mission as a Democrat."

That view became the prevailing sentiment. The story turned out to be a "one-day wonder." Without the actual report, or Lunde at the DNC pushing the message, it died.

Almost three years to the day after the Orlando meeting—and ten days after Dukakis had turned a seventeen-point lead into an eight-point loss—nothing had changed in the party's pitch or fortune.

This time the Democratic chairmen met in Phoenix, which was fitting since the party was in ashes and needed a rebirth. Yet the mood was so buoyant it sounded like a GOP victory party. The "party of the people" was meeting at the posh Spanish-style Pointe at Tapatio Cliffs Hotel in the city's swank suburbs. The adobe resort, where it seemed everything but the grass was tiled, more often hosted Republicans at medical and dental conventions than Democratic pols.

As would befit a celebration, the chairmen's schedule was fat with leisure time to enjoy the hotel's golf course, tennis courts, and swimming pool. One day the menu featured salmon, the next, barbecued steak. Each suite had a mini-bar. Camped inside the front lobby in tennis whites that first afternoon of the three-day session was Wally Chalmers, who had replaced Lunde as Kirk's

right-hand man on the DNC. Chalmers, the quintessential prep-
pie, sat on one of the two bamboo sofas with deep, dark blue
cushions directly across from the front door.

Chalmers gave the impression that the Democratic party was
healthy as a horse, congratulating the chairmen on their state or
congressional victories and alluding to the presidential disaster only
when reporters inquired. Kirk himself told the chairmen that
weekend that the Democratic party "is stronger today than it has
been in modern political history, even when we had a Democratic
president."

Incredibly, the state chairmen believed him. It was a classic case
of denial. "There's a great deal of satisfaction with the status quo. I
don't think we need to turn this thing upside down," was Indiana's
John Livengood's blithe remark.

Once again the party leaders refused to believe America wouldn't
buy a "real Democrat" if he were packaged correctly. And not just
the party functionaries. Elected officials, who should have known
better, were sticking their heads in the sand at about the same
period. Most blamed the loss on Dukakis' dumb campaign tactics.
Gephardt, soon to become the House majority leader, maintained
in March of 1989 that "in 1981 and 1985, we went through a long
process of soul searching, trying to review what we thought, why
we thought it, what we wanted to say to the American people. I do
not think we need to do that again."

In short, the Democratic leadership continued to think that a
majority of Americans shared their view that government's primary role was helping the neediest in society.

When it was suggested that white voters were telling them that
government should do as much as it could for the largest number of
people—i.e., the middle class—they countered with the same old
answer: that such a course would mean abandoning the party's
heritage. And it wasn't just what they said, it was the Democrats'
tone in saying it, a tone filled with the same moral superiority that
led them to question Reagan's intelligence or Bush's tactics. They
refused to understand why they had lost the White House five of
the last six times.

Still, there were a few sharp-eyed eagles among the flock of ostriches. Chief among them was Texas Chairman Bob Slagle, who knew something was seriously wrong. He had been at the Orlando debacle three years before and had spent most of that weekend trying unsuccessfully to get Lunde to give him more of the CRG report. Slagle was willing to acknowledge that the party's problem in his state, without which Democrats have never won the White House, was almost exclusively among white voters.

But he was a rarity, and for other reasons as well.

He was one of the few chairmen who actually had clout in his state. Not that Slagle controlled Texas Democratic politics, but he was a major player. Many chairmen were totally owned by their governor or a U.S. senator.

Slagle, more of a throwback to the old-time political bosses than most of the other party chairmen, had run the Texas party since 1980. His political agenda was limited: He wanted to win elections. That meant he walked a fine line.

He did enough for the state's black and booming Hispanic population to keep them happy. And he was enough of a moderate to satisfy conservatives and big-money people who dominated the ranks of white Texas Democrats. In Texas, Slagle was viewed as a moderate liberal. That DNC members considered him a conservative spoke loudly about how out of step they were with "Joe and Jill Average."

A colorful, plain-spoken Texan, Slagle had bombed in a 1972 legislative race and harbored no illusions of an electoral career. He didn't view his office as a steppingstone, as did many state chairs. So he didn't care about his image. For decades, more often than not, a cigarette dangled from his mouth. In 1988 he quit cold turkey to stop his new wife Susan's nagging. "It didn't improve my lungs much," he quipped, "but it improved my ears a good deal."

And because he'd been raised in the rough-and-tumble of Texas Democratic politics—his father had been a crony of House Speaker Sam Rayburn and, for a time, of President Johnson—he didn't measure everything he said or did against whom it would offend. In fact, he enjoyed pissing people off—especially Republicans.

He also took his job seriously. During the last six weeks of a fall campaign, he would rally the troops in the counties, up to six a day. While the candidates for governor or senator were in Dallas, Houston, and San Antonio playing to the major media markets, Slagle would pile into his car and tour the rural areas, offering red political meat to the faithful.

On one occasion, while fending off GOP charges that Democrats were soft on gun control, he told a rally a month before the 1988 election: "My position on gun control is very firm. There should be no gun control until such a time as we Democrats have time to use our guns to kill all the damned Republicans." When Republicans asked for an apology, he fired the other barrel. "If the Republicans are going to take that remark seriously, then they are going to be like the young lady who got pregnant by taking seriously what was poked at her in fun."

But Slagle's voice was almost as lonely in Phoenix as it had been at Disney World three years earlier. He sought as delicately as he could to persuade his fellow chairmen to face up to the party's problems. He knew that Ron Brown, a black liberal, was waiting in the wings to take over the party if Kirk decided not to seek another term. But Slagle couldn't get the Southern chairmen to unite behind a more moderate, white candidate who would send the right signal about the Democratic party's direction.

That was in part because the "win-or-else" ethic that has consumed American sports doesn't raise its head in the Democratic party. Cynics said that wasn't surprising, since Democratic economic policies seemed to disdain the marketplace and its competitive pressures. But the real reason why a chairman who had presided over the 1988 disaster wasn't running for cover was that in the Democratic party, losing wasn't the ultimate sin. Those consigned to political hell were those who rocked the boat by opening up the racial Pandora's Box.

Kirk had run the DNC for four years. He had been among those in 1987 who literally licked their lips at the thought of facing George Bush, calling him the "little Lord Fauntleroy of the Republican party," although he later denied saying it. Yet, despite losing the big one in 1988, Kirk's fans were everywhere.

"If it ain't broke, don't fix it. Keep Kirk" said the buttons urging him to accept the almost unanimous pleas of party leaders to take a second four-year term.

The reasons for their attachment to Kirk, who had been a controversial choice in 1985 because of his Kennedy ties, stemmed from two not so obvious factors—and the same old fear of confronting the truth.

First, the state chairmen had prospered during Kirk's four-year tenure. Democrats had won back the U.S. Senate and taken even firmer control of the House. And they still held commanding leads in governorships and state legislative seats, masking the gains of the past decade made by Republicans at the state level, especially in the South.

The second reason was that Kirk had restored a financially broke party to prosperity. In fact, the DNC had so much cash on hand in 1988 that Kirk decided not to spend $3 million that was in the bank on the election. He reasoned that he had met even his loftiest spending goals and given millions to state parties, and saw no reason not to save for the future. It turned out to be a smart decision because Brown's first six months in office were a fiscal disaster for the DNC.

But most important of all, it would be easier if Kirk stayed on. They could avoid confronting the racial issue that a contested election would inspire. Kirk, however, was completely aware of the problems facing the Democrats; he told friends privately that the developing racial split might not be solvable. He decided he'd had enough.

In his place came Brown. His election by the Democratic National Committee flew in the face not only of conventional political and marketing strategy, but of common sense. A business that finds itself doing poorly among a particular group, whether women or diabetics, makes a special effort to show the group that it cares. In the Democrats' case, the obvious answer was to pick a white, moderate-to-conservative Southern male to head the party.

So the DNC, loaded with liberals, elected a black liberal from the Northeast. Democrats preened themselves on having won the high moral ground—Brown's election had broken down one more color barrier. Brown's biggest asset was his smoothness, especially as compared to his prime opponent for the chairmanship, Michigan Chairman Rick Weiner. Weiner was a talented political tactician and manager, but he was saddled with an appearance and nasal-sounding voice that could have won him a starring role in the *Revenge of the Nerds.*

In one sense, Brown's election could have been anticipated. He was an attractive, smart, well-qualified, and articulate man. He had worked long and hard in the liberal vineyards. After helping run Ted Kennedy's 1980 presidential campaign, he became an effective Washington lawyer-lobbyist. He succeeded among the pragmatists there because he was not, in fact, as liberal as his benefactors. In 1989, for example, when Kennedy called for new laws to overturn the Supreme Court decision that sided with white Birmingham, Ala., firefighters who claimed reverse discrimination, an associate of Brown remembers him wondering out loud if there wasn't some "merit" in the firefighters' case. Brown denies having said it.

Meanwhile, on the DNC, where Slagle typified the few remaining members of the old school of party insiders, Iowa's Bonnie Campbell was more on the cutting edge of the DNC's ideological and demographic mainstream. Weiner told friends later that it was her decision to back Brown that made him realize the race was lost.

At forty, Campbell was the most visible state chairman in America because of the media obsession with the Iowa caucuses. It seemed she was on network TV more frequently than some presidential candidates. She was the impartial and articulate Democratic voice reporters sought for assessments during her caucuses. And she had her eye on public office. In 1990, Iowa voters elected her state attorney general.

Although in step with her state's liberal Democrats, Campbell was also a pragmatist. Maybe she learned that from her husband, Ed Campbell, twenty years her senior. He was a former state chairman and Iowa Democratic power broker, but was not nearly as progressive as she. But for all her liberalism, and unlike most DNC members, she understood how out of step with mainstream America they were. On some issues, however, this squeaky-clean but very determined politician would not swerve. She believed in the Democratic party.

Her short, red hair and clean-scrubbed smile fit the image of a woman who'd left a farm in the hamlet of South Plymouth, N.Y., at age seventeen for a clerk's job in the U.S. Department of Housing and Urban Development in Washington. It was 1965, the heyday of LBJ's Great Society. Government, she believed, was supposed to do things for people—a belief that was solidified when she joined the staff of Sen. John Culver (D-Iowa), a former Kennedy aide.

In 1989 she acknowledged the Democratic losing streak was at least partially because the party was too closely identified with blacks; it was not a problem in her state because Iowa has few blacks. But in respect to Brown, she explained: "I just think Ron's the most impressive candidate. I understand the problem we have, and that his election may further that perception. But if I were to vote against him because I was worried about how it looked, then that would be racist on my part and I can't do that after being a progressive Democrat all my life."

Her mindset was not unique. When told later of her remarks, Weiner sadly shook his head and said she was only one of many DNC members who felt that way about their votes for Brown.

Cuomo, one of Brown's law school professors at St. John's, told his former pupil: "Ron, I'll do anything I can to help you, but I don't think I want to get too involved. They'll say I'm running for president, and you don't need that and I don't need that." But then Cuomo met with the editorial board of *The New Republic*, the once-liberal magazine that in recent years has led the way in questioning Democratic orthodoxy. Cuomo said the meeting was crucial in changing his thinking. "They said, 'You can't make him chairman,' and I said, 'Why not?' 'Let's be honest,' they replied. 'Well, he's black and, although he's really terrific and conservative [for a black Democrat], you already have Jesse. . . . [If you add] Ron Brown . . . [you] can't win.'

"That's when I decided [publicly] to support Ron Brown," Cuomo recalled. And once Cuomo decides to do something, he doesn't go halfway. Weiner never really expected many votes from the Northeast, but Cuomo's muscle gave Brown strong momentum.

This was not the only version of the story, however. Others at *The New Republic* editorial board meeting held in the magazine's spiffy, long, and narrow conference room tell a slightly different story. They portray a didactic Cuomo spending much of the time lecturing on the hopelessness of life on welfare. When questions about Brown, which were meant to raise the issue of the party's electoral future, came up, Cuomo immediately interpreted them as racist. It was yet another example of Democratic leaders—in this case an Italian-American who is thin-skinned about Mafia stereotypes he thinks victimize his people—perceiving hints of racism and feeling an obligation to compensate.

As it became clear that Brown's highly expensive $250,000 campaign was headed for victory, his supporters rationalized that, while they knew the party had a problem winning back the white middle class, they felt Brown was the one best able to handle it. It was, they said in a tone more of hope than belief, like the opportunity President Nixon capitalized upon in 1971. As a conservative Republican whose anticommunist credentials were impeccable, only Nixon could open the door to communist China without rebellion from his own ranks.

So, too, with Brown. He was an intimate of Jackson, who was exacerbating, not ameliorating, the Democrats' problem with white voters. They argued that since Brown was a pragmatist, he could handle Jackson better than anyone else in the party. After all, they kept telling one another, how could Jackson call the Democratic party racist when it was headed by a black man?

Weiner tossed in the towel before Brown had it sewn up. Even Weiner, who had resigned his state chairmanship to seek the big job and had nothing to fall back upon, didn't want to raise the racial question. He told friends he didn't want the job badly enough to go down in history as the one who brought civil war to the Democratic party. Much like Kirk in 1985, he was unwilling to take the flak.

Even to argue—as did those who pointed to the presidential losing streak—that there had to be a reason why whites consistently rejected the party, made the Democratic hierarchy uncomfortable.

At the Phoenix meeting, the chairmen invited Babbitt to offer a path out of the darkness. It was a daring choice, for he relished telling people what they didn't want to hear. As might have been expected, Babbitt cut to the heart of the matter when he asked, "How many times do you have to whack the mule over the head with a two-by-four to get the message?" The silence was deafening. His prescription—"We've got to focus on our message . . . . We are offering one product, while the American people are shopping for something else"—sailed right over their heads.

But that was nothing new. For years Democrats had deluded themselves that they had been kept out of the White House by causes unrelated to their basic message. In 1980 and 1984, Ronald Reagan's acting skills had fooled the American people; in 1988 George Bush had played dirty. And now, despite Babbitt's plea to wake up and smell the coffee, the state chairmen passed a resolution—as if their voting would make it so—that rejected "the notion" that Dukakis' defeat was a "rejection of the Democratic party or the principles its supporters hold dear."

It truly was laughable.

So nothing changed after the 1988 election. Democrats prayed for a steep recession or a monstrous Republican scandal.

There were, however, a few like John Lewis, the black Georgia congressman, who suggested, "We need to talk about it. Maybe now is the time. It shouldn't be something we put on the back burner." But they were shunted aside by the Ron Browns. Brown's rhetoric was stirring: "Issues do not exist within compartments bounded by gender, or age, or income, race, or region. The problems we face, the opportunities we will be presented, are not separated by group but exist for all of us."

But his attitude typified the problem. To his credit, he had sought to move the Democrats back toward the political center where the white middle class lived. He felt Democrats were dealing with the race problem by telling—rather than showing—white voters how important they were. To put the racial divide under a microscope struck Brown—like Kirk before him—as needlessly risky. What scared Brown and other Democratic leaders, both white and black, was that a public discussion would legitimize white disenchantment—what Democratic leaders saw as racism, but what the middle class considered reality based on its own experiences. Things would probably only get worse, they figured. And they may have been right.

But what they refused to acknowledge was the extent of the damage that had already been done to the party. Democrats needed both black and white votes to win. The white Democratic defections meant Republicans could win the White House with the 60 percent of whites votes they were getting. To win back enough white defectors, the Democrats had to confront the problem, not sweep it under the rug.

"Democrats aren't willing to look at it, not because they don't think it exists, but they are trying to find a constructive way to bring people together," Brown stated. " . . . There are some wounds you just do not want to open, and it is irresponsible to walk down a road that you know opens those wounds."

In the Democrats' view, the middle class was just plain wrong in believing that the party cared more about the problems of the poor and minorities than of the middle class. Be that as it may, what the middle class wanted was not to be told once again to rethink its beliefs, but for the Democrats to rethink their own: to recognize the inherent conflicts between the interests of the poor and of the middle class, and adjust the party's agenda—not just its rhetoric—accordingly.

Brown wasn't alone. His attitude was even more prevalent among the party's congressional leaders who actually believed they could keep everyone happy by doling out more federal programs, not making tough choices.

House Speaker Jim Wright, before scandal enveloped him in 1989, spoke for the party's congressional leadership when he said that "to make such a choice, consciously or unconsciously, would be to betray the very basis of America's unique national success and the one indispensable foundation of the Democratic party."

Outside the Washington beltway, things were no different. New Jersey Gov. Jim Florio presided over a state where white flight from cities and the Democratic party had reached epidemic proportions. He had been elected in 1989 against a very weak Republican opponent and then kidded himself the racial divide was closing, not widening.

"It's something that results in counterproductive discussions that some people [Republicans] like to have happen. I am troubled by neat categories [race] that I am not sure are really the appropriate categories," he said in the summer of 1990, sitting in his state capitol office, squirming physically as well as verbally. "When you get into artificial distinctions, blacks are for government intervention that whites are not for, you allow an interesting discussion that is not relevant."

But sadly for society, he was wrong. The huge differences between the perceived self-interests of black America and white America and the political solutions each favored made it very relevant.

Clearly, Brown, Cuomo, Wright, Florio, and the Democratic establishment had consistently underestimated the size of the problem. If the middle class was to give Democrats another look, the party needed to get their attention by signaling real change.

Brown's decision to take the 1992 Democratic convention to New York only further illustrated the stubborn mindset that denied the racial problem. Brown proclaimed that New York had no negative image that would hurt the party's chances for the presidency. Perhaps having been born there and having known Mayor David Dinkins, a black liberal, since they were kids, Brown had a blind spot about the city. For, despite his good political instincts, Brown refused to acknowledge what even his own aides told him— that for most Americans, and certainly the vast majority of white voters, the Big Apple was a Big Negative.

New York sent the wrong message, as had San Francisco, which hosted the Democrats' 1984 convention. San Francisco had symbolized gay rights, a tolerance of homosexuality, and it turned off Middle America. New York symbolized the liberal big taxes, big union, free spending approach to politics Middle America had fled when it moved to the suburbs.

New York, moreover, was beset by racial problems. It displayed a strong image of black power. A media coverage of the convention displaying composite pictures of Dinkins, Brown, and Jackson would almost certainly dismay middle-class voters.

It was a foolhardy choice, and not a surprising one. Just another example of the Democrats following the ostrich theory of politics: Put your head in the sand and hope the party's problems will go away.

10

Suburbs and Democrats Don't Mix

Pam Blips is the typical American of the early 1990s. Like much of her generation, she is a suburbanite and into cocooning. Her priorities are her young son Madison, her older daughter Murphy, and her husband Mark. Like many Americans, she doesn't think much about politics, but she votes regularly because that is part of her clean, good citizen, suburban lifestyle.

Because Pam and Mark Blips are suburbanites, it is increasingly hard for the Democrats to compete for their votes, largely because suburban individualism doesn't mesh well with the Democratic view of collective problem solving, a view nurtured in the cities. But it's more than philosophy. There's the question of comfort level, which the Democrats don't understand. In fact, Democrats just don't seem to understand what makes suburban America tick. Either that, or they don't care.

As 1991 opened, the Blips were trying to move from a suburban-style neighborhood within a few feet of the Atlanta city line into the serious suburbs. Had the real estate market permitted, they would have left more than a year earlier. Their driving force was the same as has motivated millions of other Americans who have been fleeing to suburbia for more than a generation: a desire to get away from the increasingly dangerous and expensive cities, to find a safe and secure place to raise their children, and to enjoy the good life.

"We want to get away from the noise and crowds, but mainly from the insecurity and threat of crime, whether real or perceived," Mark said. "We are about the only house on our street that probably hadn't been broken into.

"We want as much house and land as we can get for our money. It's just getting more and more congested, the crime is incredible, and the taxes are outrageous. We are looking for something a little calmer," he added.

Pam, as she proclaimed and her lifestyle evidenced, was "just average middle-class folks."

Indeed, Metropolitan Atlanta was a testament to the nation's suburban boom. The 1990 census showed that about half the population in Georgia, one of the nation's largest states geographically, was packed into a fifty-sixty mile radius of downtown Atlanta. Twenty miles north of Peachtree Center on I-75, the suburbs of Marietta and Roswell boomed like California during the gold rush. Estimates were that by 1993, seventy thousand new jobs will have been created during the past decade. Most of them will not have been the product of Fortune 500 firms setting up shop, but of small companies spreading their wings. As of today, some have flown, and others have failed, but there has been no shortage of entrepreneurs.

Office buildings, warehouses, light manufacturing plants, and retail shops sprang up on what had once been farmland.

The cows were replaced by a developing skyline. The population of suburban Cobb County quadrupled in the last quarter-century—suburban sprawl was the rule in America from Philadelphia to Phoenix—and Republican margins were massive.

The last part of the twentieth century has seen the vast majority of the American middle class become suburbanites. It is in the land of shopping malls that elections will be won or lost in the 1990s. In 1992, for the first time ever, more than half the votes will be cast in suburbia. In 1960, suburbs housed a third of the population. The 1990 census showed just under 50 percent live there.

New York Governor Cuomo was on target when he said the

GOP had "won the presidency without getting the votes of the cities." All you had to do was examine any metropolitan area in America. In 1988, ABC News' exit polls showed large cities— which disproportionately feature more blacks and fewer whites than the racial composition of the overall population—were the only type of community Dukakis carried.

And the 1990 census showed that more than half of the nation's largest twenty-five cities actually lost population in the last decade, while those that gained were almost all in the Sun Belt and more likely to lean to the Republican party.

The GOP areas that are shaping American politics range from California, where the sheer voting strength of Los Angeles County is now dwarfed by Orange County to the south, to Philadelphia, where the Democratic margin in the city is overcome by suburban Bucks, Montgomery, Delaware, and Chester counties. And the population advantage the suburbs hold over the cities is magnified politically by suburban turnout rates, which are a quarter higher than in the cities.

Chicago, where the "collar counties" of DuPage, Lake, Kane, McHenry, Will, DeKalb, and Kendall outvote the late Richard Daley's once powerful Cook County machine, showed just how massive the change had been. In the early 1960s, the Chicago suburbs supplied about 22 percent of the statewide Illinois vote, but by 1988 the figure was roughly 37 percent. And the population changes did not alter the partisan balance: almost two out of three votes remained Republican.[1] But it wasn't just metropolitan areas with heavy black populations where the migration occurred. In 1960, Minneapolis-St. Paul had seventy thousand more residents than the surrounding suburbs. Thirty years later the suburbs were two and a half times larger than the two cities.

Democrats, nevertheless, continue to run their campaigns and tilt their platforms to the voters in the cities. That's because when they talk suburbs, all too often they think geography, not mentality.

In 1988, Democrats thought they had licked their suburban problem. They said repeatedly that Michael Dukakis was a man of suburbia. Once again, they were deluding themselves. Dukakis'

Brookline is not suburbia. It is an affluent town on the western border of Boston and is conveniently serviced by the city's subway system. It is overrun with lawyers, doctors, and other well-educated professionals. Residents there are three times as likely to have a college degree, and women are less than half as likely to be housewives as the rest of the country. Brookline residents are much less likely to be married, have children, or own their own homes than suburbanites nationally. They shun TV, bowling, and the Bible, preferring foreign travel, reading books, and talking politics for hobbies.

Political life in Brookline is liberal. Barney Frank, although reprimanded by the U.S. House of Representatives for hiring a male prostitute, is quite popular there. The Brookline town governing board has voted against reciting the Pledge of Allegiance before its meetings and has declared the community off limits to nuclear weapons.

Brookline doesn't suffer the same kinds of pressures that beset typical suburban communities such as Mesquite, Texas, twenty-five miles east of Dallas. Unlike Brookline, Mesquite's residents generally are married, have children, own their own homes, and aren't as comfortable economically. They endure much longer and worse commutes, crime is more of an immediate problem, and taxes cut more deeply. In Mesquite, people overuse their VCRs because the time constraints of taking Johnny to Little League makes them miss the show first time around. They bowl, play home video games, and shun the high culture events that sell out in Brookline.[2]

In Mesquite, American flags are displayed on July 4th, everyone proudly says the Pledge of Allegiance, and the high school football game is packed on Friday night. In communities like Mesquite, the GOP is on a roll because the party's message strikes a chord with the lifestyle and values of suburbia. Even those on the opposite side of the political divide see the trend and understand why.

It would have been difficult to find two people with less in common than GOP Chairman Atwater and Citizen Action's Ira Arlook. Atwater was a card-carrying conservative who enjoyed his reputation as the Darth Vadar of American politics; Arlook was a community organizer and liberal who pointed to Atwater as the type of politician he abhored. Yet these two baby-boomers have a good understanding of their generation and of the suburbs and agree on something that should send a chill through those who run the Democratic party.

"Many of the problems Democrats have in suburbs," Arlook explained, "can be attributed to a liberal elitist view among some Democrats. And that form of elitism is more objectionable to many people in suburbia than the form that characterizes the Republican party."

"The happiest I was during the entire 1988 campaign," Atwater reminisced, "was the weekend after Dukakis' nomination when the papers and television had all these photographs of him sitting around in a wrought-iron leisure chair with all his Brookline friends on Martha's Vineyard with a brand new pair of deck shoes, his little khakis, and his starched blue shirt. I knew we had this guy's ass. They don't understand that swing voters are antielite and antieffete."

In 1970, Ben Wattenberg, a former LBJ speechwriter, and Richard Scammon, JFK's director of the Census Bureau, published that era's seminal examination of the American electorate, *The Real Majority.* In it, they described the average voter as a white, forty-seven-year-old mother and wife of a machinist with a high school diploma who lived either in Dayton, Ohio, or its near suburbs. They picked Dayton because it was the heart of the New York-Chicago corridor, where America's population and economic strength was located. This housewife was a little less likely not to work than to have a job outside the home. She was a Protestant and was beginning to lose her ethnic identity. If her husband wasn't a union member, other men in her family were. And the odds were heavy that she was a Democrat.

To futurist Alvin Toffler, that Dayton housewife was the proto-type of those who inhabited a smokestack America that today has largely disappeared.

Such people, he said, "are accustomed to routine. Resigned to a lifetime of work. They have surrendered responsibility to others and take orders. They don't necessarily like it, but that's the way life is. You don't talk back to the boss. You like products that are standard brands. You are happy with your house that is no different than your neighbor's. You are family-oriented, but your conception of the family is limited to the nuclear family. That's the lower-middle-class working culture as it was in smokestack America. It's fading."

Two decades later, the difference between that Dayton housewife and the updated profile of the average American compiled by the highly respected *American Demographics* magazine[3] told volumes about the changes that had taken place in the nation.

The average American is now a thirty-two-year-old married woman living in the Sun Belt suburbs with a job and a child or two. No matter where her and her husband's ancestors originated, they are Americans, not hyphenated-Americans. Their ethnic identity has disappeared. She (and probably her husband) works in a technical, sales, or administrative job. But they aren't afraid to switch jobs for fear they won't find another. They talk back to their bosses, their television sets, and their politicians.

The differences between Pam Blips' of the 1990s and the Dayton housewife are crucial for those trying to get her vote. And the Republicans did understand the differences—well enough to win Pam Blips' vote for the presidency in 1980, 1984, and 1988.

In fact, Pam Blips fit the bill of the new average voter almost to a tee, although she was a few months younger, twenty-five pounds lighter, and an inch taller than the 5'4", 142-pound norm. And, like most Americans nowadays, she has moved several times in her life.

Until her son Madison was born in 1988, Pam had held a variety of clerical and technical jobs and planned to return when he was ready for school. But then Murphy came along and she remained at home. Indeed, the rate of women entering the work force slowed in the late 1980s because, like Pam, many women felt that staying home and raising their kids was more important than the luxuries a second income might bring.

Actually, Pam's concerns and priorities weren't much different from those of the 1970 Dayton housewife, although the women's liberation movement had provided more choices than had previously existed. But the difference in their lifestyles—which defined the middle class and its values as much as anything else—explained the Democratic fall from grace.

Much of the reason lies in the cultural mores of modern suburbia, which is not a partisan political place. The civic culture of suburbia is intrinsically less Democratic in its orientation than were the cities where the mass of voters lived a generation before. In those days—the "good old days" for Democrats—the party's strength came from its ability to play the political godfather, something the Republicans never had.

Most of the white urbanites of the Dayton housewife's era thought of themselves as immigrants, and they recognized that the Democratic party had helped their ancestors when they got off the boat at Ellis Island. In the old days of neighborhood politics, it was the Democratic ward healers who took care of people's problems. The block captain administered the city political machine. He got jobs for the unemployed, took care of widows, and made sure the garbage was collected. Politics was not about ideology in those days, it was about getting things done for people. And in return, the masses voted a straight Democratic ticket.

The Republicans were the WASPy good-government types who generally lived in the few suburbs of the time and ran against the machine that took care of the average Joe. Or worse, from a political point of view, Republicans were the tools of management at a time when class warfare was a winning formula for Democrats.

But that changed as more and more people moved to the suburbs. The Democrats weren't organized there, since the suburbs were a GOP bastion, and in suburbia, people didn't need the party in order to get government services.

There were millions of families like that of Peter Kelly, the Democratic power broker, who understood how out of step his party was with the times.

"In my family," Kelly explained, "there were nine brothers and sisters. Seven moved out of Hartford, one died, and one stayed in the city. Of the seven who moved out, six became Republicans within a year. It was, 'Hey I've arrived, my neighbors on both sides are Republicans.' "

In suburbia, "we are organized; we come and knock on their door," said Al Jourdan, Illinois Republican chair who lives in McHenry County in Chicago's northern suburbs. If the Republicans' built-in advantage doesn't match the old machine-like operation of the Democrats in the cities, certainly the present Democratic party doesn't begin to compete.

Probably no one in America understood how the suburban exodus had damaged the Democratic party as well as Harriett Woods. For it was the exurbs outside of St. Louis and the Kansas City suburbs that kept her from immortality.

Harriett Woods was a Missouri state senator in 1982, having first won office in 1976, running largely as the mother of University of Missouri (and future NFL) quarterback Pete Woods. That November she came within 26,000 votes out of 1.5 million cast of winning a U.S. Senate seat. Had she won, Harriett Woods, not Geraldine Ferraro, almost certainly would have become Mondale's historic vice presidential choice in 1984, because her office was more prestigious and she came from a key "swing state."

A former Missouri lieutenant governor and grandmother of six, Woods is a tall, slim woman with curly salt-and-pepper hair and a savvy political mind. She runs a St. Louis think tank and believes the Democrats' inability to deal with demographic change has been greatly responsible for the party's decline.

"There is a pattern of social change that occurs to people as they turn to material goals," Mrs. Woods stated. "Working-class families move into suburbia and a climate of upward mobility and they tend to try and adjust their views to a pattern, almost a snob appeal, and disassociate themselves from the lower class from which they rose.

"I think," she continued, "there is a difference in the value system of suburbia. People prefer to describe themselves politically as an independent, more than a party regular. They prefer to frame a campaign in terms of better schools [rather] than more jobs [a typical Democratic issue]. They prefer to talk about working together [rather] than us against them, the traditional Democratic class warfare.

"Typically, Democrats built themselves on immigrant populations. Our control was based in the cities on doing things for people [in terms of supplying jobs or services]. In return you supported the party. In suburbs they deal with smaller units, nonpartisan boards. More people identify themselves with management than with the unions. It's the nature of the change of the workforce and the suburban expansion," she concluded.

In the nonpartisan political atmosphere of suburbia, former Democrats were cut free from the associations that had reinforced their Democratic leanings in the cities. People moved more often and identified less with their community and its customs.

"In suburbia, there are fewer organization affiliations," said Heather Booth, former president of Citizen Action, the grass-roots activist group, and head of the Coalition for Democratic Values, a group set up by Democratic liberals like Sen. Howard Metzenbaum of Ohio, to battle the influence of the centrist DLC. Certainly, no neighborhood political clubs, no local ward leaders passing out turkeys at Christmas to loyal party members exist in suburbia.

But it is more than that. "The unions are not there," Ms. Booth laments. "There aren't neighborhood clubs or organizations like in cities. There is less church-going." And suburban churches—except for the booming evangelical Christian denominations in the eighties which were strongly Republican—are of a nonpartisan character that is vastly different from the Democratic orientation of the former city churches. Further, the organizations that have sprouted in suburbia have a nonpartisan flavor—the PTA, the Little League, or Boy and Girl Scouts.

Attitudinal and lifestyle differences aside, the type of Democratic political organization that existed in the cities was geographically hopeless. In suburbia, there weren't the row upon row of identical apartment buildings, the row houses and double- and triple-deckers that had once housed America's middle-class urban residents in neatly defined areas. People were much more spread out, making it impossible for a neighborhood boss, even if he wanted, to gain the confidence and support of enough people to matter. Grass-roots organizational politics was just not feasible. Suburbia got its political messages from television and the GOP understood this.

Even in some tract suburban areas where enough people were concentrated to allow a base, families did not stay put for decades, which allowed a political machine to cement a personal bond with the voters. One in six Americans moves yearly.

But the most important factor, even more than the geographic obstacles, in cementing partisan allegiance in succeeding generations was also gone—family ties and inherited politics.

No longer did children live a stone's throw from their grandparents. Those who had lived through the Great Depression and considered FDR their savior had little time with their grandchildren who seemed always on the move. When the generations broke bread together, it was a special occasion. Politics took a back seat to more important matters, and the historical memory that had stood Democrats in good stead faded from the nation's psyche.

Young people spent less time being reminded of their ethnic identification by their grandparents, among whom ancestry was a badge of honor, and more with contemporaries, among whom such distinctions blurred. They grew up knowing little about what the Democrats had done for their ancestors.

In other words, the average voter in the 1990s is different from his grandparents for reasons having nothing to do with politics.

"Work is a lot less important for them," in the opinion of Toffler, who began drifting from his liberal Democratic leanings in the sixties and sees a bleak future for Democrats because of these changing lifestyles. "Among this new generation, except for some driven Yuppies, work is no longer the center of life. They've grown up in a world without a severe depression and they assume this will continue.

"It's not," Toffler added, "that the Republicans necessarily understood the future better. It's that the solutions that move in the direction of greater decentralization, greater individualism, solutions that exercise innovation rather than routine, policies that move in the direction of diversity go with the flow toward the way society is changing, and Democratic policies have moved against that."

It is not, said fellow futurist John Naisbitt in *Megatrends 2000*, "an every man for himself type of individualism, gratifying one's desire for [his] own sake and to hell with everyone else. It is an ethical philosophy that elevates the individual to the global level; we

are all responsible for preserving the environment, preventing nuclear warfare, eliminating poverty. Individualism, however, does
recognize that individual energy matters. When individuals satisfy
genuine achievement needs—in art, business, or science—society
gains."

In fact, while urban life reinforced the predominantly Democratic strategy of collective solutions, suburban life reinforced the
mentality of individualism—the fundamental tenet of Republican
philosophy.

Nothing makes that point more forcefully than the everyday
chore of getting to and from work. In this new era, the average
commuter does not go from the suburbs to the city. He or she
commutes between suburbs. And except for the handful of major
cities like New York, Boston, Chicago, and Washington, D.C.,
almost all the commuting trips are made by car rather than mass
transportation. Almost nine in ten American commuters were driving to work as the nineties opened, many spending three hours a
day alone in their mobile cocoons. Is it any wonder they viewed
collectivist solutions like mass transit as foreign to them? "The
factors which would have favored the collective approach in a
previous generation have changed dramatically," Senator Robb of
Virginia remarked.

Toffler sees that as a crucial dividing line between Democrats and
Republicans: "If the industrial society was a mass society, and we
are moving towards a demassified society, that creates tensions that
lead to different responses. On one hand you have people [Republi-
cans] who say, 'Do your own thing, diversity is great.' This reso-
nates with baby-boomers, who want maximum diversity. On the
other side you have people [Democrats] who are terrified of that
and want to remassify the society. You hear a lot of discussion about
the need for community, for care."

And of course, without the sentiment for collective solutions,
there can be no constituency for the taxes to finance them. The tax
revolt of 1978—which jump-started the GOP—was at its core a
revolt of suburban homeowners who felt they were being taxed to
death.

"The one thing about the suburbs is that most of the people

living there are overextended," agreed former Atlanta Mayor Andrew Young. "They can't really afford to be there. You've got young families that can afford a $50,000 house, but they see a $80,000 house they really like and they decide to go for it. They are barely on the edge and then someone comes along and reassesses their property. They panic because they see it putting them on the streets. High taxes is a life-and-death issue for most of the *nouveau riche* in the suburbs. And they believe it is Democrats who are raising their taxes."

Young's understanding was not shared by the majority of Democratic officials, however. Once again, the Democrats' tendency to mock that which didn't fit their value system proved counterproductive. In this case, they raged against what they saw as the increasing materialism of society, but which in reality was the middle-class's objection to the collective problem solving that was the Democratic party's very bread-and-butter.

Democratic attempts to argue that "to be individualized is to be selfish, that greed is bad," were politically counterproductive, Toffler believed. "They [Democrats] identify individuality with individualism as though there were no distinctions."

"The younger middle-class population [baby-boomers] is interested in being different from other people," Toffler continued. "They want their house and car to be different. Consumer purchases can define your style. All this works to the Republican advantage. Anything that works against massification works to the advantage of a party whose ideology has been very strong on individualism and against central bureaucracy."

In an emotional sense, it paralleled the change from people being concerned with economic security to their being concerned with economic opportunity. Pam Blips and her contemporaries wanted everything about their lives to be special. They wanted to stand out in people's minds. They were not satisfied, as had been their parents, with just being part of the whole. The 1960s' suburbanites tried to "keep up with the Joneses" and everyone's home looked the same. The idea in suburbia a generation later was to be at least a little bit different.

Heather Booth understands the political differences well from her days at Citizen Action, whose grass-roots activity is probably the most comprehensive in suburbia: "If the Constitution is about liberty and justice for all, grossly you could say that liberty people are Republicans and justice people are Democrats, although that's not always true. The liberty aspects are, 'Don't step on me, I'm going to do it on my own, I don't need anyone, get government off my back.' So the style of life people have—without connections, more in isolation—leads them to seek solutions focused on individuals. The group solutions are more the Democratic approach and they are less popular."

There was yet another dominant characteristic of suburbia that didn't mesh with Democratic politics. As Anne Eshoo, a county supervisor in San Mateo County, California, and an unsuccessful Democratic congressional candidate put it, the suburban psyche grates against the Democratic mentality.

"People in suburbs are comfortable and the Democratic party, frankly, is the one that rocks the boat. If someone is comfortable, why rock the boat? The Republican party reflects the status quo and their lives are a lot more status quo in the suburbs. But the problems they see sweeping the country don't touch them in a personal way. The suburbs reflect more of a complacency. Maybe not in the terms my father would have used, but in an All-American sense, they are comfortable. The Democrats continue to push."

And that was why the racial conflicts—a manifestation of the Democrats' insistence on helping the poor even if it rocked the boat—seen so vividly in Macomb County became the rule, rather than the exception. Suburban America viewed the economic, lifestyle, and values differences between the cities and the suburbs as a race problem. That's why voters in Gwinnett County, a suburb northeast of Atlanta, in 1990 refused to approve extension of Atlanta's rapid transit system into their county. Opposition to the extension won by a roughly two-to-one margin despite bumper-to-bumper traffic and horrendous commutes into Atlanta. County Commissioner W.J. Dodd thought the reason was simply that "the minorities" the Gwinnett voters feared would pour into their county if the transportation link were established.

"People move to the suburbs and all of a sudden they have different interests," lamented Jerry Austin, Jackson's 1988 campaign manager. "They are worried about property values, who is moving next door, above all security. All of a sudden they think of Democrats as the party of minorities, who are going to take [their security] away. They see the Republicans as the party of white people who protect the status quo. I have friends who marched in civil rights marches in the fifties and sixties and now they talk about 'nigger this' and 'nigger that.' They don't want their kid going to public school. Got to protect their property values. What's that all about? They want to protect what's mine."

The baby-boom mindset was captured by National Public Radio's Garrison Keillor, radio's folk hero for the better part of a decade, in his description of life in Lake Wobegon, a quiet, peaceful, and mythical mid–Minnesota village. Most people of that generation realized that they couldn't just leave urban civilization for the country, so they sought the next best thing: suburban isolation from the turbulent city. That's why Democratic calls to rebuild America's cities fell on deaf ears. When Michael Dukakis talked about his success in revitalizing decaying cities in his state, few listened. They couldn't relate. Why would anyone want to go downtown to shop when they could get what they needed at the mall?

Pam and Mark Blips' daily lives illustrate this dynamic at work. Like their peers, work takes a back seat to family and enjoyment, what salesmen call self-fulfillment and cynics call selfishness. That was why Mark gave up a shorter commute for life in the suburbs.

Mark, who likes to work in the yard, and Pam, who runs half-marathons for fun, are prototypical baby-boomers. They don't go out much, but spend their time with their VCR and playing with the kids. This lifestyle of cocooning has become the norm among baby-boomers. It focuses on personal security and consumption, another GOP edge. And boomers, juggling jobs and family, are invariably short on time.

Business, understanding this, put a premium on service. American Express told its employees that the first person who answered the telephone should deal with the customer's problem. If not, the caller might grow frustrated with being passed from one person to the next and take his business elsewhere. When it came to politics, this meant that boomers were increasingly disenchanted with government bureaucracy. They disdain government inefficiency, and blame bad postal service or long waits for car license renewals on public employees whom they view as incompetents who are being protected by unions and Democrats.

Pam Blips' husband Mark, a slim man with a beard and wire-rim glasses, is a lawyer like his brother. They work in a two-person law firm started by their mother. Although located in downtown Atlanta, this family law firm handles the legal problems of families— wills, divorces, house sales, and criminal matters. It is not an Atlanta version of TV's "LA Law." Mark earns roughly $40,000 a year.

"Mark could go and work for a large firm and bring home two and three times what he makes, but that's not what we want. He would have to put in more time, and he would rather spend the time with us as a family," Pam confides.

Neither belongs to any party organization. Pam is a member of Greenpeace, the environmental group whose members have tended to support Democrats, and Mark belongs to the bar association. They have neither the time nor the inclination to work for candidates. As Madison gets older, they expect to get involved with the PTA, maybe the Little League.

Both are fitness oriented. Boomers are much more likely to be physically active than their parents were. It reinforces the individualistic belief that if you work hard enough, you can get what you want—in this case a firmer tummy and stronger cardiovascular system. Every morning while Mark is feeding the kids breakfast, Pam and her seventy-pound German shepherd Tate jog three miles. When Pam lived near the Atlanta city line and was worried about crime, Tate went along to protect her.

Their physically oriented lifestyle meshes with their political mindset. Mark likens a liberal friend to the Democrats' overall problem: "If someone could exercise for you, there would not be a fat person on earth. This guy is fat, yet he doesn't work in the yard. He pays people to do things. He goes to Weight Watchers, where people say he's an OK person, that he can lose the weight. This guy reminds me of the Democratic party—always looking for someone to do something for them. If this guy was willing to make an effort, he could solve his own problems for himself."

In suburbia, voters are looking for someone to offer a product that fits their needs—educating their children, protecting their environment, and keeping law and order.

They are not ideological, at least not in the traditional sense. They don't see Democrats as the party of the little guy, Republicans as the party of big business. Actually, like most of their contemporaries, they identify with neither big business nor labor. They identify with small business because entrepreneurs, people they knew and grew up with, fueled the economic boom of the 1980s.

This economic boom occurred because Pam and her peers were the best-educated group of voters in history, an asset that will increase with time. By the early 1990s, three in five high school graduates had some college education, compared to a 1968 electorate in which only one in four voters had taken some college classes. One in five people between 25-29 have a college degree compared to one in ten in 1960.

This higher educational level, in addition to producing a more prosperous population less susceptible to Democratic class warfare, was another boost for the GOP because of the attitudes that education instilled. The most far-reaching implication was the increasing tendency to discard the traditional view that the federal government was the answer. Many of them had been liberal in college during the sixties and early seventies. But with marriage and children, they adopted the conservativism of their parents—even more so, because they lacked the historical ties to the Democratic party brought on by the Depression.

As Naisbitt observed, society was moving in a way that fit the GOP general approach: "Think globally, act locally." The slogan became a bumper sticker; the federal government was not where the action was.

In the 1980s and early 1990s it was governors, not presidents, who were proposing the bold new programs to deal with domestic problems. Polls showed people believed they could influence their own lives by activism on the local level, and they took local issues seriously—from the location of a garbage dump to that of a nuclear power plant. But they had trouble doing the same with the burgeoning but abstract federal deficit or the clowns in Washington who couldn't handle that or any other problem.

The emerging allegiance to the GOP of the American middle class because of their higher education was evident in the 1988 voting. ABC's exit polls showed Dukakis carried a majority of the 7 percent of voters who did not have a high school diploma (the very poor) and won half of the 15 percent of the electorate that had postgraduate college degrees (intellectuals, academics, and teachers), but lost the 78 percent of the voters in between. It showed that when it came to education, as with income, the Democrats were losing the huge bloc of voters in the middle.

The higher educational level of the boomers produced a work force that was markedly different from that of the long-gone smokestack economy. The new work force was more willing to challenge the status quo at work, more eager to run its own business, and less likely to belong to unions. Those differences worked to the Republicans' advantage.

Ralph Whitehead, Jr., a University of Massachusetts professor, is a pioneer in examining the lives of these baby-boom voters. Whitehead, who played a role in Michael Dukakis' campaigns for governor but never had much impact on his 1988 presidential effort, realizes that the Democratic image of the blue-collar worker is out of step with reality. He has dubbed the roughly 30 million workers (40 percent of the baby-boom generation) who toil in service industries as the "new collars." Almost all are high school graduates, and many have college credits or even a degree.

"Neither manual laborers nor coat-and-tie professionals, they make their living in the rapidly growing range between those two extremes. They often avoid the grime and regimentation of blue-collar workers," Whitehead maintains.[4]

The typical blue-collar worker of yesteryear was Ralph Kramden, the bus-driving character of the 1950s' TV series "The Honeymooners." He was a World War II veteran, drank shots-and-beers, and had a wife who didn't work outside the home. He was a Democrat because he was a little guy and that's what little guys were.

Whitehead's typical "new collar" is a Federal Express truck

driver who, unlike his blue-collar predecessors in a smokestack economy, has a great deal of autonomy. His education gives him the skills to design his own route and handle the company's high-tech delivery system. His business didn't even exist a generation ago. In fact, it was the slowness of the U.S. Post Office and United Parcel Service—unionized, large, inflexible organizations—that allowed Federal Express to give their workers the flexibility that allowed the firm to become the standard in the overnight package delivery business.

Today's "new-collar" counterpart drinks less and probably didn't serve in the military. Because he or she works in newer industries, he or she is unlikely to be unionized. "New-collar" workers, like the entire baby-boom generation, are wary of anything that stifles their individuality—big unions, big government, big business.

The other big chunk of the baby-boomers, 35 percent of new workers, according to Whitehead, are "bright collars." They hold many of the same jobs as white-collar workers of previous genera-tions, but are younger, more individualistic, and less likely to respect institutions or eschew risk. They are more inclined toward entrepreneurial pursuits.

"Bright-collar" families are as different from their white-collar predecessors as the "thirtysomething" crowd is from June and Ward Cleever of "Leave It To Beaver." The nineties group is less likely to be married, has fewer children, and looks at life differently.

The typical "bright collar" is a computer software engineer who is constantly testing his ability to manage a computer. He is most likely doing a job that either wasn't done a generation ago, or was done manually.

The differences between the "bright collars" and the traditional white-collar voters of years past, just as between the "new-collar" voters and their blue-collar predecessors, include a differing view of economic and social change. The older groups see change as creat-ing problems for America because it did for them. "Bright-" and "new-collar" voters, on the other hand, like economic change be-cause for the most part it has worked to their advantage. That attracts them to Republicans, because they welcome a changing society and find ways to profit from it.

The suburbs—North and South, and especially in the electoral gold mine of California—are filled with voters who inhabit "mall-America." Because of the value of individuality drummed into them at work and at play, they are voting Republican.

"I don't think this is a shift from a Democratic milieu to a Republican milieu," Democratic pollster Greenberg explained, "but it's a shift from an institutional Democratic milieu to a deinstitutionalized setting in which partisanship is almost of no consequence. But there are values associated with that new lifestyle that tend to push people more toward becoming Republicans."

National Demographics & Lifestyles, the Denver-based marketing firm, did an analysis of almost two million such families and found a group that, like Pam and Mark Blips, is focusing inward. This white middle class likes home computers, household tools, and the Bible. They bowl, hunt, and fish; they do not play racquetball or tennis, nor do they ski. They skip the ballet, fancy restaurants, and antiquing, in preference to renting movies for the VCR and buying take-out pizza. Boomers are dedicated to hearth and home and have a distinct Sun Belt orientation. Their lifestyle, that is, differs widely from the high profile, fast-paced life of the Northeastern United States—the last remaining bastion of Democratic America.

The people who ran the Republican party in the 1980s—and its presidential campaigns—came from the Sun Belt and understood how to reach these middle-class voters. Democrats like Ron Brown and Paul Kirk came from the Northeast, as did the Dukakis crowd. By the time Mondale became the presidential nominee, he, like his people, had become a thorough Washingtonian. On the other hand, Reagan and Bush, and GOP chairs Atwater and Frank Fahrenkopf, came from the Sun Belt. The same pattern continued down the ranks of the two camps, manifesting itself in thousands of ways that reinforced the two parties' images.

"We don't understand what is happening in the South and the West, the fact that a lot of these folks have a different set of values," said former House Democratic Whip Tony Coelho, a Californian. "Some of our people say, 'they don't care about poor people.' That is a quick, knee-jerk reaction that Eastern liberals have. It isn't true.

They care as much, but they have a different way of looking at it. The Northeast basically is an older area, more tradition bound.

"In the South and the West, they are more entrepreneurial. They look for different ways to do things . . . .It's just a different attitude. That's where the country is moving, to a Western and Southern middle-class suburban lifestyle. We Democrats, because the party is controlled by the Northeasterners, have a problem. Their values are different than the values in the West and the South. We need to understand that. If we don't, we're not going to get back the White House."

There was no better example than the music.

In the spring of 1984 Sara Long, a slim, attractive twenty-nine-year-old blond from Evansville, Indiana, as typical a middle-American city as exists, was a scheduler for the Reagan-Bush campaign. She had been dating Doug Watts, a sandy-haired Californian who was heading the "Tuesday Team," the group of Madison Avenue professionals assembled to handle the campaign's advertising. One day, after she'd been blown away by a country & western song she'd heard on the radio—and she didn't usually go for country—she asked Watts if he ever listened to country & western.

"Occasionally," he answered, but he hadn't heard the newly released Lee Greenwood song. So she ran out, got her roommate's tape, and played "God Bless the USA" for him.

"The first time I heard it on the radio, I cried," she remembered. "I figured if I reacted that way, it would probably affect other people the same way. "God bless the USA" was the way we all felt about things on the campaign. Everyone was beginning to feel good about being an American again. I felt sort of strongly about it. That song summed up what a lot of people were thinking and feeling. It brought in defending the country, being proud to be an American. It was like he had written it for us. Those were the themes we were working on at that point."

Watts immediately recognized the powerful music and the lyrics that began:

If tomorrow all the things were gone I'd worked for all my life;
And I have to start again with just my children and my wife;
I'd thank my God above to be living here today;
Cause the flag still stands for freedom and they can't take that
   away.

Coming from California, Watts figured the rights to the song
were controlled by the Hollywood money men who were notorious
liberals. He told Long it wasn't worth the trouble, but she wouldn't
be deterred. She went into a neighboring office to see Sig Rovich,
who had just come east from Las Vegas, where he had run the city's
largest advertising agency. Rovich, who would become President
Bush's chief image-maker in 1990, had a feel for average voters
since those were the kind of people to whom he'd peddled soap. He
was immediately sold on the song, and when Watts tried to talk him
out of it, Rovich waved him off.

Rovich knew that Greenwood, a former Las Vegas casino dealer,
was from Nevada and figured he could get his permission. He was
right. Greenwood, a Reagan fan, was flattered. Greenwood's only
request: would it be possible for him to meet the president sometime?

So, in what was without doubt the best political film in American history, the $450,000, eighteen-minute movie shown at the
GOP convention showed Reagan marking the fortieth anniversary
of the D-Day invasion. He was reading a gut-wrenching letter from
the daughter of a Normandy veteran who had died of cancer eight
years before. In the crowd, gathered on a bluff that overlooked the
Normandy beaches, the woman sat with her father's war buddies,
now gray-haired or balding. They wept openly as Reagan read her
letter to the memory of her father, who had often talked to her as a
young girl about what he had been through there.

" 'I'll never forget what you went through, Dad, nor will I let
anyone else forget. And, Dad, I'll always be proud,' " Reagan read
the young woman's words. Hand-in-hand with wife Nancy, Reagan walked through a military cemetery putting flowers on graves.
And Greenwood sang, "I'm proud to be an American, where at
least I know I'm free. And I won't forget the men who died, who

gave that right to me. And I'll gladly stand up next to you and defend her still, 'Cause there ain't no doubt I love this land. God Bless the USA."

The night the movie was shown at the 1984 GOP convention there weren't many dry eyes in America watching on television, even among hardened Democrats. The movie was excerpted in countless GOP commercials, and Greenwood's song was standard fare at almost every Reagan or Bush appearance during the 1984 and 1988 campaigns. The song became a Republican anthem and Greenwood a GOP campaign staple. "It thrills me to death to be around the people running the country," said Greenwood.[5]

He was very partisan, and when the Democrats played the song once during their 1988 convention, Greenwood was aghast. "I have been associated with the Republican party. We are doing things with the Bushes and Reagans," said an annoyed Greenwood.

"God Bless the USA" came to symbolize the GOP the way that "This Land is Your Land" had symbolized the Democrats decades earlier. And Pam Blips—and without doubt millions of other middle-class voters—could sing you the Lee Greenwood song without missing a beat.

It wasn't just that they remembered the song. It was that for millions of Americans it captured the way they felt about life. Liberal Democrats would mock the emotion, focusing on the nation's problems and how the glass was half-empty, not half-full. But in suburbia, Pam Blips' reaction was pretty typical.

"I wake up every morning and count my blessings I don't live in another country. I realize we are very fortunate to have what we have, and we don't have a whole lot. But, there are a lot of people worse off. I really didn't know I would be as happy and content with my life as I am. I think I doubted it would turn out this well. I never realized I would meet someone like Mark and have children as wonderful as Madison and Murphy."

"The Republicans don't do [this sort of thing] by accident," said former House Democratic leader Coelho. "Picking the song is a process. We pick it as something the candidate wants, or that reflects his experience. We don't look at politics as a business and understand our market."

As Coelho knows, the Democrats seem to make symbolic choices like these almost as an afterthought. The Democratic music from the 1984 and 1988 campaigns prove Coelho's point. Given the Northeastern orientation of those in Democratic campaigns, it's no wonder they never thought about country & western, even though a 1986 Harris poll said more Americans—especially those old enough to vote and motivated to do so—prefer Country & Western over any other type of music. During both the 1984 and 1988 campaigns, the Democrats stuck with the music of rock star Bruce Springsteen. It reflected Springsteen's popularity and ignored the fact that the core of his fans were the young, the least likely to vote. Much of Springsteen's music, moreover, was a celebration of the declining America that Democrats were trying to save.

In 1984, the year Democrats picked Ferraro as the first woman on a national ticket, the song Americans remembered from the convention was "Celebrate"—a high-energy song that began as a hit on the soul charts and went over like a lead balloon in Middle America. It may have energized blacks and feminists excited by Ferraro's selection, but it did nothing to help expand the party's base.

No one in the 1984 Democratic convention hierarchy is willing to claim paternity for the selection of "Celebrate," although convention manager Roz Wyman remembers that someone in the Mondale organization thought it was a nice song. But, as with the Springsteen music, little thought was given to it—or to the message it sent.

The irony is that in 1984, the Democrats had gone to the trouble of commissioning Carly Simon to write an uplifting song to which Middle America could relate. In fact, Middle America loved it, but not in connection with the Democrats. "The Turning of the Tide" was played—but not prominently—a couple of times early in the 1984 convention. It wasn't until four years later that the song caught on—as the theme for the movie *Working Girl*.

11

Jesse Jackson Scares the Middle Class

Jesse Jackson held the almost all-white crowd of 2,500 people in the palm of his hand. As usual, he had arrived more than an hour late. But the crowd, packed thigh-to-thigh on the bleachers, hundreds of whom had arrived more than an hour early, didn't mind. They cheered, stomped, and tried to touch him as he walked into the rally with the sound system blaring "Here Comes the Sun." Most of all they couldn't take their eyes off him.

It was difficult to understand how the people who filled the Sheboygan, Wisconsin, armory on that chilly spring afternoon five days before the state's 1988 presidential primary could have been Jackson voters. Sheboygan, located on the shores of Lake Michigan, was a prosperous and mostly homogeneous Dutch-German community. With only a handful of black families in the city, 80 percent of the voters were from white, blue-collar families, the sort Jackson had rarely been able to crack.

Sheboygan's 3 percent unemployment rate allowed Mayor Richard Schneider to brag, "We don't know what poverty is." The city of 49,000 people (and fifty-one churches) had the nation's second lowest poverty and crime rates. When Jackson stood in front of the crowd, his arms outstretched, he asked those with friends who had died or gone to jail because of drugs—a staple of his stump speech—to stand. Hardly anyone did. Someone in the exceedingly polite crowd explained that booze was Sheboygan's worst social problem.

Jackson nevertheless delivered his rhythmic "down with dope, up with hope" speech, called for more government programs for the poor, and laced it all with biting criticism of corporate America and the Reagan administration. Cheers and three standing ovations echoed through the former basketball arena built a half-century before by the WPA, a massive Depression-era government program of the sort Jackson wanted to resurrect. The reaction was almost as thunderous as he typically got in inner-city black neighborhoods.

"We can feel the vibrations here," Jackson bellowed. "We're shifting from racial battleground to economic common ground and moral higher ground. Something is going on."

And so it seemed at the time.

"This is amazing," Jackson would tell his aides in the car after events like this. He called them "serious white" events because of the crowd's middle-class nature. As it turned out, although he could reach these voters emotionally, he couldn't do so electorally. But "America is getting better," he would say.

Watching Jackson that day made even professional cynics agree with him that just maybe he *could* become president. Jackson, after all, is a master politician. Senator Robb of Virginia, who differs with Jackson on most political matters, calls Jackson "the most gifted political communicator on the scene today." And no one could disagree. In addition to his rhetorical ability, Jackson has an uncanny feel for people. He can read crowds, even hostile ones, and turn them to his advantage.

A month earlier Jackson had been in a debate in Williamsburg, Virginia, sponsored by the centrist Democratic Leadership Council. The DLC, headed by Robb, was composed of those who had created a southern regional primary to block liberals like Jackson from the nomination. That night, Jackson was walking into the lion's den and knew it. In his opening statement, he thanked Robb for helping create the regional primary, which had backfired and actually helped Jackson. His quip broke the tension and so convulsed Arkansas Governor Clinton, sitting in the front row next to Robb, that he almost fell off his chair.

In another example, shortly after the October 1987 stock market crash, Jackson told a group of Wall Street executives, "I was watching it on TV and heard them refer to it as Black Monday. Funny, though, I didn't see any black faces on the screen. I saw a lot of red faces and some green. And some pretty pale white ones."[1]

One of Jackson's favorite approaches, especially in dealing with the suspicion that he wanted to cut the defense budget in order to pour money into the cities, was to switch the audience's thinking from the threat of the Soviet military to that of Japanese business. "How many of you own VCRs?" he would ask. Virtually everyone would raise hands. Then Jackson would ask, "How many of you own MX missiles?" and when no one responded, he would quip, "See, we're making what nobody is buying."

But in Sheboygan the crowd certainly wasn't hostile, and he played it like a fiddle. Jackson was given some of the city's renowned cheese. Instead of handing it to an aide as other candidates were wont to do, he opened it, put some on his finger and ate it. Given the time and a stove, he'd probably have grilled the bratwurst and eaten it right there on the stage. He was a showman and a crowd pleaser, not only that day in Sheboygan, but every day and everywhere.

But when the television cameras left and the polls closed five days later, Jackson lost Sheboygan 2-1 to Michael Dukakis. And the Dukakis rally, be it recalled, had been a tame and under-attended affair.

It all made perfect sense to Tom Peneski, the city alderman and math professor at the University of Wisconsin's Sheboygan campus who organized the Jackson rally: "People came and cheered who knew they weren't going to vote for Jesse, but they just wanted to see him. They're nervous about his agenda, they see it as a black agenda. And they think he is too liberal."

Mayor Schneider remembered thinking at Jackson's rally that he would do better than he did. But in retrospect he realized that the crowd was "there to see a celebrity, not because of their true political feelings. They just wanted a chance to be with him, to touch

him. The thing is, they weren't there because they were considering voting for him. There's just a mystique about Jesse Jackson. If it
had been Frank Sinatra it probably would have been the same."

And that, in a nutshell, explains—partly—why Jackson dominates television coverage of Democratic campaigns and loses badly
in elections. But there is a vastly more important reason, the one
least talked about in polite company, especially by whites, but
understood perfectly by blacks.

Jackson "scares [white] people," stated Jerry Austin, Jackson's
1988 campaign manager. Barbara Jordan, the black former Texas
congresswoman, who will be forever remembered as the conscience of the House impeachment of President Nixon, told Jackson
publicly, "Don't frighten everybody off. Don't be so volatile that
people become afraid to associate with us."

"There's no question" that Jackson alienates most white voters,
agreed Atlanta Congressman John Lewis, a quiet pugnacious man
who, like Jackson, grew up dirt poor in the South but with neither
Jackson's looks nor media skills. Unlike Jackson, Lewis—whose
balding pate is scarred from beatings suffered at the hands of white
cops a generation ago—has moved from the politics of confrontation to the politics of consensus. "Maybe two years from now or ten
years from now things will change," Lewis mused. "Maybe people
will get to know him better." Maybe then "he would not create the
same misgivings and fears that he does. The voters are very intelligent. They can see through a lot of rhetoric. They know when a
person is trying to pull something over them, or be sincere. There's
something about Jesse that doesn't ring right with a lot of voters,"
he added.

It's not that the men and women who lead the Democratic party
nationally aren't as perceptive as Lewis. They're just not as candid.
Publicly, they describe Jackson only in positive terms, ignoring his
political liabilities among whites. Comprehensive data on Jackson's
white supporters is scarce because there are too few of them in
primaries to be able to come up with precise measurements.

After all, Jackson got only one in eight white votes in the 1988
Democratic primaries among the most liberal group of whites
imaginable. The overall white electorate is massively less sympa-

thetic to Jackson's politics and markedly less susceptible to liberal guilt. Candidates who need white votes to win are reluctant to ask Jackson to campaign for them. Andrew Young, during his unsuccessful 1990 campaign for Georgia governor, put it succinctly, if in an understated way: "What I need to win this race is help with white voters, and I don't think Jesse would be a great deal of help."

Exit polls from the 1988 Democratic primaries show that Jackson's white support comes mostly from moderate- and upper-income voters with college and graduate degrees. In the 1988 California and New York primaries, for instance, CBS-*New York Times* exit polls showed his white supporters were roughly 50 percent more likely than the electorate as a whole to have a college degree, 25 percent more likely to have incomes of more than $35,000, and three times as likely to call themselves liberals. They truly fit the "limousine liberal" label. Perhaps the best evidence of that was how few if them lived in suburbia—the heartbeat of America.

Democratic leaders and candidates refuse to consider what Jackson's own local organizer in Sheboygan takes as gospel: that Jackson is instinctively seen by much of white America as alien to their way of life. These elite leaders think the idea is racist. They cling to Ron Brown's mantra-like explanation of Jackson's politics as mainstream: "He's frankly where a majority of the American people are on most issues. If you take it issue by issue—there's some divergence on some—but not way out in left field. On most things, particularly in the 1988 campaign, his common sense stands out on issues. If another candidate, with a different style, had said the same things, there wouldn't have been an uproar."

Actually, given what middle-class America thinks, if another candidate without Jackson's flair and media savvy were to run on his platform, he or she would not be taken seriously. The only things Jackson and most white voters have in common are the lofty goals of peace and prosperity. But when Jackson's values are translated into specific policies, they become troublesome to Middle America.

"When you talk about expanding services as he does consistently, these are people who believe it will be coming out of their pocket," Mike Espy, the black Mississippi congressman, states. "He wails for those on the lower side; he's not speaking the language of those in the middle. Middle-class America feels like it has the most to lose."

No one would argue with Jackson's high-profile opposition to drugs, yet even there his proposals reeked of the "blame society, not the individual" attitude that Americans were increasingly rejecting. He blamed Reagan and Bush for not stopping the drugs from crossing U.S. borders, opposed capital punishment for major drug dealers or drug-crazed murderers, and gave budgetary priority to programs that would treat drug users over those that would penalize them.

On another subject entirely—foreign affairs—Jackson's proposals were even more alien to the white middle class. He was chummy with the Palestine Liberation Organization and Cuba's Fidel Castro, neither of which win popularity contests in "mall-America." He also seemed to oppose any use of American force overseas, blasting Bush's popular invasion of Panama and charging, inaccurately it turned out, that U.S. soldiers killed more civilians there than the Chinese did in their 1989 slaughter of student demonstrators in Tiananmen Square. And he adamantly opposed Bush's 1991 Persian Gulf War policy. To the millions like Pam Blips, Jackson fit nicely the description that Reagan's UN ambassador Jeanne Kirkpatrick gave to the Democrats—the "blame America first" crowd.

Moreover, to a middle class fed up with the federal government taking their tax dollars for programs perceived as mostly helping blacks, Jackson's desire to hike taxes to finance even larger social programs raised a giant STOP sign.

Jackson's central domestic initiative also sounded warning bells. On the surface it seemed like a wonderful idea. He proposed that 10 percent of all public pension funds—the retirement money socked away by teachers and civil servants—be invested in programs to rebuild America's cities. Jackson wanted to use that money for projects considered too risky to attract private investment. In essence, he was saying the taxpayers should assume the risk. Jackson spoke for the poor, unemployed, homeless, and dispossessed. His message did not resonate with the mass of Americans.

"The middle-income family that owns their own home looks at

JESSE JACKSON SCARES THE MIDDLE CLASS   243

Jesse Jackson's prescription for America and says this guy is not in my world," opined former Republican presidential candidate Pete du Pont.

That middle-income family, correctly or not, thinks it knows more than enough about Jackson to pass judgment. Jackson is without doubt America's best-known Democrat. He is also a unique figure in American history. No potential presidential candidate has ever held the public attention nor the allegiance of such a large constituent group for so long outside of a major elective position. Whether Jackson runs in 1992 or not, he will seek to mold the party and its candidates in a way that will remind the middle class why it is suspicious of Democrats.

In effect, Austin believes Jackson has become "a professional candidate. He does it very well. No one is better at getting free publicity. He goes to Africa and winds up with a picture on the front page of the *New York Times* talking about how the Angola leader thinks black Americans should be called African-Americans." The most obvious reason is that in a media age he is almost made for television.

But that analysis, as with much that is critical of him, is also too simplistic. Jackson is one of those larger-than-life figures that comes along every generation or so. And he knows it.

Austin, a blunt and perceptive Jewish boy from Brooklyn who grew up loving sports and leftist politics, makes a living running Democratic campaigns in Ohio. Austin knows how to count. He played basketball for a Hunter College team that won three out of forty games—"I made a half-court shoot at the buzzer and we still lost by forty-two points. I knew what losing was about." So, once it became clear that Jackson's 1988 campaign could not win, that it was becoming the Jackson crusade, he wanted no part of it. He began telling reporters the game was over and, without asking his boss, suggested Jackson as Dukakis' running mate. Jackson, unused to anyone but himself deviating from the party line, brought in Ron Brown over Austin's head for the convention.

For two months Austin retained his title of campaign manager, but he had no power.[6] Austin's exit talk with Jackson tells much about the man. It was early August of 1988, and if truth be told, both were happy to be parting company. " 'Jerry, this all started in 1963 and you played a role in a chapter in a big story,' " Austin remembered Jackson saying. "He was not just thinking of himself as leading a crusade for the Democratic nomination for blacks and minorities, he was seeing himself as a world leader. He sees this as an international thing he is involved in."

Jackson and Austin sat in lawn chairs on a patch of grass off to the side of Jackson's fifteen-room stone house in an integrated middle-class neighborhood on the South side of Chicago where Jackson lived before moving to D.C. in 1989. There was a basketball hoop over the back patio where Jackson and his youngest son, Yusef, who won a football scholarship to the University of Virginia, often played two-on-two against Secret Service agents. The house was filled with pictures of Jackson with world leaders, and one with rock star Michael Jackson. There was also a gold record of Stevie Wonder. Among the decorations on the walls were gifts brought back from his travels—including spears and shields from African leaders.

And some real surprises too, at least for those who think of Jackson in terms of politics and his former habit of dressing in dashikis—pictures of two of his sons, Jesse, Jr., and Jonathan, in their North Carolina military school uniforms. Family is important to Jackson, the son of an unwed mother.

Bob Beckel remembered that during his time as Mondale's campaign manager in the 1984 Democratic convention, he went to Jackson's suite to negotiate the final deal to guarantee Jackson's support for the general election. Beckel, a stocky former football player whose relationship with Jackson over the years has resembled a roller coaster ride, brought his mother along. Beckel's seventy-year-old mother waited in the living room of Jackson's suite while her son went into the bedroom for the high-stakes meeting. About twenty minutes into the negotiating session, well before the issues were settled, Beckel off-handedly mentioned his mother's admiration for him and that she was waiting outside to have her picture taken with him.

"You've had your mother sitting outside while you were talking to me?" Jackson thundered. He promptly got up and went out into the outer room. "He said, 'You have to respect your mother,' " and Jackson then spent the next twenty-five minutes talking with her. "He was charming as hell," Beckel remembered. About a year later Ellen Beckel broke her ankle in an accident. Beckel doesn't know how Jackson found out, but when he did, he called her.

Despite his taste for luxury, Jackson has a down-home quality. Although he almost lives on airplanes he dislikes flying, often taking an aspirin before take-off and curling up with a Walk-Man playing soul music to help him sleep.

He eats two small boxes of raisin bran and hot water for breakfast and the rest of the day, fittingly, he craves "soul food." At almost every campaign stop local supporters show up with mounds of fried chicken, fried fish, corn bread, sweet potato pies, hush puppies, and greens. "Food, serious food," Jackson bellows, welcoming the offerings to his suite. A staple of the Jackson travel bag is a notebook with the names of every soul food restaurant in America, although Jackson's culinary taste—the fried food—exacerbates his gout.

Austin, who likes Jackson's politics despite their falling out, thinks that "when white voters have become exposed to him in person they are not so scared. The image he has in many peoples' minds—which I think is unfounded at this point—is that of a rabble-rousing dissident from Chicago. That is his past. If you are not exposed to Jesse Jackson other than the clips on TV you are not going to see the real Jesse Jackson.

"He sees himself as addressing issues that no one else does, and standing up for people no one else does," Austin continues. "He sees himself as one of the few people who will take on issues other people don't because they aren't universally popular. He marches to the beat of his own drummer. He doesn't work for anyone but himself. He goes where and when he wants. He's going to be around a long time as a political force. . . . The speech you saw at the Democratic convention was probably only the eighth or ninth best speech of 1988."

Parts of Jackson's message, especially the accent on taking care of America's domestic needs above all else, plays in Middle America.

"They love his 'let's take care of our own' approach. They view it as an antiforeign, insular, nationalistic message. But they explicitly say 'right message, wrong messenger.' They could never see themselves voting for Jesse Jackson," pollster Stan Greenberg believes.

Maybe that explains something Austin never quite understood.

"I can't prove it, but I'm willing to bet that a quarter to a third of the [202,000] people that contributed to Jesse Jackson did not vote for him. They contributed because they wanted the issues to be out, but they couldn't vote for him," Austin said. "They believed in his ideas, but didn't think he should be their president."

Perhaps those contributions reflect the mixed emotions Jackson brings out in almost everyone.

Jackson is "a mass of contradictions. He's the most complex, multifaceted, interesting, contradictory, deep guy in this whole thing," Bruce Babbitt remarked after a long pause. "He is at once brilliant and demagogic; idealistic and self-aggrandizing. The less admirable episodes are well known. Most of them have been in the past. He is both liked and feared in the black community. You talk to the civil rights leaders of the sixties; for every one that likes him another says he's opportunistic and untrustworthy. His behavior and political and personal conduct have shown an enormous capacity for growth. People change.

"The bottom line is the guy is larger than life both in his flaws and strengths and abilities. That's what makes him so difficult to get hold of because we live in an era of homogenized politicians, who have minor vices and minor virtues."

In the spring of 1987, Richard Gephardt, then a longshot presidential candidate, was explaining how he planned to win. Gephardt, the 1980s Democratic young man in a hurry, was having one of dozens of the breakfasts he initiated with reporters to hustle for coverage.

So clean-cut in appearance he almost squeaked, Gephardt went through his game plan of how a win in Iowa's opening caucuses could propel him to the forefront of the race. He talked as he ate his bran muffins and drank his grapefruit juice and black coffee in the

House members dining room, a historic-looking restaurant with painted ceilings, large mirrors trimmed in gold, and a maitre d' in black tie, even at 8 A.M.

Then came the question that he and the other Democratic aspirants were asked regularly: "How will you deal with Jesse Jackson?" Gephardt, whose answers often seemed preprogrammed, as if he were just turning on the tape recorder, batted that one away in his usual manner. "I will treat Jesse Jackson just like any other candidate," he predicted. But of course Gephardt, an early proponent of slash-and-burn politics, didn't. And neither did the other Democrats, nor, for that matter, the media.

Democratic pollster Geoff Garin believed, "There is concern of having a policy difference become confused with a personal attack. And the truth is a lot of these guys haven't figured out how to keep that distinction clear. It is to Jackson's interest to keep that distinction blurred."

"I have never believed Democrats need to distance themselves from him. I think the Democrats need to disagree with him," Arkansas' Clinton responded. "A lot of traditional white liberals get uptight and pull back, but they don't ever explicitly disagree with Jackson" because they worry their ideological differences will be taken as a racial slight.

And it wasn't just the other candidates that treated Jackson differently. Jackson rightly complained that for much of the 1988 campaign, TV and newspaper reporters concentrated on asking what he wanted out of the campaign. This did him a disservice by implicitly refusing to consider for their audience the possibility that he could win the presidential nomination—presumably the reason all candidates run.

Of course, Jackson also benefited greatly from this double standard. Perhaps because the media didn't think he could win, perhaps because they bent over backwards to avoid charges of racism, they treated Jackson (and his ideas) more gingerly than they did the other candidates. In fact, a study by the Center for Media and Public Affairs, a D.C.-based media research group, found that 75 percent of the network coverage of Jackson during the campaign had been positive, 20 points higher than that for any of the other candidates.

The other Democratic aspirants had no doubts that he benefited from a double standard. The only question was whether it stemmed from liberal guilt, as Babbitt believed, or from political fear. Once the other Democratic candidates got on the campaign trail, they went after each other's jugulars but wouldn't say boo to Jackson.

Because of his experience in the 1984 campaign and his innate talent, Jackson was by far the best debater of them all. The others would take a day off to be briefed before debates. Not Jackson. He'd just huddle with his issues people on the plane for an hour. Despite his lack of preparation, he had a knack for saying the right thing to get on the network news.

"He knows the country better than anyone else," opined Bob Borosage, Jackson's top issues advisor and a fellow of the Institute for Policy Studies, a very liberal D.C. think tank. "He's dealt with everyone from people on the Southside of Chicago [to] the president of Ford Motor Co. Whenever he's stuck, he has a personal experience to draw from. A lot of these guys are '3x5 card' guys. If you asked Dukakis any question twice he'd give you a 3x5 card in a different order. Congressmen had a slightly easier time because they have dealt with a lot of these issues. But they get caught into their Washington background and see issues in terms of legislation and have ridiculous conversations about 'I supported this and you supported that' and no one knows what they are talking about. Jackson doesn't do that. He has a worldview. People understand what he stands for. He's a tough guy to take on. There is a lot of posturing about challenging him but there is widespread fear he might take them apart."

Jackson never attacked the white candidates. He knew he didn't need to worry about his black base. He understood the way to get to white voters was to give them as much positive information about himself as possible, which he did through his debates since he lacked the money for large-scale TV buys.

The sometimes fierce attacks during the Democratic debates that the media focused on were actually telegraphed punches. The Democratic primary contenders had an unstated agreement that if they were going to attack someone during a debate, they would warn him beforehand. The only candidate who did not observe that ground rule was Sen. Al Gore of Tennessee. Gore was also the only Democratic candidate to criticize Jackson's proposals, although making sure that nothing could be construed as personal. Yet when he found himself taking flak from party insiders, he backed off.

Pure and simple, Democrats are afraid to confront Jackson, not only because of their liberal guilt and his behind-the-scenes maneuvering, but because of his hold on black voters.

"I can give you the right answer," offered former Dukakis campaign manager Estrich. "You deal with him like you deal with every other candidate. Say when you agree or disagree. But Jesse in many other respects is not like another candidate. There is no other candidate who speaks for a constituency as strongly and clearly as Jesse does, the treatment of whom carries so many symbols with it."

Jackson's hold on the black vote is tighter than that of any American politician on any ethnic group. Blacks, even middle-class blacks whose economic situation opens them to more mainstream political appeals, view him with awe. He received more than nine out of ten black votes in the 1988 Democratic primaries.

Jackson and black America are immensely proud of his 1988 showing, and rightly so. His 1,218 delegates are the most ever received by a second-place finisher—although, in part, that was due to his unwillingness to toss in the towel when he was realistically eliminated, as others had done. He won almost 7 million votes, roughly Mondale's total in 1984 when he won the nomination.

Jackson has become an inspirational role model to black youth, replacing sports and entertainment stars, and has inspired in much of black America the belief that anything is possible.

It was this side of Jesse Jackson that made such a positive impression on white America.

"What he is doing is tremendously important to the business of politics in the long term," stated then House Democratic whip Coelho. "In effect, he is saying to young blacks, 'You can dream about being president of the United States.' It is so important for young blacks to feel they can be part of the American dream, that they don't have to be part of the welfare system."

Jackson has also made some progress with whites. In January

1984, at the beginning of his first presidential campaign, a CBS-*New York Times* poll showed 16 percent of white Democrats viewed him favorably, 48 percent unfavorably. Four years later, beginning his second presidential campaign, the same poll showed his favorable rating among whites had risen to 24 percent and his unfavorable had fallen to 36 percent. After the 1988 presidential campaign Jackson's ratings fell somewhat because he was less newsworthy. By the spring of 1990 the same poll showed 20 percent of whites viewed him favorably, 42 percent unfavorably. But, should he return to the presidential campaign trail his ratings might well climb again.

"No one would have opened up a conference eight years ago with me discussing foreign policy," Jackson said in late 1990, and he was right. "The argument then was, 'You at best know civil rights, you can't talk about the big stuff.' Well, I could talk about the big stuff then, but I can really talk about it now. I've been to places where other people [American politicians] are afraid to meet with the leaders."

By any measure, Jackson is a major player in American politics.

Jackson loved to tell of his appearance in Beaumont, Texas, in March of 1988. As he spoke, a tall, slim man with a mustache who was a chemical workers union organizer walked up to Austin and told him how much he admired Jackson and wanted to have his picture taken with the candidate.

It didn't strike Austin as unusual when the man told him he had been at the 1965 Selma marches. But Austin's head jerked when the man continued, "No, I was there with a sheet on my head. I was a klansman." After Jackson finished his speech, Austin brought the ex-klansman over to talk to Jackson.

"That sure is something," mused Jackson, buoyed by fresh evidence that his belief in the redemption of man could turn his crusade into election victories. Even those who didn't agree with him, or shuddered at the thought that he might become president, recognized that Jackson was performing a public service. His "I am somebody" message, preached in ghettos from Harlem to

Houston, and his ability to manipulate the white establishment are what average blacks relate to and admire about Jackson. Unlike Doug Wilder, who has emerged in the eyes of white America as his rival, Jackson's power base is black, and blacks know he won't sell them out.

Whether a white Democrat who aggressively criticized Jackson for his stands on economics, foreign policy, or affirmative action/ quotas would suffer electoral consequences in November is an open question. No one has called his bluff. But even those who tangle tangentially with Jackson find they pay a price with liberals, the most solidly Democratic constituency.

When former Wisconsin Democratic chair Suellen Albrecht, who ran the party in that most progressive of states from 1985-1989, suggested that Jackson's policy proposals be better scrutinized, four black Democratic state lawmakers demanded she resign. After giving up her post and moving to Kentucky, Albrecht claimed that it is widely understood throughout the Democratic party that "when you criticize Jesse you are called a racist."

John Buchanan heads People for the American Way—a group that generally stands with Jackson and the American Civil Liberties Union on civil liberties questions. But he thought Jackson's effort in 1988 to raise money at church services was inappropriate, and said so publicly: "I said something about Jesse Jackson's use of church congregations to raise money being improper and, since Jackson was the target, the reaction it was as if I had broken all ten of the Ten Commandments."

But former New York Mayor Ed Koch paid the highest price for criticizing Jackson. The outspoken mayor said during the 1988 New York primary that Jews like himself would be "crazy" to vote for Jackson because of his position on Israel. And Koch was defeated for his fourth term in 1989; the consensus among New York politicos is that his attack on Jackson triggered his defeat.

"It was not permissible at the time to treat Jesse Jackson like a human being with faults as well as his positive contributions. He was an emotional symbol," Koch said in retrospect.

Austin contends that the flak received from criticizing Jackson notwithstanding, the key to Jackson is to understand that he respects strength: "They need to understand what Jesse is all about, that in order to treat Jesse like everyone else you have to stand up to him when he should be stood up to. He's very good at doing the psychological thing on his opponents."

Dukakis' refusal to tell Jackson up front he was not being seriously considered for vice president exacerbated his problems with Jackson. By maintaining publicly that Jackson was in the running when he was not, Dukakis further alienated him.

"Dukakis' fatal error was the way in which he played with him during the entire period," opined Bill Morton, executive assistant to Jackson during the campaign. Morton, who became DNC Chairman Brown's special assistant, believes that, "If Dukakis had dealt with him straight up and said, 'Jesse, you've got all of these positives, I want you to be an important part of the team, but there are some negatives we can't deal with and I need to win this election,' he wouldn't have had as [many] problems as he did. He would have absolutely respected that if Dukakis had been honest with him."

In fact, the 1988 relationship between Dukakis and Jackson—two very different people and politicians—is a model on how *not* to deal with Jackson.

Dukakis, the analytical, meticulous planner who loves the intricacies of government, has thought about being governor since high school. He hates to condense complex matters into a thirty-second TV clip and he lives in elitist Brookline where everyone professes to love blacks, but knows relatively few of them. Dukakis' idea of a good time is mowing his postage stamp-sized lawn with a push mower. Dukakis is not a social person. He prefers to stay home and study a five-hundred-page briefing book. At a superb outdoor concert by the country music group Alabama at the 1986 National Governors Association meeting in Hilton Head, South Carolina, many of the governors stomped and clapped; Dukakis complained the music was too loud.

Jackson, who never makes decisions until forced to, is almost the polar opposite. He knows and cares little about the intricacies of the bureaucracy. He deals in concepts and big picture ideas, but leaves the details to others. One of the first things Jackson's wife Jackie told Austin when he became campaign manager was that "my husband is not a manager. He's a spiritual leader. He's not into a lot of detail."[2]

Growing up in segregated South Carolina, the civil rights movement's politics of confrontation became Jackson's political model. He learned how to exact concessions from the white establishment by playing to liberal guilt. Having grown up poor, he enjoys the good life. He travels in limousines, his wardrobe is out of *Gentleman's Quarterly*, and he seeks the most luxurious of all hotel suites. He loves to be in front of TV cameras and is a master of the soundbite.

Austin remembers joking with other top Jackson aides that their candidate was the political equivalent of a rock star. "Like a rock star, he would give exhausting performances in his crowd-moving speeches—usually five to seven times a day. Then Jesse would reap the adulation of his audience, moving into it like a celebrity, reaching out, touching and being touched by adoring fans. Like a rock star who insists on Jack Daniels or champagne in his dressing room, Jesse wanted to be catered to. He wanted orange juice or Pepsi and a television set in his holding room before performances."[3]

And, like a professional entertainer, Jackson—as was once said about Robert Kennedy—is at home anywhere. His shoulders are always relaxed, the smile genuine to the onlooker, whether he is on Wall Street or in Watts.

Dukakis' goals were tangible—the nomination, the election, passage of a legislative agenda. Jackson's goals were more ethereal. Not surprisingly, given the history of black-white relations, he insisted above all on being shown respect. Dukakis was color-blind and truly didn't understand Jackson's desire to be treated differently than the other losing candidates.

When they got together privately, the meetings were disasters. Jackson towered over Dukakis physically and—true or not—those on both sides think it affected the diminutive Dukakis. After one of the debates during the California primary, they went up to a hotel room and couldn't sit together. Jackson sat on the edge of a table, Dukakis stood up straight. But Jackson was still taller and Dukakis backed away.

The two men were like oil and water. When Dukakis failed to notify Jackson he had picked Bentsen as his running mate, it struck Jackson as a lack of respect. But despite his anger—and those close to Jackson don't mince words about it—Jackson responded like a man on a mission. He was building toward the eventual goal—the presidency.

Following the 1988 convention, a serious debate raged within Jackson's inner circle over whether he should vigorously support the ticket, given the perceived insult felt by Jackson and insiders like D.C. Mayor Marion Barry, California Congressman Ron Dellums, and some of the most influential black ministers. But Jackson had his eyes firmly set upon the future and knew the problems that he would face if he failed to go all-out for Dukakis. Besides, he told his kitchen cabinet, better to win with Dukakis than suffer another GOP presidency.

That Jackson, the private one, is different from the one seen on TV. Even those who have dealt with him adversarially describe a more restrained but very determined man. It helps explain why he seems to get his way from powerful people who generally don't agree with him.

"He's so good one-on-one. He's so good behind the scenes," insists Charles Manatt, who as Democratic chairman in 1984 frequently clashed with Jackson. "He's so good personally, privately, when the setting is different, that it relieves people because they are so used to the public thing of him banging away. He is obviously charismatic, and a strong . . . enrapturement sets up between you and Jesse when he is talking to you one-on-one."

Duane Garrett, Mondale's 1984 cochair and Babbitt's chairman in 1988, has dealt with Jackson extensively. "Jesse in his handling of other candidates and people of prominence is one of the most skilled handlers of human relationships that you would ever meet. He is a genuinely warm person. He is always personally affectionate when that's proper. He knows how to play that range of human emotions. He likes people and people like him. He is very aware of the small gesture. In every one of the dozen or so small meetings I have been to with him, he has been no less than the coequal. Usually he dominated them. I've seen more people walk into meetings with

Jackson who had a negative mindset about him walk out turned around 180 degrees."

Bruce Babbitt knows just how good Jackson can be in those situations. Despite the wide gulf in their political outlook, in 1988 they were as friendly as rival candidates can get. Jackson likes and respects Babbitt more than any of the other 1988 Democratic candidates because of Babbitt's civil rights record in the sixties. Jackson also understood that Babbitt's support, although narrow, was very deep. Many Democratic activists thought the world of Babbitt, but they didn't support him because they didn't think he could win.

It was February 16, 1988, and as the New Hampshire primary returns came in, Babbitt sat in a third floor suite at the Howard Johnson's Motor Lodge in Manchester, New Hampshire. He realized that a naked man standing outside in the single-degree, snow-piled terrain would have a better chance of surviving the night than his candidacy. He began looking at the final draft of his withdrawal speech.

"It was about 9 P.M.," Babbitt recounted, "and I get a call from only one candidate, Jackson, as my political ship is taking on water and going down. He asks if he can come over. He arrives shortly after that and we go into my hotel suite. We moved everybody out except for Hattie. I said to Hattie, 'I want you to stay. You will remember this.' We got three wood-backed chairs and set them in the middle of a large room. As the three of us sat there, he made the normal Jackson pitch as to why he is a candidate.

"He then looks me straight in the eye and says, 'You can do more for my candidacy than any other American leader at this point. The reason is you were in the streets in Selma, Alabama [during the sixties march]. You understand what this is about. You had the courage to go against the grain then, and you now have an opportunity to do it a second time in a bigger, more dramatic way. You have a chance by endorsing my candidacy to make a statement about principle over personalities. About bringing blacks and whites together. Taking the last step in this evolution of relations between black and white in this country.' "

Babbitt, who believes the "achievements of the sixties have altered our society in the most profound ways," was stunned.

"His appeal was powerful stuff," he recalled. "That 'we have come so far—we have made such a difference. And now we have to put the capstone in place. I am the one who can do it. I can bring American society together. I can lay to rest the divisiveness and racism. Bring us together in one great moment of healing.'

"I'm sitting there shaking my head up and down, saying, 'I understand what you are saying and you are right.' I was thinking, 'You had a lot of say in this campaign and you are entitled to make this pitch,' to say, 'there ought to be prominent white backers.' The appeal was to my heart and I'm shaking my head yes, yes, yes.

"Meanwhile, my head is saying, 'Wait, wait, wait. I am in sympathy with your symbolic role in American politics and although I like you enormously, what it is you are saying—your politics—are not my politics.' Did I rise to it? Yes. 'It's a millennial vision of American society. It's the kind of thing that appeals to Democrats. It's the kind of thing that appeals to me. If there were one chance in a hundred of pulling it off. If I suspend my faculties and judgment about the objective questions, about what is your experience and the platform . . . .'

"I didn't give him a clear answer. I couldn't. I was so moved by it. I wanted to say yes, but I couldn't.

"The next morning at 6:20 A.M. I'm dead asleep in bed. The phone rings and Jesse sounds like he's been up for four-five hours. 'Bruce, we ought to continue that conversation we had last night.' Then he says, 'I've got to go, I'm at the set, watch me.' "

So Bruce and Hattie, sitting on the edge of the bed in their pajamas, watch Jackson's TV interview.

"He's asked about the Middle East and he proceeds to basically ignore the question and answer it as though it was a question about Bruce Babbitt. He looked straight in the camera and made this pitch to me directly, setting aside the other 20 million people watching. 'He's a valiant candidate. He spoke directly to the issues. He cares about the things I care about. He shares some of my experience.'

"The interview's over," Babbitt continued, "and the phone rings soon after. It's Jesse and he says, 'What did you think about that appeal?' At that point I was speechless at that incredible appeal. The bottom line is I, perhaps to my own detriment, view politics as the head over the heart and I could not endorse him."

"If Bruce Babbitt had followed his heart rather than his advisors," Garrett opined, "Jackson might well have gotten him."

That was not an isolated incident. In 1984, Jackson made a similar appeal to Ohio's Democratic power brokers after Sen. John Glenn of Ohio dropped from the presidential race.

That March, Gov. Dick Celeste, House Speaker Vern Riffe, State Treasurer Mary Ellen Withrow, Attorney General Anthony Celebreeze, Secretary of State Sherrod Brown, and Auditor Thomas Ferguson met with Jackson in a suite at Columbus' Sheraton Hotel. While the Democratic heavyweights who had been in Glenn's corner ate their lunch, Jackson made his pitch.

"White politicians stand in line to get my endorsement, but there aren't any white politicians standing in line to endorse me," he told them. "If you want fairness in politics you should endorse me."

"There were a lot of people staring at their shoes during his presentation," one participant remembered. "He did a good job of making folks who might be uncomfortable with Jesse Jackson very comfortable. There was no tension, he was very good at what he was doing. If it had come down to Jackson and Gary Hart, based on Jackson's performance and Hart's at a similar session, Jackson would have walked off with all the endorsements."

And in fact, Jackson's appeal made a strong impression on Celeste, who, however, along with most of the others found they needed to pay back Mondale for past favors. But the governor later leaned heavily on Secretary of State Brown to endorse Jackson. Celeste argued he couldn't do it himself, but since Brown was young, liberal, and a Yalie, it would not hurt him politically. Brown didn't, for a practical political reason: Jackson had supported a black Republican against Brown in 1982.

Why Jackson is such a controversial figure in white America is at best a difficult, and at worst an impossible, question to pin down.

The easy explanation—and with more than a little truth in it—is race.

Democratic Chairman Brown contends that, at least in 1988, "there was an overriding issue with Jackson. There was an overriding impediment with Jackson, which in fact superseded any of these other things, and that was the issue of race. I think it was a factor which was out there above and beyond everything else. So you never got to the other issues with Jackson. It wasn't necessary. You knew there was this one major impediment that would in all likelihood keep it from happening in 1988."

Austin remembers a meeting with Jackson in the candidate's room at the swank Le Meridien Hotel in San Francisco on the eve of the California primary. Although the media had been saying for weeks that his chances for the nomination were gone, all of a sudden it seemed to hit Jackson. And in his view, at least at the time, the reason was clear.

"I am not going to be the nominee of the Democratic party because I'm black, and whites will not vote for a black candidate."

But it was wrong to blame it simply on white racism, as Jackson did when he said, "strong, black males have long been the object of fear" among whites. We do not yet live in a color-blind society. But nonwhite candidates have won by appealing to majority white constituencies across racial and economic lines and by rejecting Jackson's class warfare-oriented solutions. That is how Doug Wilder was elected governor of Virginia and how Henry Cisneros prospered in San Antonio.

Jackson, however, has so far been unable or unwilling to transform himself from a black candidate to a candidate who happens to be black. The differences between the political agendas of whites and blacks mean that candidates who speak for blacks can't win enough white votes in most places to get elected. Jackson understands that distinction, yet he believes he is on the side of the angels and that that supersedes the electoral math.

"We can't be all things to all peoples. We have to determine what side of history we are on," Jackson reasons. "If we are all things to all people we become rather ill-defined, indecisive. Like warm spit."

The other facile explanation for Jackson's inability to win a stronger following among whites is his lack of experience in government.

"One of the things Jesse Jackson has to overcome, which he didn't want to hear, is that Americans consider their vote for president their most cherished vote," Austin stated. "They are used to voting for a vice president, a senator, a governor, but not the head of Operation PUSH. That does not compute in people's minds as being prepared to be president."

But that explanation, too, is a bit simplistic. After all, Dwight Eisenhower, albeit in a different time and place, was elected without political experience. In the last two decades, numerous senators and governors have been elected without previous political experience. It seems highly unlikely that Jackson could win a statewide election anywhere in America except in the 70 percent black District of Columbia.

The real reasons why Jackson can't win the presidency are much more complicated.

"He is for radical change at a time when most middle-class folks want incremental change. If you had a white candidate espousing Jesse Jackson's positions I don't think he would do as well. I don't think the vote is there for that ideology," Celeste says.

Kean of New Jersey believes voters "fear the reaction of the crowds—the fact they see enormous groups of people that are looking like what their memories bring back of Huey Long and Mussolini. That kind of thing. We are brought up to think that people who get reactions from crowds are not to be admired but feared. Americans think of themselves as mainstream. They see Jesse Jackson preaching something that is extreme, something that is black first, or poor first, that is going to be done at the expense of someone else. They may say I see why he does it, but I reject it. They see him as manipulative, being so single-focused that he is willing to do so at the expense of others who are oppressed."

Former vice presidential candidate Ferraro thinks white people are "not quite sure. They think he's racist in a way. They think that if he were to get control, be in power, somehow their futures would be less secure because they would be in the position of being in a minority. In some instances they see him as angry."

In truth, it is all of these things: race, lack of experience, a leftward ideology, and a style that scares average white voters who worry he wants to take from them.

Jackson understands he scares whites, says former traveling aide Morton. "His response would be that Martin Luther King, Jr., was viewed as militant and someone who scared the status quo. But if fear was a factor in improving the lives of people then he [Jackson] would see it as something people will accept as their own inadequacies."

Former campaign manager Austin cautions: "The Jesse Jackson of 1988 may not be the Jesse Jackson of 1992. He moved from 1984 to 1988 to a more centrist position on running within Democratic party lines. I think you'll see more growth in 1992."

Almost as if on Austin's cue, as the nineties opened, Jackson began a concerted effort to work on his problem with white voters. He followed the example of Ronald Reagan after Reagan left the California governorship. Jackson began doing radio commentary and syndicated newspaper columns. As Reagan sought to solidify his support at the time with Republican conservatives, Jackson used the platform to cement his position as the preeminent liberal voice in America. In fact, he went the Gipper one better. Jackson put together a syndicated television talk show aimed at explaining his political slant to the millions of white voters whom he turned off politically.

"For Jackson, who is too often seen on the nightly news yelling at a crowd in a clip and seen as an angry black man, the television show could be a very valuable mechanism of transmission to people who don't hear him on a retail basis," Borosage believes.

And, at times, a different tone could be discerned if Jackson wasn't renouncing government programs, or denying that black progress was thwarted by racism. Especially on the subjects of drugs, urban violence, and the underclass, he began offering a more "bootstrap" approach. Although that line pleased white America, he seemed to make such comments only in heavily black settings, especially churches, and generally when no TV cameras were present. It was as though he could say those things to members of his black family, but doing so before outsiders would be treasonous.

"When a basketball team keeps missing free throws," Jackson told a black church audience in Washington, "they don't blame conditions or the rules of the game or unfair coaching. They work on analysis: timing, technique, trajectory. Well, when our team keeps making babies out of wedlock, keeps having crack-addicted babies, keeps on killing each other, it's time for analysis. Blacks themselves are the only ones who can do that. It's all well and good to talk about oppression, but we've got to rid ourselves of that which we want our oppressors to be rid of. We've got to go to the question of introspection, without being defensive or feeling that to talk honestly about these issues somehow compromises the race.

"Let's talk about it in terms of moral struggle," Jackson continued. "It's hard to fight the moral struggle without moral authority, and our failure to become introspective and responsible takes away our moral authority. . . . And we shouldn't underestimate the non-budget-item remedy. The Prodigal Son couldn't blame his condition on resources. He had resources. He couldn't blame mistreatment; he had parents who loved him and provided for him. It wasn't until he came unto himself that he got straight. That's what we have to do."[4]

Austin predicts, perhaps optimistically, that Jackson "may not scare as many people as he did in the past. He may be the nominee, he may get his clock cleaned, but I don't know the fear will be there."

The fear was certainly there among Democratic leaders from Syracuse to San Diego as they woke from a collective nightmare on March 27, 1988. They had spent a restless night with the same thought. Jackson had won an amazing victory in Michigan's Democratic caucuses and seemed for the first time to have a serious chance of winning the presidential nomination. What would happen to the party if he became the standard-bearer?

"People became frightened. They had been willing to vote for him as a protest, but now they decided he could be the nominee," Austin said.

"The panic was over the image of the party. There were certainly people calling who were concerned: other state chairs, Washington types, it ran the gamut," remembered Ohio Democratic Chairman Jim Ruvolo, who would become the party's national vice chairman the following winter. But, at the time, no one was willing to tell this straight to Jackson or his intimates. Sort of the quintessential liberal guilt. "We only see that in the press," said California Assembly Speaker Willie Brown, chairman of Jackson's 1988 campaign. "Maybe people don't want to say that in front of us." Whatever the reason, it allowed the Jackson campaign to maintain that he was riding a wide tide of public enthusiasm.

In fact, Jackson's victory in Michigan was due to a caucus system held on a spring Saturday afternoon that attracted only committed white liberals and blacks to the polls—a total turnout of about 213,000 out of 5.8 million registered voters. It was the apex of his campaign.

The chill Michigan sent through the national Democratic hierarchy is still alive. They fear that, were Jackson to become the Democratic nominee for president, or even vice president, he would alter the American political scene as much as computer trading has changed Wall Street. With computer trading, massive stock movements that previously took place over months occur in minutes. So too could be the impact of Jackson's candidacy.

Jackson himself refuses to believe that would occur, and openly predicts that the time is coming when the Democrats may have to have him on the ticket. "By 1992, having me, if I were to run again, or another African-American on the ticket is like a reasonable expectation. That won't even be radical in 1992."[5] Jackson argues that 1988 Democratic vice presidential nominee Lloyd "Bentsen didn't deliver Texas or the South, Miss Ferraro [the 1984 nominee] didn't deliver Queens, Catholics, or women. But I would have delivered urban America. Blacks and Hispanics and a lot of workers. No doubt in my mind about that. So just think about that. The people who they did put on the ticket did not deliver their base constituency. I would have delivered my base constituency."

But many believe that his presence on the ticket in November would just speed up white defections, leaving a Democratic party composed of blacks and a limited number of white liberals.

No one outside of Jackson's inner circle thinks he can be elected president, and many inside understand the formidable odds. Although his detractors compare Jackson to Harold Stassen, the former Minnesota governor whose quadrennial campaigns for the presidency between the 1940s and 1970s made him a political joke, they miss the point. Jackson isn't to be taken lightly. In truth, he is very much like William Jennings Bryan.

Like Jackson, Bryan voiced the frustrations of a large chunk of the Democratic party—in his case, the agrarian interests with whom the party threw in its lot around the turn of the century. Bryan, like Jackson, was known as "the great commoner." The agrarians, like blacks and liberals in today's Democratic party, had enough clout inside the party to win the nomination, but couldn't muster the majority needed for a victory in November.

In fact, Bryan's words to the 1896 Democratic convention could just as easily have come out of Jackson's mouth during his high profile speeches to the 1984 and 1988 Democratic conventions. "Upon which side will the Democratic party fight; upon the side of the 'idle holders of idle capital' or upon the side of the struggling masses?"

Should Jackson be nominated for president, or even vice president, what happens to the Democrats running for Congress, state legislatures, and local offices is "the big fear," Austin believes. "I think it's a real possibility [that the under-ticket would be devastated]. The evidence seems to point to that. But until he's on the ticket, he and a lot of people will not be convinced that Jesse Jackson will do unforgivable horrors to the Democratic party. I think he can get 40 percent. He starts out at 30 percent and has a shot at 10 percent more or 40 percent. He might get 20 percent of the white vote."

Democratic pollster Maslin is pessimistic about the next few years for the Democrats because he thinks Jackson will get his day in the sun if he runs. "Let's play it out. Jesse Jackson is either so strong in 1992 that he either wins the nomination, or to deny it to him means the election is lost. So Jackson is the nominee and everyone believes if he is, he would lose big.

"Let's assume Jackson lost [the popular vote] 60-40, every state, and let's assume Democrats lose the Senate and lose enough of the House that we do not have an ideological majority. My guess is, after Jesse lost by twenty points he would realize he's gone as far as he can go. We would have made history. We are still standing as a party with extraordinary support and I think we probably would have gotten beyond the issue.

"What is the alternative? We have to play this thing out. And it may be the worst case in the short run."

As damning as Maslin's view is, it may be the optimistic one. After all, 40 percent of the vote is four points better than George McGovern did at a time when the Democratic party still held some sway over voters.

"What would happen if Jesse were nominated?" asks Bruce Babbitt. "You would have to look at other turning points in American history. The disappearance of the Whigs in the 1840s. There would almost certainly be a recasting of the political parties."

Peter Kelly, the former Democratic treasurer, doesn't think Jackson can win the nomination, but he doesn't mince words about what would happen if he did. "If Jesse is nominated in 1992, then we have our Armageddon. The thing unwinds in small pieces. We lose every state legislature, the House, and Senate. The facts are, one out of every three votes we've always gotten would not be there."

If Paul Soechting—the Democratic mayor of El Campo, in Weatherford County, historically a Texas bellwether—is any indication, Kelly's right.

"If Jesse were the nominee, we'd become Republicans," he says of moderate whites like himself. "It's not a racial thing, it's an ideological thing. He's against national defense and has rather liberal stances on abortion and social programs. Jackson would be the end of the Democratic party in Texas and, without a doubt, the South. It would be absolute disaster. It will begin to have an impact when Jackson lands on the ticket. We will dive for cover like you have never seen."

If that is the case, then why don't Democrats stand up to Jackson? In 1988, perhaps they could be excused for not doing so since they didn't believe he could win the nomination. But in 1992 and beyond, the continued migration of moderates from the Democratic primaries will lose them their safety net.

Bill Galston, the University of Maryland professor who was Mondale's 1984 chief domestic advisor, poses the key question.

"The first time Jackson makes an aggressive move, will anybody stand up and say in so many words, 'Reverend Jackson, I don't doubt your sincerity or your commitment, but the path you recommend for the Democratic party is fundamentally wrong'? Somebody absolutely has to take him on. I would say the best way to deal with him is honorably and directly. It's time to stop evading him, time to stop patronizing, time to treat him as a serious contestant who needs to have his ideas scrutinized on their merits. Until some central figure develops the intellectual capacity and the backbone to do that, the party will continue to suffer at the national level."

What kind of president would he be?

"It would depend entirely on the first dozen people that he appointed to exercise responsibility," Babbitt believes. "The first really top appointments. He's clearly not an administrator. He's very much like Ronald Reagan. He brings the same kinds of abilities as Ronald Reagan to governance. As he says, he is a tree-shaker, not a jelly-maker."

Given the fear among Democratic leaders of saying the obvious, only blacks are left to acknowledge Jackson's political position.

"There's an old saying that the folks who kick down the door seldom can go through it," says Espy, expressing the political reality of a Jackson presidential candidacy.

Or, as Virginia Governor Wilder puts it: "Whether Jesse can achieve the presidency is a far, far different question than whether he commands attention."

Actually, the better question may be whether Jackson's commanding presence will prevent the Democrats from winning the White House.

12

The Minority Mirage

Jesse Jackson was speaking in March of 1989 at the Democratic Leadership Council's annual conference held at Philadelphia's swank Wyndham Franklin Plaza Hotel not far from Independence Hall. He could have been any one of countless Democratic liberals from the last decade—Ted Kennedy, Mario Cuomo, Walter Mondale—offering the same false tune that dominated party thinking.

There was nothing wrong with the Democratic message: once the millions of nonvoting poor and minorities were brought to the polls, happy days would be here again. But something was missing—a party candidate and a message that would excite these nonvoters.

"We lost ten states with 160 [electoral] votes; 160 of the critical votes by less than the amount of unregistered Afro-Americans in those states alone," Jackson offered.

It was another verse in the Democratic refrain of self-delusion.

"The mainstream is too narrow," Jackson told crowds during the 1988 campaign. "We've got to turn the stream into a river and bring more people in. There were 85 million people last time who didn't vote. . . . The most fundamental challenge today is to revive the spirits of those who dropped out. . . . Fundamental, therefore to our victory, is a commitment to voter registration, voter rights enforcement, and voter turnout."

That day in Philadelphia, Jackson claimed that "Dukakis did not aim for our basic Democratic base, nor did he sell our message." Jackson argued that if Democrats emphasized their liberal orthodoxy, they would excite the masses and drown the Republicans in a sea of black, brown, and yellow voters. These poor souls, even if they didn't as yet understand, would finally wake up to their own interests.

Actually, neither Jackson's premise, that all poor and minorities were downtrodden and certain to vote Democratic, nor his math, that there were enough of them to win the White House, was correct. That's because Jackson talked about the potential electorate, not those who vote or are likely to in the near future.

In 1980, 1984, and 1988, whites were 85 percent or more of the electorate, according to network exit polls. The argument that Democrats need to focus their appeal on whites is not based on any racist judgment that white votes are the most important; rather it is based on simple math—there are many times more whites than people of other races in the U.S. electorate. In those three most recent presidential elections, blacks were at most 10 percent of the electorate. Other racial groups—principally Hispanics and Asian-Americans—made up the difference.

Some contend that the population projections hold another story. *Time* magazine said in 1990 that by the year 2056 America would have become a country where the average resident was nonwhite. That, of course, would depend on the accuracy of demographic assumptions about birth, death, and immigration rates. After all, in 1947, the Census Bureau predicted there would be 163 million people in the country in the year 2000. There were already 250 million by the year 1990 and the new projection was for about 269 million at the turn of the century.

But even if the 1990 projections are correct, the near and intermediate term is likely to see only minor change in the percentage of the electorate that is white. It was a perfect example of the media focusing on a trend and making more of it than existed. In fact, a Gallup poll in March of 1990 asked Americans what percentage of the U.S. population they thought came from various ethnic groups. While blacks made up only 12 percent and Hispanics only 9 percent of the U.S. population, Americans estimated they were 32 percent and 21 percent respectively.

The Census Bureau estimated that in the year 2000, 76-78 percent of eligible voters would be white, 11-12 percent black, 7-8 percent Hispanic, and 4-5 percent Asian. The uncertainty depended on the projections about what percentage of Hispanics age eighteen or older would be citizens, and therefore eligible to vote. The projections for the year 2010 were for a potential electorate 74-76 percent white, 11-12 percent black, 9-10 percent Hispanic, and 5-6 percent Asian. And in any case, it seems almost certain that whites, given their overall higher educational and socio-economic status, will be a larger part of the actual electorate than they are of potential voters. By 2010 the U.S. Hispanic population will outnumber that of blacks.

Moreover, as the voting age population of America becomes less white, the bulk of the new voters will not be black, but brown and yellow. Perhaps the Democratic party's greatest mistake is believing that all racial minorities share the same political agenda. More on this later.

If either premise—that racial minorities could control American politics in the near term, or that all racial minorities were as solidly Democratic as blacks—were correct, at least the theory of mobilizing voters that dominated Democratic strategy councils for most of the 1980s might have made sense.

But the plain truth, is the Democratic party has been chasing windmills in an effort to avoid confronting their central problem: the party lacks a message that appeals to most Americans.

Their mobilization strategy ignores the facts. A CBS-*New York Times* poll taken shortly after the 1988 election showed that if everyone in America had voted—instead of the roughly 50 percent of eligible adults who participated—George Bush would have won by an even larger margin than he did.

But, say Democratic strategists, that's not what we are talking about. We intend to concentrate on the poor and other minorities and forget the white middle class.

"We must go after and retrieve the white male, I hear the wise men say," Jackson scoffs. "Well, we'll never get the white males back."

Ron Walters, a former Jackson deputy campaign manager and Howard University political scientist, claims Democratic leaders "have to say what is the future of the Democratic party. It is not competing for the residual white vote. It is expanding the base of the Democratic party. You have to take the party in the direction of the liberal tradition. If you look at the demographics of this country, it's becoming far more minority and will become far more in the future."

And it's not just Jackson and his adherents who mouth that line. Cleta Mitchell, formerly chairman of Oklahoma's House Appropriations Committee and an unsuccessful candidate for lieutenant governor in 1986, was typical of white Democrats who believed minorities were the key to their party's future. Entering the 1988 campaign she had looked to moderates like Robb and Babbitt, but changed her mind.

"I don't think we're going to get them [whites] back. We need to recognize that," Mrs. Mitchell stated. "I think white middle-class America fully believes the Democrats are the party of people who don't work. That's racist. But people believe that the people who don't work are black. White Americans simply do not believe there are the kinds of societal barriers to black progress that blacks believe exist and that the Democratic party talks about. White people still believe Abe Lincoln, you can be born in a log cabin and become president. With just these people [voting] we're not going to get it back. Unless we find a way to enfranchise more people" the Democrats are not going to win.

The Democrats made the politics of mass mobilization their strategy for the 1984 presidential campaign. With Jackson as their leader telling audiences "the old wineskin must make way for the new wine," the Democrats poured millions of dollars into an effort to get more blacks to register. And it worked—sort of. Millions of new voters, undoubtedly many of them black, Hispanic, or Asian-American, registered for the first time and voted. The problem was, the vast majority of new registrants and voters were white and voted Republican.

ABC News exit polls showed that in 1984, first-time voters supported Reagan by a 61–39 margin, a higher rate than the 57–43 percent edge among those who had voted in previous elections. In

1984, the new black voters were more Democratic than the blacks who had voted in previous elections. Mondale got 95 percent of the new black voters compared with the 88 percent he got from previously registered blacks. The problem for the Democrats was that new white voters backed Reagan 69-31, while whites who had voted before supported him only by a 62-37 margin.

Simply stated, what the 1984 campaign proved was that in a country that is heavily white, a Democratic strategy of trying to enlarge the electorate is certain to backfire. It is the political version of Newton's Third Law of Physics—for each action there is an equal and opposite reaction.

In fact, in five southern states (Florida, Louisiana, North Carolina, Kentucky, South Carolina) that kept separate registration lists by race during that period, the evidence was crystal clear. In those states, whites—two-thirds of whom voted for Reagan—increased in registration by almost 1.5 million, while black registration increased by less than a third of that figure. Even given 90 percent Democratic allegiance by blacks, the net was still a probable Reagan gain of about 150,000 votes in 1984.

Following 1984, the Democrats went back to the drawing board. But they still couldn't get rid of the vision of a vast number of minority voters who could save the party, the message bedammed. They again avoided substance in favor of tactics.

They wouldn't abandon the mobilization model.

So, in 1988, instead of mass mobilization, they designed a strategy of selective mobilization. In some neighborhoods they offered bounties to volunteers to sign up new voters—as if it were possible for Democrats to tap only potential Democratic voters. They must have thought they would be like the angel of death in ancient Egypt who smote the first-born of the Egyptians, leaving the Hebrews unscathed.

Of course, what the strategy meant was they had to increase turnout among minorities—the only group they felt sure would vote Democratic—without increasing white turnout. The problem was, it can't be done. Given the political dynamics of American society, a Democratic drive to register blacks will—as sure as night follows day—spur a GOP drive to register whites. And there are seven times more whites in America than there are blacks.

Before the election, Bill Lacy, the former Reagan White House aide who would oversee Bush's comeback in California from a seventeen-point deficit to a narrow victory, had been skeptical but cautiously pleased with the Democratic strategy.

"I don't accept the whole notion the Democrats win by minority turnout activities. It's fundamentally like they want to change the playing field. They are sort of admitting that within the circle of voters we're operating in, they can't win. Therefore, what they want to do is bring new people in to change that universe. I don't think it works. But I hope they follow that course."

Lacy was a believer in the laws of political physics. And, in state after state, selective mobilization didn't work. White America decided to protect its interests from what it perceived as a black-dominated agenda of the Democratic party.

Take Louisiana from 1981-89, the period when the feeling that Republicans cared only about whites was strongest in minority America because of the belief that Reagan was a bigot. Democratic registration among blacks there increased by 77,779, but Democratic registration among whites dropped 161,230, and GOP registration increased by 176,477. That meant that the net effect was a GOP pickup of about 100,000 voters.[1]

The pattern was duplicated throughout the country during that same period. A study by the Committee for the Study of the American Electorate released on the eve of the 1988 election concluded there had actually been a drop in registration and the Democrats were the big losers.

Facts and the 1988 Bush victory notwithstanding, the message still did not seem to get through to Democratic leaders. It took the well-argued analysis of a respected political scientist known for his Democratic sympathies, Ruy Teixeira, finally to make an impression.

Writing similar pieces in *The New Republic* and *Public Opinion*, Teixeira showed just how foolhardy the mobilization theory was if Democrats wanted to win the White House. Using CBS-*New York Times* exit polling from the 1988 election, Teixeira estimated that in the election in which half of all eligible voters participated, turnout was 52 percent among whites, 46 percent among blacks, and 23 percent among Hispanics. By combining that data with the actual voting results and demographics of the country, Teixeira came up with some disconcerting conclusions for Democrats.

Even in the highly unrealistic event that turnout among blacks and Hispanics had been ten points *higher* than among whites, and that whites with family incomes of $12,500 or less had had a ten point higher turnout rate than those of $50,000 or more, Bush still would have defeated Dukakis by 2 million votes. Teixeira further estimated that even if black, Hispanic, and poor white turnout had increased twenty points without any corresponding increase among the rest of whites, Dukakis would have won only three more states than he actually did, giving Bush a 320-218 electoral college victory.

"Turnout of the 'usual suspects' will not win elections for the Democrats. Brown and his party will have to range further afield, to those broad sectors of the electorate whose members remain unconvinced that Democrats have the solutions to their problems," Teixeira wrote. "Democrats may have an understandable urge to trade in the current electorate for a new one, but it isn't advisable. They lost the presidency because they didn't have enough support in the nation as a whole, not because enough of their people failed to show up at the polls."

And, in fact, Teixeira's argument began to take hold in much of the party establishment.

"There are some in our party who say the way Democrats win is with expansion," Chairman Brown remarked. "Nobody is more committed to voter registration than I am, but that's not enough to win elections, that's not enough to make the Democratic party the majority party at the presidential level. We've got to get back some of the voters we've lost."

The rhetoric sounded good, but the party didn't make the substantive changes needed to bring back the white middle class. And in the meantime, Democratic leaders perpetuated the myth that the future was theirs because the higher minority birthrates would eventually override their problem with whites.

In many ways, this myth was a devastating problem because it contained the seeds of the party's long-term collapse—perhaps a time when Republicans would gain a national plurality and Democrats would be uncompetitive in many places. The party that prided itself on caring for racial minorities was operating under a major misconception.

When most Democrats, except for some perceptive Texans and Californians, talk about minorities in a political context, they are using it as a euphemism for blacks, specifically poor, inner-city blacks. They wrongly assume that all three major American minority groups—blacks, Hispanics, and Asians—are identical, or even similar, in their political beliefs.

Whether the Democrats can continue their lock-tight hold on black voters is an interesting question, given the growth of the black middle class whose economic interests are often more in sync with Republican thinking. But in terms of the overall political dynamic, the voting behavior of blacks is not critical. Democrats already get 90 percent plus of the black vote and have been unable to win the White House.

If Republicans could increase their share of the black vote to, say, 20 percent, the Democrats would be left with nothing, assuming the GOP retained its hold on whites. That was the goal of Bush's effort to change the GOP's image by offering his vision of a "kinder, gentler" America.

But here again, the GOP has better understood a changing country. It knew that the key to any Democratic reversal of its electoral slide was the other two minorities: Hispanics and Asians.

"I don't think there is any question that the Democrats lump African-Americans, Asian-Americans, and Hispanics into one group and think the points of view of those three groups are very much consistent," said Robert Matsui, the Democratic congressman from a heavily white district encompassing Sacramento, Calif. Matsui, a Japanese-American born in California who was sent to an internment camp following the outbreak of World War II, believes "there is a mindset in the Democratic party that if you are a minority, you are downtrodden and therefore you are with us. That's absolutely not the case."

The message was driven home in Matsui's California in 1990. Exit polls by Voter Research and Surveys, a pool of the three commercial television networks and CNN, found that Republican

Pete Wilson was elected governor with 58 percent of the Asian-American vote and 47 percent of the Hispanic vote. He also got 14 percent of the black vote and 53 percent of the white. Although the Hispanic and Asian-American subsamples on which the data were based were small, the message was plain—Democrats were facing a serious problem that most of them didn't even recognize.

"The fact that the party is run by Easterners, by establishment types, contributes to the problem," believes Bill Richardson, a New Mexico congressman and former chairman of the Congressional Hispanic Caucus. "There is not hostility toward Hispanics [or Asians], there is basically a lack of knowledge and an assumption there is no potential erosion in their support."

In simple terms, Democrats assumed that because Hispanics and Asian-Americans were racial minorities they had a common bond with blacks, and implicitly with the Democratic party. But party officials greatly overestimated how solid those links were.

Hispanics, those with Spanish surnames, are composed of several major groups of widely different political persuasions: Cubans, Puerto Ricans, Mexican-Americans, and those from Central and South America and Spain. Although Hispanics are considered a separate race, about 90 percent are white, most of the rest black.

In many ways, Cubans and Puerto Ricans have already chosen their political home.

Puerto Ricans, concentrated in the New York metropolitan area, are strongly Democratic, although not as heavily as blacks. Cubans, who live primarily in Florida, are just as heavily Republican. The differences stem from their heritage and economic situation.

Puerto Ricans, roughly 13 percent of the Hispanic population, are the least affluent, with incomes on the average a quarter less than other Hispanics, according to census data. They have twice the ratio of households headed by females and significantly higher welfare rates than Hispanics as a whole. In some places they have built political coalitions with blacks where it serves both groups' interests.

Cubans are concentrated in southern Florida, where they have become a significant political force. They have an almost 50 percent higher average income than Hispanics as a whole. Because they fled Fidel Castro's communist regime, their staunch anticommunist views have made them solidly Republican. And although they are much less numerous than Puerto Ricans, about 5 percent of the nation's Hispanic population, their much higher voting percentage allows the two groups basically to nullify each other in a partisan context in presidential elections.

Besides, since Cubans are mostly concentrated in Florida and Puerto Ricans in New York, those two states are not real contests in anything resembling a close national election. Florida will be solidly Republican in anything but a national Democratic landslide, in which case it will be a battleground. And the opposite holds for New York.

Neither group, then, is likely to make much of a difference in America's political mosaic in the coming years unless their voting behavior changes greatly.

But Mexican-Americans—about 63 percent of the nation's Hispanics—and to a lesser degree Central and South Americans, and others who make up the remaining 20 percent of Hispanics, are another story. They are the Super Bowl for the Democratic party. Not that Democrats can hope to win from them the same sort of allegiance they have from blacks and Puerto Ricans.[2]

These Hispanics, however, virtually all of whom are in the Southwest—Colorado, Texas, and California—could at least keep the party competitive in the coming decades. But if enough of them, even 40 percent, vote Republican, then the Democrats may only be able to recapture the White House in times of depression.

The good news for the Democrats is that most Mexican-Americans and South and Central Americans are not yet middle class. The poorer someone is, regardless of his or her ethnic heritage, the more likely that person is to look to the government for answers and to be in tune with Democratic politics. The bad news for the Democrats is that Hispanic political culture is inhospitable to Democratic interventionist government. And, perhaps most importantly, Hispanics have shown they are very upwardly mobile.

Paul Maslin, the Democratic pollster, moved his office from

Washington to Los Angeles in 1989. One of the things that immediately struck him was that when he got his car washed—a southern California ritual—"you'd get through the wash and there would be ten male Mexican-Americans who would dry it. In Washington it would take twenty seconds; in Los Angeles it takes ten minutes because it's serious, hard work. I can't imagine white or black Americans spending that much time or effort for a small tip. That tells you something."

"Because they are immigrant populations, they have brought with them the traits of their native countries that have to do with intact family units, hard work, deep religious belief," former San Antonio Mayor Cisneros maintains. "It is only after several generations in poverty that traditions begin to break down." Democrats "probably don't" understand the differences between blacks and Hispanics. "We rely on models of social actions that derived essentially on a generic poor person's model rather than looking at the particular cultures."

In fact, there are huge demographic differences between poor blacks and poor Hispanics which have not been widely studied or understood. The Census Bureau did not even begin collecting data on Hispanics as a group until 1970.

Blacks are poor because, relative to other ethnic groups in society, they work less, tend not to marry but to have children, depend on government programs, and drop out of school more often than whites. By comparison, Hispanics are more like the working poor, those who drop out of school and take low-paying jobs. In 1989, more than four of five whites and three of four blacks, but only slightly more than one of two Hispanics, graduated from high school. The Hispanic Policy Development Project, a Washington, D.C.-based research group, found that in Austin, Houston, Dallas-Ft. Worth, Phoenix, Tucson, Albuquerque, Sacramento, and San Francisco, Hispanics were much less likely to have finished high school and college than blacks, but in general had incomes about 10 percent higher. In San Antonio, San Diego, and Los Angeles—centers of large numbers of illegal aliens—the income edge was smaller for Hispanics, but the education pattern persisted.

Hispanics were much more likely to marry than blacks—or

whites—and to have more children. In fact, the Census Bureau said in 1989 that only a little more than one in three black children lived with both parents, while two of three Hispanic kids and four of five white children came from intact families.

In 1989, the Census Bureau reported that nationally Hispanic median family income was $21,920, roughly 20 percent higher than for blacks. And that figure does not include government benefits, which Hispanics enjoy to a much lesser degree than do blacks or whites. Hispanics are much less educated, even than blacks, and drop out of school at higher rates than any ethnic group.

Their marital status—both in providing a role model for their youngsters and in the economic benefits an intact family accrues—is what made the difference. Blacks and Hispanics had the same per capita income, and Hispanic married couples had incomes 10 percent lower than married black couples. But, significantly, many more Hispanic families were headed by couples, as opposed to the single mothers who headed a much larger percentage of black families.

David Hayes Bautista, director of UCLA's Chicano Studies Center, examined black and Hispanic poverty in California and found Hispanics were the most likely of any ethnic group—including whites and Asians—to hold jobs. And they had by far the lowest rate of government employment as well as "virtually no dependence on governmental programs." In fact, the Census Bureau, which found that 36 cents of every dollar in black America and 21 cents of every dollar in white America came from government transfer payments and employment, said that the figure for Hispanics was just 23 cents.

Part of that stems from the large number of Hispanics who, because they are in the United States illegally, keep their distance from the government. The rest, as Cisneros noted, is a product of the political culture of Latin America, where government is not a provider for the poor.

"First of all, welfare is not even a notion in many of the sending countries," stated Rafael Valdivieso, a former Carter administration appointee and vice president for research at the Hispanic Policy Development Project. "The idea that the government should take some of your money and give it to other folks, that's just wrong" in the view of most Hispanics. "There is a strong feeling we are the workers, we still have a strong work ethic and strong family ethic. There is a very strong feeling that blacks don't. There is a strong feeling that [welfare, unmarried mothers, etc.] happens to blacks, not Hispanics. There is in some cases an animosity, in others a disdain, a looking down on, certainly a 'we are not in the same boat' attitude.

"The only places where they get along are New York and Chicago," Valdivieso continued. "Everywhere else, there is really bad tension. Mexican-Americans don't have much, they really feel that blacks get all the breaks. They don't know blacks. They don't understand blacks. There is tremendous resentment towards blacks. They view the Democratic party as the party of blacks."

There are also serious ideological differences between blacks and most Hispanics. One is the question of identity. Hispanics, polls show, are much less likely to perceive themselves as an oppressed minority. They are much less likely to say they have been personally discriminated against because of their race. The fact that no umbrella advocacy group like the NAACP has surfaced as a unifying force underscores those differences.

"The Hispanic considers himself, although a racial minority, basically white, mainstream middle class, trying to be part of the mainstream, not always seeking, I think, the same objectives blacks have: redistribution, poverty programs," Congressman Richardson avers. "Their economic level may be the same but the objectives seem to be different."

"In the Hispanic community there is a large American dream, work-hard mentality—pride, self-reliance, family, church, neighborhood," something that Richardson concedes plays right into GOP hands. "There is less of 'somebody has got to help me.' There is more of a self-reliant attitude, particularly when they have left their native country and know they have to make it on their own, and not with the help of the government because the government is perceived as the immigration service.

"The Democratic party's perception of the Hispanic rank-and-file fits into two categories: that they are agricultural farm workers,

or people in the barrio who are poor and have no other option,"
Richardson says. "Their perception is that dealing with poverty
issues will get you the Hispanic vote. And that is not going to
happen, because Hispanics are now asking about tax policy and
economic growth, defense. Issues like immigration and bilingual
education, while they still have importance, lessen in importance as
Hispanics become part of the American mainstream."

He believes that "unless the Democratic party pays more attention to Hispanic needs and changes its emphasis from social redistribution polices to economic growth polices, the danger is that the
Hispanic vote will become like other [white] ethnic votes and take
more stands on bread-and-butter issues not reflected in the Democratic philosophy."

Polls show Hispanic political attitudes lie somewhere between
whites and blacks, but on many questions closer to whites. Data is
scarce but clear, and much comes from the Gallup-*Times Mirror*'s
landmark 1987 national study.

The fiscal conservatism of Hispanics is inescapable when it
comes to government spending and their belief that the Republicans
are more careful with government money. The survey asked
whether spending should be increased, kept constant, or cut for
fifteen categories of government programs. In twelve of the fifteen
areas—including the question of government programs for
minorities—the answers for Hispanics were closer to those of
whites than those of blacks. And, once again, while the Democratic
message seems tailored towards blacks and a minority of liberal
whites, the GOP message attracts most whites.

The cultural conservatism of the Hispanic community is also a
plus for Republicans and a problem for Democrats. On the issues of
the death penalty, abortion, prayer in school, mandatory drug testing for government workers, resuming the draft, and limiting the
access of AIDS patients to public places, Hispanics were closer to
the position of whites than blacks, according to the *Times Mirror*
study.

And when it came to national defense, nothing symbolized the
differences between blacks and Hispanics more than their attitude
toward the Persian Gulf War. In January 1991, when polls showed

that three out of four whites but fewer than half of blacks supported
Bush's decision to attack Iraq, a *Los Angeles Times* poll (January
26-29, 1991) showed two out of three Hispanics agreed with the
white view.

"There is very, very close to unanimity between the majority
[white] culture and political tradition and the Hispanic
community—support for the free enterprise system, the business
community, small business, criminal justice, and military affairs,"
reports Democrat Dan Morales, the attorney general of Texas and
the first Hispanic elected to statewide executive office in either
California or Texas.

"There are big differences, and potentially a similar type of split
can take place between blacks and Hispanics" as has developed
between blacks and whites, Maslin believes. Should that split even-
tuate, the type of "rainbow coalition" envisioned by Democratic
liberals becomes very suspect. Jackson himself, it seems, is far from
a hero to Hispanic America.

Among Hispanics who voted in the 1988 Democratic presidential primaries—as a group much more liberal than the Hispanic
electorate as a whole—network exit polling showed Jackson got just
three in ten votes.

"They just don't get it. They don't connect with him. It's like
Jimmy Carter trying to get votes in the North. It's just not there.
It's a different culture, the way he talks. How he uses imagery just
doesn't click" with the majority of Hispanics, Valdivieso explained.

Even within the Mexican-American community, some major
political differences evince themselves along partisan and geographic lines. In 1988, for instance, Dukakis defeated Bush by a
66-33 percent margin nationally among Hispanics, according to
ABC's exit polls. As expected, Cubans in Florida and Puerto Ricans in New York canceled each other out. Bush got three of four
Hispanic votes in Florida, Dukakis the same in New York.

But in California, Dukakis defeated Bush 64-33 among Hispanics, while in Texas, Dukakis won 75-24. The reason for the ten-
point swing has to do with the greater economic and cultural
assimilation and intermarriage rates with Anglos among Hispanics
in California than in Texas.

Exit polls of the November 1988 electorate done by the Southwest Voter Research Institute, which focuses on registering Hispanic voters, found that in California 44 percent of Hispanic voters had household incomes of $30,000 or more and 51 percent had at least some college education. In Texas, only 29 percent of Hispanic voters had household incomes of $30,000 and 42 percent had some college courses.

That is a bad sign for the Democrats.

For what it portends is that Hispanics show every sign of behaving politically more like white ethnic voters than either blacks or Jews. Blacks and Jews are the exception to the rule of American politics which states that an ethnic group's voting behavior becomes more Republican the more it loses its ethnic identity and climbs the economic ladder. And, as the data clearly shows, Hispanics are climbing the ladder.

"Most Democratic leaders think the average Latino is Cesar Chavez and that's their mindset of how they view the average Hispanic in California, a migrant worker," Matsui believes. "But if you go anywhere in the state of California, the average Latino is an upwardly mobile individual aspiring to a college education or to own a small business. That's the perception of the new Latino community, especially the profile of those Latinos who vote most often."

And that is important, because Hispanics are not yet active voters. By some estimates a third of all Hispanics in this country are not citizens and are unable to vote. Among those who are citizens, studies show they register and turn out to vote at roughly a 15 percent lower rate than non-Hispanic whites.

The Dukakis showing in Texas and California was down from the 85 percent share Democratic presidential candidates got from Mexican-Americans in those same states twenty years before, a time, that is, when Hispanics were less assimilated.

Also contributing to the Democratic decline has been a corresponding erosion of the Roman Catholic Church's hold on Hispanics—once 99 percent Catholic. By the early 1990s that figure was down to the 80 percent range, a drop caused by a growing evangelical movement, which has not only altered the

Hispanic community's religious orientation but its political alliances as well.

If the Democrats' hope for the future lies with minorities, they must hope also that the Hispanics halt their climb up the economic ladder. And that hope is a pipe dream. The governnment figures for Hispanic income are deceiving. They understate the economic status of Hispanic voters more than any other group because the Hispanic average is brought down by the millions of illegal immigrants who can't vote.

Census Bureau data show that Hispanics earned roughly two-thirds the incomes of whites, but that is misleading. When the data were analyzed for U.S.-born and new immigrants, it was a different story. Median income for U.S.-born Hispanic men is 80 percent of whites. For U.S.-born Mexican-American high school graduates, and U.S.-born Mexican-Americans with one or two years of college, the incomes are 90 percent and 97 percent respectively of whites with the same education.[3] Since it was primarily the U.S.-born Hispanics who were voting, the conclusion is inescapable. Hispanics are rapidly climbing the ladder, and a Democratic message that assumes they are still at the bottom is doomed to fail in the long term.

There's also a catch-22 at work here. Since the Hispanic population is the youngest of any ethnic group, it will be a decade or more before their population bulge will affect the voting age electorate. By that time, quite likely the voting Hispanics will have become economically more comfortable and will no longer be a likely target for the Democrats.

"There is clearly a trend among those who have become relatively successful to affiliate as much with the other party as with our party," says Morales, at thirty-four a rising star in national politics. He advises Democrats to "go after the Hispanic middle class just like the white middle class."

Although Hispanics may begin to act politically like white ethnics, Asian-Americans are doing so already. They have been called the "model minority" by some cynics, the "new Jews" by others. In reality, when it comes to educational and financial achievements, Asian-Americans have literally run up the ladder. They have almost a 20 percent higher median household income than whites.

Like Hispanics, Asian-Americans are really several disparate groups. They have also become the fastest growing part of the U.S. population—seven times the pace of the general population. And they are concentrated in California, the fastest growing state. In 1990, the more than 7 million Asian-Americans were not a very big part of the 250 million national picture. But within California it is another story. And there is no conceivable way Democrats can win the White House without winning that state.

Many fourth-and-fifth generation Japanese-Americans—many of whose relatives, like Matsui, were interned during World War II—are quite comfortable economically. So too are recent immigrants from Taiwan, South Korea, Vietnam, and Hong Kong who arrived with skills and an admirable work ethic. They don't think of themselves as minorities. There are also some Cambodians and Hmong tribesmen who have floundered economically.

Unlike Jews, they show no signs of retaining an allegiance to the Democratic party. In fact, in 1988, Asian-Americans voted for George Bush by a slightly higher percentage than did whites. Moreover, like Hispanics, the more the Asians are assimilated into the American way of life, the more likely they are to vote Republican.

Asians, again like Hispanics and the other hundreds of thousands of others who have recently come to this country, are highly motivated, generally entreprenurial people. Many have skills and an upward mobility and do not find traditional Democratic economics to their liking. Even among the poorest Asian immigrants, the signs are economically encouraging.

Nathan Caplan, a University of Michigan professor of psychology, studied seven thousand boat people, mostly from Vietnam, who came to the United States in the late 1970s. They arrived with a limited knowledge of English, little education, and few occupational skills.

These people comprised 1,400 households and had a 90 percent unemployment rate in their first few months in the United States.

But by their forty-second month, the jobless rate was down to 15 percent, slightly higher than the national 11 percent rate at that time, but lower than the rates of blacks or Hispanics. These boat people earned only 46 percent of the poverty level standard during their first few months in America, but by their fortieth month they were averaging 171 percent of the poverty level. The Bureau of Labor Statistics reported that in the spring of 1990 the Indo-Chinese—including the Hmong and Cambodians who have not been as economically successful as the Vietnamese—had a jobless rate of 8 percent, again higher than the national average of 5.2 percent, but remarkable compared to other minorities and recent immigrants. [3]

Roughly 42 percent of the California population in 1990 was composed of Hispanics, blacks, and Asians. By the turn of the century that figure will approach 50 percent.

About 10 percent of the state's population was Asian, and in some cities the number of pages in the phone book with common Asian names outnumbered the Smiths and the Joneses. The projections were that Asians would soon pass blacks as the second largest minority group. By the turn of the century, in California, they will almost double the number of blacks. Unlike Hispanics, few are illegal aliens and can become citizens and vote. But like Hispanics, they have a history of political noninvolvement.

In general, the Chinese and Southeast Asians have been mostly Republican, the Filipinos mostly Democratic. The Koreans, Taiwanese, and Japanese are more split, but are increasingly moving toward the GOP because of their relatively conservative political attitudes on economics and social questions, as well as their legacy of anticommunism.

Polling data on Asian-Americans is even more difficult to obtain than data on Hispanics, but what's available is clear.

ABC News' exit polls in 1988 showed Bush won 61 percent of the Asian vote in California and 54 percent nationally. In 1984 exit polls showed that Reagan won seven in ten Asian votes, again substantially higher than his share of whites.

A study of whites, blacks, Hispanics, and Asians in California by Cal Tech political scientists Bruce Cain and Roderick Kiewiet in 1984 highlights the conservative nature of Asian-Americans.

On a dozen values questions—such as the death penalty, abortion, welfare, school prayer, and immigration—the attitudes of Asian-Americans were generally much closer to those of whites than Hispanics or blacks. The study said when it came to party identification, Asian-Americans were more likely than whites to consider themselves Republican. And the trend is continuing. The Field Institute poll, California's most respected nonpartisan polling operation, did a 1986-87 study of political attitudes in the state and concluded that in terms of ideology Asians were only slightly less conservative than whites and more so than either blacks or Hispanics.

Monterey Park, Calif., a suburb of sixty thousand persons a few minutes to the east of downtown Los Angeles, illustrates the movement. Its population is roughly 51 percent Asian-American, the first city in America with an Asian majority. Most of them are Chinese- and Japanese-Americans. Its streets are lined with Chinese signs, and condos have sprouted up where there used to be cozy single-family homes.

Don T. Nakanishi of the UCLA Asian American Studies Center found that between 1984 and 1989 Democratic registration among Asian-Americans in Monterey Park fell from 51 percent of the electorate to 42 percent, while GOP registration rose from 30 percent to 36 percent. The share of independent voters jumped from 18 to 21 percent, with those voters also coming from the Democratic column.

What is happening in Monterey Park "applies generally to what is happening throughout California," reports Michael Woo, Los Angeles' first Asian-American city councilman. Woo, a Democrat, was elected from an overwhelmingly white district with a 5 percent Asian and 25 percent Hispanic electorate and is a potential candidate to become someday Los Angeles' first Asian mayor. "It is true Republicans understand this transformation. . . . on a regular basis, while the Democratic party leadership reflects the tradition of being out of touch."

Since Woo is an ambitious politician, he has made a habit of attending Asian-American events outside his own district, even his own city, on a regular basis. He remembers looking around at the annual celebration of the Tet holiday in Orange County's New

Saigon section: "There were a large number of elected officials from various levels of government there, and I was the only Democrat. The rest were Republicans. It was another reminder to me of the lost opportunity the Democrats are squandering in terms of not effectively reaching out. The same thing happens at the large naturalization ceremonies. The Republicans very frequently have volunteers standing outside the auditorium. So, literally, the first American the new citizen will encounter will be a Republican trying to sign them up as an active voter. Democrats are forfeiting the next generation of new Americans. Democrats are definitely way behind among many of the new Asian groups."

"From an ideological point of view, a lot of Asian-Americans feel more comfortable with what they perceive to be the ideology of the Republican party," Matsui states. "It's entrepreneurial, no new taxes, strongly anticommunist at a time when many of these people came from Southeast Asia. Secondly, the Republican party is reaching out to a large extent. This may sound strange, but I think that in the Republican party there may be more tolerance for diversity than in the Democratic party."

"I don't think it's an inherently antigovernment attitude," says Woo, "but the question of opportunity and entrepreneurship and the desire for independence versus security. Especially among the Vietnamese, Koreans, Chinese there is a strong drive to be your own boss. A lot of Asians get their start working for a large institution, but their real goal is to get their money together and start their own business . . . . That makes Asian-Americans more in tune with Republican economics."

There are three other issues which, to varying degrees, are dear to Democratic hearts that raise red flags for Asian-Americans.

The most obvious is the affirmative action/quota question. Although polls show that Hispanics aren't strong supporters of such programs, and many surveys show they oppose them even though they may sometimes benefit from them, the Asian stance is clear. Asians believe that, given their enviable record of achievement, programs set up to help racial minorities get jobs or enter college limit their ability to climb higher.

A Field Institute poll in 1988 of Californians showed that four out of five Asians oppose the idea even if such programs were set up to grant special preferences to Asians. The margin of opposition was greater from Asians than from any other group, including whites.

The second issue is welfare—perceived to be central to Democratic politics. Woo puts it simply: "Generally welfare is looked upon as dishonorable" by Asian-Americans. "Asian-Americans have a strong tradition of family and as a result of that they would prefer that if there is someone in the family who needs assistance that they provide that assistance," Matsui explains politely.

In reality, much of the antiwelfare attitude stems from the tension between Asian entrepreneurs in black neighborhoods and the residents. Blacks resent the presence of yet another immigrant group climbing over them. Asians blame the blacks' inability to advance on their own failings and see welfare as part of the reason. Serious cultural differences also come into play, more so than between whites and blacks. Blacks interpret the inscrutability of Asians, a tenet of their culture, as impoliteness.

And on the question of protectionism as a trade tactic, the only American politicians who raise it are Democrats. They are the ones who at times seem to be bashing the Japanese for their trade surplus with the United States. "It takes advantage of the issue of nationalism and creates an 'us versus them' situation," Matsui believes. "We're Americans first, but the problem is that when an Asian-American hears a politician say that, it does raise the specter of intolerance. Why don't they say that about the British, the Canadians, or the Dutch [who have trade surpluses with the United States]? One begins to wonder about motivation."

If there is any good news for Democrats, it is fleeting: Currently, Asian-Americans don't vote. In fact, in 1990, although they were about 10 percent of the California population, they cast only about 4 percent of the votes, according to a review by the Center for the Continuing Study of the California Economy. As for Hispanics, they also vote irregularly. The 1990 exit polls showed Hispanics were about 5 percent of the California electorate although they were almost 25 percent of the population. But their behavior is more easily explained given their economic status and fear of immigration officials. The reasons for small Asian turnouts are more complex and have to do with cultural values.

Nghia Tran was born in Saigon in 1963, the son of a colonel in the

South Vietnamese army. He and his family fled Vietnam in 1975 just ahead of the North Vietnamese and were separated from his father before reuniting a month later in the Philippines. They came to the United States and settled in the heavily Hispanic Huntington Park section of Los Angeles. His family opened a "QuikStop" convenience store where he worked after school and on weekends.

Because he worked his way through college, it took Tran six years to get a degree. Two years into his engineering studies at Long Beach State he switched his major to political science. The reaction from his family to that decision—and to his subsequent political career working for California state assemblywoman Gwen Moore, a black Democrat—was negative.

"When I told my parents I was going to pursue a career in politics they told me I would be poor for the rest of my life and no one would marry me," Tran remembers. "My father wanted me to stick with engineering. He said, 'You'll always have a job. You'll never find a job if you major in political science.'

"In the Vietnamese tradition people want their daughters to marry people with financial security and have stable positions in the community. New immigrants tend to have an inferiority complex. They want their children to go into medicine and engineering where language is not as much a requirement."

Tran has married, but his parents weren't totally off base.

"When I was in college, I dated a Vietnamese girl for about six months and she wouldn't introduce me to her parents because I was a political science major," Tran admits. His wife is part Vietnamese, part French, and was born in France.

"It may not be a typical situation" in the Asian-American community, says Matsui of Tran's experience. "But it is not an unusual one."

There is a real dichotomy in the attitudes of Hispanic and Asian voters.

In their efforts to better themselves economically they are very much like the tens of millions of Irish, Italians, Poles, and countless other immigrants who came to the nation a century ago through

Ellis Island. They move into homogeneous urban ghettos, work hard, save their money, and in due course move to the suburbs where the schools and housing are better and the streets safer.

But, unlike those who came to these shores a century ago, Hispanics and Asians have not embraced the political system as a means to progress. In the past, immigrants were courted by the political machines. Their bosses, virtually all of them Democrats, handed out jobs in return for political allegiance. The mutually dependent relationship that developed lasted until the suburbanization of America and the racial split of the 1960s eroded the Democratic control. With the new immigrants on the West Coast, it is different.

Political machines have long disappeared from the American landscape; in fact, they never existed in California. Perhaps more importantly, the people who arrive at our shores today, except for some illegal aliens from Mexico and Central America, are different from those of a century ago. Many, especially those most likely to participate politically, are not from the bottom of the society they left; they tend to have skills, to be professionals. They come to the United States in search of economic betterment, not economic survival. Like most whites, they focus on economic opportunity.

"Latinos [and Asians] don't have the same cultural linkage or reasons for Democratic loyalty as do blacks or Jews," Maslin claims. "They are aspiring Americans who want to make a better life, who originally get organized around the Democratic party. Democrats originally understand them better and respond to them. They use government at a time that they are down and need the help. But as they experience the American dream they move to the San Fernando Valley as the Irish and Italians did before them in the suburbs of cities like Philadelphia. Then all of a sudden the Democratic party seems more distant and Republicans have a better ability to appeal to them. It's a pretty standard progression."

13

The Broader Democratic Problem

A week after the 1988 election Frank Sullivan gathered for his semiannual poker game with some of Fort Worth's leading Democrats. It was a collection of the city's power elite. The portly Sullivan, a state judge, had for years mentally questioned his party allegiance. But he had never said anything publicly, nor done anything about it.

Sullivan had been drawn to politics as a teenager, one of the few jocks who bothered with such things. In 1965, his senior year of high school, he was both a tackle on the football team and vice president of the Texas Young Democrats.

But now, entering his forties, balding, and almost seventy-five pounds over his football playing weight, the decades of internal party strife had taken their toll. Dukakis hadn't moved him, any more than McGovern had in 1972, or Mondale in 1984.

Sullivan had wondered about the internal contradictions of the Democratic party as far back as 1966. That year, he was an eighteen-year-old Washington intern for former House Speaker Jim Wright, then a backbencher and Sullivan's congressman. Lyndon Johnson was president. Fellow Texan Sam Rayburn had died a few years earlier, having served as House speaker for almost two decades. Texans chaired four of the House's twenty committees, including two that really mattered—Appropriations and Banking. But the Vietnam War and the civil rights and women's movements were splitting apart the Democratic party.

That summer Sullivan sat in on a meeting of the House Un-American Activities Committee, chaired by Joe Pool, another Texas congressman. Pool was the type of conservative Democrat that dominated the Texas party, the type Sullivan had grown up with. But it was at that meeting that Sullivan learned about another kind of Democrat, the Northeastern liberal who seemed to be from a different planet. Such people, he learned, were in Texas politics too.

That committee session became deeply embedded in Sullivan's memory, because it drove home the inherent contradictions within FDR's Democratic coalition. It showed just how times had changed. As, for instance, when antiwar leader Jerry Rubin made a ruckus and police had to carry him out of the hearing room. Rubin, whose politics if not his methods clearly evoked sympathy from some of the leading liberals, made his scene about five feet from where Sullivan was sitting. The meeting got a lot of publicity.

Sullivan remembers feeling pretty good that day, believing his Democrats had stood up to Rubin and those subversives from New York who didn't believe in America. But a couple of hours later, after work, Sullivan wandered into the Democratic Club located in the old Congressional Hotel, now converted into an auxiliary House office building. To his amazement he saw Rubin and Pool sitting companionably together on bar stools. As the years passed, he came to realize that a marriage of political convenience had come to dominate the Democratic party. Sure, liberals and conservatives fought before the TV cameras, but in private they accommodated their differences. And more and more, that accommodation compromised his values.

But the hypocrisy didn't alter Sullivan's course. The Republican party in Texas hardly existed at the time. So he worked his way up the political ladder and, to all appearances, was a true-blue Democrat.

Sullivan wasn't involved in politics during the turbulent sixties and early seventies. In those years he worked as a computer operator for the Texas highway patrol and went through Texas Tech's law school. By the time he hung out his shingle in Fort Worth in 1973, he was married with three children.

He did well. His Democratic contacts came in handy and he was a good lawyer. In 1983, those Democratic contacts—especially his decades-long friendship with Texas Democratic Chairman Bob Slagle—helped Sullivan fill a vacant judgeship. He was elected in 1984 and reelected in 1986. Sullivan had always wanted to run for Congress, but as he got older he figured that wasn't in the cards. After all, Jim Wright, a long-time friend, wasn't going anywhere, or so he thought.

So, during that 1988 poker game, as he and his friends munched cold cut sandwiches during a break, Sullivan voiced a thought that had been welling up inside him for years, maybe even decades.

He and his poker pals were basically moderate conservatives. They believed in hard work, a strong defense, low taxes, and toughness on crime. When Sullivan was a kid, that description fit a majority of Democrats, not just in Texas but nationally. But now he knew that wasn't the case in most of America and he had begun to wonder about Texas as well.

"Why are we Democrats?" he asked his friends and fellow political warriors.

Tom Schieffer, a former state lawmaker, was hosting the game, which was held in the Men's Grill of the Petroleum Club, an exclusive club overlooking the Dallas-Fort Worth Metroplex from the fortieth floor of the Continental Plaza building. Sullivan and Schieffer, brother of CBS correspondent Bob Schieffer, had been friends since junior high school. They had once shared a law office.

Also present was Pete Geren, a local lawyer and Democratic insider who would replace Wright in Congress the following year when Wright resigned because of an ethics investigation. As a congressman, Geren often voted like a Republican in order to keep his seat. Two other lawyers, big wheels in Fort Worth Democratic politics, sat at the table—Tom Williams and Roger Neeley.

"We're sitting up here. We look like Republicans, we talk like Republicans, we act like Republicans, we think like Republicans. Why are we fighting this battle?" Sullivan asked.

The others were silent for some time. Then Schieffer, speaking for the others and echoing decades of tradition among the state's Tory Democrats, looked straight at Sullivan and said, "Well, we just are. I don't know exactly what a Democrat is, but I know I'm not a Republican."

And that is true for many Americans. That is why Democrats in much of America have been able to retain their hold on state and local politics and in Congress, despite their presidential losing streak. But, as is becoming increasingly clear, times are changing. Sullivan's conversion to the GOP six months after the poker game illustrates what is happening across America, especially in the Sun Belt, as Republican presidential control begins to move down the ticket.

Sullivan was actually surprised when a GOP lawyer friend asked if he had ever thought about switching. Sullivan shocked his friend by saying he sure had, but didn't think the GOP would want him because his Democratic bloodlines ran so deep. But he is exactly the type of convert the GOP recruiters want, because such cases drive home just how deep the transformation in American politics has become.

A couple of months later it was done. Sullivan doesn't think his political philosophy has changed one iota, but many of his old friends won't talk to him anymore—he hasn't played poker since. Slagle, president of the Young Democrats when Sullivan was vice president, blasted him publicly and won't talk to him privately. "He's not my friend anymore," Slagle states flatly.

The reason Sullivan raised the issue with his friends that particular November evening was his survival instinct. He realized he had reached the point of no return. His county—which got its first countywide GOP officeholder in 1984—was becoming a Republican bastion. To ensure his political survival, Sullivan felt he needed to climb aboard the speeding Republican train before it ran over him.

In 1988, when Dukakis lost Tarrant County 62 to 38 percent, Sullivan's colleague on the bench, Earl Bates, Jr., "a hell of a judge, admired by both prosecutors and defense lawyers," lost his reelection bid to Everett Young, a Republican whose sole qualification seemed to be the inherent GOP strength in Tarrant County. Sullivan saw the handwriting on the wall. "If I had remained a

Democrat I would eventually lose. The Republicans run this county," Sullivan explained. He was reelected without opposition in 1990 as a Republican.

If Frank Sullivan were an isolated case, Democratic officials would have nothing to fret about. But clearly he is not. Within two years of Bush's 1988 election, more than 240 Democratic elected officials joined the GOP. Given the partisanship in American politics, for an elected official of one party to go over to the other can be a wrenching act. But in the Sun Belt, where the vast majority of these switches occurred, changing parties didn't require changing ideology. Most offered a rationale similar to Tommy Robinson, the tough-talking former Little Rock sheriff turned congressman, who put it simply when he moved from the Democratic to the Republican party in 1990: "The hard fact is there is and will be no room for conservative Southern Democrats in today's national Democratic party."

A few big name Democrats, such as Louisiana's Governor Buddy Roemer, have become Republicans. Some, like Robinson when he ran for Arkansas governor, found themselves losing GOP primaries in bids for higher office. But some have been successful. Tampa Mayor Robert Martinez was elected governor of Florida in 1986, although he was defeated for reelection in 1990. Phil Gramm has twice been elected to the U.S. Senate from Texas and seems almost a certain candidate for the 1996 GOP presidential nomination.

But most of the switchers were county officials, mayors, or state lawmakers. In a decade or so they will be running for Congress and statewide offices. A big chunk of them are baby-boomers who, like Sullivan, can read the handwriting on the wall.

The party switchers are symptomatic of a much more serious potential problem for the Democrats—the same type of infrastructure problems that handicapped the GOP for decades.

The best and brightest young people entering politics for the better part of two decades, beginning with John Kennedy's 1960 inauguration, chose to be Democrats. First it was the appeal of Kennedy, followed by the antiwar and civil rights movements which were primarily coordinated by Democrats and were popular with the young. Then Watergate, which badly tainted the GOP as far as most of the politically ambitious youth were concerned. That string of events hobbled GOP efforts to find good young candidates to begin their journey through the political pipeline.

Then two events intervened. The 1978 tax revolt—which sparked a Republican resurgence—and Carter's failed presidency not only changed the voting allegiance of young people, but also the career of the best and the brightest. It became harder—especially in the Sun Belt—for the Democrats to recruit good young, white candidates unless they were liberal enough to feel comfortable with the Democrats' image. And, in something of a catch-22, if the candidates fit that image they were less likely to become winners.

This phenomenon, like most of what was happening in American politics during the period, had a racial dimension to it.

"In Texas there is a growing belief there is no longer room for young, upwardly mobile Anglos in the Democratic party," former San Antonio Mayor Cisneros stated. "Many believe it to be true and don't want to make concessions in their views" to conform to the Democratic national line. "It hasn't yet reached crisis proportions, but certainly the trends do not look good."

It was not just happening in Texas, either. Slowly, but surely, it was happening almost everywhere. It was most prevalent on the local level, but Cisneros was on target about the long-term implications.

The GOP turned off most young people during the late sixties and early seventies because of its support for the Vietnam War and Watergate. But that didn't translate into serious problems for the party until the early eighties when the Republicans sought to extend their presidential success to the local and state level and lacked a sufficient supply of good candidates coming through the pipeline.

This syndrome now became the Democrats' problem. Their failure to retain the allegiance of most young whites in the eighties and early nineties meant that unless something changed, come the turn of the century they would face serious problems finding candidates who were neither doctrinaire liberals nor members of a minority.

As Democrats continued to lose the White House they kept telling themselves that nothing was fundamentally wrong with their party.

After all, they controlled Congress and most of the state and local offices as well. And indeed, since the GOP began its run on the White House in 1968, Democrats have kept control of the House of Representatives and only lost the Senate from 1980-86. They've also taken a majority of the nation's governorships, although sometimes by a narrow margin, and have held a huge lead in state legislative chambers.

As a result, Democrats have deluded themselves into believing that the split-level political alignment in America means the voters want it that way. They seem to take as gospel the quip of Charlie McDowell, the *Richmond Times-Dispatch* columnist whose wit livened American living rooms for more than a decade on "Washington Week in Review." "We elect Democrats to Congress and state and local offices to give us stuff, and we elect Republicans so we don't have to pay for them."

Democratic leaders grudgingly acknowledge that the public doesn't trust them to run the country which, for them, explains the White House drought. They also believe voters consciously elect Democrats to Congress to keep an eye on GOP presidents. It may sound great to political scientists, but it just ain't so.

This Democratic attitude stems from a belief that if realignment comes, it will occur like the last time around, in one fell swoop— not surprising, given how strongly the party is tied to the past. In 1932, the Democrats recall, when FDR swept into office, he brought with him Democratic control of Congress as well as hundreds of state and local offices. These officials ended a decades-long Republican control of American politics.

But once again, the future is not the past. Dealignment has already occurred—the end of Democratic control of American politics. And it is being followed by a trickle-down form of realignment that, unless checked at the presidential level, will mean eventual GOP control of the lesser organs of government. What guarantees it is the massive swing in party identification of the middle class from the Democratic to the Republican party.

To a large degree, money and incumbency explain the Democrats' congressional hold. In the late 1980s, the reelection rate in the House of Representatives among members who ran was about 98 percent, higher than that enjoyed by members of the Supreme Soviet before the end of the USSR's one-party rule.

"Incumbents in Congress have tools that are just very, very difficult to overcome," former New Jersey Governor Kean admits. "If they send nice mail for five years and in the sixth year someone's out there saying they're a bum, you can't always get that across."

Incumbents have the advantage of tens of thousands of dollars of free mailing privilege and taxpayer-paid staff members who spend their time trying to make the lawmaker look good in the public eye. They are in an excellent position to command news coverage and collect kudos for solving the problems of constituents. "Let's face it," quipped John Rowland, a Connecticut Republican whose election to the House in 1984 at age twenty-seven made him the youngest member at the time, "you have to be a bozo to lose this job."

But Democratic incumbents are more effective than Republicans in protecting their turf for two reasons. First, their view of an activist government gives them freedom to fight for goodies from Washington for their districts. According to studies, Democrats devote a greater percentage of their staff resources to such pursuits than Republicans. Secondly, Democratic members have lower attendance records overall than Republicans, indicating they spend more time attending to constituents in their districts.[1]

Given the Democrats' edge in using their official position to ensure reelection, a stalemate has developed over how to reform the political system. Everyone agrees it is spinning out of control, but although both parties want the rules changed, their approach tells volumes about the state of congressional elections.

The Democrats, who have traditionally fostered government regulation, want to cap spending in congressional races. That is self-serving, since it is a boon for incumbents who begin any campaign with a huge advantage in name recognition.

Republicans, for their part, want to nullify the current advantage Democrats enjoy in fund-raising for congressional campaigns. That edge surprises many who see the Democrats as the party of the little guy, and the GOP as the tool of big business. But the edge exists. Despite the GOP's image, Democratic congressional candidates traditionally outspend Republicans by a wide margin.

The reason: Incumbents are much better investments for political action committees trying to curry favor. And there are more Democratic incumbents than Republican ones. Surprisingly too, the Republican donor base includes many more small givers than the Democrats, who get most of their money from the fat cats. Thus the GOP solution to campaign reform is to ban contributions from political action committees (PACs). Interestingly, most of these PACs represent business groups whose individual members vote for GOP candidates, especially on the presidential level, but the PACs themselves contribute to Democrats because Democrats run Congress.

As matters stand, Democrats have been able to hold their congressional majority with ease.

Their success can also be laid at the doorstep of Republicans. They have not been as smart or aggressive in going after the Democrats at the congressional level as at the presidential level. If Republicans had retained all the seats they held at one time or another during the 1980s, they would have a majority both in the House and the Senate. For that they have only themselves to blame. They let districts that were solidly Republican on the presidential level slip away, and a disproportionate share of those congressmen were defeated because of ethical problems.

On the congressional level the GOP failed to capitalize on the attitudinal changes taking place in America. Most people agreed that government wasn't working, but Republican congressmen were unable, or unwilling, to do anything but criticize the Democratic majority, especially when it came to their seeming preoccupation with the poor.

The Republicans in Congress almost gave away the game by apparently believing that the private marketplace would solve the problems of the middle class if left to its own devices. By failing to provide serious alternative ideas on environment, health care, and education, Republicans shot themselves in the foot time after time on the congressional level.

Ironically, for years Republicans were treading the same path

traveled by Democrats on the presidential level. Republican congressional candidates failed to offer clear, common sense alternatives to solve domestic policy problems, just as Democratic White
House hopefuls had no new ideas concerning the big economic and
foreign policy issues.

"Conservatives and Republicans have failed to articulate an attractive alternative to the liberal welfare state," conceded Vin
Weber, a prematurely balding Republican congressman from Minnesota who became a leader of the GOP's younger members.
"Most conservatives have chosen not to enter the debate on domestic policy, with the result that Americans still have more confidence
in Democrats than in Republicans when it comes to poverty, homelessness, and education. Our failure to think more creatively about
the role of government in domestic policy has probably cost us
control of the Congress and the state legislatures."

So in the early 1990s, the Republicans began offering alternatives
built around the concept of rewarding work, using financial incentives rather than regulations, and providing for local, rather than
national, control of such programs in an effort to limit the influence
of the hated government bureaucrats.

In many ways, the Republicans were racing to recast their image
on "caring" issues at the same time the Democrats were trying to
reshape theirs on race, foreign policy, taxes, and crime.

The betting was on the Republicans.

One practical reason for the split-level nature of U.S. politics
during this period was that winning the White House was like
building a basketball team. One great player could carry the day,
whether a charismatic Ronald Reagan or a more solid George Bush.
But controlling Congress was like football. It was a numbers game.
One great player didn't always make the difference. And the Democrats had greater bench strength because of their years in power. The
infrastructure problems caused by a shortage of good, young moderate candidates had not yet reached the congressional level.

Thus, when a Senate seat or governor's chair opened and the
Republican candidate was a congressman, more often than not the
Democrats were able to win back the vacated House seat. In 1990,
nine GOP members of Congress gave up their seats—and almost

certain reelection—to seek a U.S. Senate seat or governorship. The GOP retained only four of those nine seats that November.

Much of the reason for the Democrats' congressional success through the lean presidential years of the 1970s and 1980s was their solid control of legislatures. This assured a virtual political farm club of young state lawmakers looking to move up. And the young, hard-working state representative was generally a better-known and more attractive candidate than the political newcomer, often a local businessman, that the GOP typically offered. But it is doubtful whether that edge will continue, given the Democrats' increasing inability to attract young moderates.

Increasingly too, when the Democrats do find a young moderate, he or she is apt to be ideologically close to the Republicans. Jill Long, the determined Democratic congresswoman from the northern Indiana district that gave America Dan Quayle, is a good example. After Quayle became vice president and Congressman Dan Coats was named to take Quayle's Senate seat, she won Coats' House seat by running against taxes and the bureaucracy—positions learned during her two previous losing campaigns for the seat. "I would be comfortable being a moderate Republican," admits Long, whose Fort Wayne office has a picture of herself with George Bush prominently displayed near the front door.[2]

But an even more important reason accounted for the Democrats' congressional winning streak at the very time they were almost impotent in presidential elections—their skill at reapportionment politics.

At the beginning of every decade the U.S. Constitution requires the federal government to undertake a census to determine the size and location of the country's population. That information is used for a variety of government purposes, including redistributing the number of congressional seats beginning in the first election after the census year; i.e., 1972, 1982, 1992, and so on.

From 1970 to 1992—roughly the period encompassing the exodus of white voters from the Democratic party on the presidential level—forty-four congressional seats, more than 10 percent of the 435 seats in the House, have moved from the generally Democratic Northeast and Midwest to the increasingly Republican Sun Belt.

Yet, entering the 1992 campaign, the Democrats have been able to hold their House margin. One big reason: Their control of state legislative chambers that draw the redistricting maps has allowed them to dictate the shape of the political playing field.

What the Democrats have done successfully is to group Republicans into a small number of heavily GOP districts and create a larger number of Democratic districts with smaller, yet sustainable, Democratic majorities. The impact of this strategy is predictable. In 1988 Democratic congressional candidates got just 53.3 percent of the votes, but won 69.8 percent of the seats. In the 350 congressional districts with major party competition in 1990, Republicans won 47 percent of the votes, but only 37 percent of the seats.

The classic example is the redistricting plan drawn up for California's 1982 reapportionment by the late Phil Burton, a hard-charging San Francisco liberal Democratic congressman. Burton, whose knowledge of California demographics was legendary, put together a map Republicans decried in public, but privately admired for its political acuity. One district was composed of 387 sides to make sure it maximized the Democratic advantage.

By late 1981 the California redistricting was complete, and Democrats were aware just how effective they had been. Ed Rollins, then Reagan's White House political honcho who later ran his 1984 reelection campaign, remembers running into his old friend and political nemesis Tony Coelho at a typical Washington reception. At events like these, war horses from opposite sides of the political aisle renew their friendships, which in this case traced from both men's California roots.

As the two shared a drink, Coelho was positively euphoric.

"I'll never forget Tony telling me" about the redistricting plan, Rollins remarked almost a decade later. " 'Not only am I going to take back every [congressional] seat you won in the seventies [in California], but I am going to pick your future leaders and decide who is in Congress for the Republicans.' And he was right," Rollins sighed.

In 1980, the last year the previous congressional map was in effect, Democrats had 22 and Republicans 21 of California's 43 seats. In 1982, when California picked up two more seats for a total of 45, Burton's new map went into effect and the Democrats won 28 while the Republicans trailed with seventeen.

Just the political tides? Hardly. On that same 1982 election day California elected a Republican governor.

The runaway population growth in California's GOP areas during the 1980s dictated that anything approaching a just map for the state's 1992 redistricting should mean a gain of at least five Republican seats. And that doesn't take into account that a majority of the seven new seats California will get beginning in 1992 will likely be Republican.

Given the racial nature of the defection of white voters from the Democratic party that has produced the GOP presidential domination, race is most likely to play a major role should the Democrats eventually lose their congressional bastion. In fact, in a world where unlikely political bedfellows often emerge, black and Hispanic Democrats and Republicans are joining for the ultimate political one-night stand.

The 1982 amendments to LBJ's Voting Rights Act are likely to play a crucial role in this changing scene. Like virtually every other piece of civil rights legislation over the past generation, the 1982 changes were authored by Democrats. But this legislation, in the bright light of 20-20 hindsight, has become a Republican gold mine.

The law requires that wherever the Census Bureau finds a large enough concentration of blacks or Hispanics to elect a member of Congress, or of the state legislature, the redistricting map *must* be drawn to create a district in which the minority population constitutes a majority of voters. If not, the courts no longer need to find that the lawmakers intended to discriminate against minorities; they can simply throw out the map and order a new one. No matter how ridiculously shaped the district looks, minority strength is the key factor. Districts that in the past would otherwise fail the courts' "geographic compactness" test will now be allowed if they create a minority-dominated district.

Further, in areas where voting rights violations have been proven in the past and where there are enough black or minority voters, lawmakers must create "super majority" districts. These will have a population that is 60-65 percent black or Hispanic to compensate for lower minority turnout on Election Day.

The reason this brings joy to Republican hearts is simple. It gives the GOP a powerful tool to limit the ability of Democrats to parcel out minorities to a large number of districts which would provide the margin of victory for white Democrats.

Take, for example, the typical major metropolitan area with a half-dozen or more congressional seats. Typically, the heavily black city is surrounded by even more heavily white suburbs. Overall, these metropolitan areas have much larger suburban than urban populations. Under the 1982 law, blacks—the most loyal Democrats—would be packed into one or more congressional districts in which they are a voting majority. That means they cannot, as in the past, be sprinkled over a multitude of districts to provide the margin of victory for white Democrats. Recall: the whiter a district, the more likely it is to be Republican. And that's not racist, that's fact.

Although in 1980 minorities and Republicans worked together on reapportionment, it was done on a limited basis. Since then, the court decisions have provided much greater opportunities. Entering the 1990 reapportionment, Republicans were better prepared. They actively worked with black and Hispanic groups, portraying themselves as victims of the same white Democratic gerrymandering.

Blacks understand they may be getting into bed with those who have consistently been their mortal enemies in state legislature after state legislature, but they find the opportunity tempting.

"My interest lies with whoever can strengthen and empower African-Americans," admits Annette Polly Williams, a Democratic state lawmaker from Milwaukee who led Jesse Jackson's 1988 campaign in Wisconsin. "My position will be to ally with anyone" whose support can increase the number of black districts. "We, as African-Americans, have got to look out for ourselves."

Or, as Kay Patterson, a state senator from South Carolina who chaired that legislature's Black Caucus, put it: "I'm not going to sacrifice a black district to be a Democrat. I was black before I was a Democrat."

Patterson's South Carolina, once among the nation's Democratic bastions, showed just how vulnerable the Democratic house of cards was.

The state's population was one-third black, but the state had not had a black congressman since Reconstruction. All six congressmen following the 1990 elections were white, four of them Democrats. The defection of whites from the party had become so massive that polls showed less than 20 percent of South Carolina whites considered themselves Democrats. Here as elsewhere the Republicans gave the state's Black Caucus—which was 100 percent Democratic—all possible help in drawing up redistricting maps.

Sophisticated computer software, designed to work in conjunction with detailed census data, was developed by GOP operatives and received up to $250,000 on the open market. But the Republicans sold the software to minorities and their advocates at minimal cost so they could draw up maps to maximize minority strength.

Patterson's attitude was typical of many frustrated black Democratic leaders who felt the white Democratic leadership had used blacks for decades without reward: "I wouldn't give a damn if all six are Democrats, but if they are all six white, that doesn't help me any," he said.

Caught in the middle was the white Democratic leadership. Especially now, with declining Democratic identification among whites, from a strategic point of view they needed to continue using black votes to retain their majority status in legislatures and Congress. Yet, to oppose black interests in drawing redistricting maps threatened to fracture the party coalition.

Robert Shaheen, the Democratic speaker of the South Carolina House, could see what was happening. Creation of a black district "would probably mean five Republicans and one Democrat in South Carolina" eventually, he said. "The opportunities would be greatly diminished for Democratic candidates because of the depletion of black voters and putting them into a black district."

Entering the 1992 elections, blacks were almost 13 percent of the nation's population, yet made up less than 6 percent of the House of Representatives, and not one of the one hundred senators. In the South, where blacks are roughly 20 percent of the population, they had just 5 percent of the House seats. The situation for Hispanics—roughly 8 percent of Americans but less than 3 percent of House members—was similar.

It was clear as the 1992 redistricting approached that a dozen years of Reagan and Bush in the White House had produced a federal judiciary much more in tune with GOP thinking. Democrats understandably worried that the courts would overturn state legislative plans that did not properly create minority districts where possible.

"The Republicans have threatened to litigate us to death on redistricting plans and we expect them to do it," Democratic Chairman Brown acknowledged.

Yet another factor was playing into GOP hands in 1992. It was the last year in which incumbents elected prior to 1980 could convert the money in their political accounts to personal use upon their congressional retirement. After the 1990 elections, 166 House members were eligible to take the money and run—an average of about $250,000 each (some more than $1 million) could be put in the family bank accounts. By a more than two-to-one margin Democrats outnumbered Republicans among those with that option. No doubt many more Democrats than usual would be giving up their safe seats.

The other reality that boded well for Republican control of the House in the coming decade, a fact accepted by both Democrats and Republicans, was that the GOP didn't need to win 218 of the 435 House races to take control.

"If George Bush's reelection in 1992 gets us to 195 [House seats], I'm convinced there are enough Democrats [mostly in the South and West] who will switch parties," predicted Ed Rollins, brought in at the unheard-of annual salary of $250,000 to run the National Republican Congressional Committee in 1989. If conservative Democratic members no longer had to worry about losing their power as members of the ruling majority party in the House, they would be more likely to switch.

Although Rollins, who left the NRCC in 1991, may be overly optimistic, not many disagree with his general premise.

Virginia Democratic Senator Robb remembered the situation

when he was lieutenant governor of Virginia right after Reagan carried the state handily in 1980. Nine of the state's ten congressmen were Republicans, as was its governor. One of its U.S. senators was a Republican, another an Independent. Speculation was that the GOP might be ready to make a breakthrough at the state and local level in the Old Dominion and take control of the legislature. Although that did not occur—precisely because the Virginia Democratic party turned to conservative Democrats like Robb, Gerald Baliles, and Doug Wilder to lead them—Robb recalled the conversation he had with numerous conservative Democratic members of his legislature, many of them holding key posts.

"They said it didn't matter to them. They could be either Democrats or Republicans" depending on which party was in control, Robb said. He believes there are a number of Democratic congressmen, mostly from the South, who are in the same boat: "It is a matter of power and incumbency. I think there is a number short of a statistical majority that you [Republicans] could achieve and certainly cause some sleepless nights among some members. The theory is certainly valid in an abstract sense, whatever the number is."

In the Senate, Democratic control has not been as firm as in the House. The GOP won the Senate in 1980 and kept it until 1986. They could recapture it in 1992.

After the 1990 election the Democrats held a 57-43 edge in the Senate, having gained one seat in 1990. In 1992 Democrats were forced to defend 20 of the 34 seats up for election. Of the 20, 11 were freshmen—the most vulnerable—and all but one of them came into office in 1986 with 55 percent or less of the vote. Several other Democratic incumbents have been tarred by various scandals. Most of them came from Southern, Midwestern, and Western states where Bush was expected to carry the top of the ticket handily. If so, he could carry enough GOP challengers with him to gain a Senate majority.

In 1990, an analysis of the state of the Democratic party done by Tubby Harrison, Dukakis' 1988 pollster, for the congressional leadership put it bluntly. "We may be deluding ourselves if we think we can hold Congress forever," it read. What was needed was to fix the problems that had made Democrats almost noncompetitive on the presidential level, Harrison concluded.

The Democratic ability to dominate state legislatures far more than any other level of government is a tribute to the party's deep bench. But even there things were changing. The GOP actually held control of one legislative chamber in most of the major Northern states for most of the 1980s. The vast Democratic edge was in the South where, ironically, even Democrats agreed that control could not last. In 1979 only 14 percent of state lawmakers in Dixie were Republicans. By the time of the 1992 election, that figure had roughly doubled.

Furthermore, as the 1990s opened, disgust with politics-as-usual led Oklahoma, California, and Colorado to adopt initiatives limiting the length of state lawmakers' tenure. Other states seemed sure to follow and there were increasing calls for a limit on the tenure of members of Congress. Republicans were behind the movement and Democrats fought it, both for selfish reasons: anything that forced incumbents to retire would mean the loss of more Democratic seats than Republican. There was every indication that the term limitation movement for state and federal legislators was likely to pick up steam and, where successful, it would be a useful tool for the GOP.

The same purpose that united minority Democrats and Republicans to create minority congressional seats also existed on the state legislative level, where the GOP was certain to benefit in the long run. In fact, from all indications the coalition of convenience was likely to be more effective on the state than the federal legislative level. In Congress virtually every issue carries a partisan label. But in state houses, some issues—like roads, education, and law enforcement—often feature bipartisan cooperation.

The change on the state and local level throughout the South was especially ominous for the Democrats, and the legislative gains were only the least of it. Just as in Congress, incumbency and the nonpartisan nature of many local elections kept local Democrats in office long after voters in presidential elections had given the party up for dead.

In Frank Sullivan's Texas, the transformation was impressive over time. It began slowly, with support for Dwight Eisenhower in the 1950s. By 1992, Texas had gone Republican three straight times for president and four of the last five. In the 1960s the GOP won its first statewide office in a century when John Tower was elected to the Senate. In 1978, Texans elected the first GOP governor and by 1992 had won two of the last four gubernatorial elections and three of the last five U.S. Senate seats. The legislature still remained in Democratic hands, but Sullivan's sentiments were proof that on the local level too, change was coming.

In 1978, a mere 92 of the more than 3,000 elected officials in state, local, and county offices were Republican—only 2 of 24 U.S. House members, 3 of 31 state senators, and 19 of 150 state House members. Following the 1990 voting, there were 803 GOP officials in Texas—8 of 27 congressmen, 8 of 31 state senators, and 56 of 150 House members.

Perhaps the best proof was that although the 1990 GOP gubernatorial nominee, Clayton Williams, handed the governorship to Democrat Ann Richards on a silver platter, the movement toward the Republicans continued. Williams, who held a fifteen-point lead in the polls entering the final month, admitted, "I just would shoot myself in the foot and then I'd load up and try it again."

Yet the Republicans continued to pick up local offices and, for the first time ever, elected two "down-ballot" candidates for statewide office. The elections of Agriculture Commissioner Rick Perry and Treasurer Kay Bailey Hutchison were overshadowed by the Williams debacle, but they indicated the GOP growth.

If any doubt about the trend remained, all you had to do was look at the polls in which voters were asked which party they identified with. Traditionally, that is the best measurement of political change since voters often change their voting habits without changing their party registration. In 1974, the Texas Poll found that by a 59-16 margin Texas voters called themselves Democrats rather than Republicans. By the fall of 1990, the Harte-Hanks/Texas Poll showed the numbers were virtually even, 32-30, with the rest independents who tended to vote GOP. But a closer examination of the numbers showed just how dramatically Democratic fortunes were likely to drop in the future. Among voters under age forty-five, the Republicans had a ten-point edge. Among whites, the GOP margin was fourteen points.

"Texas is the classic example of how the pressure is exerted from the top down. That process hasn't happened as much in all the other states. But Texas may be the image of the country's political future if this process continues for another decade," predicts Bill Galston, Mondale's 1984 chief issues aide and now a University of Maryland professor.

It wasn't, of course, just happening in Texas. The Sun Belt was the best indicator of attitudinal change. In South Carolina, once a Democratic bastion, polls showed a big GOP plurality and only 15-20 percent of whites considering themselves Democrats. In 1978, turnout in the Democratic primary was nineteen times that of the GOP contest. By 1990, when there was no GOP contest for governor but a black-white face-off in the Democratic primary, only twice as many voters took part in the Democratic as in the Republican primary.

But even that didn't fully show the extent of the Democratic erosion. Between 1986 and 1990, turnout in the Democratic primary for governor fell almost by half. Since the black candidate, State Sen. Theo Mitchell, won the 1990 primary to become the first black to head the ticket in post-Reconstruction history, it was evident the missing voters weren't black. And that became clear the following November when GOP Gov. Carroll Campbell was re-elected with more than 70 percent of the vote.

The change was so rapid in Florida that it was even showing up in party registration, a longer process than party identification. During the 1980s, new Republican registrants outnumbered Democrats 20-1 in Florida, and when it came to the ballot box, that strength showed. The GOP turned a 12-3 handicap in the U.S. House delegation into a 10-9 edge. And it improved its share of state legislators from 26 to 40 percent even though it too lost the governorship in 1990 when Democrat Lawton Chiles spiked Martinez for breaking a promise not to raise taxes.

The GOP realignment was happening fastest in places like South Carolina, Texas, and Florida, but it was going on everywhere. Even in California, the Democrats' last hope for retaining their hold, the signs were dismal. In 1990, Democratic registration in that state dropped to below 50 percent of the electorate for the first time since 1934. And these are people who had been voting

Republican for president for decades. The last Democrat to carry California was Lyndon Johnson in 1964.

From state to state, Democratic leaders felt powerless to stem the tide. The party's national image had become such an albatross around their necks that local leaders felt they could only make marginal progress or tread water.

"If something isn't done on the national level, it's going to continue to work its way down the ticket. Those of us fighting the Republican dream of realignment have to have ammunition. If there is no sense of change at the national level in the Democratic party, my guess is that the Republicans can achieve their realignment," Virginia's Robb predicted.

14

The Treatment: Painful But Necessary

Washington columnist Mark Shields, a one-time Democratic operative, is a jovial but very direct man. Shields, who shed fifty pounds in 1988 by watching what went into his mouth, recognized that the self-deception within his beloved party stemmed from Democrats not watching what came out of theirs. Like the fat man who gobbles ice cream and candy, Democrats were seeking to fuel their electoral comeback with outmoded political junk food.

To the now-trim Shields the Democrats continually go through the four stages of losing campaigns.

First, they blame the candidate—a common Democratic practice since 1972. Democratic leaders seem to believe that George McGovern, Jimmy Carter, Walter Mondale, and Michael Dukakis magically appeared before the country as the Democratic nominees who could not win in November. They never acknowledge that these candidates reflect Democratic primary voters' out-of-touch views.

Secondly, Democrats blame the voters—and have for almost two decades. Shields saw it in 1972 when he was national political director of Ed Muskie's initially popular campaign for the Democratic presidential nomination. After a loss to George Wallace in the Florida primary, Muskie turned to a phalanx of television cameras and blamed his defeat on the voters' poor judgment. Democrats might be on to something if they blamed the voters in their own primaries; at least that might lead them to useful analysis. But in the years past, they have blamed the general election voters. Anytime the party's candidate or agenda has been defeated, Democratic leaders complain that voters just don't seem to understand what the Democratic candidate is trying to say. Or, they argue, it is the racism of white voters responding to Republican hate-mongering.

Thirdly, losers look for a gimmick—any gimmick. It is one more instance of the same ample evidence of Democratic self-delusion. They insist that their problems can be papered over. At one point, for example, they unearthed the gender gap, hoping that women might be the ultimate answer; by concentrating on females, a bare majority of the voters, perhaps the election would be theirs. When that failed, they looked to the mobilization theory, pinning their hopes on the untapped electoral power of nonvoters, especially minorities. But not much there. After the 1988 defeat, some began trying to get state legislatures to change the way their electoral votes were cast. No luck there either.

Finally, says Shields, comes the overwhelming desire to find a winner, regardless of who the candidate is, whatever his or her message. Dukakis, a bland man whose form of static liberalism satisfied neither Democratic liberals nor moderates, fit that description to perfection. After all, this candidate was cheered by the 1988 Democratic convention when he said the campaign was "not about ideology but about competence."

But the Democratic problem is not that the overwhelming number of white, middle-class voters don't understand what the party is saying. The problem is the voters understand quite clearly. And they don't agree.

Following the 1990 elections, Democratic pollster Bill Hamilton found that more than four in ten voters agreed that "the Democratic party is the party of the past—holding onto tired, outdated ideas that no longer work." Those who agreed the Democrats were living in the past were more likely to be younger voters with decades of voting ahead of them, whereas those who disagreed were older. Almost a decade earlier—a year after Reagan's election—Hamilton's polls found only three in ten voters felt that Democrats were stuck in the past.

As the New Deal shaped the political order of the Industrial Age, so too today Democrats must develop a coherent philosophy that meets the challenges and changes of this new information age. Thus far they have failed to develop new ideas that appeal to anyone other than the shrinking number of doctrinaire liberals. Until they do so, they will remain out of power.

Nothing else really matters.

Because they have nothing persuasive to say to the middle class, Democrats fall back on the fond memories older voters have of FDR, Truman, and JFK. But the only Democratic presidents most young and middle-age voters remember clearly are Jimmy Carter and Lyndon Johnson, and generally the memories are not pleasant.

The Democrats will have a real chance to win the White House when:

1. The voters in the Sun Belt cast the key votes to choose the Democratic presidential nominee, not those in New York, Pennsylvania, and Illinois, as has been the case for several election cycles. As the political balance in America continues to shift South and West, it is critical that Democrats respond. The data is clear; voters in the Sun Belt think far differently about life than those in the Frost Belt, especially the Northeast.
2. The Democratic nominee isn't invoking the ghosts of the past in late October of a presidential election year. That means the Democrats will have new ideas to discuss; they will be prospecting for votes based on what they will do in the future, not what they have done in the past.

It wasn't always so. The once-innovative Democratic Left used to produce practical solutions to America's problems. But currently there is an intellectual void.

It wasn't coincidence that Louisiana's Buddy Roemer became the first sitting governor in U.S. history to switch parties in March of 1991. As he explained, "after more than ten years of public service it has been my observation and increasing conviction that it is the Republican party that is becoming most open to new ideas, new thinking, new people."

When Democratic Chairman Brown says, "We are centimeters rather than miles from putting together the formula for winning a presidential election," he not only is wrong, but greatly so. The only strategy Democrats have had for the last decade is to pray for a Republican scandal or a deep recession.

Americans, for one, do not believe in redistributive economics, which is at the heart of the time-honored Democratic strategy that seems to be making a comeback. Of course Americans want the rich to pay their fair share of taxes, but that is the political equivalent of supporting motherhood. When New Jersey Gov. Jim Florio in 1990 tried a tax program aimed at implementing that idea, he was hit by a middle-class revolt. His programs raised levies on individuals who made $35,000 and couples who earned $70,000. Despite all his charts and graphs explaining that the middle class wouldn't be forking out any more in taxes, they didn't believe him. The bulk of those who were hit didn't consider themselves rich, and those below the threshold figured the Democratic tax man would get them next as they climbed the economic ladder.

Democrats confuse the generally popular notion that those with higher incomes should shoulder a greater burden of the cost of government services with the much less accepted idea that all incomes should be equal. In fact, America is by far the least likely of the seven Western industrialized nations to believe great disparity in incomes is bad. Only 28 percent of Americans feel that way, half the rate of strongly capitalist West Germany and a smaller fraction yet of Great Britain, Holland, and Italy.[1]

Class warfare no longer works politically because it seems to the middle-class voter that the Democratic party is bent on punishing him for his success. These voters look at programs like Florio's as punitive redistribution. To the millions like Mark and Pam Blips, Democrats, having failed to raise the incomes of the poor, seem bent on trying to legislate equality by limiting *their* upward mobility.

" 'Soak the rich' will not suffice as a message for 1992" because "it's not clear to the voters that Democrats are on the side of the middle class," Democratic pollster Mark Mellman believes.

In conceptual form it is egalitarianism, not capitalism, that the Democrats are proffering at a time when the rest of the world has decided that the high standard of living available to most people under capitalism is worth the inequities the system entails.

Even if a populist cycle is underway in America, as many Democrats contend, it isn't like the old days. To say that the Republicans are letting a few people get very rich doesn't work by itself. The middle class doesn't believe the rich are getting richer at their expense because the American economy is no longer driven from the top by Fortune 500 companies, those big fat cats with inherited wealth. The engine now is smaller—entrepreneurial companies, created by middle-class people like themselves who are seeking to climb even higher.

Lyndon Johnson used to say that in Texas the Republicans understood old oil, while the Democrats related to new oil. The wildcatter who was seeking his fortune was a Democrat, and the party worked for him. The Republicans were the friends of the big oil companies. "Unfortunately, it seems today as if we have lost both Texaco and the wildcatter to the Republicans," Senator Nunn of Georgia maintains.

Democratic economic policy must be targeted to help the companies that are creating jobs and wealth, not hinder them through mindless restrictions. Democrats, because of their labor base, traditionally worry that large corporations are abusing workers, and certainly some cases exist, although fewer than in the past. Yet those companies will find a way to deal with, or get around, needless government red tape. But for these small companies upon whose future America depends, government policies can spell the difference between life or death. Democrats must discard their model of a highly centralized industrial policy and their belief they stand with labor battling the interests of business. Republicans have abandoned their belief that they stand with management in defense of laissez-faire capitalism, accepting the concept—if not always the specifics—of protecting society from corporate excesses.

Above all, Democrats must adopt polices that foster economic growth. Obviously, just dividing the existing pie won't do. What is less obvious—and politically painful for many to admit—is that policies that foster growth limit redistribution. And policies that foster redistribution are a disincentive to growth.

Simply put, think of it in terms of taxes. The fewer taxes a worker knows he will pay on his marginal production, the more incentive he has to produce. But low tax receipts mean less money for government to redistribute. Yet society in the long run will be better off because of the economic growth. And in the long run so too the welfare recipient if he can be brought into the growing economy. The challenge for government is to foster policies that provide incentives for production *and* bring the poor and disadvantaged into positions where they can take advantage of a growing economy.

Americans are compassionate about the needs of the less fortunate, but they believe Democratic government spending programs have gone too far toward sacrificing the well-being of the middle class. The middle class will support smart investment, but not throw good money after bad.

Democratic pollster Celinda Lake told a meeting of Democratic state chairmen after the 1990 elections that the party still had not changed its image with the middle class when it came to fiscal responsibility. "People don't feel the Democrats understand that taxes are real money. They think [Democrats believe] it is Monopoly money," she stated.

If the middle class feels it is being played for a sucker—as it has about Democratic spending programs—it gets mad. And it gets even at the voting booth.

For example: The middle class is more interested in programs like Head Start that seek to reach poor kids before they get caught up in the cycle of poverty than more generous benefits for adults whom they consider a lost cause. These voters may want a tough-minded approach that calls for harsher penalties for criminals under age eighteen. But at the same time they favor more generous programs to head off deviant behavior before it begins. But, in order to get public support for programs like Head Start, Democrats must demonstrate their fiscal responsibility by giving up some of their pet programs that have proven ineffective.

Middle-class voters believe in the notion of individual account-ability. And they are growing increasingly frustrated with a society where people blame their problems on someone else: the drunken driver who sues the bar for serving him too many drinks; the criminal who says his deprived childhood made him do it; the tax cheater who says everyone does it.

The middle-class frustration with this trend comes out in its complete lack of patience with the way Democrats view their con-stituents as victims: blacks, feminists, gays, and workers are always the victims of discrimination by the white-male-heterosexual-business-dominated culture.

In the Democrats' view, victimization explains lower test scores for blacks, lower earnings for women, the lack of a cure for AIDS, and the disappearance of good-paying, low-skilled jobs. They re-fuse to see that black family structure fails to put a premium on scholastic achievement, that women pick careers for different rea-sons from men, that AIDS is the medical challenge of a generation, and that an increasingly competitive world has left firms no choice but to adapt or die.

Democrats therefore oppose any efforts aimed, for example, at imposing reciprocal obligations on welfare beneficiaries—such as required work or school. Democrats need to appear tough-minded when dealing with their strongest supporters.

Americans want a nation where everyone has a chance to excel, even if that means some fail. They believe in equal opportunity for all, but not mandated equal outcomes. Until Democrats come to terms with the dichotomy between their support for racial prefer-ence programs and the almost universal dislike among white Amer-icans for such policies, electorally they will remain behind the racial eight-ball.

And, because of demographics, this situation will only get worse. Older white voters are both the most likely to be racists—i.e., to think blacks are inferior—and the most likely to carry liberal guilt, having lived through the era when blacks were bla-tantly abused. Those born after World War II grew up believing the civil rights movement had secured equal rights for all and that a level playing field now existed. And this group of voters—those who can't understand racial preference policies, who are repelled by the Democrats' belief in special treatment for blacks—will shape the country politically for the next two generations.

Similar racial preference plans have failed in other multicultural nations. They just don't work. In fact, white resentment against racial preferences remains relatively tame in the United States. By contrast, in New Delhi in late 1990, thousands of protesters rioted over an Indian government plan that gave preference to specific racial groups for government jobs, regardless of applicants' specific economic situation or abilities. Protesters hijacked government buses and stormed Parliament, which authorized the plan. Several dozen people were killed.

This is not to predict similar violence here, but rather to suggest that the resentment that exists is neither unique nor likely to just disappear.

One way to deal with the political problems both of white resentment and of helping the disadvantaged is to redefine who should benefit from such programs. Currently, eligibility for special help—whether in college admission or landing a job—stems from one's race because of the generalization that blacks are more likely to be poor than whites. But, with the growth of the black middle class, not all blacks are disadvantaged.

But, if the criteria for special help were changed so that eligibility for special consideration was determined by meeting a well-defined set of circumstances regardless of race, such programs would then truly help only those who needed it—whether inner city blacks or Hispanics, or rural whites. Not only would this be a more efficient way to help those from disadvantaged backgrounds, it would go a long way toward eliminating white middle-class resentment that such efforts are going to middle-class blacks at their expense.

The key to understanding American voters is realizing they respond to symbols that represent their most cherished values. While Democrats are fond of charging voters with being simplistic for responding, Republicans understand how crucial this is. Voters have neither the time nor inclination to wade through lengthy position papers.

Take crime. Americans believe in being tough on criminals. Four in five support capital punishment and believe candidates are tough on crime when they support the death penalty, not when they talk about how unfairly it has been applied or seem more concerned with rehabilitation—which reflects many Democratic leaders' 1960s mentality.

This pattern was repeated on issue after issue. It was especially true when it came to the hot-button ones that got middle America's blood churning.

Despite the growth in tolerance for alternative lifestyles in this country over the past generation, Americans believe in family values, if perhaps not defined so narrowly as many on the Republican Right would like. Americans, by and large, don't consider homosexuals bad, but they do worry that attempts by politicians, invariably Democrats, to legitimize the gay lifestyle may make it glamorous and thus attract their own teenagers. If Democrats want to prevent baby-boom parents from feeling threatened they must tone down their image of being in the hip pocket of people who make the middle class uncomfortable.

As for foreign policy, the vast majority of Americans tell pollsters that they believe the American way of life is superior to that of any other country, and that America has a special role to play in the world. Republicans understand those emotions much better than Democrats. Although Democrat-turned-Republican Jeanne Kirkpatrick was indulging in hyperbole in 1984 when she claimed Democrats always "blame America first," the charge held enough truth to make a point with the average voter.

When, for example, the vast majority of Democratic congressmen voted against authorizing Bush to attack Iraq in early 1991, Robert Torricelli, a partisan Democratic congressman from New York's Jersey suburbs, characterized it as a "peace-at-any-price mentality." That had not been the case in the days of FDR, Harry Truman, or JFK, who understood and reflected the healthy patriotism in this country. Yet today, Democrats seem unnecessarily embarrassed by that emotion.

Three avenues are open to Democrats if they wish to change the political situation. They have been trying variations of two, but have had, and will continue to have, little success with either: They can continue to tell the white middle class it is wrong, that the party's concerns are in fact focused on them, not on the poor and minorities; or they can tell voters that in this time of limited resources middle-class needs must be overlooked in order to help the more needy poor. So far, of course, both approaches have been politically ineffective.

The third alternative is actually to pursue policies aimed at the perceived needs of the middle class. The only practical answer, discussed later in this chapter, is to modify party doctrine without completely abandoning its predominantly have-not base. It would be foolish, however, to think this possible without at least part of that base feeling it is being deserted.

Underlying much of the Democrats' problem is the belief it can be all things to all people. That has never been true, although in the past the approach worked much better. Now, however, instantaneous communications provide Americans with huge amounts of information. Voters increasingly see themselves in a zero–sum situation—what is good for them is often harmful to someone else, and visa versa.

Democrats refuse to believe both that the middle class views events in a zero–sum context, and that in fact many political events and decisions do have a zero–sum impact. Democratic rhetoric is filled with calls for politicians to play to the electorate's dreams, not its fears. Perhaps that's because playing to voters' dreams allows Democrats once again to sidestep the contradiction inherent in their traditional coalition. But Machiavelli was correct: "Men are more motivated by fear of loss then they are hope of gain."

White voter perception of the zero–sum equation makes the racial component especially powerful. Jesse Jackson is right: "If we are all things to all people, we become rather ill-defined, indecisive—kind of like warm spit." But the Democrats' refusal to face facts has been self-defeating. To change their fate, they must reverse course.

If Democrats continue down the road they have traveled for the past generation, they will drive away more whites from the party. If things continue on their present course, Jackson's faction may soon win the internal struggle for party control. When enough moderate whites have fled the party, the coalition of minorities and white

liberals will achieve critical mass within Democratic councils—
leaving a party that will not win the White House.

Democrats must decide whether they want to remain competitive and try to win presidential elections or, as a sizable faction
within the party insists, stick with its traditional message and never
mind the consequences.

And it is not just Jackson who invokes the high ground, arguing
that any other path is treasonous. Paul Simon, a Democratic senator
from Illinois who sought the party's presidential nomination in
1988, got great mileage among the Democratic faithful by arguing
against modification. "The American people didn't reject Fritz
Mondale's ideas," he claimed, somehow believing, as is the Democratic wont, that Reagan had blinded the American people with his
charming personality.

Simon railed against those who would "shift the Democratic
traditions to the rich and the powerful" and thus forsake the FDR
legacy. "I am glad there is a Republican party, but one Republican
party is enough."

Implicit is the belief by Simon, and those who share his view, that
winning elections is not worth changing the party's historical principles, that any deviation from party orthodoxy, even to deal with a
changing society, is unacceptable. Liberals like Simon see adapting
to a new era as treasonous instead of smart.

Simon and his like believe that history is cyclical. Eventually, they
muse, times and attitudes will change, and Democratic philosophy
will be more appealing to a majority of Americans. In the meantime,
the party's fate is out of its own hands. Meanwhile, Democrats must
wait for a scandal, or economic collapse, or a foreign policy fiasco by
the Republicans to stem their party's losing streak.

The wiser Democratic alternative is to make a meaningful
change in the party's message. Democrats must revisit the party's
entire agenda and examine each of its policies and values in the light
of America today and not as it was in the 1930s or the 1960s. The
Democratic party that came to power through innovation has become the bulwark of the status quo. Even from a Democratic
perspective, there are no longer sound reasons for many parts of the
Democratic agenda.

In an intellectual sense, although, obviously, to a large degree
political as well, America's two political parties have changed
places.

"The Republicans used to be the status quo group. Now there's
a complete change," Virginia Senator Robb states. What happened, agrees former Michigan Governor Blanchard, is "we became the party of the status quo. We were able to win everything
but the presidency, and most assumed all you had to do was refine
the message a little bit."

From 1932 until 1965 Americans knew exactly who the Democrats were. They were the party that controlled the agenda of
American politics, not just the levers of power. They were the party
that issued new ideas, generally entailing government. They were
the party that stood for a strong U.S. role in the world. And they
were the party that in the early 1960s cut taxes and, even more
important, provided broad-based programs for all Americans, not
just the poor or minorities.

Because of these universal programs, most people thought they
were getting more value from government than they gave in taxes,
and such policies ensured continuing Democratic majorities.

During that period, Republicans called for smaller versions of
what the Democrats were offering and, unless they had an unusual
candidate, they lost. The one time they won the White House was
with a nonpolitical candidate—Dwight Eisenhower—who could
just as easily have been a Democrat.

But, over the last twenty-five years the shoe has been on the
other foot. With the exception of environmental awareness, virtually every major change in American policy has been
Republican—tax cuts, less government spending, a more traditional approach to social issues, or a stronger defense. The only
Democratic initiatives have been targeted toward the poor and
minorities.

Arkansas Governor Clinton didn't mince words in the spring of
1990 when he assumed the chairmanship of the Democratic Leadership Council. "The biggest problem for Democrats isn't that
George Bush is popular. It's that most Americans go about their
business every day and we [the Democratic party] don't ever cross

their minds." And that was because the Democrats weren't generating any ideas that caught the public's imagination.

In the early 1990s it was mostly the GOP that cranked out ideas on how to deal with the nation's domestic problems, ideas that responded to the middle-class mandate not to enlarge the role of government further. Many of the same ideas had in fact been advanced by moderate Democrats, and the DLC crowd as well, but the clout of special interest groups within their own party beat them down.

In education, Republicans called for legislation to allow students to go to public schools anywhere in a state—an idea pioneered by Clinton in Arkansas. They also sought to open up the teaching profession to BA or BS graduates with real experience in a field, but without a degree in education. Unlike the Democrats, the Republicans could run on these themes because they had no need to worry about teachers' unions whose leaders were Democrats.

In the area of crime, Republicans pushed for requirements that parolees pass literacy and drug tests before gaining release, secure in the knowledge that the middle class was not filled with prisoners' rights advocates or civil libertarians.

In yet another area, Republicans felt little internal opposition to their efforts to require work and school attendance from families on public assistance and to expel drug users from public housing, because welfare rights groups hold little sway in GOP councils.

In general, the GOP brought market forces to the war on poverty, believing that whatever money government provided should go to the poor rather than the bureaucracy, and that government programs should be graded on the results rather than on the money spent. All of the GOP ideas appealed to the white middle class. The voters who sought solutions felt the Democratic approach of government interference rather than individual accountability had proved ineffective.

"Policies forged in the economic crisis of the 1930s and the cultural schisms of the 1960s are less and less relevant to the changes and challenges that are facing America," Virginia's Robb says. And the Democrats are stuck in that time warp.

Futurist Alvin Toffler, a one-time liberal and union activist, believes "the Democrats have been hostile to ideas generally. They had a kit of ideas that were very successful for a long time. They just seem to feel 'all we need is someone to communicate' without questioning what it is they should communicate."

Between 1968 and 1992, the only Democrat to win the presidency, Jimmy Carter, was a moderate who offered a vision that challenged large portions of the Democratic Holy Grail. Had he gotten his political start in a state with a viable GOP, instead of Georgia, Carter might easily have been a Republican. Or so Democratic liberals certainly thought. They sought to deny him renomination in 1980 on ideological grounds when he failed to deliver the liberal agenda.

With such opposition to anybody who deviated from the ideological line, it's not surprising new Democratic thinking died on the vine. The Democratic leaders who emerged seemed to say the same things as the previous generation. Party platforms tried to freeze-frame a 1965 America when governmental activism was an accepted goal. And they viscerally fought anything that suggested a new way of thinking.

"You can't say 'Let's look at all of the underpinnings of our platform and really challenge whether or not they should be there,' " stated Duane Garrett, the San Francisco lawyer who held key posts in the Mondale and Babbitt campaigns. "People don't even want to be on the same forum with you and discuss those things unless they can vilify you for raising them. Until you've got that debate how do you attract new thinkers?"

John Lewis, the Atlanta Democratic congressman, voiced the key question. "What is happening? What happened to the young leaders we once had? Have we run out of steam? I don't know, but something is missing. A lack of vision, a sense of direction. Right now we literally are stuck. I don't see any light at the end of the tunnel. And I've been accused of being hopeful and optimistic. I have a feeling we are stuck and we're not moving."

Blanchard is correct in thinking that Democrats have been playing mind games with themselves in recent years.

"We assume we are the governing party of America and assume that there is something wrong with the person communicating ideas and not with the ideas themselves. We have misunderstood that. Even today there are people who believe if we just get our vote out, we win. That's absurd, and simply not true."

Bob Matsui, the California Democratic congressman, agrees: "I don't think there is any question that the trouble with the Democratic party is we have become too comfortable and don't want to take risks. Here in Congress we are out there trying to protect our majority. I think there is a belief here we are still the majority party, but I know we're not. We love it when we hear that the latest Gallup poll says 52 percent of the public want to support their incumbent member of Congress, and we mistake that to mean we are still a majority, but we are not. Generally speaking, the Republican party rolled the dice a lot [when they were out of power]. They perceived themselves as having very little to lose."

Matsui puts his finger squarely on a major problem. Because Democrats control most states and both houses of Congress—and have for all but six years since 1954—there is little incentive in Washington among party leaders to innovate. "Incumbent congressmen get reelected by maintaining the status quo" is the way Arkansas' Clinton put it.

Clinton's analysis—that in the long term "we don't have to innovate to survive, you can stay elected to Congress by maintaining and massaging the benefits of the system already in existence"—is flawed: Democratic control of Congress is greatly endangered through a trickle-down realignment now underway. But Clinton hits the nail on the head when he says that, absent fresh ideas, Americans "will never elect us to run the country because the presidency is about tomorrow."

So, although a new direction might win the Democrats the White House, their Capitol Hill leadership feels it could also cost them their state and congressional control, and they consider that more important. After Dukakis' defeat, Sen. Tom Daschle (D-S.D.), one of the younger Democratic senators, described the mood among his colleagues as "euphoric."

"I know that sounds funny after you've just lost the presidency," he admitted. But it made perfect sense once you realized that the Democrats in control of Congress are resigned to losing the presidency; they are only interested in personal survival.

That is why new thinking, such as Senator Moynihan's idea to cut Social Security taxes in 1990 and 1991, died for lack of unified support from congressional leaders. Democratic leaders mistakenly thought they had something to lose, this time something other than their jobs. Among the rank-and-file Democratic members in Congress, the seniority system provided little incentive for any course other than being seen and not heard. Without a reward system for championing good ideas and support from above, the only thing that mattered was protecting incumbency.

Various other Democratic groups exist, but like the congressional leadership, they are mostly brain dead. The presidential Democratic party, for example, that sprouts every four years around the nominee is forged in the primaries, and is dominated by lawyers looking for White House jobs and liberal activists looking for dedication to the Great Society. None has developed a new idea in decades.

Yet in one place in the Democratic party, new ideas were welcomed. And that was among a number of innovative Democratic governors during the 1980s. Clinton, Babbitt, Robb, Blanchard, Lamm, and Mississippi's Ray Mabus, among others, pioneered new approaches to the problems of education, environment, and economic development. But when they sought to transfer their ideas from the state to the national level, the Washington-based Democratic infrastructure, while celebrating their electoral success, squashed their ideas.

The Democratic Leadership Council gave these governors a forum from which to press for change, but it lacked the clout either to redraw the congressional leadership's agenda or to nominate a presidential candidate. Its think tank, the Progressive Policy Institute, nevertheless began to offer new thinking; it questioned the wisdom of raising the minimum wage and called for increased use of incentives in the welfare system. DLC leaders also talked about requiring national service in return for federal college aid and linking a worker's pay to his firm's profitability. But, again, the DLC didn't have enough strength within the party to persuade it to endorse these and countless other new approaches. The general public never got the message that people other than liberals existed in the national Democratic party.

Meanwhile, the DLC's predominantly Southern leadership was unable to change the public perception that the Democratic party had become a Northeastern party. Most Americans saw the Northeast as symbolic of the nation's past and its problems, not its future and its potential.

In late May 1990, Maslin's firm asked Americans whom they identified as the leaders of the Democratic party. Of the top five living Democrats cited, four were Northeasterners—Ted Kennedy, Michael Dukakis, Mario Cuomo, and Jesse Jackson, who by then lived in Washington D.C. The fifth, Jimmy Carter, was a Southerner, but he was viewed as a failed symbol of the past. The top five Republicans named in Maslin's survey came from Middle America, either the Sun Belt—Texas' George Bush and Secretary of State Jim Baker, and California's Ronald Reagan—or the Midwest—Indiana's Dan Quayle and Kansas' Bob Dole.

And Congress, the remaining Democratic bastion, was much the same. In late 1990, frustrated Southern Democrats circulated a map showing the districts of the ten lawmakers who held the key House leadership posts and committee chairmanships. All were from places north of a line drawn from Washington, D.C., to Sacramento, California. On the other side of the aisle, the Republican congressional leadership included people from the South and the Southwest.

This combination—the party's Northeastern orientation and its refusal to change its outmoded message—has kept presidential candidates from being able to communicate with middle-class voters.

"I think the infrastructure is one of the reasons we lose presidential elections," Maslin commented. "It may be 8, 12, 16 years. That may be how long it takes. But the out party ultimately comes up with a clear, concise case about itself and the country's future. The real vexing question is, 'Is [Democratic strength outside the White House] so much of a block that if we don't lose it at the state and local level,' we can't get it back at the national level?' We need to decide what is the ideology of the Democratic party. The most central ideology has been self-preservation, people with offices trying to protect those offices.

"Aside from some good people—and I don't want to minimize it—some good people losing their offices, would it really be the death of the Democratic party if we lost our majority in the House and Senate and became a true minority party? Would that kill us for 20, 30, 40 years? I think not."

In some ways, a serious reevaluation of the party agenda might not be as painful as most insiders believe. That's because part—although only part—of the problem is semantic. Democrats have been out-of-step with the American middle class so long they don't even talk the same language.

Natalie Davis, the Alabama Democratic pollster, decided the communication problem was so severe and harmful that she wrote up a list of do's and don'ts for party officials in her state. Although her linguistic approach didn't deal with the underlying issues, it at least let the Democrats make their case without raising red flags to the white middle class.

Davis' suggestions:

- Instead of talking about Democrats lifting someone out of poverty, describe the party's goal as helping average Americans live the good life;
- Instead of saying Democrats want to eliminate homelessness and educate the underclass, talk about finding a way for young couples to buy their first home and offer financial help to middle-class families to send their kids to college;
- Instead of saying the Democrats want to provide health care for the poor, focus on making sure all working Americans have coverage.

In each example, rephrasing the case at least partially eliminated the charge that Democrats only cared about the poor. And, in each case, the new language also covered those at the bottom end of the economic scale.

But such semantic fixes were clearly an easy and small part of the problem. What the Democrats never understood was that Reagan's popularity had a great deal to do with his optimistic spirit, something Americans not only shared, but revered.

"We are always preaching doom and gloom; we sound like we are wearing hair shirts. We are a bit like the guy with the sign that says, 'The world's going to end on Thursday.' Well, it's the following Tuesday afternoon," acknowledged Barney Frank, the Massachusetts congressman and one of the few Democratic liberals who understood public opinion, even if he didn't always like it.[2]

And the pessimism that seemed to pervade the Democrats, who waited passively for a GOP recession or scandal, wasn't lost on average voters. Even some Democrats understood early what was happening. In January 1983, Sen. Joseph Biden of Delaware, giving part of the Democrats' televised response to Reagan's State of the Union speech, put it bluntly: "We can criticize the Republicans and we will. We think frankly, though, it's time to put up or shut up." But no one was listening in his own party.

More than eight years later, the Democrats' image had not changed. They had neither offered a compelling new vision for Americans nor shut up.

Democrats were in the same spot as the GOP during the heyday of the New Deal—when the American people weren't buying what the Republicans were selling. It wasn't until the Republicans obscured their ideology and persuaded Eisenhower to become a Republican that they were able to win. Then, after going through the Goldwater debacle in 1964, the GOP started again from ground zero. But those who think the Democrats are at the 1964 stage are wrong; they are where the Republicans were in 1952. They still lack credibility with the average voter. Absent such a figure as Eisenhower, the Democrats will have to do in one step what the GOP did in two.

It won't be easy. Because even if the Democrats were to change their spots, they are caught in a catch-22 that will make it difficult to convince voters of their sincerity. That is: To regain the White House, Democrats must convince middle-class Americans the party has changed. But, concedes Senator Nunn of Georgia, the Democratic "congressional majority cannot set the nation's agenda. Only a president can do that. Until we regain the White House, we may be able to block, modify, and amend, but not challenge, inspire, and lead."

All of which leads to the question of how the Democratic party can deal with its racial problems. There is no way it will convince white, middle-class Americans it cares about their interests if it doesn't, as it hasn't in the past generation, pursue policies that actually do that. And if it can't make that case, it can't win the White House.

Given the different political agendas of black America and middle-class white America, to continue the current effort to pretend neither side has to compromise is folly. As Blanchard says, in the view of middle-class white America, the Democrats have a giant hole to dig out of in order to become credible.

Few white Democrats will publicly say this for fear of being viewed as racist or of abandoning black voters.

Louisiana Senator Breaux is one of those few who is willing to state the obvious. The way for Democrats to win is to tell blacks, "If you want to win an election you have to moderate those positions or we are going to continue to lose. Are you better off with a candidate who goes down in flames or a moderate Democrat?. . . . [Black] voters have to be able to give some leeway to elected officials in order to keep the real goal—the White House—in sight."

Breaux continued, "Black voters in Louisiana would rather have me as a moderate that they cannot agree with on everything than my Republican opponent, who will not agree with them on anything. It has to be true in presidential politics for Democratic candidates in order to win, but it has not."

Along the same lines, Georgia's John Lewis said that Democrats must go after whites "even if it risks losing some blacks in order to win. I'm tired of losing. We have to go all out. Try to protect the base, but if in the process you may lose a few . . . that's not the end of the world. But go and get those white voters, that's where we are missing the vote."

This strategy is of course neither foolproof nor easy. Wilder won following it, but he truly is an ideological moderate. Blacks who are not don't do so well. Andrew Young's unsuccessful attempt to become governor of Georgia in 1990 shows the pitfalls. He carefully cultivated moderate whites, fudging his opposition to the death penalty and offering a message that seemed keyed to the white areas outside Atlanta. But in doing so he didn't speak strongly enough to his black base to get the voter turnout he needed for victory.

It is truly a huge problem for Democrats to walk such a tight-rope. But they must if they want a biracial coalition large enough for victory. They have little choice. Continuing as they have will neither get a large enough black turnout, nor attract enough whites, to win a national election.

San Antonio's Cisneros puts it simply: "We need to relearn the art of compromise and sharing across ethnic lines, in some sense in the reverse direction [so that] the minorities who have had almost veto power over the Democratic party understand they too must compromise their agenda in order to win elections."

One possible approach may be for the Democratic party to follow the advice of the 1985 research report Paul Kirk threw into the trash: Rebuild the biracial coalition around the values that white middle-class America shares with black middle-class America. Even in these times of racial polarization a common ground exists. That meeting place is not where individual groups are encouraged to claim victimization by society; it is where broad-based policies are designed that help everyone feel they are in the same boat.

Even though this is a country of people who primarily came here from elsewhere, until recently the nation has been unusually cohesive. Certainly more so than Canada, Ireland, or Spain, which have far less diverse populations but greater internal strife. And that's because the millions who came to these shores celebrated the melting pot, rejecting group rights for individual rights. Even more, everyone wanted to be part of the common citizenry, and they shared the desire—first and foremost—to be an American.

In recent decades that has changed, in large part pushed by the political engine of the Democratic party. Various groups, blacks yes, but also certain women's groups, some Hispanics, and homosexuals, have pursued the opposite goal, which has stirred the anger of the white middle class.

As bad as this splintering has been for the Democratic party politically, the greater harm has been dealt America itself. Unless the trend is reversed, the national cohesion will be threatened and we risk becoming balkanized as a society.

The new Democratic domestic agenda must be built upon interconnected principles. The public must come to view the Democratic party as:

- the party of those who work, not the party that seems to be helping those who don't;
- the party whose policies reward people for working, even if this offends and penalizes some who don't;
- the party with the wisdom to adopt good ideas even if they stem from their competitors;
- the party that knows when to say no to its friends.

Democrats must put the emphasis on programs for the working poor, not the welfare poor, although obviously they can't abandon those who truly can't work. They must make sure that those who work do better than those who do not. A worker who is poor by any reasonable standard should be eligible for government aid. Above all, Democrats must provide incentives for people to improve their own position and penalize those who don't try. (A little-noticed feature of the controversial 1990 budget deficit reduction package took a small step in this direction, but further efforts are needed.) And, most importantly from a political point of view, Democrats must be willing to take credit for such policies.

Not only is a reward-based compensation system good politics, it is good policy. Human nature requires incentives to spur initiative.

Along the German–Belgium–Netherlands border, management analysts have noticed a disturbing trend. There is little difference among the people who live and work in the three countries. But in the Netherlands, the number of workers calling in sick is twice that of the other two countries. The reason is clear: The Netherlands'

cradle-to-grave program of income maintenance and health benefits provides little incentive for productivity, compared to the other
two nations, where a good living depends on productivity.

Today in America, it seems to much of the middle class that
Democratic leaders wish to follow the Dutch example. They see
virtue in poverty and think that it should be rewarded. The middle
class thinks differently. It puts in an eight-hour workday and, in
many cases, two more hours commuting. Middle-class people
figure they get what their hard work deserves. They are the ones
who build the wealth and pay the taxes that support American
society.

In their view, those who don't work or who don't work produc-
tively fail to keep up their end of the social compact. Basically, the
middle class sees those on welfare as being, in varying degrees,
responsible for their own predicament. And it does not feel guilty in
so thinking. Rather, it believes in reciprocal responsibilities for
those getting public assistance.

Clearly, much of this stems from middle-class resentment, and
this very human emotion should not be mocked, as many Democratic politicians seem to do. One way for Democrats to sell programs that redistribute society's wealth is to convince the middle
class that the recipients are doing something in exchange for the
money.

Tim Penny, the Democratic congressman and rising star in Minnesota politics, understands this: "It is not disrespectful of those
who find themselves on hard times that the help we provide not be
free and clear of encumbrances."

Yet Penny is more the exception than the rule. Until Democrats
lead the charge for more accountability by recipients—not larger
payments to them—they will be unable to change their image. And
without this change, middle-class support for such programs will
continue to dwindle. The difficulty in making the change lies—as
with so many of the party's image problems—with the groups that
allegedly represent its core constituency.

Michigan's Blanchard remembers when he set up a pilot program requiring every able-bodied welfare recipient to see a job
coach periodically in order to get state checks. "We had enormous

opposition," he remembered. And it was all from Democrats, mainly "white liberals and professional black welfare advocates, but not the black community at large. It was met with enormous resistance from the existing liberal structure."

Democrats must stop thinking about blacks as people who are poor and impoverished because society has conspired against them. They must think of blacks as they do everyone else—as people who want a better life. And then provide incentives for those who are willing to strive for that better life.

The civil rights establishment will resist because clearly everyone cannot succeed. The answer: don't abandon those at the bottom of the economic ladder, but don't make their economic security the party's prime focus. In truth, some people will suffer, at least in the short term. But as it stands, the income maintenance policies of the past generation have only made their situation worse. It's unlikely that, in the long run, the new course could do worse.

In political terms, the costs of the Democratic party's traditional approach have not been worth the benefits. Until the Democratic party changes both its substance and image, the future is bleak, at least in the sense of recapturing the true majority status it enjoyed in America from 1932-1965.

That is not to say the Democrats won't again win the presidency. American voters love change. At some point, the Democrats will inevitably win back the White House. It does not appear likely in 1992, but perhaps in 1996 when the voters would have tired of sixteen years of GOP presidents, maybe later. At that time, as in 1976 after eight years of GOP rule, there will be enormous pressure from party constituencies to make up for all those lean years of government goodies. Every Democratic interest group will be looking to reverse whatever harm it believes the Reagan-Bush years did to their agenda. If the Democrats give in to that pressure they will deserve what they get—another four year presidency followed by a generation or more in the wilderness.

"Sooner or later that reality will be at our doorstep. That will be the real test," forecasts former Arizona governor and presidential candidate Bruce Babbitt. "For that may well be the last chance. If we haven't come up with new ideas and a way to manage a continuing biracial coalition as opposed to a one-shot election, we could be in the wilderness for a long time.

"My fear is that when the opportunity comes, we may not have positioned ourselves to reap the rewards. It's going to come; the question is, will we be able to go through that window of opportunity when it opens?

"If not, we risk becoming a mirror image of the Democrats of the nineteenth century. From the Civil War to the great Depression we were never in power" except in special circumstances—the bad economy in 1884 and a Republican internal split in 1912.

"The comparison is the late nineteenth century. In political terms, Jimmy Carter is Grover Cleveland. As we cross into the next century, we are looking potentially, in the absence of some serious change, at an unbroken string of Republican presidencies. A lock on the presidency."

End Notes

CHAPTER TWO

1. Dave Barry, *Dave Barry Turns 40* (New York, N.Y.: Crown Publishers, 1990), 124.
2. Poll commissioned by Democrats For the 80s (Washington, D.C.: June 1989).
3. John Petrocik, "Issues and Agendas: Electoral Coalitions in the 1988 Election," published for the American Political Science Association Convention, August 1989, table 5.
4. Merle Black and Earle Black, *Politics and Society in the South* (Cambridge, Mass.: Harvard University Press, 1989), 237.
5. Petrocik, op. cit., table 5.

CHAPTER THREE

1. Juan Williams, "What Chills the Blood of Liberals," *Washington Post*, Sept. 24, 1989, D.1.
2. Richard Lamm, "Can America Revive Its Dysfunctional Institutions? Probably Not," Scripps Howard News Service, Aug. 22, 1989.
3. Black and Black, op. cit., table 1.3.
4. Petrocik, op. cit., table 5.

CHAPTER FOUR

1. Pete Hamill, "Breaking the Silence," *Esquire*, March 1988, 94.
2. "Suffering in the Cities Persists as U.S. Fights Other Battles," *New York Times*, Jan. 27, 1991, 21.

3. Donald Kinder, et al., "Race and the 1988 Presidential Election," University of Michigan Research Program on Race and American Politics, 1989, table 2.
4. Ibid.
5. David Pitt, "Gang Attack: Unusual for its Viciousness," *New York Times*, April 25, 1989, B. 1. Also, Rita Giordano, "Teens' Clothes 'Key' In Park Attack Case," *Newsday*, April 24, 1989, 2.
6. Howard Kurtz, "Park Attack Reopens Racial Wounds in New York," *Washington Post*, May 3, 1989, A.11.
7. Dan Pearl, *Wall Street Journal*, Dec. 7, 1990. "CDC Report Shows Alarming Increase in Homicides of Young Black Males." P. A6.
8. Sari Horowitz, *Washington Post*, Aug. 30, 1989. "Homicides in the District Rush Past the 300 Mark."

CHAPTER FIVE

1. Morton Kondracke, "The Two Black Americas," *The New Republic*, Feb. 6, 1989, 18.
2. Walter Updegrave, "Race and Money," *Money Magazine*, December 1989, 154.
3. Aug. 14, 1988, and July 17, 1988.
4. William Galston and Elaine Kamarck, "The Politics of Evasion" (Washington, D.C.: Progressive Policy Institute, September 1989), 7.

CHAPTER SIX

1. Dinesh D'Souza, "Sins of Admission," *The New Republic*, Feb. 18, 1991, 33.

CHAPTER SEVEN

1. *Congressional Record*, 88th Cong., 2nd sess., March 30, 1964, S6549.
2. Linda Gottfredson, "When Job-testing Fairness is Nothing but a Quota," *Wall Street Journal*, Dec. 6, 1990, A.18.
3. David S. Broder, "Quayle Calls for Mending GOP Fissures on Budget, Gulf," *Washington Post*, Nov. 11, 1990, A.13.

CHAPTER EIGHT

1. Paul Taylor, *See How They Run* (New York, N.Y.: Knopf, 1990), 149.

CHAPTER TEN

1. William Schneider and Patrick Reddy, "Altered States," *The American Enterprise* (Washington, D.C.: The American Enterprise Institute, July/August 1990), 47.
2. *The Lifestyle Market Analyst*, published by National Demographics & Lifestyles, Denver, Co., 1990, special run.
3. June 1989.
4. *Psychology Today*, June 1988, 44.
5. Joe Edwards, Associated Press, Nov. 6, 1988.

CHAPTER ELEVEN

1. Jerry Austin, *Somebodies*, unpublished reminiscences.
2. Ibid.
3. Ibid.
4. William Raspberry, "Black-on-Black Violence: Jackson's Answer," *Washington Post*, Feb. 2, 1990, A.23.
5. Roger Simon, *Road Show* (New York, N.Y.: Farrar, Strauss, Giroux, 1990) 250.

CHAPTER TWELVE

1. Galston and Karmarck, op. cit., 13.
2. Linda Chavez, "Rainbow Collision," *The New Republic*, Nov. 19, 1990, 14.
3. Nathan Caplan, "Boat People Prove Their Worth," *Wall Street Journal*, Aug. 1, 1990, A.14.

CHAPTER THIRTEEN

1. Mark Zupon, "Why Congress Is the Democrats' Game," *Wall Street Journal*, Oct. 20, 1989, editorial page.
2. Jeffrey Birnbaum, "In Quayle Country Democratic Congresswoman Finds Growing Acceptance Among Constituents," *Wall Street Journal*, Feb. 16, 1990, A.14.

CHAPTER FOURTEEN

1. Gallup International Research Institutes, International Research Associates, National Opinion Research Center, International Social Survey Program, 1987-88.
2. "What's Wrong With the Democratic Party?," *Harper's*, January 1990, 45.

Index

Adams, Brock, 158
Affirmative action, 142–50. *See also*
  Racial quotas
  Asian Americans, 286–87
  John Lewis, 99
  schools, 80
Ailes, Roger, 136
Albrecht, Suellen, 251
Arlook, Ira, 41, 71
  suburbs, 217–18
Asian Americans, 95
  affirmative action, 286–87
  demographics, 284
  families, 287
  security, 286
  upward mobility, 282–83
  values, 285, 287–88, 288–89
  welfare, 287
Atwater, Lee, 127–28, 232
  1988 presidential campaign, 30–31
  Democratic primary, 184
  George Bush, 185–86
  suburbs, 217–18
  Willie Horton issue, 136
Austin, Jerry, 175, 226–27, 240, 261
  Jesse Jackson, 243–44, 251–52, 253,
    258, 261
  Jesse Jackson in 1992, 260

Babbitt, Bruce, 71, 210–11, 334–35
  class warfare, 31
  Jesse Jackson, 149–50, 246, 255–56,
    264, 265
  lifestyle, 68
  personal characteristics, 32
  social stratification, 32–33
Baby boomers, 35, 69–70, 228
  lifestyle, 232
  work, 230
Barbour, Haley, 51, 182
Barry, Dave, 41–42
Barry, Marion, 96
Barton, Jackie E., 143–46
Bates, Earl, Jr., 293
Bautista, David Hayes, 277
Bayh, Birch, 48
Bayh, Evan, 48–49, 119–20
Beckel, Bob, 43, 83, 244
Beckel, Ellen, 245
Biden, Joseph, 329
Black, Merle, 173
Blacks
  families, 86, 98, 317
  men, 101–2
  political attitudes, 110–14
  responsibility, 261
  self-sufficiency, 103–4

Blacks (*continued*)
  upward mobility, 85–86
  voting, 269
Blanchard, Jim, 26–27, 322, 324
  Democratic convention, 178
  education, 191
  equal opportunity vs equal results,
    146
  Michael Dukakis, 174
  television, 135
  welfare, 333
Blips, Pam, 214–15, 219–20
  work, 227
Booth, Heather, 222, 225–26
Borosage, Bob, 119, 248
Boxer, Barbara, 179–80
Brazaitis, Tom, 46–47
Breaux, John, 4, 157, 330
  David Duke, 168
  Democratic convention, 187
Bright collars, 231
Brountas, Paul, 122
Brown, Ron, 46, 72–73, 128
  1990 elections, 38–39
  civil rights, 169–70
  Democratic convention delegates,
    187
  Democratic National Convention,
    206–10, 213
  Helms ad, 168
  Jesse Jackson, 241, 258
  media, 60
  redistricting, 305
  Steve Cobble, 183
Brown, Tony, 78–79
Brown, Willie, 262
Buchanan, John, 251
Buckley, F. Reid, 186
Burger, George, 199
Burris, Roland, 179–80
Burton, Phil, 301

Bush, George, 232
  1990 budget negotiations, 37–38
  image, 59
Busing, 7–8, 10–11

Cain, Bruce, 284
Campbell, Carroll, 136, 309
Campbell, Ed, 208
Capitalism, 40
Caplan, Nathan, 283
Carrick, Bill, 160, 161, 167
Carter, Jimmy, 19–23, 72–73, 324
Celeste, Dick, 257, 259
Chalmers, Wally, 203–4
Chiles, Lawton, 309
Chinese, 284
Cisneros, Henry, 66, 276, 295, 331
Citizen Action, 41, 225–26
City revitalization, 242
Civil rights
  1964 Civil Rights Act, 137, 154
  1965 Civil Rights Act, 80
  1990 Civil Rights Bill, 152–70
  Bill Clinton, 82
  laws, 76
  Ronald Reagan, 84
  Voting Rights Act, 302
  white perceptions, 81
Class warfare, 30–31, 314
  1984 presidential campaign, 43–44
  the Depression, 54
  South, 50–52
Clay, Henry, 183
Clinton, Bill, 48, 323–24
  civil rights, 82
  class warfare, 31
  crime, 100–101
  equal opportunity vs equal results,
    146
  Jesse Jackson, 247
  Michael Dukakis, 123–25

Clinton, Bill (*continued*)
  public employee unions, 67
Coats, Dan, 300
Cobble, Steve, 183
Coelho, Tony, 192–94
  Jesse Jackson, 249
  music, 235–36
  redistricting, 301
  television, 57
Collective solutions, 224–25, 226
College admissions process, 139–41
Congress, 296–99
  Democratic control of the Senate,
    306
  redistricting, 301
Conn, Paul, 26
Connolly, John, 185
Consumer Price Index, 36
Crime, 100–103, 318–19, 323
  suburban migration, 215
  Willie Horton, 131–34
Cubans, 274
Culver, John, 209
Cuomo, Mario, 209, 215–16
  crime, 101

Darr, Carol, 123
  white voters, 178–79
Darr, Justin, 105–7
Daschle, Tom, 325
Davis, Arthur, 203
Davis, Natalie, 65, 328
Death penalty, 72, 115, 132
Delauro, Rosa, 24
Democratic convention
  delegates, 120–21, 183–84, 187–88
  Jesse Jackson, 171–72, 178
  voter turnout, 121–22
Democratic Leadership Council, 238,
  326

equal opportunity vs equal results,
  146–47
Democratic National Committee, 41
  Ron Brown, 207–8
Democratic party
  1990 elections, 38
  effect of media, 62
  internal split, 74–75
Democratic primary, 182–83
  voters, 119
Demographics
  Asian Americans, 284
  blacks, 85–87
  South, 76
  suburbs, 78–79, 219, 223–24
  use in campaign planning, 60–61
  voters, 33, 267–68
The Depression, 54
Dodd, W. J., 226
Dole, Bob, 186–87
Donilon, Michael, 155, 165–66
Donilon, Tom, 59–60
Drugs, 70, 102–3
Dukakis, Michael, 232
  Democratic convention, 174
  education, 190–91
  Hispanics, 28
  image, 59
  Jesse Jackson, 177, 252, 253
  lifestyle, 252
  national health insurance, 189–90
  suburbs, 216–17
  union vote, 44
  Willie Horton issue, 131–34
Duke, David, 161–63
Dyer, Dennis, 107–9, 115

Economic equality, 79
Economic policy, 315
Economics, Republican, 34
Economy, in the 1800s, 53–54

Education, 167, 323
    baby boomers, 229
    Michael Dukakis, 190–91
    Republican party, 230
Eisenhower, Dwight, 259, 307–8
Elections, 1990, 38
Employers, 1990 Civil Rights Bill,
    153
Employment, 65, 90
Endorsements, 255–56
Equal Employment Opportunity
    Commission, 137
Equal opportunity vs equal results,
    79–81, 138, 147, 153, 317
Eshoo, Anne, 226
Espy, Mike, 40, 241–42, 265
    crime, 135
Estrich, Susan, 104, 122, 176
    Jesse Jackson, 177, 249
    Republican convention, 187
    South, 52
    Willie Horton issue, 133, 136

Fahrenkopf, Frank, 189, 232
Fairness, 39, 80, 159
Farrakhan, Louis, 95
Feinstein, Dianne, 158–59, 160
    fairness, 159
Fenwick, Millicent, 29
Ferraro, Geraldine, 79, 236
    Jesse Jackson, 259–60
    Willie Horton issue, 133–34
Filipinos, 284
Florio, Jim, 148, 212–13, 314
Focus groups, 24
Foley, Tom, 39
Ford, Maxine, 141
Foreign affairs, 319
    black and white perceptions, 115–
    16
    Jesse Jackson, 242, 250

Frank, Barney, 122, 179–80, 217, 329
From, Al, 49–50
From, Ginger, 50
Fulwood, Isaac, Jr., 103
Furlough programs, 131–34

Galston, Bill, 72, 265, 309
Gantt, Harvey, 164–65
    television, 165
Garin, Geoff, 166, 174, 247
Garrett, Duane, 177–78, 254–55, 324
Gephardt, Richard, 167, 246–47
    fairness, 39
Gingrich, Newt, 57, 73
Gordon, Robert, 117–18
Gore, Al, 249
Government function, 112–13
Graham, Bob, 41, 74
Graham, James, 94–95
Gramm, Phil, 70, 111–12, 125, 294
    fairness, 131
    television, 62
Gray, Bill, 145
Green, Pete, 292
Greenberg, Stanley, 24, 49, 232
    affirmative action, 146, 169
    crime, 102
    Jesse Jackson, 246
    racial quotas, 158
    Willie Horton issue, 133
Greenwood, Lee, 233–35
Guilt, 128–29, 170, 197–98
    young voters, 156
Gun control, 186, 206

Hamilton, Bill, 312–13
Harrison, Tubby, 306–7
Hawkins, Augustus, 193–94
Head Start, 316
Helms, Jesse, 164–65
Herman, Tom, 190–91

Hispanics, 274–77
   families, 276–77
   income, 282
   Jesse Jackson, 280
   Michael Dukakis, 28
   Persian Gulf War, 279–80
   political attitudes, 279–80
   upward mobility, 281
   values, 288–89
   voters, 282
   welfare, 277–78
   work, 278
Holman, Larry, 141
Hutchison, Kay Bailey, 308

Image
   blacks, 89–90
   Democratic party, 71, 262
   George Bush, 59
   Michael Dukakis, 59
   Republican party, 273
Income
   black and white family, 83
   Hispanics, 282
   voters, 33–34
Income equality, 39–40
Individual accountability, 317, 323
Individuality, 232
Industrial age, 54
Information age, 54, 313
Institute for Southern Studies, 51–52
Integration, 99

Jackson, Jesse, 320–21
   black image, 90
   city revitalization, 242
   debates, 248–49
   Democratic convention, 171–72
   Democratic Leadership Council,
     238–39
   Democratic ticket, 262

   endorsements, 255–56
   equal opportunity vs equal results,
     147
   foreign affairs, 242, 250
   Hispanics, 280
   lifestyle, 252–53
   media, 247, 260–61
   Michael Dukakis, 253
   radio, 260
   responsibility for minority failure,
     261
   Ronald Reagan, 84
   Sheboygan, WI, 237–38
   white voters, 197
Japanese, 284
Jeffers, Howard, 105–7
Johnson, Lyndon, 128, 315
Johnston, J. Bennett, 163–64, 165
Jones, Curtis, 107–9, 115–17
Jones, Jim, 74–75
Jordan, Barbara, 240
Jourdan, Al, 221

Kean, Thomas, 75, 93–94, 297
   Jesse Jackson, 259
   Willie Horton issue, 134
Keillor, Garrison, 227
Kelly, Peter, 60–61, 137–38, 149, 220,
   264
Kemp, Jack, 186–87
Kennedy, John, 294–95
Kennedy, Robert, 25
Kennedy, Ted, 48, 151, 170
   Diane Feinstein, 160
Kiewiet, Roderick, 284
Kildee, Dale, 193
Kiley, Tom, 30
Kirk, Paul, 196–203, 232, 331
Kirkpatrick, Jeanne, 319
Koch, Ed, 87, 98, 251
Koreans, 284

Labor in the South, 51
Lacy, Bill, 32, 132, 186–87,
    270–71
Lake, Celinda, 316
Lamm, Dick, 85, 102, 130
    black politics, 174
Lane, Vince, 86
Leadership Conference on Civil
    Rights, 169
Levin, Sander, 24
Lewis, John, 324
    government function, 111
    Jesse Jackson, 240
    South, 52
    upward mobility, 43
    white guilt, 129
    white voters, 97–98, 330
    Willie Horton issue, 137
Lieberman, Joseph, 71–72, 84, 135–
    36
Lifestyles
    baby boomers, 232
    middle class, 40
    Sun Belt, 232
    white voters, 42
Long, Huey, 98
Long, Jill, 300
Long, Sara, 233
Loury, Glenn, 96
Lowry, Nita, 142
Lunde, Brian, 198–99

Manatt, Charles, 254
Marino, Barry, foreign affairs, 19–23
Marketing, 55–56
Martinez, Robert, 294
Maslin, Paul, 75, 195
    blacks and Hispanics, 280
    Hispanics, 275–76, 289
    white and black voters, 175–76,
        263–64

Matsui, Robert, 66, 286
    minorities, 273
McCarthy, Eugene, 7–8
McCurdy, David, 39
McCurry, Mike, 171–74, 184–85
McDowell, Charlie, 296
Media, 60, 62, 247. See also Radio;
    Television
    Jesse Jackson, 247
    talk radio, 89
Mellman, Mark, 169, 315
Metzenbaum, Howard, 222
Mexican Americans, 275
Mfume, Kweisi, 89
Michel, Bob, 172–73
Middle class
    lifestyle, 40
    taxes, 46–47
Midwest, 65
Minorities. See also specific groups.
    political attitudes, 273
Minority failure
    racial discrimination, 130
    responsibility, 261
Mitchell, Cleta, 269
Mitchell, George, 39
Mitchell, Theo, 309
Mondale, Walter, 4, 198, 232, 321
    1984 presidential campaign, 42–43,
        43–44
    fairness, 39
Moore, Gwen, 288
Morales, Dan, 280, 282
Morton, Bill, 252
Moynihan, Daniel Patrick,
    325–26
    black families, 98
Music, 233–36
Muskie, Edmund, 311–12

Nakanishi, Don T., 285
National health insurance, 189–90

Neeley, Roger, 292
Naisbitt, John, 55, 223–24, 229
New class, 167
  description, 35
  values, 35–36
New collars, 230–31
Noonan, Peggy, 33
North, unions, 65
Northeast, 232
  political leaders, 327
Nunn, Sam, 40, 191, 315, 329–30
  equal opportunity vs equal results,
  146
Nuttle, Marc, 75

O'Brien, Frank, 199
O'Neill, Thomas "Tip," 42–43

Party identification, 290–94, 306, 308
Patterson, Kay, 303–4
Peneski, Tom, 239
Penny, Tim, 194, 333
Perry, Rick, 308
Persian Gulf War
  Hispanics, 279–80
  public opinion, 116
Phillips, Kevin, 36–37
Pledge of Allegiance, 122–23
Political action committees, 298
Political attitudes
  Hispanics, 279–80
  whites and blacks, 110–11
Pool, Joe, 291
Preferential hiring, 83
Presidential campaign, 1984, House
  Democratic caucus, 42–43
Presidential campaign, 1988
  class warfare tactic, 30–31
  voter demographics, 33
  Willie Horton, 131–34
Primas, Randy, 77–78, 91–92

Prisons, 115
Private investment, 117
Progressive Policy Institute, 326
Public opinion, 56
  Persian Gulf War, 116
Puerto Ricans, 274

Quayle, Dan, 48–49, 170

Racial discrimination, 116
  David Duke, 162–63
  minority failure, 130
Racial preference plans, 318
Racial quotas, 146, 153–56. See also
  Affirmative action
Racism and Democratic defections,
  26–27
Radio, 89
  advertising, 186
  Jesse Jackson, 260
Raspberry, William, 97
Reagan, Ronald, 73, 232
  civil rights, 84
  Democratic voters, 25
  popularity, 64
  social programs, 88
Redistributive economics, 314
Redistricting, 300–304
Reed, Thomas, 53
Renaud, Louise, 13–19
Rephrasing Democratic agenda, 328
Republican convention delegates, 187
Republican party
  1990 elections, 38
  image, 273
Republican primary, 182–83
Reverse discrimination, 138–39
Richards, Ann, 308
Richardson, Bill, 274, 278
Riots, of the 1960s, 10, 92

Robb, Charles, 238, 305–6, 322, 323
    black self-sufficiency, 103–4
    equal opportunity vs equal results,
        146
    Willie Horton issue, 132–33
Robertson, Pat, 75
Robinson, Tommy, 294
Roemer, Buddy, 294, 313–14
Rollins, Ed, 301, 305
Rooney, Andy, 85
Roosevelt, Franklin Delano, 29
Rose, Doug, 164
Rouse, James, 91
Rovich, Sig, 234
Rowland, John, 297
Rubin, Jerry, 291
Ruvolo, Jim, 262

Sasso, John, 173
Scammon, Richard, 218
Schieffer, Tom, 292
Schneider, Richard, 237–40
Schramm, Marty, 58
Schroeder, Patricia, 127
Security, 66, 286
Sexual harassment, 157
Shields, Mark, 311–12
Simon, Carly, 236
Simon, Paul, 321
Slagle, Bob, 205, 292–93
Slattery, Jim, 72
Smith, Joshua, 97
Smith, Wade, 197
Snyder, "Jimmy the Greek," 85
Social programs, 88–89
Social stratification, 32–33
Soechting, Paul, 264
South, 72, 232–33
    class warfare, 50–52
    demographics, 76
    unions, 65

Southeast Asians, 284
Special consideration, 142, 318
Springsteen, Bruce, 236
Staheen, Robert, 304
Stahl, Lesley, 58
Standard of living, 72
Stark, Fortney "Pete," 110
Stassen, Harold, 263
State competition, 47–48
State legislatures, 300, 307
Strauss, Robert, 151
Suburbs
    demographics, 78–79, 219, 223–24
    Lee Atwater, 217–18
    Michael Dukakis, 216–17
    migration, 68–70, 92–93
    values, 221
    work, 227
Sullivan, Frank, 290–94
Sullivan, Louis, 110
Suma, Geri, 7–13
Sun Belt, 66, 313
    lifestyle, 232
    political leaders, 327
Supreme Court, civil rights, 152

Taiwanese, 284
Taxes, 115, 316
    middle class views, 46–47
    Reagan tax cuts, 37
    wealthy, 38
Technology, 66–67
Teeter, Bob, 64, 135
Television
    black image, 89–90
    Jesse Helms, 165
    Jesse Jackson, 243, 260
    Jim Blanchard, 135
    racial quotas, 159–60
    Republican use of, 57
    Willie Horton issue, 134

Tests
    employment, 144
    General Aptitude Test Battery, 140–41
    group scoring, 155
Thurmond, Strom, 185
Toffler, Alvin, 55, 65, 218–19, 323–24
    suburbs, 223, 224
Torricelli, Robert, 319
Trade, 66–67
Tran, Nghia, 287–88
Transportation, 224
Tuchfarber, Al, 63

Unions, 65
    class warfare, 44
    George Bush, 59
    Michael Dukakis, 124
    public employee, 67
Upward mobility, 43
    Asian Americans, 282–83
    blacks, 85–86
    Hispanics, 281

Valdivieso, Rafael, 277–78, 280
Values, 124–25, 319
    Asian Americans, 285, 287–88
    Democratic party, 193
    middle class, 28
    new class, 35–36
    suburbs, 221
Van de Kamp, John, 158–59
Vietnamese, 283–84, 287–88
Violence, 102–3
Voluntarism, 125–26
Voters, 266–72
    1984 presidential election, 269–70
    1988 presidential campaign, 33, 270–71
    Asian Americans, 282–89
    baby boomers, 230

Democratic primary, 119
demographics, 33, 267–68
Hispanics, 274–84
income, 33–34
racism, 26–27
registration, 272
turnout, 272
union, 44–45
white, 84, 196–203
young, 63–65, 156, 295
Voting
    middle class drop-off, 47
    Voting Rights Act, 79, 302
Voting rights, 79

Wal-Mart stores, 50–51
Walters, Ron, 268–69
Wattenberg, Ben, 218
Watts, Doug, 233
Wealthy, taxes, 38
Weber, Vin, 299
Weiner, Rick, 208
Welfare, 13–19, 86–87, 112–13, 193
    Asian Americans, 287
    Hispanics, 277–78
West, 232–33
    unions, 65
White collars, 231
Whitehead, Ralph Jr., 230
Whites
    frustration with black progress, 89
    liberal guilt, 128–29
    political attitudes, 110–14
Wilder, Doug, 99–100, 181, 330–31
    Jesse Jackson, 251, 265
Wilks, Robert, 144–46
Williams, Annette Polly, 303
Williams, Clayton, 308
Williams, Tom, 292
Willkie, Wendell, 29
Wilson, Pete, 158, 159, 167, 274

Woo, Michael, 285–86
Woods, Harriet, 221
Woods, Pete, 221
Woodson, Robert, 88
Work
  baby boomers, 230
  Hispanics, 278
  suburbs, 227
Work ethic, 193
Work incentives, 332–33

Wright, Jim, 212, 290–92
Wyman, Roz, 236

Young, Andrew, 224–25, 241, 331
  liberal guilt, 129
Young, Everett, 293–94
Youth
  voters, 63–65, 156, 295
  work, 223

About the Author

Peter Brown is the chief political writer for Scripps Howard News Service, which serves more than 350 daily newspapers in the United States. A former Neiman Fellow at Harvard University, Brown received undergraduate and graduate degrees from Syracuse University. He joined United Press International as a reporter in 1974 in Albany, N.Y., subsequently working for UPI in Boston, Hartford, and Washington, where he covered the 1980 presidential campaign. He joined Scripps Howard as the news service's White House reporter in 1982 and was named chief political writer in 1986. He is now at work covering his fourth presidential campaign.

Although this is Brown's first book, he has written for *The New Republic* and *The National Journal*. He has also been guest lecturer on campuses ranging from Harvard to the University of Oregon. He lives in the suburbs of Washington, D.C., with his wife Mary Beth and children Stephen and Charlotte.